WHERE HOOPOES FLY

Exploring Almería 2

Kevin Borman

Published in 2017 by FeedARead.com Publishing

First Edition

A CIP catalogue record for this title is available from the British Library.

Contents

Introduction

Writing the predecessor to this book, *Flamingos in the Desert,* was a leap of faith. I was fascinated by discovering what eastern Almería had to offer and was keen to write about it. I thoroughly enjoyed doing so but I had no idea whether people would be interested in the results; a 300-page book that tried to get under the skin of Almería province. What would constitute success? 100 sales? Dare I hope for 500? How would I be able to gauge whether the effort had been worthwhile?

I put my email address in the book, so that people could contact me for the link to the online photo album that I created to accompany it, and so they could give me feedback. Three years on from publication, with sales at over 2,400 and many emails and Facebook messages, I think I know the answer. The people who didn't like the book have been kind enough not to tell me so, but I've received a lot of positive feedback, many snippets of intriguing information, had plenty of enjoyable conversations, both face-to-face and online, and made a few fine new friends. I was delighted to find that my interest in eastern Almería was shared by so many other people. It made the more than four years I spent working on the book all the more worthwhile.

Initially I thought that *Flamingos* was fairly comprehensive. Certainly I didn't have much more to say about eastern Almería at the time it was published. However, as I realised that there was a lot of information that wasn't in the book, and as it became apparent that there was a market for this kind of 'creative non-fiction', I decided that I wanted to work on a follow-up.

It would have to be slightly different in some respects. I'd already written about my Spanish neighbours and obviously didn't wish to repeat that, but I realised that there were geographical areas that I'd barely touched in *Flamingos*: the coast from Macenas to the Murcia border, the Sierra Almagrera, the Sierra María, the Almanzora

Valley. The urban areas too: Mojácar, Vera, Cuevas del Amanzora, Almería itself, of course, and others. And there were updates to ongoing issues such as the AVE and the Algarrobico hotel.

People contacted me in significant numbers to say they liked the details of the walks and the clues to places to visit – the ancient olive tree near Agua Amarga, the deserted village of Marchalico-Viñicas, the Salinas de Cabo de Gata and so on – so I wanted to have a similar element in this book: places where people could go, sometimes off the beaten track, and find a bit of genuine Almería.

It seems that the amount of detail in *Flamingos* was appreciated. Many people told me they liked that, and they used the index to dip in and out. Others told me that they read the whole thing from start to finish and, in a few cases, they were going to start again because "there's so much in it". *Where Hoopoes Fly* has a similar structure, plus an index, so it's possible to either begin at the beginning or dip into shorter sections more selectively. There is an online photo album to accompany this book, which you can find here: https://www.flickr.com/photos/156283557@N06/sets/7215768265296524 4

Once again, I've hand-drawn a few maps. These are intended to give the general layout of some of the areas and themes. They are selective and not all places or roads or other details are on them, so please bear this in mind and don't rely on them for precise navigation.

So in some senses *Where Hoopoes Fly* is 'more of the same'. That said, I've tried to avoid duplicating information that was in *Flamingos in the Desert.* However, there are many links between this book and its predecessor. The two volumes are complementary. So, for example, if you are looking for detailed information in this book about the coast of the Cabo de Gata-Níjar Natural Park or the best maps of the local area, Lorca's *Blood Wedding* or the Gypsum Karst of Sorbas, details of floods or earthquakes or wildfires, you'll find relatively little here because those subjects, and many more, were thoroughly covered in *Flamingos in the Desert*. Barring unforeseen circumstances, this should still be available both in paperback (from amazon, feedaread.com and in almost 30 local outlets) and as an e-book on Kindle.

I have tried to ensure the information here is as accurate as possible at the time of going to press but things do of course change, so particularly with details such as opening hours (or days) do try to check online or by phone before setting out if you are planning a significant journey.

I have a Facebook page at Flamingosinthedesert on which I regularly post new photos and snippets relating to these books. If you are on Facebook do check it out and please give it a 'Like'. All feedback is welcome either on the Facebook page or via my email address at kevindborman@gmail.com. And if you have enjoyed either or both of the books, I'd be very grateful for reviews, however brief, on amazon. At which point, I think I've said enough, so on with the main event.

Kevin Borman
Sorbas, August 2017

MAP A - EASTERN ALMERIA

GRANADA

María
Sierra de
María
Vélez Blanco
MURCIA
N

Vélez Rubio

Sierra de las Estancias

Albox
Huércal-Overa
Pulpí
San Juan de los Terreros

Purchena
Olula del Río
Zurgena

Tíjola
Macael
Cuevas del Almanzora

Villaricos

Sierra de los Filabres
Lubrín
Vera
Palomares

Uleila del Campo
Los Gallardos
Garrucha
Mojácar Pueblo

Turre
Sorbas
Sierra Cabrera
Mojácar Playa

Tabernas
Lucainena de las Torres
Carboneras

Sierra Alhamilla
Níjar

Agua Amarga

Almería
Mediterranean Sea

Las Salinas
San José

Cabo de Gata
0   10   20
KM

1. Coasting: Sopalmo to Garrucha

'Almost a hundred kilometres of wild arid coast separate Cabo de Gata and Garrucha, windswept in winter and sunbaked in summer, as amazingly beautiful as it is unknown.'

(Juan Goytisolo, 1960)

Sopalmo to Macenas

My previous book, *Flamingos in the Desert*, began with several chapters describing the coast of the Cabo de Gata-Níjar Natural Park, finishing at the Playa del Algarrobico, just north of Carboneras. Beyond there, the mountains of the Sierra Cabrera come steeply down to the sea, so following the coast closely for the next stretch is not a realistic proposition. Now, in an attempt at some kind of symmetry, it's time to take up that journey again, beginning at Sopalmo, slightly inland and a little further north, aiming to soon reach the coast and then follow it, over the course of several chapters, all the way to the provincial border with Murcia.

A few kilometres south-west of Mojácar, in the eastern Sierra Cabrera, several river valleys converge to create the Rambla de Macenas, a substantial dry riverbed. This runs north-east for about six kilometres before reaching the sea at Macenas itself. Near where these valleys meet, tucked into a fold of the mountains, lies the hamlet of Sopalmo, astride the sparsely-used coastal road between Mojácar and Carboneras. Sopalmo is little more than a cluster of houses, though with a couple of good restaurants to tempt the hungry. Sopalmo and Macenas can be linked by a superb circular walk of about four to five hours which offers great views of the coast and the hills. There's a fair bit of height gain and there are some rather tricky slopes, but if you are reasonably fit and confident, it's a highly recommended circuit.

The obvious place to leave your car in Sopalmo is the small car park on the Mojácar edge of the village. Incidentally, to do the walk one way only, you will need to be dropped in Sopalmo and collected at Macenas; there is no public transport. The walk itself begins bang in the centre of Sopalmo. On the seaward, east side of the road (that is the left, if you are facing south, towards Carboneras), is a track that dips down towards a *rambla*. The walk starts from here and immediately takes a vehicle-width track on the left which twists up, gaining height as it cuts east. Look to your right for views across deeply-dissected hilly ground, with vivid colours in the rocks and a glimpse of the road threading its way towards Carboneras. Geologists have referred to these brightly-coloured bare slopes as 'painted badlands'. The complex geology here coincides with one of the Carboneras Faults, a part of the boundary between the African and Eurasian tectonic plates.

The track becomes narrower, winding among plants typical of the zone, such as the grass-like esparto (Stipa tenacissima in Latin, *esparto* in Spanish,) and *albaida* (which has no English name but is Anthyllis cytisoides in Latin) with its many yellow flowers. The path is indicated by blue and white flashes. At the second flash, a diversion to the south for 40 metres or so brings you to a point where you look steeply down into a narrow valley heading directly for the sea. This is the Barranco de los Moros, Ravine of the Moors, named for the fact that Moorish pirates came this way in 1573 (see chapter 37). Retracing your steps back to the path, continue seawards and you soon reach a steep, loose descent needing care. This gives on to a wider track that, with the aid of a hairpin or two, leads down to the few coastal buildings at Piedra del Sombrerico. There's a small olive grove and a *chiringuito*, a beach restaurant, which is open during the summer months.

The track goes inland around a small knoll to an adjacent beach, the Playa del Sombrerico. Straight ahead is a house built high on the truncated top of a rocky hill, right on the coast, like something from an old James Bond film. The map shows it as 102 m above sea level but it looks higher. The track climbs inland past a gate where a plaque names the villa as La Rosa de los Vientos, the Rose of the Winds.

Almost immediately an elegant tower on a rocky coastal cone comes into view. Just before it there's a superb natural arch in the rocks, with the sea seething through below. The tower, the Torre del Pirulico, is one of the many watchtowers built in times past for the defence of the coast against incursions led by pirates such as Al-Borany, Maimono and Gálvez. The booty as often as not would be the local people themselves, taken off to be sold as slaves. The Pirulico tower dates originally from the Moorish Nazari epoch, the 13th-14th centuries, though what we see now is a restoration made just a decade or so ago. It's been done very well. A sturdy iron ladder leads up to what would have been the original entrance about halfway up the tower. Once inside, you can then take a further set of steps, inside the wall, to a platform with a parapet at the top. The situation is spectacular. The rock the tower sits on is only 32 m above the sea, so that even at the top of the tower, you are looking out from a height of less than 50 m, but it is a dramatic place, spoilt just a touch by the evidence of the spray-can merchants on some of the prominent rocks below. This tower can, incidentally be reached from Macenas along the easily-drivable coastal track.

The route continues for a kilometre on this wide level track to Macenas, where a *chiringuito* will happily serve you lunch if you are so inclined and where a different sort of defensive structure, the Castillo de Macenas, sits squat and strong on the beach. A couple of photos of this same stretch of coast, taken looking north towards the Castillo de Macenas, one in 1984 and one in 2009, clearly show that sand has disappeared from this length of coast in the intervening years, leaving just a rocky beach. Two British geologists, Adrian Harvey and Anne Mather, believe that the erosion of the sand is due to the sea walls and groyne-style jetties that have been built at

Mojácar for coastal protection there as the resort has developed. So, with the natural movement of beach material being north to south along this coast, that movement is now being impeded and the once sandy beach at Macenas has vanished due to 'sediment starvation'.

The next three paragraphs describe the circular return route to Sopalmo. If you don't plan to do that, you can skip them. By the *chiringuito*, waymarks indicate the footpath of the return route, heading off at an angle, uphill, to gain the ridge called the Cuerda de la Chacona. The signpost suggests an 'Observatorio'. This is at the end of the first steady climb up the very obvious track. The observatory, which is actually just a viewpoint, is 70 metres to the right, clearly indicated from the main track. At this point, looking seawards, you are more or less level with the Rose of the Winds, the hilltop villa seen earlier. In the other direction, inland, lies the Rambla de Macenas, of which more below.

The track climbs on in switchback fashion, though gradually gaining height to reach a top called El Sombrerico at 166 m. Here, by a huge concrete tank there's a *mirador*, another viewpoint. This has a couple of tables with benches, a wooden shelter and an information board with some delightful mistranslations. It's an ideal spot for a picnic after the climb. You are now significantly above the Rose of the Winds and it still looks to be right out of a Bond movie.

The wide track ends at this *mirador* and the onward way is a much narrower but still obvious path, sticking to the crest of the Cuerda de la Chacona which rises over a series of undulations to reach 228m at its highest. Two and a half kilometres from the *mirador*, the path suddenly begins to tilt down steeply. This is the most awkward part of the circuit, with a gullied and loose descent to be negotiated. It's perfectly possible, and a walking pole helps to provide some security and balance. It brings you down to regain the wide track taken on the outward leg of the circuit. By going to the right on this track and then, very soon, left at the T-junction, you are soon back at Sopalmo. There is of course nothing to stop you from starting and finishing this circuit from Macenas, with Sopalmo as the halfway point. That option would make the first half the tougher proposition, finishing with a level coastal stroll back to Macenas.

The desecration of Macenas

In 1764 a simple structure manned by three tower-keepers was built at the seaward end of the Rambla de Macenas. Just ten years later, it was replaced by a stone artillery tower in the redoubt style, described in Spanish as *con forma de casco de caballo*, 'in the shape of a cavalryman's helmet'. It held two cannons capable of firing 24 lb balls. It was restored in the 1990s and is still there, in good condition, today.

I have the second edition, published in 2006, of *El Litoral Mediterráneo*, one of the many excellent books in the *Guías de Almería Territorio, Cultura y Arte* series. The date of publication is significant. Macenas is described in glowing terms as an unspoilt place with the old redoubt prominent and a series of sandy beaches between contrasting rocky headlands.

In another book, *Calas de Almería*, the picture described is rather different. Search as I might, I've not been able to find anywhere in it a publication date, but I know it's later than 2006. The Castillo de Macenas is described thus: '*está siendo rodeada por una enorme urbanización que ha ido cambiando, para mal, el magnífico paisaje de su entorno*', 'it is being surrounded by an enormous development that has been changing, for the worse, the magnificent landscape of its setting'.

The huge Playa Macenas Beach Resort project in the Rambla de Macenas and on the adjacent hill-slopes just outside the boundary of the Cabo de Gata-Níjar Natural Park was begun in 2005 when much of the ground was levelled. The original project was promoted by Medgroup Macenas Playa SA and included plans for almost 1,400 luxury houses, three luxury hotels and two golf courses, though this was later scaled back. Medgroup was almost 50% owned by the international investment group of high-profile financier George Soros.

The development was formally inaugurated in a blaze of publicity in July 2008. Celebrity buyers were hinted at and there was even mention of a marina. However, the project was mired in controversy from the start. A rare plant called Limonium was threatened by the development; the developers agreed to finance a programme to re-establish the plant nearby. Conservationists still opposed the plans though, primarily on the basis that the watercourse in the *rambla* would be ruined by the golf course, but to no avail. The developers confidently trumpeted that they would create 2,000 jobs, with €68 million flowing into the local economy.

Building work was halted for a year while the Ministry of the Environment investigated whether or not Medgroup were building within 100 metres of the high tide mark and thus contravening the Ley de Costas, Law of the Coasts. Then ecologists showed that the company was illegally using drinking water to irrigate the greens on the golf course, forcing the company to alter its plans.

A number of the houses were completed and some were sold but more indications of trouble came towards the end of 2008, when work halted on the construction of the five-star beachside hotel. The gaunt, grey concrete frame of the building remains to this day as a reminder of the impact of the global economic downturn. The book *Calas de Almería* describes what stands as '*el feisimo esqueleto de un hotel, paralizado por la crisis*', 'the very ugly skeleton of a hotel, paralysed by the crisis'. George Soros must have seen the writing on the wall early on, because he had sold his substantial stake in the project by late 2008.

The golf course lost some €450,000 euros over the six years from 2008 and from 2012 onwards there were threats from the water company Galasa to cut off its water supply because of unpaid bills.

The Ministry of Employment and Social Security had already embargoed the complex and in 2014 Mojácar town hall revoked the building licence for the 'paralysed' hotel. Finally, on April 9th 2015, the golf course and part of the complex went under the auctioneer's hammer, with an asking price of €153,000 but with debts of €2.6 million.

The price of the luxury houses, initially between €325,000 and €395,000, has dropped by over 50%, so you could say there are bargains to be had. Sareb, a financial outfit that collects bad debts, is said to own about 40 of the units and the Banco Popular has another 80. Michael Gen, one of the project's major shareholders, insisted before the auction that the resort had a viable and positive future, and said he was confident that banks would be bidding for the golf course. Despite his upbeat assessment, no applications to buy were lodged in advance of the auction date and since then, Macenas seems to have dropped out of the news. A check on Trip Advisor at the time of this writing showed 22 reviews from people who have holidayed at the development and, while Trip Advisor is of course open to abuse, the following score: Excellent 2, Very Good 10, Average 3, Poor 4, Terrible 3, tells a mixed story, and in fact the lower scores tend to be from the more recent reviews. Meanwhile, a stark grey concrete skeleton and a desiccated, unkempt golf course blight the once attractive Rambla de Macenas.

The development of Mojácar Playa

The coast road from Carboneras to Mojácar, a superb scenic drive these days, was not always as easy to traverse as it is now. In his memoirs of the 1960s, Alan Simpson recalls that then it was 'a single-track dirt road as far as the Hotel Indalo. The dizzying road had no protection on its seaward side and wrecked vehicles could be seen far below.'

As a built-up area, Mojácar Playa is a young upstart compared to the much older *pueblo* that lies above its northern end. From the early 1960s things were starting to happen in Mojácar Pueblo, but it was a few years more before the potential of the beach began to be realised. Ric Polansky, one of the early developers, has a picture in his collection showing an idyllic stretch of coast with the Torre del Pirulico and Castillo de Macenas away to the south. It dates from 1969 and there are very few buildings to be seen. In the foreground is a small white house that Ric says was owned by a flautist from the London Philharmonic. Beyond that is another small building, the Cortijo de las Ventanicas, that was to become Tito's Bar (see chapter 3) and a little further away still is a temporary cement plant that was set up for the construction of the Hotel Indalo.

Another photo of Ric Polansky's, this time from 1976, shows the Guardias Viejas complex in place. The land there had been owned by the Polanskys and was sold to Laing, who put up several large buildings that included apartments, shops, bars, a restaurant, offices, and one of the first banks on the Playa. Steady development followed, although always with buildings restricted in height, thus avoiding the worst excesses of some other stretches of the Spanish coast.

The modern Mapa Topográfico Nacional (sheet 1032-1 Mojácar), though mostly sea, more or less shows the extent of modern building. It is, however, based on photogrammetric flights from 1998, so an updated edition is long overdue. One interesting detail stretches right along the sea-front, a double row of pecked lines labelled 'Colada de Vera'. This is one of the traditional routes by which animals were moved on their annual transhumance migration between the coast and the higher hills to the north, a yearly rhythm linked to the availability of good grazing. This no longer happens of course, though theoretically it could. Sheep are famously still driven through central Madrid on one day each year in order to maintain the ancient transhumance rights there.

In the mid-1990s the first section of Mojácar's *paseo* (promenade) was made, from just south of the Hotel Indalo (these days called the Hotel Best Indalo) to the Cueva del Lobo beach. I wanted to follow the coast from the southern edge of Mojácar northwards, stopping to make notes and take pictures of whatever caught my attention. A car's no good for this kind of thing and walking's a bit slow when you are faced with such a long flat prospect. The perfect solution was a bike and so I found myself, in September 2016, ready to begin. The *paseo* separates pedestrians and cyclists from the road and each other. At the start and frequently repeated on the red-surfaced cycle lane is the stencilled outline of a bike with the words 'CARRIL BICI', so you can't go wrong.

After about 300 metres there's a Parque Biosaludable, a sequence of 11 pieces of equipment on which those of a certain age can exercise without dire consequences. Cycle or walk along here every day in the wonderful Almerían climate, incorporate a regular 30-minute workout on these machines, and you might easily live forever. Just before the end of the original section of the prom the two carriageways join at a sign announcing that pedestrians have priority on this shared stretch: 'Zona Compartida: Prioridad Peatonal'.

It was not until March 2015 that work began to extend the *paseo*, by 880 metres, from Cueva del Lobo to the Red Cross roundabout, at a cost of €990,000. As part of the scheme, a time-capsule was buried, containing newspapers from the day the work began, coins minted in 2015 and a letter signed by the great and the good who attended the laying of the first stone by mayor Rosa María Cano. This work was completed and the new stretch opened in June 2016 just as the summer weather was kicking in. Near the beginning of this, by the Ankara bar, there's a wide section with seating and parking for bikes. Just beyond and across the road is a statue of the archetypal Mojácar woman in the appropriately named Plaza de la Mojaquera. There's an identical statue in Mojácar pueblo.

At the Red Cross roundabout, the paseo currently ends with a sign 'FIN CARRIL BICI'. From here, I'm on the road and as it's past the height of the tourist season, things aren't too bad. Proposals for the 'third phase' in the prom's extension, for a 2.7 kilometre stretch from the Red Cross roundabout to the Maui beach bar, were revealed in August 2016. At an estimated cost of €3 million, it will include (I appreciate that by the time you are reading this it may well have been built) parking for 145 vehicles and a cycle lane. However, the plans provoked an outburst of concern from the owners of several beach bars (*chiringuitos*) and the Somos Mojácar opposition group on Mojácar council, who claimed that the work would impinge on land where the bars have traditionally set out tables and chairs. Mayor Rosa María Cano pointed out: "Everyone has turned a blind eye to the fact until now, but we all know that parts of these *chiringuitos* have been built on public land. That is a problem that needs to be addressed."

Making people behave

Somewhat earlier Mayor Cano, no stranger to receiving flack after introducing by-laws restricting live music in bars and even drinking water in the street (presumably on the grounds that people might try to pass off alcohol as water), continued her campaign in late 2015 to raise standards with a series of new ordinances to counter antisocial behaviour. The mayor explained that the new laws were partly aimed at tackling the rowdy behaviour associated with noisy hen and stag nights, which occur mostly during the summer.

Detailed in a 27page document, the measures restrict the wearing of swimming costumes or walking bare-chested away from the beach, or wearing 'offensive' fancy dress. Street vendors are not allowed and anyone caught buying from them can be fined €300 and have their purchases seized. Additionally, under the by-laws, parents can be fined up to €1,000 if their children are deemed to be causing a nuisance whilst skateboarding or playing ball games. The mayor said: "I'm fed up seeing children with skateboards on the road, people wearing headbands with penises, or carrying inflatable dolls in the streets." She also added that she would not tolerate people showing off their muscles. All of which suggests that your passage through Mojácar will not be disturbed by incidents of questionable behaviour. Unless you are guilty of them yourself.

On the other hand, the current sanctions pale into insignificance compared to the treatment of bathers who did not meet the norms in the days of Franco. Alan Simpson's memoir *Mojacar Misremembered* contains this snippet: 'A British tourist bathed nude and was spotted through binoculars by two members of the Civil Guard who manacled him. After a brief appearance before a judge, with the Civil Guard saying he had been offended by the nudity, he then languished in prison until an amnesty after Franco's death. A backpacker sleeping on the beach was awoken with a rifle muzzle in his mouth, rattling his teeth. He was told: "The beach is a military area. You can't sleep here."'

By now I'm cycling past the Mojácar Parador. It was opened on 8th March 1966, one of a national network of luxury hotels. Most are in places of historic interest or natural beauty but in the case of Mojácar it was a new-build initiative to give tourism a kick-start in the area. The Minister of Tourism for the central government, Manuel Fraga, the same man who had attracted notoriety and some ridicule for bathing in the sea after the Palomares nuclear accident to assure everyone that it was safe, had signed the decree authorising the purchase of the land for €9,000. The hotel was built by Albert Vandenbergue for €148,000 and some of the first guests were military personnel deployed to the area after the Palomares disaster, which occurred just a couple of months before the hotel opened. The opening of the Parador and then of Almería airport in February 1968 were two key events in the early days of tourism in the area.

Next up is the roundabout by the Parque Comercial, the commercial centre at the foot of the road that comes down from the *pueblo*, the old village on the hill. In early 2017 a large Indalo figure was installed on this roundabout, replacing a fountain which, the council said, was costing too much in "constant repairs". The price of the new Indalo was about €50,000. Reports in the local press suggested that some residents thought the installation "unimaginative and too expensive". My impression is that the figure is very small in proportion to the large plinth on the roundabout where it sits. It's apparently made from Dekton, a new ultra-compact surfacing material that reproduces the creation of natural stone over thousands of years using high pressure and heat. Doesn't this beg the question: why not use natural stone in the first place? Wouldn't natural stone have been cheaper? And given the size of the roundabout, the Indalo seems rather stranded, a small figure on an island in a sea of traffic.

I'm continuing along the coast. It's flat and there's no stopping me, even though it's ridiculously hot for September. On the right is the Club Petanca Mojácar with its boules courts immediately above the beach. On the inland side of the road are various big complexes, including Marina de la Torre, but these are either stepped or stand back, so they don't overwhelm the scene. There's a reasonably spacious feel to this stretch.

Just beyond the Río Abajo roundabout is a long bridge over the Río de Aguas. There's a big pool here, impounded by a sand bar, so it's worth stopping to look over the parapet if you have any interest in birds. You're bound to see coots, almost certainly moorhens, and often something more interesting such as a few pochards or a cormorant. Immediately beyond the bridge during the main tourist season, there are camel rides at the Parada de Camellos, with half a dozen of the enigmatic beasts plodding across the ground at the back of the beach and not seeming entirely out of place amongst the palm trees and hot sands. Beyond here we are soon at the southern end of Garrucha.

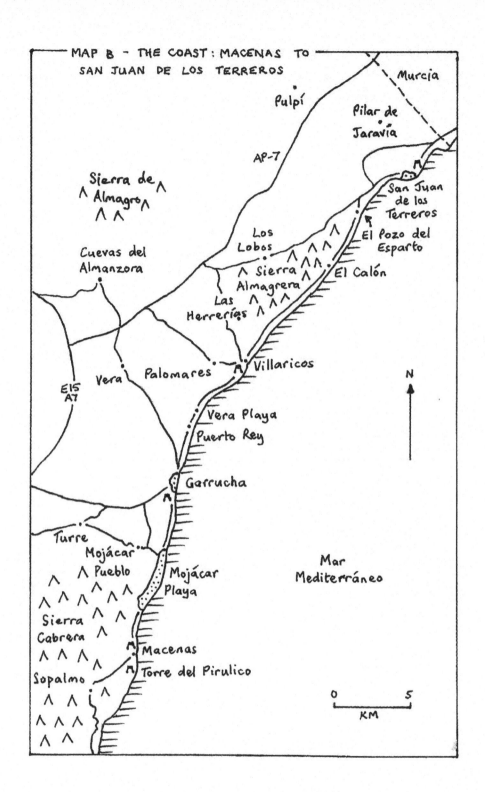

MAP B — THE COAST: MACENAS TO
SAN JUAN DE LOS TERREROS

Murcia

Pulpí

Pilar de
Jaravía

AP-7

San Juan
de los
Terreros

Sierra de
Almagro

Los
Lobos

El Pozo del
Esparto

Cuevas del
Almanzora

Sierra
Almagrera

El Calón

Las
Herrerías

Villaricos

Vera

Palomares

N

E15
A7

Vera Playa
Puerto Rey

Garrucha

Mar
Mediterráneo

Turre

Mojácar
Pueblo

Mojácar
Playa

Sierra
Cabrera

Sopalmo

Macenas

Torre del Pirulico

0   5
KM

2. Mojácar Pueblo

"Mojácar... is a little corsair settlement where the women still wash clothes in the Moorish fashion, by treading them with their feet..."
(Gerald Brenan, referring to the 1920s)

Mojácar: a short circuit

More walking; here's a route to give you the flavour of the old hilltop village of Mojácar. There is plenty of car parking space in front of the municipal swimming pool and also across the road from there, on the far side of a small roundabout. You reach these parking possibilities most easily by coming from the Turre direction and, just after passing the *tanatorio* (morgue) on your left, turning right, uphill, at the roundabout. The road sweeps up and soon reaches the parking areas described.

Before starting the walk, the roundabout is worth a look. The huge rock on it is the Piedra de los Silos and on a plaque it carries the words 'HOMENAJE A LAS MOJAQUERAS DEL CAMPO', Homage to the Mojácar Women of the Countryside. Such a woman, cast in bronze, stands atop the scarred and scratched rock, with her shoes a prominent feature. The caption tells that many country women walked together up to the hilltop village as part of their daily routine and at the point marked by the rock, would stop to change their shoes (I suspect this might actually mean they put shoes on after coming this far barefoot) before the final climb up the Cuesta Chillas into the 'city'.

So to the walk. From the roundabout take the wide pavement downhill on the road signposted to 'A7 Almería and Murcia'. If you arrived as described above, you are now walking back down the road you just drove up. As you lose height, there are wide views ahead over the broad plain to Vera and to the right, out to the sea at Garrucha. Close ahead is the flat-topped hill of Mojácar la Vieja, of which more later.

At the bottom of the hill, go right at the roundabout on the AL-6113, signposted to Mojácar. The red brick sidewalk with its metal fence decorated with the Indalo figure was laid in recent years, no doubt at great expense. Look up to the right and there is Mojácar Pueblo, perched high on the skyline. After a short while, by a turning on the left, in a small compound, is an information board about Mojácar la Vieja. The plaque says, in Spanish and slightly distorted English, that this conical hill has remains from when it was first settled in the 6th-7th centuries AD. It mentions signs of first a Visigoth settlement and later a Moorish one called Muxacra, usually translated rather oddly as 'Mountain in the height', from which the modern name has evolved. For details of how to visit the top of this hill, jump to the next section at this point. To continue with the basic walking circuit, read on.

The pavement by the road steadily gains height with a series of gentle curves. Scattered around the base of the hill to the left is the hamlet called Las Huertas with many orange and olive trees traditionally irrigated with water from the nearby Río de Aguas. Today there is almost never water in this stretch of the river. About 50 metres before you reach the roundabout at the bottom of the *pueblo*, look left over the Indalo fence and you'll see a small ravine, with running water. This is fed by the overflow from the *fuente*, the spring which made the ancient hilltop settlement viable. As I stood peering over the fence two grey wagtails, a robin and a black redstart were flitting around, obviously attracted by the water.

At the roundabout, turn right, uphill, and in a further 60 metres or so, bear right along Calle La Fuente. A little way along here is the *fuente* itself, now a substantial marble-clad feature with a single water spout immediately on the left and a dozen more at the far end. Many people still collect their drinking water from the *fuente* and if you're there for more than a few minutes you will almost certainly see someone turn up in their car with a batch of 5-litre plastic flagons. Above the row of spouts is an inscribed marble plaque recording a meeting here on June 10th 1488 between Garcilaso de la Vega, the envoy of the Catholic Monarchs and Alvarez, the last Moorish mayor of the town. The south of Spain had been ruled by the Moors for centuries but it was now the time of the Reconquest. At the meeting by the *fuente*, those present drew up a pact of 'free association' between the local Moors, Jews and Christians. In effect the Catholic Monarchs were demanding peaceful submission by the Moors. Some accounts say that the mayor of Mojácar did not attend the meeting at the fountain and when later questioned about his absence, he reputedly stated that although he was a Muslim, generations of his people had been born in Spain and were in effect Spanish.

The English version that has come down through history is that, when asked to surrender, Alvarez said this: "Christian, listen carefully to my words and transmit them faithfully to your kings. I am as Spanish as you are. When those of my race have lived in Spain for over seven hundred years, you tell us, 'You are foreigners, go back to the sea'. In Africa, an inhospitable coast awaits us, whose inhabitants will tell us, as you do, but with more reason, 'You are foreigners; cross the sea from whence you came and go back to your own country'. We find ourselves between two coasts both of which deny us bread, shelter and neighbourliness. Is this human? I never took up arms against the Christians. Tell your kings so. Allah is my witness.

"I believe, therefore, that it is just to treat us as brothers, not as enemies, and that we should be allowed to continue to cultivate our fields and graze our sheep. If, as it is said, Doña Isabella and Don Fernando are as good-hearted as they are virtuous, I have faith in Allah - they will accede to our request. We, in exchange, promise to be loyal to the Christian kings. But, if we are forced to, we shall defend ourselves with honour. Rather than live like a coward I shall die like a Spaniard. May Allah protect you!"

The Spanish Monarchs were sufficiently impressed with this argument to reply as follows: "Garcilaso: Tell Alvarez that we agree to his request, in view of his noble words. We offer him our friendship and we are confident that he will respond to the mercy which it is our pleasure to show him. May God keep him and his kinsmen." Historical accounts, however, suggest that non-Christians were heavily taxed and were under great pressure to convert or face expulsion.

A somewhat airbrushed version of these events is remembered nowadays in the annual Moors and Christians festival held in the *pueblo* and on the *playa* each June. It's a spectacular celebration of elaborate and colourful costumes, parades and jousting. It's a commercial opportunity too, as evidenced by this snippet from a press account of the 2016 festival: "Business owners reported an excellent weekend of trading."

Only 30 years after the meeting between Garcilaso de la Vega and Alvarez, the earthquake of 1518 which totally devastated Vera also took its toll on Mojácar which, at that time, had 350 inhabitants. All the houses were inside a wall and below a fortified citadel, the ultimate retreat where the population went when pirates from North Africa attacked. The earthquake caused the collapse of this stronghold, killing nine people who were inside at the time. Elsewhere in the village, 30 houses collapsed and five more people died, a total of 14 fatalities. The castle was soon rebuilt and the Duque de Alba had someone stationed in it as a keeper and also as the governor of his various holdings in the Turre and Mojácar area.

Back to the *fuente*. Leaping ahead 350-odd years, the *fuente* underwent major renovation in 1876. A second marble plaque, immediately below the one described above, records this and gives the name of the mayor at the time as D. José Yribarne de los Ríos, 'of the Rivers', a suitably appropriate name to be inscribed on a fountain. A century later Alan Simpson, in his reminiscences of the years around 1970, recalls that the *fuente* was shaded by palm trees, had donkeys carrying away water and women doing their laundry. He says also: 'Two women with horses walked around Mojácar *pueblo* selling drinking water from the *fuente* in huge clay pots slung either side of their animals. Mains water had not yet arrived at the village.' He adds that later, when the *fuente* was modernised (this was in the 1980s), there were 'fisticuffs between expatriates who wanted the *fuente* to remain *antigua* and Mojaqueros who favoured a modern look'.

At the beginning of 2015 the old water mill next to the *fuente* was renovated at a cost of about €100,000. In the Middle Ages the mill processed grain and the adjacent bakery, together with the *fuente*, would have been the central hub of village life for the long centuries before piped water was installed.

Immediately above the *fuente* is the Centro de Arte which holds regularly changing exhibitions. It's worth popping in if you find it open (at the time of writing, its opening hours are Tues - Fri 0900 - 1400, Sat and Sun 1000 - 1400, closed Mondays). Follow the street past the art centre as it twists steeply up and to the right. This will bring you out on to a brick pavement. At this point go on just a few metres then, under the street name Cuesta La Fuente, take the steep road of grey setts uphill to the left. Follow it until a tall stone wall faces you. Go right here, still steeply up, and you soon reach an arch. This is the city gate, the Puerta de la Ciudad, with an inscription over it in both Roman and Arabic scripts and, on the uphill side, a tile indicating that it dates from the 15th century.

Opposite the arch, go up Calle Unión and shortly you will reach the Plaza Nueva, with several bars and cafes and an airy viewing platform looking out over a wide arc from Vera to the coast. The shops here are crammed with trinkets featuring the Indalo, the figure that has come to be associated with Mojácar more than anywhere else. The climbing is all but done now and the circuit is almost complete, so this is a good place for a drink and a break to enjoy the panorama. As an aside, at the time of writing, a major project is under way to build a new town hall and police station under the Plaza Nueva and renew the plaza itself but I assume that, when it is finished, the route described here will not be affected.

Leading off from the Plaza Nueva is Calle Alcalde Jacinto. The name refers to the mayor (*alcalde*), Don Jacinto Alarcon, who was almost single-handedly responsible for the rejuvenation of Mojácar in the 1960s. In a few metres Calle Alcalde Jacinto reaches the small Plaza Iglesia which, as the name suggests, is by the church. It also has a marble statue of La Mujer Mojaquera, the archetypal Mojácar woman, dating from 1989. It's identical to the one down on the *playa* but this one is rather spoilt by the black cast-iron fence that tightly encloses it. Such a figure seems reminiscent of Gerald Brenan's description quoted at the head of this chapter.

Cross the square at the right-hand side of the church and find Calle Arco de Luciana, near the Tourism Office. This street very soon leads steeply down several flights of steps. At the bottom of these, turn left alongside the road, Avenida París, and this will bring you back to complete your circuit at the parking area within a couple of minutes.

Mojácar la Vieja

To visit Mojácar la Vieja, take the side-road on the left by the information board mentioned early in the circuit above, dropping steeply, and then go sharp left after 50 metres on Camino Eras Del Lugar. Continue until this road sweeps round to the right by a sign saying 'FV <---- '. At this point continue ahead, bearing slightly left to do so. After 200 metres there is an open area on the right with several tall eucalyptuses and, at its nearest edge, a slightly overgrown track. Take the track, which passes to the right of a horse corral and veers to the right across the base of the hill. Continue along, more or less contouring and staying above various wire fences. The lower slopes of the hill show definite remains of terracing, some of the retaining walls even having mortar to consolidate the stones. Pass above a flat-roofed brown tank in a wire enclosure and go on until you see a T-shaped feature at the base of the eastern ridge. This turns out to be a dead tree-trunk with a hefty branch fixed above it as a cross-piece. From here a path, faint at times, works its way up the seaward nose of the hill. (I didn't find this way up until later and actually went up in a more frontal assault, scrambling up awkward and loose slopes, to pop out suddenly at the summit. Entertaining but not recommended.)

The big surprise at the summit is a long, sunken *aljibe*, a water tank excavated from the bedrock, with its roof missing. Other than this there isn't much to see in terms of remains but the views are superb, away to Vera, out to sea, and across to the hilltop *pueblo*. The best way down is to reverse the way up, then from the T-post, contour back across the base of the hill to the track and the road, returning up to the paved walkway by the AL-6113.

Rising like a phoenix

By about 1960 the population of Mojácar had declined from a much earlier peak of about 10,000 to only 1,000 or so, with a long drought and a period of deliberate neglect under the dictator Franco having taken their toll, the town having been Republican during the Civil War. The mayor in the early 60s, Don Jacinto Alarcon, perhaps inspired by the way he saw other previously unknown small coastal villages such as Torremolinos attracting foreigners and money, announced that he would give ruined houses or plots of land to outsiders who were prepared to come and put some new life and, hopefully, funds into the place. Advertisements were placed in prominent newspapers to spread word of this and soon people were coming to take advantage of the initiative.

What follows are a few snippets about the time when Mojácar recovered from its apparent terminal decline. Others, who were here at the time can, and have, written, from personal experience, more extensively about those heady days. I can't do that as I was a wet-behind-the-ears schoolboy in Grimsby at the time.

Within a few years a number of well-known characters had arrived, including the British diplomat Sir Michael Adeane (private secretary to Queen Elizabeth II for the first twenty years of her reign), the Spanish diplomat Rafael Lorente, bullfighter Antonio Bienvenida, actor Charles Baxter and the renowned Colombian concert pianist Enrique Arias. Film stars who were in Almería in the early heyday of the industry locally often spent time in Mojácar too. The immediately recognisable actor, novelist and playwright Robert Shaw, femme fatale Anita Ekberg, Mark Lester (who had played Oliver in the eponymous musical), and larger-than-life Americans Dennis Hopper and Orson Welles were amongst them. Former police officer Paco Haro, whose book *Mojaqueros de hecho* recalls (in Spanish) those days in detail, said he wrote it "to express well-deserved respect for a number of people who were fundamental to the modern history of Mojácar." As characters came from across Europe, South America and the USA, Haro met many of them as his family owned the old Indalo Hotel in the Plaza Nueva.

Mojácar journalist and blogger Lenox Napier, who himself arrived as a 13-year old when his parents came as part of the new wave, tells of his father playing draughts with Orson Welles. Welles was in the area playing Long John Silver in the 1972 film of *Treasure Island* but liked a game of 'checkers' in his time off. This was draughts with a difference though: rather than having simple circular pieces, black and white for the respective players, the idea was to have a dozen small liquor glasses each. One player had brandy, the other anis. When you took a piece, you had to drink it. As Lenox Napier explains: "The player who could still see the board at the end of the game was declared the winner." When director Sergio Leone was making his 'Dollar Trilogy' near Tabernas, he and the stars of his films, such as Clint Eastwood and Lee van Cleef, who generally stayed in the Gran Hotel in Almería, often came to Mojácar too.

In his quirky book of reminiscences *Naked in the Snow*, Alan Simpson takes up the story: 'In 1968 most of Mojácar was a heap of brown ruins. There were more dogs and donkeys than houses. The Americans had already atom-bombed Palomares by mistake; if they had bombed Mojácar no one would have noticed. Mayor Jacinto had given away ruins to selected foreigners on the condition that they were rebuilt. It was a masterstroke. Mojácar was a town that rose from its ashes, and started again almost from scratch. Because of the strange nature of its revival it attracted an international polyglot of writers, artists, intellectuals, eccentrics, layabouts and Kooks, as well as some useful people like plumbers and electricians, builders, shopkeepers and chefs.'

By 1972, in Alan Simpson's words: 'The Mojácar miracle had happened, almost overnight it seemed. A hundred young people with glazed eyes loitered around smoking pot, or lay semi-comatose on the pavement. The air vibrated with strange sounds resembling music which emanated from 32 bars all competing to be the loudest. One had to step over their legs to proceed along the *calle*. These were Mojácar's first tourists. The *escaleras*(steps) below Rincon de Zahari were packed to capacity with colourful characters and at night the blaze of lights lit up the sky. The din could be heard as far away as Turre.'

A white elephant

One of the most prominent though not one of the most attractive buildings in Mojácar *pueblo* is the 300-room Hotel El Moresco. On the seaward side of the town's hill, it has panoramic views out over the Mediterranean. The only problem since September 2008 is that it has been closed and uncared for. Prior to that, in the high season it had an average of 300 guests at any one time, and this obviously had a massive knock-on effect in boosting the town's other businesses.

At the time of its closure, the hotel was owned by businessman Arturo Fernández who, as the head of the Grupo Arturo Cantoblanco, allegedly received part of a grant, amounting to €320,000, from the Junta de Andalucía to refurbish the hotel. This work was never done. In 2013 it was revealed that Sr Fernandez owed Mojacar council €62,000 in property tax on the hotel, and he was also accused of having paid most of his workforce a significant proportion of their wages in cash to minimise social security payments.

Meanwhile, in early 2016, the PSOE opposition party in Mojacar proposed that the council should buy the abandoned hotel to create jobs and stimulate further tourism. They suggested that the hotel could be bought at an advantageous price as the owners, Grupo Arturo Cantoblanco, had entered bankruptcy proceedings. I checked the hotel's website in the autumn of 2016 and, somewhat surprised, discovered that it appeared to be fully open for business. Just to be sure the information was accurate for this book, I walked up there at the end of the year to double check, only to find it as closed up and sad-looking as ever. Large faded posters in the windows, clearly years old but originally designed to give punters a positive message, were still claiming that it was closed for improvements and implying that it would be open again soon. Another example to prove that you can't believe everything you see on the internet.

Who is Indalo Man?

The simple answer is that the cave-drawing that has come to be known as the Indalo is one of a number of faint brownish-red stylised representations of people and animals in the Cueva de los Letreros (Cave of the Signs), in the Sierra de Maimón Grande, near Vélez Blanco. *Cueva*, or cave, is really a misnomer in this case, as the feature in question is no more than a shallow rock-shelter part way up a slope at the base of a steep outcrop.

The cave paintings were first identified by the archaeologist Antonio Gongorra Martinez in his 1868 book *Antigüedades arqueológicas de Andalucía*. Then in 1924 the area was designated a National Historical Monument and in December 1998 UNESCO declared it a World Heritage Site. Many caves in the same area show indications of Bronze or Stone Age humans. Dating of the remains suggests that people lived here and the paintings were made during Neolithic times, around 5500 – 6000 BP (Before Present). The red ochre colour of the designs is because they were made with iron oxide, *almagre* in Castilian. As an aside, it's thought that the Sierra de Almagro and Sierra de Almagrera both owe their names to the abundance of iron oxide in these mountain ranges.

Before we had a house here, we were exploring eastern Almería in our campervan and were near Vélez Blanco. This would have been in early 2005. We knew that the only way to get close to the ancient paintings was to join a guided visit so, despite having almost no Spanish at that point, I rang the number to enquire about this, only to be told by the guide that she was actually with a group at the cave at that moment. She invited us to join her. Somewhat unadvisedly, we bumped our ageing Hymer motorhome as far as we could up the rough approach track, pulled off when it seemed really unwise to try to drive any further, and climbed hurriedly up to the site. We managed to catch the latter half of her talk, the thrust of which we more or less followed.

The cave paintings are rather enigmatic, with figures and animals such as archers, horned men, deer and mountain goats repeated frequently. They have a constant sense of movement and expression. And, of course, the best-known symbol in the cave is that of a man apparently holding a rainbow. It's worth noting that the late Michael Jacobs, a respected authority on Spain, in his excellent book

Andalucía, at no point uses the term 'Indalo' for this figure. Two suggestions have been advanced for the origin of this word. The first is that it comes from the language of a tribe who lived in Iberia some 2,500 years ago. The second is that, as 'Indal Eccius' in Latin means 'Messenger of the Gods', linking to the shamanic appearance of the cave figure, it may derive by association from the patron saint of Almería, San Indalecio.

Jacobs's book was published in 1998 and already at that date, the rock-shelter was 'protected from the graffiti-writer by an iron grille' but he goes on to write: 'I was strongly recommended in Vélez Blanco to bring with me a flask of water to throw at the paintings so as to bring out their colours; the present, near-illegible state of the paintings is sad evidence of the frequency of this practice.'

At some point local villagers took to daubing the outside of their homes with the rainbow man symbol, converting the figure into a talisman designed to ward off evil and natural disasters. In 1946 the Almerían painter Jesús de Perceval and other artists founded 'el Movimiento Indaliano', a kind of earth-magic movement based in Mojácar, which adopted the rainbow man as a symbol, together with its existing connotations of protection against the evil eye. Local blogger David Jackson, who has researched the Indalo extensively, describes this artistic movement as coming from a 'vital position, the cosmovision of the Almerían, and the essence of ancient and past civilisations before our own'. The Indalo Movement artists saw in their symbol an ancient hero who, by capturing and controlling a rainbow, symbolised the pact between the Gods and Man. Despite such exotic theories, experts generally agree that in the original cave paintings the Indalo is simply a hunter who uses his bow and arrows to bring down birds in flight.

Initially the Indalo was just a symbol of Mojácar but its reach expanded steadily across the Levante Almeriense (Eastern Almería) and gradually it became a trade-mark for the whole of Almería province. The official logo of the 2005 Mediterranean Games was Indalete, a cheery, youthful character based on the iconic figure. The Indalo now appears on key-rings, tee-shirts, mugs, jewellery and even the heavy lorries that transport Almerían vegetables to the markets of northern Europe. The lucky charms of the Indalo are only effective though, if the Indalo has been presented as a gift – or so they say. Thus has an unknown prehistoric artist unwittingly created a distinctive image for modern commerce.

3. Characters

'...el Parlamento inglés decidió remitir una solicitud al Gobierno español para que su compatriota, el Matador Henry Higgins, más conocido como Enrique Cañadas, no fuese discriminado como torero en España por su condición de inglés.' '...the English parliament decided to submit a request to the Spanish government that its countryman, the matador Henry Higgins, better known as Enrique Cañadas, should not be discriminated against as a bullfighter in Spain because he was English.'
(Francisco Haro Pérez)

Henry Higgins

Having driven along the road from Turre towards Mojácar, as you come towards the steep ground on your right, with the *pueblo* high above you, there's a turning on the left signposted to a *tanatorio* (morgue). Just beyond the *tanatorio* is a cemetery, the Cementerio de San Agustín, with plenty of parking space in front of it. Go through the entrance, turn left, and on the far left-hand wall, about 20 metres along, in the top tier, is a stone on one of the niches, inscribed:

HENRRY HIGGINS

26 – 10 – 1944

15 – 8 – 1978

LOS TUYOS NO TE OLVIDAN

The sentence below the dates means, more or less: 'Your people will not forget you'. There's the unfortunate spelling mistake, the double R, but there's no clue here that this marks the final resting place of an English bullfighter.

Henry Higgins was born in Bogotá in Colombia to Bill Higgins, a British oil executive who worked for Shell, and his wife Irene McHatton, who was Mexican but of Irish descent. He spent his early years in South America before being sent to school first in Kent and then the Isle of Man. His father was interested in bullfighting and took the young Henry to see a *corrida de toros*, an experience that fired the young lad's interest. However, when Henry first came to Spain it was because he had a passion for the Spanish guitar. He became a pupil of Antonio Sánchez, the father of Paco de Lucía.

Higgins had read Hemingway's *Death In The Afternoon* though and, once in Spain, he became more interested in bullfighting. The idea of doing it himself didn't come to him immediately but soon it overtook the Spanish guitar in his affections and became a consuming interest. His first bullfight was in Tenerife on 19th March 1967. Things seemed to be going well when the Beatles' manager Brian Epstein agreed to represent him and gave him a generous contract. Epstein, however, died less than a year later. After this, Tito del Amo, about whom more appears below and elsewhere in this book, took to the bullfighter and decided to back him.

Although Tito wasn't particularly interested in bullfighting, the two got on well and became friends. They spent three years traipsing across Spain and southern France, wherever Henry could get a booking. Despite this, he tended to be looked down upon because of his nationality. He would find himself in small flea-bitten village bullrings in the middle of nowhere, as often as not cheated by shady promoters and dealing with unscrupulous rivals. Higgins was slight in build but he was honest and brave. Too brave, perhaps, as he was gored on average once every three fights.

He passed the *alternativa* exam in 1970 to become a qualified *matador*. It was nevertheless a difficult journey. He had taken the professional name Enrique Cañadas, borrowing the surname from a family he was friends with in Sevilla, to appear more Spanish. He had successes. On 20th September 1970 he filled the bullring in Fuengirola, though he had worked hard for this, spending the previous few days personally plastering the town with posters. His skills came to the attention of Antonio Ordóñez, who offered him a contract for eight fights in the most important bullrings along the

Costa del Sol. However, the first two fights did not go well and the contract was rescinded. In the UK the *News of the World* newspaper took up his cause to such effect that in 1972 the British government interceded with the Spanish government on his behalf (see quote at beginning of this chapter).

Following this he returned to Mojácar and his old friend Tito del Amo, missing no chance in interviews to recall how Tito had supported him in his early years. In that same year, Higgins collaborated with Jim Myers on his autobiography *To Be A Matador*, which was generally well received. He was not making a living from the bullring though, so back in Mojácar he went into business, opening a small souvenir shop called Regalos Johanna with a friend.

He gave up the bullring for good in 1974 and tried other business ventures, including being a sales rep for the English inventor Clive Sinclair, as well as spells as an estate agent and a promoter of board games. But Higgins was enthusiastic for anything involving risk and speed, and it was not long before he needed the adrenaline rush again. He developed an interest in hang-gliding and wanted to enlist in the Escuela de Aviación Civil de Cuatro Vientos in Madrid. To his disappointment, it turned out that they would only accept Spanish nationals. He nevertheless pursued his interest, but always flew in tandem with an instructor.

Then, at about midday on 15th August 1978, something went wrong. This was his 42nd flight - he'd always kept records - but it was the first time he'd flown solo. Under the watchful and horrified gaze of his partner Isabel del Barrio, he came to grief. I had imagined that he launched himself from one of the rocky crags above Mojácar but Barrie Naylor sent me this: 'We thought that he started his flight from high in the Cabrera, near where we recently repaired his cross. But the truth was less glamorous. He took off from a couple of streets back from the *playa*. He crashed into a wall a couple of streets down from his take-off (no thermal uplift). His body was covered with a towel and he lay dead in the street for a couple of hours awaiting the *guardia*/coroner.'

It was estimated that he fell from a height of eight metres or so; not much, but enough to break his neck. If you stand before his gravestone, there is no clue to the adventurous life of this Englishman who died in his early thirties but there is, on a brass plaque, which incidentally has his name spelled correctly, this verse:

Sobre la tierra dorada que pisa el Minotauro y
sobre los cielos azules mediterráneos
brotarán cada Primavera los recuerdos
de tu juventud para siempre eterna

Above the golden earth that the Minotaur treads and
above the blue Mediterranean skies
every Spring, memories will arise
of your never-ending youthfulness

It seems appropriate for someone who carved out such a distinctive path and who died at just 33.

Frank Evans

Slightly earlier another Englishman, Frank Evans, born the son of a butcher in Salford in 1942, had his first professional bullfight in Montpellier in France in 1966 when he was mistakenly booked by a promoter who thought he was hiring Henry Higgins. By 1969 Evans was Spain's top *novillero*, apprentice bullfighter, but despite this he struggled to earn a living from it and returned to Salford, where he established a successful kitchen business and became 'unofficial manager' to the mercurial and troubled footballer George Best.

After his father died in 1976, Evans decided life was too short not to follow his dream and returned to Spain. By 1979 he was bullfighting professionally again and drawing large crowds as *El Inglés,* 'The Englishman'. In 2003 he was ranked 63rd in the world amongst some 10,000 bullfighters. After receiving a replacement titanium knee and then, in 2007, a quadruple heart by-pass, he was fighting again in 2009 at the age of 67. Evans was the subject of a Channel 4 documentary called *The Bus-pass Bullfighter,* and has written a well-reviewed autobiography, *The Last British Bullfighter.* He has also been consulted on proposed bans on bullfighting in parts of Spain. In 2014, he made the news for a different reason: a £500,000 cannabis farm was discovered on the upper storey of a large property he owns at Worsley, near Salford, one of about a dozen properties he rents out. At the time the *Manchester Evening News* broke the story, Evans, who has Spanish citizenship, was preparing for fights in Mijas and Sevilla. I've no doubt stretched a point by including Frank Evans here, as he has no immediate connection to Almería. And I'll put my cards on the table as no supporter of bullfighting, but I can't deny that I'm intrigued by the lives of these Brits, two colourful fragments of Spanish cultural history.

Tito del Amo

Tito del Amo's involvement with the fallout from the Palomares nuclear accident is explained in chapter 6, but the man himself deserves more than a mention. As that chapter says, Tito was born in Los Angeles but came to Spain in 1965. Jaime Carlos Tito del Amo had been strongly influenced by the hippy lifestyle prevalent in mid-1960s California and, rebelling against his strict Catholic upbringing and having received a substantial inheritance following his grandfather's death, he arrived in Spain at the age of 22, with long blond hair and a backpack. He was returning to the land of his ancestors: his grandfather was from Calabria. He came to Mojácar intending to spend a few weeks here and stayed for the rest of his life. He said he "fell in love with the light" in this lost corner of the country, a hidden world where women still covered their faces.

Tito was one of the first bohemians in the area and became fully immersed in the drop-out culture of the time. Spain was in the grip of the Francoist dictatorship but was open to the currency of foreigners, though perhaps not entirely aware that they also brought with them marijuana and psychedelic drugs. Mayor Jacinto of Mojácar pueblo was busy giving away plots of land. The old village was a hive of activity with cranes and bricks everywhere. Tito, meanwhile, bought the ruined chapel of San Sebastian and, with the help of the architect Roberto Puig, turned it into a distinctive home.

It wasn't all parties and recreational drugs though. Tito was an accomplished photographer and did a professional and important job in covering the Palomares incident. He then also managed Henry Higgins for a time before opening Mojácar's first *chiringuito*, Tito's Bar, in 1981 on the site of the old Cortijo de las Ventanicas on the beach front. Tito put on live music and his bar became synonymous with freedom, a retreat for the youth of the area under his watchful eye. His bar became a regular haunt of several famous musicians of the time, including Miguel Rios (one of the pioneers of rock and roll in Spain), flute and sax player Jorge Pardo, and Pablo Carbonell, leader of Los Toreros Muertos.

In 2011 Tito produced and starred in a feature-length documentary about Walt Disney's origins. When he was a child in the States his family had lived next door to Disney and Tito always promoted the notion that Disney was born in Mojácar, although he could find no firm evidence to support his claim.

When he died aged 74 on 22nd June 2016 after a short battle with cancer, the local press, both English and Spanish, carried fond articles about a man who was described by those closest to him as "highly spiritual" (he was a Buddhist), "loyal" and "an intelligent man with a great sense of humour". An affectionate tribute in the newspaper *La Voz de Almería* described him as *'un chamán de voz reposada'*, a quiet-voiced shaman. Here's my free translation of the final paragraph about him from the piece in *La Voz de Almería*: 'So Tito has gone, one of the big characters of Mojácar, of a more cosmopolitan Mojácar, founder of Tito's Bar, that musical universe of peace where, in those *pre-botellón* days, the youngsters of eastern Almería danced until dawn whilst a guy with Viking locks chose celestial music.'

Following a suggestion from the local PSOE party, Mojácar council voted unanimously to posthumously award the town's Indalo de Oro award to him in 2018. The council agreed also to name a street after him but stressed that would only be when a new street was built at some future date.

When I was giving a presentation of *Flamingos in the Desert* at Angie's Cafe in Mojácar in the summer of 2015, Tito was there - it was the first time I'd met him - and he told me he'd enjoyed the book particularly because it didn't focus on Mojácar. I always intended to ask him to check over what I've written about Palomares for this book but sadly, fate intervened before I could do so.

4. Coasting: Garrucha to Villaricos

'In a very few years the whole of this still unexploited coast of Almería province will be developed from the Gulf of Almería to the boundary with Murcia.'
(Nina Epton, 1968)

Garrucha

As you approach Garrucha, the embanked structure on the inland side of the road is what's left of the loading arrangements for the iron ore which came down a century ago from the Bédar area via a mineral railway. There's much more about this in this book's final chapter. And then, just as you arrive at Garrucha, on the left, is an 18th century castle, now converted into Nautarum, an Interpretation Centre of the Sea. It has sections relating to writers (Verne, Conrad, Cervantes, Melville) and painters (Monet, Seurat, Gauguin, Sorolla) who have depicted the sea, maritime trade routes, the history of navigation, Garrucha's fishing industry, and the history of diving, complete with underwater sound effects. There's also a short film called *El Siglo Minero*, The Mining Century, which is very well done. All in all, for a mere €1 entry fee, it's definitely worth a visit. The entrance is round the back, by the way, on the inland side.

I'm still on my bike, after the diversions of the last couple of chapters, so a few metres beyond the castle, I bear right at the roundabout to take the street along the sea-front and soon enough there's a broad *paseo* with a marble balustrade. There's no dedicated cycle lane but there's space enough to ride safely along here at a sensible pace without striking fear into pedestrians. Below the prom is a sandy beach and the port of Garrucha can be seen too, with continuous loading of gypsum into huge bulk tankers moored against the far arm of the port. It's this mix of catering for visitors and having commercial enterprises too - fishing and the export trade - that gives Garrucha the feel of being a real town. As at Carboneras, there's something genuine here, a dimension that seems to be missing in places that are nothing more than a resort.

The *paseo* briefly narrows then widens again. Along here is a bust of Antonio Cano Cervantes, a poet born in Garrucha in 1883 who died in Barcelona in 1950. Alongside his statue, in a bed from which tower three huge palms, there's a garden gnome, in a rather bizarre contrast to the tribute to the poet. The port and marina are on the right, and across the road to the left is a restaurant which hit the headlines in the summer of 2016 in a red prawn related incident.

Red prawn drama

These days Garrucha is noted for its famous and expensive red prawns. They are commemorated on a recently made roundabout which appeared just outside the Lidl store when it opened. The price of these prawns depends on the fluctuating cost at the market, so there may be an unpleasant shock when you get your restaurant bill if you haven't checked beforehand. This is what happened at the restaurant mentioned above, which I won't name as it's perfectly possible that the establishment itself wasn't to blame for the altercation in which 11 people were injured. According to the press, a group of customers took exception to the price they were being charged for a *ración* of 'inferior prawns'. The owner of the bar said they were drunken youths from one of the tougher Madrid suburbs looking for trouble. During the ensuing brawl he was struck over the head with a broken glass and rushed to the local medical centre, while Guardia Civil officers brought the situation back under control. The incident had attracted a sizeable crowd of onlookers who were, by then, blocking the traffic outside.

To divert from the *paseo* for a few minutes, immediately inland of the coastal strip at Garrucha, recent developments clothe the side of a hill that is crowned with a prominent tapered chimney. After intending to go up and look at it for years, I finally did so some time ago. I just drove towards it, following the roads through the housing, and found a place to park that left just a very short walk to the summit. As I walked up, I passed two workmen busily digging up, with pneumatic drills, what had obviously been a tarmac road up to the chimney. Cast-iron bollards at either side of the road had been dislodged and were just lying about. I would have asked them what the plans were for the place but they were so intent on their noisy task that I didn't feel an interruption would have been appropriate.

Almost at the top of the hill, a spiral sloped walkway leads the final metres to the chimney which itself looks to have been renovated within the last few years. There's a wall protecting the walkway, the base of the chimney has been re-pointed and the upper part given a modern facing. Adjacent there are arched tunnels on the hillside. These have also clearly been renovated. One is aiming straight for the chimney, as if it was the flue providing the air-flow for the fire at the base. However, no-one thought to spend a little of this outlay on an information board to explain exactly what went on here. The place is beginning to look uncared for again too. The wrought iron gate at the base of the chimney was hanging off its hinges when I visited, which at least meant I could squeeze in and look up and yes, way up there, I could see a tiny square of sky. Much later, by chance, I read that this used to be the site of a lead mine and the San Jacinto foundry.

The views are impressive too, apart from the part-built structures nearby that were abandoned when the economic crisis struck a few years ago. You can see north past Villaricos to the Sierra Almagrera and south along the coast towards Mojácar, and inland across the plain to Vera. Garrucha's deepwater port lies immediately below. It can take huge ships. The coast shelves steeply here. Within one kilometre of the port, there is a 200metre deep submarine canyon. That is the limit to which light can penetrate. Within 10 km the sea-floor drops to 1,000 metres and 50 km out, in the Sea of

Alborán (the westernmost portion of the Mediterranean), it's 1,500 metres deep.

A century ago Garrucha had a considerable export trade in silver, lead, copper, iron, esparto and fruit. The minerals came from the hills inland around Bédar and the mining and export enterprises led to a small community of foreigners living in Garrucha. By 1930, there were British, Dutch and German consuls there. One of the Britons, whose name I have yet to discover, piped drinking water from Mojácar to Garrucha and, with the proceeds of this lucrative scheme, made history as the person to own the first vehicle in Almería province with a number plate; his lorry had the registration AL-1.

Paseo and beaches

On along the *paseo* again, there's a shady linear park with a kids' play area and a marble statue of two fishermen, one of whom is grappling with a large fish, commemorating the fact that they were the founders of the port: *'A los Pescadores de Garrucha, Fundadores de este puerto'*. Back in the 14th century, there was a defensive tower inside a larger enclosure where the fishermen kept their boats. Each day people from the surrounding area would arrive to buy fish. This tower was destroyed by the 1518 earthquake and totally vanished. At that time there was also a building in Garrucha called the Casa de la Sal, on the site where the present town hall stands. It had vaults used for storing salt brought from the saltworks of Cabo de Gata. Of course this was long before the invention of freezing processes so salt was hugely important then for preserving food.

The *paseo* ends in a few metres but by going to the right and finding a way past the restaurants - there's plenty of space - I find a way to cycle easily right beside the harbour, thus avoiding the narrow and busy main street through the town.

At the end of the port is the compound used by the Santa Irene Club de Vela, the local sailing club. Immediately beyond that, you can look down into the entrance of an underground road tunnel. This leads out to the far arm of the port where the bulk tankers load. Work began in 2011 to create this because, these days, Garrucha focuses almost entirely on the export of gypsum, brought in by about a thousand lorry-loads every day from the quarries in the Karst en Yesos de Sorbas. A million metric tonnes is exported annually. The underpass was designed to segregate these lorries from other traffic in the town and take them straight to the port but work halted in 2012 when the money ran out. It restarted in October 2014 and the underpass finally opened, at an eventual cost of €7.4 million, in the early summer of 2016, at last ensuring that residential and shopping areas were free from the noise, pollution and danger the heavy traffic had been creating.

There's more beach ahead, a broad stretch of sand. On the bike I pass through a wide area of road with many parking bays to reach a red-surfaced cycle lane, passing a tall disused brick chimney among the houses on the left with no indication of its history or former function. This is the Playa Las Marinas-Bolaga, an expansive beach with clumps of palms and frequent showers. The bike lane finishes by the Bar Restaurante Laguna. As the name hints, straight ahead is the *laguna*, a shallow pool where a noisy cluster of ducks and coots is usually waiting to be fed at the closest point. Further out, you may see pochards and little grebes. Friends who regularly check out the birds here have also seen a kingfisher. Some folk refer to this as Millionaire's Pool, after the bar of a similar name nearby.

At this point I take to the road and head inland to the main road, the ALP-118, which will take me fairly painlessly to Villaricos. For much of the way there's a cycle and pedestrian track, with parts of it hidden from the road by a screen of oleanders. There's a reason for taking this route rather than sticking to the beach and it has nothing to do with the fact that one of Europe's best-known naturist beaches, Playa El Playazo, lies ahead. After all, in this climate, by the Mediterranean, taking your clothes off for most of the year seems like an eminently sensible thing to do. But a year earlier seven of us had decided to cycle from Garrucha to Villaricos, sticking as close to the sea as we could.

As far as Pueblo Laguna all went to plan. Then we struck out seawards of the pool, along the beach, some of which we were able to cycle. Parts were too soft though and here we pushed our bikes. Inland there is a flat agricultural area and patches of pine woodland but this stretch, for now at least, is not built up. Eventually we had to divert inland to cross the Río Almanzora at the road bridge, by which time we were virtually at Villaricos, so we judged the scheme a success. Lunch at a bar in Villaricos followed and then it was time to ride back. At this point we found three of the bikes had punctures, and one had both tyres flat. I upended my bike and looked carefully at the tyres. A small spiky seed-case was sticking to the rubber of one wheel. I pulled it away and 'Pssssssssss', within seconds the tyre had gone down. To this day I'm not sure which sandy zone plant it was that had scuppered our ride but a lesson had been learnt.

A threatened coast
The PSOE mayor of Cuevas del Almanzora, Antonio Fernández, is hoping that massive development will take place on the coastline I've referred to above. An urban management plan (PGOU) published in 2015 proposes a major reclassification of land, which would open up the coast between Quitapellejos beach in Palomares and Villaricos.

Sr Fernández says that any development will be done in a sustainable way, with low density building and the existing protected zones, amounting to 17% of the area, maintained as they are at present. Plans for a development in this area, nicknamed 'Little Venice', first surfaced 20 years ago when the idea was to have a new marina, with homes around it and along canals, so that boat owners could tie up right by their property. Permission was refused for this scheme because of the disruption to the coastline and the drainage patterns, so the plan was shelved.

The new scheme envisages hotels with a combined capacity of 5,000 places, a shopping centre and 1,600 homes, to be built over five years. A similar plan was scrapped in 2012 after the Junta de Andalucía published a decree to protect the coastline. The current developer, Grupo Almanzora, feels that, with Spain coming out of recession, the time is right to look at such a development again.

Others have a different opinion, not least the environmental group Ecologistas en Acción. In 2015 they included Quitapellejos beach in their 'anti-awards', giving it a 'black flag' because the adjacent pine forest, a notable local feature, has no protection. The developers say the pine forest will be preserved, though presumably surrounded by new building. Mayor Fernández, meanwhile, says: "The coastline from Vera to Mojácar is urbanised but much of the Cuevas del Almanzora coastline is not. The plan will increase tourist interest in the area." He appears to discount the notion that people are already interested in the area because of the pinewoods, the unspoilt beaches and the birdlife at the mouth of the Río Almanzora: in other words, people already come precisely because it is not covered in concrete like the coast a few miles to the south. For him, it seems 'tourist interest' means just another spoilt coastline.

5. Villaricos

'A cormorant, wings half spread, stands
like a man proving to his tailor
how badly his suit fits.'
(Norman MacCaig)

A long history

Villaricos is not a big place but it does have a long and intriguing history. It was founded by seafarers from Tyre (which is in modern Lebanon) in the 7th century BC and was known to the Phoenicians and Romans as Baria. Just inland from the modern village, there are late Roman remains on the summit of the Cerro de Montroy, where silver and lead were worked.

Close by lies the Phoenician necropolis, a warren of underground tombs cut into the hillside 2,700 years ago, which were first investigated by Louis Siret. Most striking are the six tapering entrance cuttings in the hillside which lead into the hypogea. A hypogeum (from the Greek *hypo* (under) and *Gaia* (mother Earth or goddess of Earth)) is an underground tomb. At Baria the external entrance passages lead to large rectangular sepulchral rooms. Very lavish funerary furnishings, including gold and silver jewels, amulets, vases and richly decorated ostrich eggs, were found in the hypogea and are now held in the National Museum. Other types of tombs were found over a wide funerary zone here, amounting to over 2,000 burials in total. The site is not normally open but it is possible to arrange a visit (which is conducted in Spanish only) for a minimum of four or five people by contacting the tourist information office in Cuevas del Almanzora.

Just south of Villaricos lies what is sometimes called the Castillo de Villaricos. It's not really a castle though, just a defensive tower of the style known as a Torre Reducto (a 'redoubt'), built to the same design as those some way further south along the coast at

Macenas and Mesa Roldán. Like them, and the other more traditionally-shaped towers, it formed part of a linked coastal defensive system.

This tower was proposed by José Crame in 1765 and its construction was subsidised by Joaquín de Luna y Zapata, a gentleman from Almodóvar del Pinar, a small place up towards Cuenca. He was initially a cadet in the coastal cavalry regiment but, in return for his involvement in this project, he was made a captain of cavalry. By 1774 the tower had been built and was in service. It was 11 metres high, with an access door halfway up that was reached by a rope-ladder, and it was armed with two cannons of 16 and 24 lbs respectively.

By 1830 it was staffed by an officer, three tower-keepers and two soldiers from a detachment in Vera, who also acted as artillerymen when necessary, although at this point they only had one iron cannon that had been cast in sand and proved unusable. At this date there was no settlement at Villaricos.

In time the tower passed to the Guardia Civil, who made interior changes and installed a door at the base. It was used by them until the 1970s, when it was closed up and abandoned, only relatively recently being restored for its current use as a tourist information centre. In truth, it usually has very little information – just fliers for trips in a glass-bottomed boat (there are a couple of these based in the small nearby marina), leaflets about the Cueva Museo (Cave Museum) and the Goya Room in the Museo Antonio Manuel Campoy in Cuevas del Almanzora, and contact details for guided visits to the Phoenician necropolis just along the road. There is a small exhibition space on the first floor too, but what I find most interesting, in the entrance gallery, are eight old black and white photos showing various aspects of the former mining works here at Villaricos, at Las Herrerías and in the Barranco del Jaroso near Los Lobos. The most intriguing shows a hillside with a couple of covered channels snaking along the slope, contouring towards the sea beyond. The caption says: 'Villaricos: Galería de Conducto de Humo de la 'Fabrica Nueva'', so it seems these were vents to take smoke away from the 'New Factory'.

Close by are the buried remains of tanks used in Roman times for the fish-processing industry which produced *garum*, a fiercely pungent condiment made by macerating the innards of sardines, mackerel, anchovies or tuna with salt. It was a very popular ingredient in Roman cuisine and was also used as a cosmetic and a medication. There is little sign of this enterprise now, unlike at the similar Roman fish-processing site at Torre Garcia in the Cabo de Gata-Níjar Natural Park, where low walls remain and an information board gives some clues to this specialised activity. Spanish *garum* was particularly highly prized and was a valuable commodity.

Outside the tower, on the evening I visit, a group of locals are using the conveniently flat ground to play boules, with the lengthening shadow of the building keeping them cool. By now I've abandoned the bike and decided to explore the village on foot. A short stroll towards the village from the tower takes me to an attractive arc of beach with a few palm trees, and an enclosed marina, the Puerto de la Balsa. It's from here that the glass-bottomed boats set out. Beyond this a promenade on several levels, with curves and slopes, leads northwards, with the village buildings set a little way back. Seaward of this *paseo*, there are rocks adding interest to the coastline. Some show signs of former use. As I pass a guy hulling sunflower seeds with his teeth in a manner that would make a macaw envious, he tells me, unbidden, that the remnants of stone walls on the offshore rocks were all linked to the mining industry. At one point there's a huge rusty mooring ring set into the natural platform of tidal rocks. More stretches of beach follow and then another enclosed basin for small boats, the Puerto de la Esperanza, which is at the northern end of the village.

Suddenly, the houses end and the rolling hills, the Sierra Almagrera, begin to rise. Clearly visible from the village are various mining remains including, just a few hundred metres away on the undulating slopes, a three-tiered masonry structure. This is shown on one of the black-and-white photos back in the information point, where it is labelled: 'Chimenea de la Fabrica Esperanza'.

In the mid 19th century the skies over Villaricos were polluted by the dense columns of smoke that rose from the foundries and factories such as the Esperanza, the first thing that the ships coming to take away the minerals would see. By the time the mining rush of the Sierra Almagrera (see chapters 9 and 10) was finally coming to an end in the 1930s, the rich mine and foundry owners had already begun to build summer residences at Villaricos, attracted by the beaches and the climate. This was the beginning of the village as a resort, which today continues to be its main function.

Dreambeach

I turn and walk back through the village; doing so on a warm late May evening is a delight. Red-rumped swallows are skimming low along the streets for a supper of insects, the heads of young house martins are peering out of their cup-nests under the eaves, and the area in front of Aurora's house is a mass of colourful greenery tumbling from pots of many sizes. I've not met Aurora but I assume it's her house because immediately alongside, part of the same frontage, is her fresh fish shop with PESCADERIA AURORA announcing its purpose.

Just behind the beach which is south of the village lies a large flat area, normally empty. It is here that the Dreambeach Festival is held each August. In 2015, the third year of the event, over 100,000 fans of DJ music came to listen to headliners such as Fatboy Slim and BlasterJaxx. Wags in Garrucha and Mojácar, many kilometres down the coast, claimed they didn't need to buy a ticket as they could hear the festival perfectly well from their balconies at home. In 2013 a group of residents from Palomares and Villaricos called 'Afectados por el Festival Dreambeach Villaricos 2013' petitioned the local council not to allow the event, citing noise pollution, damage to gardens, revellers swimming at night in private pools and drug-taking in public places. They were unsuccessful and the event has continued, each year bigger and apparently more law-abiding than before. By 2016 the festival had been extended to four days. It attracted 160,000 people and put €6 million into the local economy, according to the organisers.

Some local bar owners say the festival has a completely negative effect on their businesses, because of access restrictions and the amount of rubbish putting people off. Local politicians in Villaricos and Cuevas del Almanzora meanwhile consider Dreambeach to be "good publicity" and "a total success". So, this is a vibrant occasion with much enjoyment or a nightmare that makes the life of some locals a temporary misery, depending on your point of view.

Birding at Villaricos

There's more to Villaricos than history and festivals though. The sky was overcast, the breeze was chill. It was November and it felt like it. The Arboleas Birdwatching Group had met, as it does every few weeks, by the 'ford' in the *rambla* of the Río Almanzora, just about a kilometre inland from the coast. Usually the riverbed of the Almanzora has pools among its rocks and gravelly patches and there's shrubby vegetation such as nicotiana too: a good range of habitats for birds.

In the bed of the *rambla* we found black-winged stilt, white wagtail, ringed plover, snipe, common sandpiper and, after considerable discussion, a water pipit. An eagle-eyed member of the group announced a distant kestrel on one of the pylons that marched away parallel to the *rambla*. On a nearby wire-mesh fence were a black redstart and a stonechat. Already the birding was good.

Angled concrete slopes lead up on either bank of the *rambla*, making what in the USA would be called a levée. In odd places, shrubs have managed to gain purchase even on these blank canvases. From one such bush just a few metres from us, a male Sardinian warbler, its black cap prominent, gave its harsh rattling call.

There's a recreational path along the top of the levée on the left bank. In a few hundred metres this passes a sewage works which, inevitably, is not always fragrant. Such places though are the stock-in-trade of birdwatchers. Today its two fenced-in pools held not only more stilts and another common sandpiper but also a couple of little ringed plover. By now our group had spread out, scanning, nattering, and thus some individuals were not always in the right place at the right time.

So it was when a bluethroat was seen briefly at the side of the *rambla*: I missed it. It's a small, neat bird that breeds in northern Europe and passes through Almería province on migration, southwards in autumn and back northwards in spring. It has a distinctive white supercilium (a stripe above the eye) and, in most plumages, as the name suggests, a blue throat. It was here a couple of years earlier that I'd seen my first ever bluethroat, the first in a remarkable sudden run of three bluethroats in four weeks, so I wasn't too distraught on this occasion. In compensation, two stilts flew over, calling loudly and with their vivid red legs extended an astonishing distance behind their elegant black and white bodies.

Creatures of habit, we repaired to our usual cafe in Villaricos for a coffee before driving to the beach. From the beach there's a view across to rocks in the bay where, as happens more often than not, we saw cormorants and an Audouin's gull, a local speciality. By now, the cloud was breaking up and the sun's welcome heat was making itself felt.

Behind the beach is the area where the Dreambeach Festival is held each August. Most of the year, the Dreambeach site is literally just a large flat area, which can be crossed to reach the estuary of the Río Almanzora. Today, we saw the usual cormorants, posing nicely on various logs and rocks or swimming like half-submerged creatures from the time of the dinosaurs. Grey herons stood among the vegetation and in the shallows. Across the estuary lie low mud cliffs and, on a bush above these was a southern grey shrike. Kingfishers are seen here occasionally, fleeting flashes of electric blue and orange as they skim across your vision – if you are lucky. Little grebes and a black-necked grebe were here too.

We headed back round to the beach through taller vegetation where we once found a penduline tit. On the rocks towards the harbour several more cormorants were arrayed like ancient ragged crosses. Prospecting the shoreline boulders there was a solitary little egret and, bobbing on the sea, a gull which, after discussion, was deemed a first-winter black-headed gull rather than the hoped-for Mediterranean gull some of us had been wanting. A little earlier in the autumn we'd regularly been seeing whimbrels here, smaller cousins of the curlew, also passing through on migration. Today the highlight was seeing quite sizeable fish, maybe 20cm long, repeatedly leaping clear of the water just a few metres from the shore. We imagined they would only do this to escape predators but apart from their impressive leaping, there was no sign of kerfuffle. On the beach back nearer to the harbour was a party of waders, a mixture of pale-grey and white sanderlings and darker, orange-legged turnstones.

The day's final stop was at the lagoons near the big Consum supermarket at Vera Playa. The first lagoon on the right of the road is fairly open. On this occasion it was a matrix of shallow pools, mud and gravel, attracting a ruff, as well as Kentish plover, dunlin and little stint. The deeper water held shoveler and white-headed duck. A very late barn swallow flew over, presumably on belated passage to Africa. The next lagoon, directly opposite Consum, is good in winter and early spring but has high vegetation obscuring the view in summer and autumn, unless one of the birders has been recently with his loppers to cut strategic viewing gaps in the reeds. This hadn't happened, so our attempts to scan this pool were doomed to failure.

This is by no means a full run-down on what we saw during this typical day's birding. When we totted everything up, it amounted to 52 species, ranging from the mundane such as house sparrow and collared dove to the more rewarding sightings like bluethroat and ruff. The beaches and the climate of the area are rightly celebrated, but what riches of archaeology and natural history there are too. By not making more of these things surely the local tourist offices are missing a trick.

6. Cover-up and clean-up

"They told us everything was safe. We were young, we trusted them."
(Arthur Kindler)

The cover-up

In her 1968 book *Andalusia*, Nina Epton mentions in passing, not entirely accurately: 'the now internationally famous fishing village of Palomares at the mouth of the river Almanzora, where the Americans carelessly dropped an H-bomb into the sea'. What she writes is partly true but there were four bombs, not one. One fell in the sea and the other three fell on land. I covered the incident in some detail in *Flamingos in the Desert* but since then I've come across a further intriguing dimension to the original story.

It involves Tito del Amo, who featured in chapter 3. In early 1966 Tito's brother André was working in Madrid for the news agency United Press International (UPI) under a very experienced reporter called Harry Stathos. André del Amo had already told Tito that Mojácar was one of the places he should see and when he did, he instantly fell in love with it. This was the situation when, on 17th January 1966, an American B-52 bomber and a KC-135 refuelling plane collided high over Almería province.

As soon as the accident occurred, in which seven USAF airmen lost their lives, the US Embassy in Madrid informed the government of the Spanish dictator Francisco Franco. Franco's immediate concern was not for the danger to the people of Palomares but to protect Spain's tourist industry, the fascist government's main source of income. The US State Department's position was to tell the media nothing about the potentially devastating incident. So both the Spanish and US authorities chose silence as their strategy.

However, André del Amo had caught a whisper of what had happened and was heading for Almería with Leo White, correspondent for the British *Daily Mirror*. Colonel Barnett Young, the chief press officer of the US Air Force, tried to warn them off. When asked if the B-52 might have been carrying atomic weapons, he said: "This is not the place for scandalous stories or crazy theories".

According to Tito, his brother André got the breakthrough just as he was about to go back to Madrid: "As he was leaving Almería, he came across a US military policeman who was looking for somebody to translate for him. He wanted local people to leave the area because of the radioactivity. André said nothing, and just translated. He innocently asked if the authorities were worried about the bombs. The policeman told him everything."

The New York Times published the story the following day. It confirmed that atomic weapons were involved and that one was still missing. Franco was incandescent when the story broke. He ordered the news to be suppressed in Spain and banned the distribution of foreign newspapers. He also got Ángel Sagaz, the Director General of North American Affairs at Spain's Foreign Ministry, to protest in the strongest possible terms to Angier Biddle Duke, the US Ambassador in Spain. Duke in turn called Harry Stathos, demanding that he reveal his sources. Stathos assured him that the leak had not come from within the US Embassy but refused to say exactly where he had got the story.

The US government took 40 days to admit the existence of the bombs. Documents that have now been declassified show the extent to which the authorities tried to hide the reality of the situation with statements like this: "The US Defense Department has said that it is looking for classified material. For reasons of security, we cannot make further comments."

Franco's censors and the US Embassy were still trying to sit on the story and the fourth bomb was still missing. As a result, Harry Stathos and the correspondent for Associated Press, the other US news agency in Spain, asked Tito del Amo to monitor the situation. He recalls: "They weren't making much progress, so they hired me to keep an eye on things here. I lived nearby. They paid me 500 pesetas a day, which was a fortune in those days. I hired a Seat 600 and spent six weeks in Palomares".

Tito kept tabs on the clean-up operation on land and the continuing search for the bomb lying on the sea-bed. He took so many photos that he had to drive to Murcia every two days to give his rolls of film to the engine driver of the Madrid train. "For me it was just a job. The whole thing was very difficult though, because nobody wanted to say anything."

The search for the fourth bomb

The search for the fourth bomb, the one lost at sea, was focused on an area where a local fisherman, Francisco Simó Orts, locally known since then as 'Paco el de la bomba'('Paco the Bomb') saw it entering the water. Orts was hired by the US Air Force to assist in the recovery operation. Despite this, many ships and 150 specialist divers were involved. The bomb was thought to lie in an uncharted area of the Río Almanzora canyon on a 70-degree slope at a depth of 2,550 feet (780m). After an 80-day search, the bomb was finally located by the DSV (Deep Submergence Vehicle) Alvin on 17th March, but was dropped and temporarily lost when the Navy attempted to bring it to the surface.

Alvin located the bomb again on 2nd April, this time at a depth of 2,900 feet (880m). On 7th April, an unmanned torpedo recovery vehicle became entangled in the bomb's parachute while attempting to attach a line to it. A decision was made to raise the recovery vehicle and the weapon together to a depth of 100 feet (30m), where divers attached cables to them. The bomb was brought to the surface and eventually taken back to the USA by the USS Cascade .

Once the bomb was located, Simó Orts appeared in court in New York with his lawyer, a former US Attorney General, to claim salvage rights. According to Dr John P Craven, an expert who was part of the recovery team: "It is customary maritime law that the person who identifies the location of a ship to be salved has the right to a salvage award if that identification leads to a successful recovery. The amount is nominal, usually 1 or 2 percent, sometimes a bit more, of the intrinsic value to the owner of the thing salved. But the thing salved off Palomares was a hydrogen bomb, the same bomb valued by no less an authority than the Secretary of Defense at $2 billion - each percent of which is, of course, $20 million."The US Air Force settled out of court for an undisclosed sum but subsequently Simó was heard to complain that the Americans had said he would be financially compensated and had not kept that promise.

Fifty years later

In mid-2014 the local Almería press announced that the US government was refusing to release the findings of a detailed report about the 1966 clean-up operation at Palomares. The report followed a visit to the Palomares site by a group of scientists from the US Department of Energy in 2011. The original clean-up effort, 45 years earlier, had failed to remove all the radioactive plutonium and the more lethal americium, and three 'hotspots' have remained cordoned off ever since. Jesús Caicedo, the mayor of Cuevas del Almanzora at the time, whose council area includes Palomares and Villaricos, said he had no knowledge of the US report.

Soon afterwards, mayor Caicedo was in the news again when his right-wing Partido Popular council decided to name a street in Palomares after the late Manuel Fraga Iribarne, who was Tourism and Information Minister in the dictator Franco's government at the time of the 1966 Palomares incident. Fraga had achieved notoriety when, in a publicity stunt to reassure the public that there was no radiation danger, he went for a dip in the sea off Palomares with the US ambassador to Spain, Angier Biddle Duke.

Cuevas del Almanzora council said Fraga should be honoured because he was the only Spanish minister who visited the area after the incident. However, Antonio Fernández, spokesman for the left-wing PSOE opposition, said Fraga had done nothing for Palomares and that naming a street after him would only remind people of Franco's dictatorship, adding: "He only went for a swim to show everyone that there was nothing amiss after the accident, when it turns out that the area is still contaminated 48 years later."

Back at the main story, namely the clean-up, in January 2015 the environmental group Ecologistas en Acción (EA) launched a petition to mark the 49th anniversary of the nuclear accident. EA demanded that the US "assume its responsibilities and proceed with the decontamination" and further insisted that the Spanish government "stand firm and force the US to comply with its obligations or itself resolve this environmental atrocity".

A further odd twist occurred a few months later, in June 2015, when US Secretary of State John Kerry was due to meet the Spanish Foreign Secretary. It was thought the Palomares contamination issue would be up for discussion but the meeting never took place because Kerry, aged 71 but nevertheless a keen cyclist, fell off his bike in the French Alps, broke his leg, and was flown back to the US.

In October 2015 there was at last some movement on the issue. John Kerry, now recovered from his cycling tumble, was back in Spain where, together with Spain's Foreign Minister José Manuel García-Margallo, he signed a 'statement of intent' to remove the contaminated land from Palomares. Sr García-Margallo said the deal would "correct a mistake committed 50 years ago". Kerry said the two countries should resolve "this important issue".

This deal was hailed as a breakthrough but the 'statement of intent' is not legally binding, can be terminated at any time, and is dependent on the availability of funds. This latter is a major issue as the estimated cost of the operation to remove 50,000 cubic metres of soil, which is contaminated with half a kilo of plutonium, runs to hundreds of millions of euros. The radioactive soil is equal in volume to 27 Olympic swimming pools but the Spanish energy agency Ciemat (Centro de Investigaciones Energéticas, Medioambientales y Tecnológicas) is looking at the possibility of compressing it down to 6,000 cubic metres. The intention is to take the soil to the USA and store it at a facility in the Nevada desert, about 100 km from Las Vegas. The cost of this operation has escalated from an initial figure of €30 million to €640 million. Of this, according to the respected newspaper *El Pais*, €500 million is for the decontamination costs and subsequent storage, and €140 million is for the costs of transporting the soil.

The 'statement of intent' did not cover how the costs would be split between Spain and the US. *El Pais* also reported that a new 100km road is being planned to take the soil from Palomares to Cartagena. This in itself is a major stumbling block for planners. Veteran journalist Christopher Morris, who was one of the first reporters at the scene of the original incident, said: "It would make a lot more sense to use the existing toll road, the AP-7, which is hardly ever used." Summing up his opinion of the latest deal, he added: "The news will come as a relief to many, but the fact that it's a 'statement of intent' sounds like a holding exercise." However, Antonio Fernández, formerly opposition leader and now the mayor of Cuevas del Almanzora, said that Ciemat was confident that the clean-up would start within a year and that the operation could take up to two years to complete.

Further attention was focussed on the issue in January 2016 with the appearance of two books in Spanish to mark the 50th anniversary of the accident. Both books concentrate on what happened after the disaster. *Accidente Nuclear de Palomares - Consecuencias (1966-2016)* by José Herrera, argues that the American authorities made a shambles of the initial clean-up operation. He told the press: "The clean-up was done very badly. It took the US military a week to begin cleaning up the area, but during that time there were 96 kph winds sweeping Palomares. That lapse may have had an impact on human health." His book suggests that the authorities cut many corners, aiming to complete their task as quickly, rather than as thoroughly, as possible. He was also scathing about the October 2015 declaration of intent, calling it "nothing more than grandstanding", given that it is not legally binding.

The second book, *La historia secreta de las bombas de Palomares*, by Rafael Moreno, comes to similar conclusions, arguing that both the Spanish and US authorities, once they realised the magnitude and complexity of removing all the contaminated soil from the hilly areas around Palomares, conspired to downplay the reality of the situation. He also castigates the Spanish authorities for refusing to publish the results of the annual medical tests carried out on local residents ever since the incident.

Back once again at the main story, if there is a new road to be built before the soil can be moved and if there are no funds available, mayor Fernández's time-scale of two years seems extremely optimistic. However, a key unspoken obstacle seems to be this: removing the contaminated soil will create a precedent. The US has carried out nuclear tests in other parts of the world and could potentially face huge lawsuits requiring it to clean up other areas of poisoned land. I'm checking over this section in October 2016. It's already a year on from the 'statement of intent' and as far as I'm aware, no significant progress has occurred.

And now, in January 2017, I read this, regarding US President Donald Trump, in an 'Opinion' piece by local journalist Richard Torné: 'Given his woeful track record on environmental issues, his thin-skinned response to criticism, his 'USA-first-at-the-expense-of-all-else' mantra and his ambivalence towards Hillary Clinton, it's reasonable to assume he will bin the much-hailed 'statement of intent' signed by both countries in October 2015'.

Cancer amongst veterans

During the summer of 2016 a report in *The New York Times* revealed that of 40 US Air Force veterans identified as having helped with the Palomares clean-up operation, 21 have had cancer and nine of those have died from it. The article was careful to say: 'It is impossible to connect individual cancers to a single exposure to radiation,' but the strong implication was that the true extent of the exposure to radiation suffered by the USAF personnel has been covered up by the authorities to avoid having to pay medical costs. The USAF has always insisted that the danger of contamination at the site was minimal and that the 1,600 people who cleaned up the crash site were adequately protected. These 1,600 were low-ranking American troops who were rushed to Palomares from US Air Force bases across Spain.

However, the piece in *The New York Times* said that veterans from the clean-up team reported that they spent months shovelling toxic dust without breathing equipment or protective clothing. The article also claimed that tests performed during the clean-up showed that the men had very high plutonium contamination but that the USAF called the results "clearly unrealistic" and threw them out. Instead, the Air Force relied on the results of about 1,500 urine tests taken at the time of the clean-up, of which it said only 10 indicated the absorption of unsafe levels of plutonium. However, the men who actually carried out those tests have said the results were "deeply flawed" as they had "neither the time nor the equipment to follow protocol". A study in 2001 also determined that the urine tests were flawed but the USAF reputedly later removed this finding from public access.

Anecdotal reports show that as soon as the clean-up ended, men began to get sick, being crippled at a young age by joint pain, headaches and weakness. Those who sought medical advice were consistently rebuffed by the army doctors. One of the veterans, Arthur Kindler, who subsequently suffered from testicular cancer and a rare lung infection, and who was 74 at the time he was spoken to by *The New York Times*, said: "They told us everything was safe. We were young, we trusted them."

Some of the airmen had been sent to local houses with hand-held radiation detectors in order to reassure local people. However, they were not shown how to use the devices and in fact were allegedly told to keep them turned off. Peter M Ricard, one of the airmen involved, said: "We were just supposed to feign our readings so we didn't cause turmoil with the natives. I often think about that now."

7. Coasting: Villaricos to San Juan de los Terreros

'North again from here, the road cuts between the sea and the Sierra
Almagrera, riddled with mine workings.'

(from *The Rough Guide to Andalucía*)

Coves and chimneys

Immediately north of Villaricos is a beach of black pebbles, Cala de
Las Dolores. However, right alongside it is the Deretil factory, which
manufactures the antibiotic amoxicillin and about 30 different types
of fertiliser, so given that there are many other beaches along this
stretch, maybe you wouldn't choose to bathe here. I should admit
that by this stage I've abandoned the bike and reverted to driving. I
do pull in at Cala de Las Dolores though, because I want to have a
closer look at all the flues contouring the slopes on the inland side of
the road, leading to and from various smelting chimneys.

It's easy enough to scramble up to the nearest flues in a
couple of minutes. Close up, they are an impressive feat of
engineering, simply because of their scale. They are semi sunken,
with an arched cap of stone and cement, with regular holes,
presumably to allow a good draw of air. In places they have collapsed
and you can get a better idea of their size; you could just about stand
up in one, and they go on for hundreds of metres. Some lead quite
steeply directly up to the chimneys, presumably to supply air to the
furnaces, but others snake across the hillsides, more or less
contouring, and to me at least, the purpose of these is less clear
though I think, on the evidence of the captions in the Villaricos castle,
that they are for taking the smoke and fumes away from the
chimneys. I'm sure there are people out there who know all about
these flues and I'd be happy to hear more from them.

Driving on past a couple more small coves, my next stop is
above Playa de la Invencible. You can't miss this. There's a huge
building, a sort of peachy colour, the size of a hotel or a barracks. It's

intact but disused. On its seaward side are big paved areas, an ornate tiled fountain, and pathways with handrails leading to various viewpoints perched above the sea. Clearly it was quite an elaborate project but it's all now abandoned and steadily deteriorating. There are views back to lots more remains associated with the mines and of course there is the beach below. A few hundred metres further on there's a slim chimney, almost down at the shoreline. Here there are extensive remains and spoil heaps of dark, heavy iron-rich rock. Directly inland is yet another chimney and a hillside veined with even more flues. It's an intriguing coast.

The next named cove is Cala de Las Conchas, Cove of the Shells, which is described in more detail - it will become apparent why - a couple of chapters on. Just a little further north is Cala Cristal, where a walkway leads down to an attractive tiny beach. A neck of sand leads out to an offshore rock and other scattered rocks indicate good snorkelling potential. For several kilometres there has been almost no modern development along this coast, though virtually everywhere there are remains linked to the old mining activity. Now though, a village hoves into view. It's El Calón, a small place that is dominated by the unfinished concrete shell of a large development, a victim no doubt of the *crisis económica*. One day a year or two ago, searching for lunch, we spotted a sign at the turn-off into the village advertising a bar, so down we went. There was no sign of life, either at the bar, which was closed up, or elsewhere. As I pass through this time, in the latter half of 2016, several of the properties are for sale, hinting at an air of gentle abandonment.

Cala Panizo and El Pozo del Esparto lie not far ahead. The main road is a little way inland here and a loop road winds through these settlements. There are plenty of trees, something of a pleasant surprise after the bare coast, and the general feel is of somewhere slightly more upmarket than El Calón. If you want a quiet life by the sea where nothing much happens and the highlight of the week is shopping in San Juan, this could be the place for you. That said, El Calón also has its charms and opportunities, I'm sure.

San Juan de los Terreros lies close now. There are more palms on the approach and the mostly modern town is not without character, although it has definitely put all its eggs in the tourist basket. The highlight of the town is the castle (of which, more below), the turn off to which is almost at the northern edge of town. Beyond that, the coast road from San Juan heads towards Águilas, across the provincial border in Murcia, but it has a couple of final delights to reveal. There's a private area on the right with the remains of what looks like an old *noria* (waterwheel) and then, at a roundabout almost at the provincial boundary, there's a turn off and a short track into the parking area for two superb beaches.

They are adjacent and separated by a strikingly eroded headland. As you look at the sea, on the left is Playa La Carolina and on the right, Playa de Los Cocedores. These are popular beaches and so best avoided at the height of the season unless you like crowds. There are a couple of *chiringuitos* too but it's the sand underfoot, the golden rock slopes protecting the coves and the easy shelving into the water that are the real attractions. My Spanish teacher María Navarro, who lives in Águilas, tells me that Cocedores is where the local families bring their young children as it's the safest beach in the area, with the water shallow and well protected. So during holiday times in particular it's noisy and busy. At Cocedores there is historical interest too; old caves, excavated into the soft rock, some closed off with metal grilles, and shallow areas of the bay partly dammed with boulders. Here, the local people used to boil and soften esparto before it was worked into straps, baskets, panniers, *alpargatas* (espadrilles), ropes, harnesses and mats. There are more beaches further north but we are right on the border with Murcia at this point and as this is a book about Almería, our coastal journey ends here.

At loggerheads

In *Flamingos in the Desert* I described the project which has been ongoing on the Almerían coast in recent years to reintroduce loggerhead turtles. The gist of it is that, over a period of several years from 2006, about 700 turtle eggs were brought from the Cape Verde Islands to the beaches of Cabo de Gata, where they were monitored until they hatched. Once hatched, they were taken to the Estación Biológica de Doñana in Seville province to grow on, before being released after a year, back at the beaches where they were born. This is because loggerheads return to breed on their natal beach once they have reached sexual maturity at the age of 15-20. Research at the University of North Carolina has shown that they do this by navigating using the earth's magnetic field.

So, to update you, in July 2015 a loggerhead laid 80 eggs on a beach in a tiny cove near San Juan de los Terreros. As far as we know, this is only the second time in 15 years that this has happened successfully. Members of the local Pulpí civil protection team, together with specialists from the marine rescue organisation Equinac guarded the site for three days and nights to protect the nest from disturbance. After this the eggs were moved to the Estación Biológica de Doñana because of the danger of exposure to storms and predators on the Pulpí beach. The eggs were kept in an incubator until they hatched after about 90 days. The hatchlings then spent a year at the centre in Doñana before being returned and released from the beach where they were born.

Hatchlings are less than five centimetres long and weigh only 20 grams, so are easy prey for predators such as gulls. Protecting the hatchlings for a year allows them to gain weight and gives their shells time to harden, so they are less vulnerable. Despite this Equinac estimates that, of every 1,000 turtles born, only one will survive to adulthood, due to predation and other dangers such as oil spills, fish hooks and the ingestion of plastic.

In 2013 an international research effort called Project Oasis established that an estimated population of 12,000 turtles live off the Mediterranean coast of Spain between Gibraltar and Murcia. The hope is that, with the reintroduction programme, a viable population of turtles may re-establish itself in Almería and boost this total.

San Juan castle

A tower was first built in San Juan de los Terreros in 1579 as part of an initiative to defend the coasts. It was to see turbulent times. In 1585 it came under harquebus fire (a harquebus was a muzzle-loaded firearm, a forerunner of the rifle) from the occupants of five North African galliots (small galleys with 16 to 20 oars per side). Nearby, these same Moorish pirates had also seized five French boats returning home carrying pepper, cochineal, sugar and rice. Soon afterwards, in 1590, the tower was besieged by a force of 550 janissaries (Turkish infantry), though what the outcome of this was, I have been unable to discover.

In 1620 the tower passed to the Kingdom of Granada after a lawsuit about this stretch of coast which was won by the town of Vera. A British ship bombarded the tower in 1743, demolishing one of its corners. This damage was repaired but in 1759 the generally poor state of the tower led to a decision to knock it down completely and build an altogether bigger defensive structure. This was La Batería de San Juan de los Terreros, built between 1761 and 1764 and still standing in a dramatic position on a high headland to the north of the town. It was then staffed by 13 members of the urban militia with an official, two corporals, four artillerymen and their officer, a storekeeper and a chaplain.

However, little more than a century later, in 1873, the fort was recorded as already being unmanned, perhaps because the threats to the coast had passed. In the 20th century, after the Civil War, it passed to the Guardia Civil before being abandoned in the

1970s. It was restored in 1980 by the Pulpí local council, in whose municipality it lies, but then once more it began to deteriorate. Finally in 2001 it was restored yet again with, I was happy to see, the carving above the entrance 'REINO CARLOS III ANO DE 1764' still intact. In the circumstances it seems rather churlish to mention that large patches of render on the outer walls have fallen away and the adjacent gardens and gravel areas are showing distinct signs of neglect.

There are huge views along the coast, out beyond Isla Negra to the north and Isla de Terreros to the south. These small islands are of volcanic origin and are now protected breeding sites for rare birds such as Cory's shearwater and storm petrel. That apart, the castle is now used to display information about the area, with detailed panels about the ecosystems of the cliffs, the history of esparto production, the system of defensive forts and towers, the local mines and much more. The big pull for visitors though, is the Pulpí Geode.

The Pulpí Geode

One day early in 2016 a friend sent me an online link to the Pulpí Geode. This looked fascinating, and soon afterwards we headed up to San Juan de los Terreros and found our way up to the castle, which involves following signs through a sequence of increasingly improbable small streets until the final twisting climb to the headland on the northern edge of the town. It was a murky, misty January day and to make matters worse, despite the online information giving full details of the opening hours, we found the castle closed, with a small notice attached to the door saying that, actually, it was open only at weekends. Frustration.

At Pilar de Jaravía in the Sierra de Aguilón, a small mountain range just inland from the coast at San Juan, important minerals were discovered in 1874. Mining began soon afterwards and continued until 1970. Then, in 1999, geologists were exploring the old workings when they made a remarkable discovery. Half a kilometre into an old mine and about 50 metres down, through a tiny opening, they chanced upon the largest geode in Europe.

A geode is an underground cavity in a rock, normally totally sealed, in which minerals have gradually crystallised in a process that can take thousands of years. Typically the crystals would be of quartz or calcite but in the case of the one found at Pilar de Jaravía, they are of gypsum. To anyone who has seen geodes of modest size in museums or in the shops that sell plundered natural wonders, the dimensions of what is normally called the Pulpí Geode (named for the fact that it is in the municipality of Pulpí) are astonishing: it's a cavity eight metres long, 1.8 metres wide and 1.7 metres high, in the form of a long, bent funnel. Gypsum crystals up to two metres long have grown into the cavity, creating a spiky and translucent wonder of nature, and leaving room to fit about ten people inside it. Except that this gypsum is soft. On Mohs scale, which measures diamonds at the hardness of 10, it has a hardness of 2, which means you can scratch it with your fingernail. The whole structure is very fragile. Human visitors clambering about inside it would trash it in no time, so at present the Pulpí Geode is off limits.

In March, a couple of months after our first failed foray, Troy asked me what I'd like to do for my birthday and I said: "How about the Pulpí Geode?" Which is where the Castillo de San Juan de los Terreros comes in. This time, success! In the castle, for a ridiculously small fee, €1 at the time of writing, you can make a virtual visit to the geode. This involves wearing earphones and a large headset. What follows is a seven-minute journey from the entrance of the Pilar de Jaravía mine for 500 metres along galleries shored up in a variety of ways, past abandoned wagons and an old underground lift. You can look around 360 degrees and you genuinely feel immersed in the underground world. At one point, where the gallery walls were coming near, I leaned to my left to avoid them. A good, clear commentary leads you through the mine, finishing with the luminous sensation of being right inside the geode itself, with huge transparent crystals pointing at you from all directions.

If this sounds unconvincing, that is not because of the quality of the virtual visit. All I can say is: go and try it. It's totally absorbing and I'd be very surprised if you don't come out with a smile on your face. As we stood on the battlements of the castle afterwards, peering out to sea, we pondered that it might even be better than actually visiting the geode, because you don't have to crawl hundreds of metres along a small gallery, scraping your knees, banging your head, getting covered in dust and worrying that you might accidentally damage one of the priceless wonders of our planet.

8. Red tides and hallucinogenic fish

'Para la gran mayoría el mar es un gran desconocido.' 'For the most part, the sea is a great unknown.'

(Antonio Frías)

Life's not always a beach

Almeria's beaches are rightly renowned as some of the best in Spain. Stories about the beaches are often popping up in the media, mostly positive, but occasionally pointing out matters of concern. We've been travelling along the coast until now, so this might be a good place to mention some of these issues and then finish the chapter on a positive note.

Toxic algae

'Red tides' led to bathing being banned at three Cuevas del Almanzora beaches for a time from 23rd June 2015: El Playazo in Vera, Quitapellejos in Palomares and Villaricos. A 'red tide' is the result of algae reproducing in large quantities. The problem came to light after more than 50 people went to local health centres with allergic reactions such as sneezing and fever, and breathing difficulties. Doctors realised that the common factor was that all of those concerned had been to beaches and alerted the Junta de Andalucía's health department. Local councils warned people not to swim or go within 50 metres of the sea, as the number of people affected gradually rose to 95.

The group Ecologistas en Acción suggested the source of the problem might be a spill from the Deretil chemical factory on the coast immediately north of Villaricos. The factory's director, Manuel Santiandreu López, said their processes use only biodegradable products and rejected the ecologists' claims. And to be fair to the factory, it was later found to have been in the clear. The environmentalists suggested that another possible source might be a sewage outfall from the Río Almanzora.

The Junta de Andalucía's environment department rejected notions of a sewage spill, saying it had last conducted tests in the area on June 11th. After people started to feel ill a couple of weeks later though, tests revealed the presence of a species of dinoflagellate algae called ostreopsis. Professor Paul Hunter of East Anglia University said a combination of a sewage spill and high water temperatures could create the perfect conditions for such a bloom of toxic algae. Marine biologist Alexander Sánchez explained that the ostreopsis alga produces a very dangerous natural substance known as polytoxin that has been known to kill people.

Despite the source of the outbreak not having been established, El Playazo beach was reopened on June 29th, Quitapellejos a few days later, and Villaricos on July 7th. The Junta explained that these decisions were the result of "the absence of any new cases and the results of the latest tests". However, the Junta was slammed by the local Veraplayazul residents' association, which had sent a written request asking for the precise toxicity levels to be made public. In spite of this, the Junta did not make public the results of its water tests.

As time passed the matter died down until October 2015, when the Junta finally admitted that it knew that Galasa, the local water company, had been pumping raw sewage into the sea four months earlier. It transpired that a break in the main pipe to the Villaricos sewage treatment plant on June 13th had led to Galasa pumping 179,000 litres of untreated sewage into the sea over a period of 46 hours. Only after the pumping ended did the company notify the Junta of what had happened. It turned out that levels of algae were much higher when the beaches were reopened than they had been when the beaches were closed. The Junta had no local facilities to test for the presence of algae and had to send the water samples to a laboratory in Madrid. Trying to explain the actions of the Junta, minister Antonio Martínez said: "The law was respected at all times. My department has carried out its legal responsibilities and water control checks showed nothing alarming. This was not harmful to humans or sea life." At least 95 humans might disagree with his interpretation of the facts. As for the sea life, it hasn't released a statement.

Risky summer parking

Beaches such as Cala del Plomo near Agua Amarga and Playa del Playazo near Rodalquilar are quiet and delightful places for most of the year but in summer, things change. The access roads to both beaches are narrow in places and what the press calls 'random and disordered parking' has caused concern that emergency vehicles would not be able to access the coast when they need to.

This was highlighted in July 2015 when there were two drownings in a single day on the Almerían coast, including one at Cala del Plomo, access to which is via a seven kilometre unsurfaced track. It takes about 20 minutes to drive this track, which is corrugated in places, so Cala del Plomo is something of a connoisseur's destination. There is space for quite a few vehicles in the area behind the beach but there is no formal car park. This is part of the attraction and once you're there, it's lovely; a beach of rounded cobbles and sand and an inviting sea.

The victim at Cala del Plomo was a 35 year old Frenchman. Two other people were rescued in the same incident by the emergency services, together with others at the same place later on the same August day. Alexis Pineda, the Níjar councillor responsible for beaches, said the tragedy was the result of strong currents and criticised bathers who continued to ignore the risk. He said: "The police and a doctor were performing resuscitation on the body on the beach, having just pulled him out of the water, and despite this scene someone still went back into the water and immediately got into difficulties, having to be rescued by the same emergency services". Cala del Plomo is a beach where there are no lifeguards and there is no system of flags to alert bathers to danger. Where flags *are* present, yellow means that only confident swimmers should venture into the sea. A red flag means 'no bathing under any circumstances'.

On one occasion, several years ago, when we knew nothing of the risks at Cala del Plomo, we were there on a quiet day out of season. We'd been walking along the tide-line and were towards the right-hand end of the beach when Troy decided to go in for a dip. She's a reasonably good swimmer but after a few minutes, when she wanted to come out of the sea, she found she was making no headway despite swimming steadily, only about 20 metres out from the shore. She shouted to me. A yelled conversation was in progress between us when two people further along the beach, the only others there, shouted: "She needs to swim to the right to get out of there!" I conveyed this and Troy tried to do just that. There was no obvious clue in the water that we could see to explain why she wasn't moving, but she wasn't. She continued paddling. I'm not a good swimmer so my jumping in was not going to help at this point. Concern was now creeping in to the equation. There were no small boats we could commandeer to try to effect a rescue. Troy was still 'swimming on the spot' and beginning to tire.

"What if she swam the other way, to the left?" I called across to the couple. "Yes, that should work too," they said. I shouted to Troy and she turned, swam left, and almost immediately broke out of her watery impasse. Troy had been shaken by the incident - we both had. Only later did we discover a crude hand-made notice, some way up the beach and therefore not at all obvious if you are on the tide-edge, warning of danger.

Subsequently, in the process of trying to find out what had been happening, we did come across mention of the Cala del Plomo tide-rip online. As with tide-rips anywhere, one of the best clues that a rip current is present is to look out for a gap in the waves. The calmer space in the line of a wave may look like a safe and easy place to swim but a small patch of calm water in an otherwise choppy sea is often a rip current.

The reason for this is that when waves crash along the beach at an angle, the longshore drift (the movement of water along the beach) flows in the same direction, all one way, but when waves break at a right angle to the shore, the water spills away to both left and right of the wave. When two such 'spills' or longshore currents collide into each other, a strong offshore flow will develop and water from these colliding currents will rush back out to sea as a tide-rip. This flow can be as fast as ten metres per second, more than enough to carry the strongest swimmer out to sea. Swimming sideways, parallel to the shore, is the way to escape from a tide-rip. Going in to help a swimmer in trouble is not recommended.

By November 2015 the death toll for the year from drownings in Almería province had reached fourteen. The latest was a 22 year old German man, who got into difficulties whilst swimming at Las Negras. "Las Negras is dangerous when the Levante (east wind) blows and you should never try to fight the currents there," explained the director of the local diving school, Victor Torres.

After the 2015 drowning tragedy at Cala del Plomo, Alexis Pineda of Níjar council highlighted the need for 'No Parking' signs and supervised parking to avoid bottlenecks. Policia Local officers and Protección Civil volunteers monitored the situation for the remainder of the high season, until the end of August. Councillor Pineda stressed the need to "find a solution to a problem that gets out of hand each year". He even mentioned that 'parking rage' has led to fights when spaces are at a premium. My personal solution to the problem is this: avoid Cala del Plomo in July and August. And at any time of year, be careful where you swim there. If caught in a rip, swim parallel to the beach for a distance, then turn in towards the shore. And for assistance in any emergency, remember the number to call is 112.

Unspoilt Mónsul?

The beaches between San José and Cabo de Gata, the cape itself which marks the southernmost point of the Parque Natural Cabo de Gata-Níjar, are considered amongst the hidden gems of the area. Genoveses, Mónsul and Media Luna are special not least because they are entirely undeveloped. These beaches have no houses, bars or shops. Apart from the unsurfaced parking areas, set some way back from the beaches and accessed only via a rough track from San José, they are genuinely unspoilt. Mónsul even featured in *The Telegraph's* 'Secret Seaside' survey of unspoilt beaches in June 2010. But for how much longer?

At the end of 2015 it was announced that the regional government, the Junta de Andalucía, had authorised the opening of a beach bar at Mónsul, in a disused building that was once a small Guardia Civil barracks. The Junta had put the idea out to tender, following the rebirth of a development plan first discussed in 1995 but subsequently shelved. This seems to have raised its head again because of the fact that in 2014 the Coastal Law was reformed, loosening the restrictions on coastal development. If someone comes along and seriously says they will do it, they would now have permission to run a *chiringuito*, which, according to the conditions in the tender must include, as well as the bar, a souvenir and basic foodstuffs shop, and public toilets. One issue for potential investors is that there are no public utilities to the site, so the *chiringuito* will have to be entirely self-sufficient.

Mónsul beach is a UNESCO Biosphere Reserve and is renowned for the shooting of many films, including *The Hill*, *Indiana Jones and the Last Crusade* and *The Adventures of Baron Munchausen*. Mónsul falls within the huge *municipio* (local government district) of Níjar, whose policy presumes against such developments. Níjar mayor Esperanza Pérez spoke out strongly against the plans, as did environmental groups and nearby residents. However, legally, it seems all of these people were to have no say in the matter. The plan was not put out to public consultation despite Mónsul beach's widespread reputation as an unspoilt treasure.

Mónsul and its neighbouring beaches are not secrets though. In fact, in 2015 almost 200,000 people visited Mónsul, part of a continuing upward trend, so to the right entrepreneur, the idea of a *chiringuito* at Mónsul, catering to hundreds of thirsty and hungry beachgoers every day, several kilometres from the nearest competition back in San José, would no doubt seem like a gold mine.

In early 2016 the Junta de Andalucía rejected a petition of over 30,000 signatures that opposed the *chiringuito,* with their environmental delegate saying he would not modify the plans. Emilio Roldán, the director of the Cabo de Gata-Níjar Natural Park, who you might imagine would be in favour of preserving the unspoilt qualities of the coast he is employed to protect, actually appeared to be in favour, saying of the proposal: "This is a similar menu that is available in establishments in all natural parks across Andalucía. My park is the only one in the region without such a service."

However, just two weeks later, the environment minister's superior, José Fiscal, announced that the plan had been scrapped, admitting that the scale of the reaction, "a cacophony of voices from across the spectrum", had persuaded him that the idea had not been a good one.

Cetacean deaths
In January 2015 the body of a young female striped dolphin, 1.7 metres long, was found on the beach at Macenas, south of Mojácar. An autopsy revealed that it had an intestinal blockage and some form of infection.

According to Eva María Moran, a spokesperson for the marine rescue organisation Equinac, by the mid-point of 2015 20 dolphins had been washed up on Almería's shores. She pointed out that they only approach the coast if they are unwell and said that this is often due to poisoning by heavy metals which pollute the sea in places. They also tend to be suffering from lack of food because of overfishing, especially by drift-net trawlers. She called on members of the public not to leave litter on beaches or throw it in the sea, and further added that if you find a beached marine mammal, you should not touch it, as infections can be passed on to humans or pets. The number to call to alert the authorities in such a situation is 112.

In January 2016 a dead blue shark was found on Pueblo Laguna beach in Vera with its dorsal fin cut off. Equinac said they could not ascertain whether the fin had been severed before or after death but there was concern that its death may be connected to the market for shark's fin soup in China. Shark's fin soup is considered a delicacy and serving it is perceived to be a sign of generosity to dinner guests. Fins can be worth up to €600 per kilogram. Despite the fact that the practice of 'finning' (removing fins from live sharks) has been entirely illegal in Europe since 2013, it is thought that some unscrupulous fishermen still continue this practice when the opportunity presents itself.

But the snorkelling is amazing

However, the last thing I want to do is to put you off exploring the coastal waters. It's wonderful what you can see while you are still in your depth. Once you have a mask and snorkel on, just lower your head to look under the sea's surface and there is a new world. For many people this is not news but it's so remarkable that it almost seems like a new discovery each time you do it. Philip Marsden describes it like this: 'The upper world disappeared. An entirely new one took its place, full of drift and silence. I could hear only the bellow of my own breathing.'

It's cheap too. A mask and snorkel cost only a few euros. You don't need flippers (fins, they tend to be called these days) though if you have them they will propel you along a bit more quickly. A pair of those neoprene sea shoes would be handy though, in many places, just to give your feet some protection from stones and rocks as you get in and out of the sea.

So, let's say you are at Agua Amarga beach. As you look at the sea, the best area for snorkelling is towards the right-hand side of the bay, near the cliffs with the caves. Not too near though, as there is a sign announcing 'iPROHIBIDO EL BANO, ZONA DE DESPRENDIMIENTOS!' with the helpful translation below 'SWIMMING NOT ALLOWED, DETACHMENTS!' This means beware of rocks falling from the cliffs. I suspect this is a very rare event but it's obviously wise to be cautious here.

A general rule for snorkelling is that you will see more fish where there are rocky areas. This applies to both rocks on the sea-bed and those that project above the water. I write not as an expert in these matters but I am guessing that in such places the food supply for fish is better. So any beach, preferably with some rocks nearby, should be good for snorkelling – Mónsul, Cala Rajá, La Isleta del Moro, Playazo and many more. Almería is often windy though and then the sea can be rough, especially, it seems, later in the day. This churns up the sand and vegetation and, with the waves as well, makes snorkelling something best enjoyed early on a calm day.

The Mediterranean in eastern Almería is basically warm enough for a dip between about May and October. Outside of this period, if you're hardy or if you have a wetsuit, it's still perfectly possible to enjoy a swim or a snorkel. I even went in, without a wetsuit, one Boxing Day, though that was admittedly just to say I'd done it rather than to revel in the experience.

At a friend's house one day I saw what looked like a helpful book, a guide to marine species in the Cabo de Gata area, so I tracked down a copy (at the Cepsa garage by the roundabout below Mojácar *pueblo*, should you be interested) and bought it. The next time I went snorkelling I took it with me. As far as the beach, that is. As well as fish, it illustrates other marine species – corals, jellyfish, urchins, starfish, octopus, seahorses and so on. It also helpfully tells you where each species is present within the Cabo de Gata-Níjar Natural Park, though obviously they are found in many other places along Almería's coast too.

So it's interesting and useful but I was frustrated that some of the fish I saw appeared not to be in the guidebook. It's also only available in Spanish; this is an opportunity to broaden our grasp of the language though, isn't it, not a disadvantage? Anyway, with the help of the guidebook, I've now established that these are just some of the species I've seen whilst snorkelling: a kind of bream called *salpa* or *salema* in Spanish and known as goldline in English and Sarpa salpa in Latin. It's a slightly chubby oval fish, generally greyish but with elegant yellow lines along its body. This is one of a group known as 'dream fish' because eating it can bring on ichthyoallyeinotoxism, a hallucinogenic inebriation similar to the effects of LSD. Indeed, it was apparently used as a recreational drug in the times of the Roman Empire and, according to the journal *Clinical Toxicology*, in 2006, two men who ate goldline caught in the Mediterranean experienced hallucinations lasting for several days. I have no plans to try it.

Groups of saddled sea bream (Oblada melanura in Latin, *oblada* in Spanish) are common. They are greyish blue with a prominent black patch just in front of the tail fin and are usually between 5cm and 20cm long. Quite similar, but with faint vertical lines and with a black thumbprint at the base of the tail, is the white sea bream (Diplodus sargus and *sargo común*). It's frequently seen, averages 22 cm long, and is caught for eating, though its flesh tastes good only when fresh.

Zebra sea bream (Diplodus cervinus in Latin) are common too. In Spanish, this fish has no less than five correct names – *sargo imperial, sargo breado, sargo real, bedao* and *sargo soldado*. As its English name suggests, it has dark vertical stripes. There are five of these bands; they are fairly wide and are dark brown on a much lighter greyish-yellow background. Zebra sea bream can reach over 30cm long but the ones I've seen have been quite a lot smaller than that.

The most colourful fish you may see whilst snorkelling is the ornate wrasse or parrotfish (Thalasoma pavo), called *pez verde* in Spanish. The simple translation 'green fish' does it a disservice though. The female is mainly green, though with complex blue and pink markings around the head, but the male is a dramatic canvas of orange, pale pink, vertical blue stripes and, like the female, blue patterning on the head. It's an odd-shaped fish, with a small tail and not much in the way of fins, but it brings a real splash of colour to the scene.

Another place that is excellent for snorkelling is the Playa de la Invencible, a couple of kilometres north of Villaricos and already mentioned in the previous chapter. That name means, more or less, Unbeatable Beach, which is a bold claim. There are many other small coves along this stretch of coast that vie for the title. Watch for a long, low pinky-beige building on the seaward side of the road. You can easily pull off there and a drivable track leads down to the right, with parking space just a few metres from the sea. Go in for a snorkel right there or just walk the few metres over a tiny headland to the next, slightly bigger beach of shingle and sand. Wade in and you find, in the shallows, meadows of vibrant green Neptune grass. Floating above these in less than a metre of water (so you can stand up whenever you like) is a wonderful experience. Neptune grass

(Posidonia oceanica) is an endemic Mediterranean species, an important habitat for fish and other marine creatures, and an indicator of low pollution levels. There are rocks here too, and these plus the Neptune grass make the perfect combination for a bit of marine life observation.

The meadows of Neptune grass are dotted with snakelocks anemones (Anemonia viridis). These anemones (*anémona común* in Castellano) have a waving shock of jade green tentacles with mauve or purple tips. This colouring is due to the presence of symbiotic algae within the tentacles that use sunlight as an energy source. The tentacles, which sway endlessly with the movement of the water in the shallows, have urticant properties (stinging or irritating) though I touched them gently and felt no reaction. The anemones prefer brightly lit shallow waters, precisely the conditions at Playa de la Invencible.

9. Ruins in the hills

' 'Industrial archaeology' always seems to me the wrong term for studying such sites. The evidence is too complete; it lacks all the gaps and enigmas of prehistory.'
(Philip Marsden)

Walking across a mountain range

As you travel north from Villaricos, there is a lot to see in terms of mining remains. The Sierra Almagrera, the small mountain range more or less due north of the village, is a good place to begin. On a map of the whole of Spain these hills barely register but in 1839 the discovery of veins of silver-bearing lead here set off a sudden bout of mining fever. Hordes flocked to the parched slopes and valleys in the hope of making a fortune. The richest of the dry riverbeds was the Barranco del Jaroso, on the inland side of the range, to the east of the now quiet village of Los Lobos. You wouldn't suspect it from the village, as it's mostly hidden by the folds of the hills, but this valley is liberally scattered with remains that indicate how dramatic the 'silver rush' was. It was silver and lead that stimulated the initial interest but subsequently iron ore became much more important.

On the basis of details in a guidebook to 'El Levante Almeriense', I've hatched a plan to walk from Cala de Las Conchas on the coast, up to the highest point of the range, then down to the village of Los Lobos a few kilometres inland. I've managed to pique the interest of two friends, Frank Selkirk and Catherine Arthur, and my wife Troy, so on a fine January Sunday we get together to give it a go.

This is a linear walk so, with no public transport available, we have to leave one car at Los Lobos, then drive in the other round to Cala de Las Conchas. This is on the coast road between Villaricos and San Juan de los Terreros, a road that swoops and curves as best it can along the rocky coast. It's an enjoyable drive.

At Cala de Las Conchas, Cove of the Shells, a wooden rail edges the *mirador*. Immediately down to the right from its highest point are the huge stone walls of a storage hopper. Looking into the hopper, there appear to be nine chutes, long overgrown and choked, in its base. Even a cursory look around shows that this was once a place of great activity. Nowadays there is just a single villa down below the road and adjacent to a small beach. Presumably it was built before the Ley de Costas, Law of the Coasts, restricted such development. Alongside it are the ruins of three calcination ovens. In 1912 construction of a metal loading wharf was completed for export of the minerals from these mountains. However, hardly had it begun to function when there was a crisis in the price of iron and maintenance of the drainage system in the mines was suspended, leading to flooding of the workings.

Having left the second car, we begin the walk by going a hundred metres north along the road then turning off to the left on a track that leads under a big cracked wall. This is the coastal side of another vast hopper. You can go into an obvious tunnel in this structure and look up into three loading funnels. The track skirts round the left side of this massive hopper and climbs a little, before levelling out, with an inclined plane visible ahead. This level section indicates the way along which the iron ore wagons came to tip their loads into the hopper, to await export. At the end of this level stretch is a group of beehives. Beyond these, I understand there is a tunnel. Its entrance, according to the guidebook, is *'prácticamente tapado por una higuera'* , almost blocked by a fig tree. By crouching down and parting the branches you can reputedly get into and through the tunnel to the base of the inclined plane. However, this would mean walking right past the beehives and, even though there is no obvious bee activity when we are there, we decide on discretion and so don't go that way.

We know we have to gain height and all the surrounding slopes are steep and scrubby, so we take to the hillside on our left, a hundred metres or so before the hives, each making our own way up through the frankly awkward vegetation. After maybe ten or fifteen minutes of not entirely enjoyable struggle, we gain a subsidiary ridge-line, regroup and continue at an easier angle across the slope, heading for the top of the inclined plane.

At the top is a slot-like pit. This, I imagine, is the site of the winding gear which was once used to lower the full wagons down the slope. Again, I have the sense of seeing history under my feet, and being in the enjoyable and slightly daunting position of trying to interpret what I am looking at. From here, another level track contours on for 200 metres or so, ending at a brick-arched tunnel entrance, no longer passable. From my subsequent reading, I gather that this tunnel is 320 metres long and linked the north side of the hills to this southern slope. Once it had been successfully driven, in 1908, ore could be brought from the richest deposits and this marked the beginning of the operation of this 'wagon-way' down to the coast by a company called S.A. Argentifera de Almagrera. This name suggests 'silver' but, just to clarify, although silver and then lead were the catalyst when the mining operations began in the first half of the 19th century, by the beginning of the 20th century those minerals were worked out and the company was focussed on extracting iron ore, particularly around Las Herrerías and Las Rozas, as described a little further on.

From the blocked tunnel entrance we again have to take to the slopes and negotiate more brush and scree up to the main ridge of the Sierra Almagrera. Here are more mining remains including a stone pillar and a number of unprotected shafts, so do watch where you're stepping if you go up here. Below lies the broad valley of the Barranco del Jaroso, with industrial remnants scattered widely. The scale of these gives a good sense of how extensive the workings were at the height of the mining fever.

When mining began, it was mostly local companies that were involved, producing lead ingots to be exported for the international market. The numbers employed were staggering. In the 1840s about 10,000 people were working these lead mines. However, by the last quarter of the 19th century the most accessible minerals had been won, the costs of extraction had risen and the price of lead on the international markets had fallen, all of which meant that most of the mines were no longer profitable.

Companies from further away, such as the Basque Country, international firms even, were now involved and the coming of the railways was another significant factor in boosting these developments. At the same time, over on the far side of Almería, where similar finds of lead had been made in the Sierra de Gádor, there were 20,000 employees. It was the mining of lead that was responsible for the big increase in Almería province's population in the period 1820-1850.

The highest point of the range, called Tenerife, is a few hundred metres along the ridge, via *algunas subidas y bajadas*, which we might call 'some ups and downs'. The way is not too difficult though and the colours of the ore-bearing rocks are rich and elemental; reds, blacks, a range of browns. When you get to Tenerife's summit you find it is a superb viewpoint even though it's only 366 m above sea level.

The other three, who are not such baggers of summits as I am, give Tenerife a miss and take a path which contours across its north side to a group of ruins on a col. From the top of Tenerife, I drop down northwards to more ruins, including a tapering chimney and a vast circular water tank with steps built down the inside wall. From there, it's a fairly level walk across to where the others are waiting. A wide track then works its way down into the *rambla* in the base of the Barranco del Jaroso, with closer views of all manner of old structures and buildings. The track weaves to and fro across the *rambla* and gradually comes out of the hills to a flatter area and in to Los Lobos, a village that is doubtless much quieter nowadays than it was 150 years ago.

It's been a fascinating walk but the first section was undeniably tough. When I come back for more explorations, I'll come into the Barranco del Jaroso from the western side, from Los Lobos.

Barracks in the fields

If you drive towards La Mulería from Villaricos, part way along, by the roadside, you will see a squat, two-tiered structure, with a chimney or shaft-head of some kind. Just near this, a sign points off north. However, you only see the blank back of this sign if you are coming from Villaricos. On the other side, seen clearly if you are coming from La Mulería, the pink sign announces 'EL ARTEAL, poblado minero', mining settlement

The track to El Arteal is unsealed but perfectly driveable. In a little while you will see, across the fields to the right, what look like rows of barracks. Parallel lines of two-storey buildings stand almost surreally in the middle of a farming landscape. Look for the track, unfenced, that leads between the fields to these buildings. They are astonishing. The windows and doors have gone, the staircases don't look sound enough to invite exploration, the graffiti merchants have been here, some of them quite artistic, and the whole complex is fairly densely overgrown but what is absolutely apparent is the sheer scale of these accommodation blocks. They must have housed literally hundreds of people. There is no information on site about what they are, when they date from, and the no doubt tough lives of those who were billeted here. Perhaps this is fine; it means the curious visitor can use their imagination to fill in the details. Those in search of more details will find them online, but only in Spanish.

Back at the main track you can go straight on, between two buildings that slightly resemble gatehouses. The larger, on the right, was inhabited when, having parked, I walked past armed with camera and notebook in the summer of 2015. Dogs barked, washing flapped on a line, and what sounded distinctly like 1920s swing music was floating out of the house. A hundred metres on, there's an intact chimney on the left with, above it on a bluff, a big rectangular building still carrying the legend 'CENTRAL DE TRANSFORMACION'. To the other side, beyond low square tanks, are more buildings, but a 'Prohibido el Paso' sign and a glimpse of white walls among the ruins indicate that someone has restored a building there. In fact, as you drive inland from Villaricos, just after having crossed the *rambla*, you will see El Arteal's 'barracks' across the fields ahead of you. But, as mentioned above, there's no sign to guide you there from this direction and no indication that you are *allowed* to visit. This is fascinating industrial archaeology, almost hidden away amidst the farmland and olive groves, just awaiting a visit from anyone interested.

Pilar de Jaravía

Having had a 'virtual visit' to the Pulpí Geode, I was curious to see the remains of the mining area where it was found. It wasn't too difficult to locate the place. I set out on the road from San Juan de los Terreros towards Pulpí, the A-1205. As I approached Pilar de Jaravía I could see mining remains up across the hillside so I took the exit and then, at the roundabout, took a minor road labelled 'Camino'. It turned out that I'd guessed correctly. I followed this uphill past an area of scattered houses to the sizeable skeleton of an abandoned development with a large billboard for 'aguilóngolf'. This small range of hills is the Sierra de Aguilón and you can see the mining remains over to the right as you drive up this road.

I parked near the roundabout where there are roadside bays opposite the deserted building project and took the track across the hillside from there on foot. In less than ten minutes I was at the ruins. Two tower-like kilns are still in a good state of repair but most of the other buildings, such as the pithead gantry and what I suspect were the mine offices, are the worse for wear. The mine here was called 'Quién Tal Pensara' or 'Mina Rica'. Iron ore was the main mineral, with a little lead and silver later. It began operating in 1890 and was very busy until 1922. A black-and-white photo in the castle at San Juan shows it in full swing in 1895. Activity gradually decreased but final closure did not come until 1970.

At some point a few years ago there was substantial investment here though; a large area is enclosed with chain-link fencing with notices saying 'Zona recuperada'. There's a tall narrow chimney and a slope with many individually-made wooden terraces to support trees. None of the latter survive though. It seems like another example of a project where a big initial outlay was made but there was no commitment or funding to follow it up and maintain it. The young trees were planted but, it seems, were never watered and failed to survive. Presumably the ultimate intention would have been to open the area to the public but it remains fenced off and forgotten.

Also in this fenced area, there's a sloping hollow way ending at what looks like an impregnable metal door in the hillside. I'm pretty sure this must be the entrance to the mine where the Pulpí Geode lies, half a kilometre in and 50 m deep. Perhaps someone out there can confirm my suspicions. Discussions are continuing about how best to manage this natural wonder and whether public access might be possible in some way but for now, it remains safely locked away.

I'm always intrigued by these old sites, so I clambered higher to check out the ruined buildings more closely and to get a different perspective, only to suddenly come on the modern Águilas to Lorca railway line, which isn't apparent at all from below. Putting two and two together, I realised that this was the way the iron ore from the mines up along the Almanzora Valley would have come via the Almendricos - Águilas spur on the Great Southern of Spain Railway (see chapter 34). That branch line was opened back in the 1890s and for a time was very busy with ore and later marble. Now there was nothing more to see, so from this upper boundary of the site I picked my way back down the loose slopes, pondering the astonishing extent of the old industrial remains that still pepper the landscape of eastern Almería.

10: Tracking down Siret

'A man of slightly crazy enthusiasm'
(Gerald Brenan, describing Louis Siret)

In search of industrial archaeology

Immediately at the southern end of Villaricos village, there's a roundabout. We turned inland here one early June day and followed the road, past the frontage of the Phoenician necropolis and round a bend or two. Along here, according to the road map of Almería province, was Las Herrerías, which I knew vaguely was a key site of some of the old iron-ore workings and was where the famous Belgian archaeologist Louis Siret built a house. Fairly soon I spotted a tall brick chimney on a small rise over to the left and took a turning. We came past a slope of dark rocks below the chimney and parked a hundred metres or so further on by a line of tall eucalyptuses. This was a small village but with clear signs of an industrial past. Alongside the trees was a straight channel, obviously man-made. This turned out to be the drainage channel from a huge open-cast mine, of which more below.

Nearby were two rows of low, terraced houses, some still with what appeared to be the original corrugated iron roofing, the sort of buildings workers would once have lived in but almost all now neatly upgraded. A straight track led off at an angle towards the coast, with buildings about a hundred metres away along it: a strange castellated house a few metres off it to the right and a long lower building immediately alongside it to the left. As we strolled towards it Pete Thom, who I'd dragged along on this occasion, said: "This has the look of an old railway." Pete used to be a highways engineer and has an eye for these things. He was right, and it was heading in a logical direction to be taking ore to the coast. We reached the long low building and it certainly seemed station-like, though now it was clearly closed up. Only later did I read that this *was* a railway,

103

designed by Siret in 1897, using draught animals to pull wagons of ore to Villaricos.

I also subsequently found out that the striking castellated house to the right was in fact Casa Siret. This was where Louis Siret lived for many decades until he died in June 1934. Subsequently, it came into the ownership of the Junta de Andalucía. It has had a particularly chequered recent history. In 2004, an arts foundation called the Fundación Internacional Artecitta was set up as the result of an agreement between Cuevas del Almanzora council and Dicomano council in Italy. The aim of the international agreement was to establish an art school based at the house under the auspices of the Junta de Andalucía's culture department. Not long before this, €297,500 had been spent on renovating the country house. An architect, Van der Burch, was appointed as head of the new project and moved into Casa Siret, along with his mother. However, he soon disagreed with the authorities and was sacked, but the two of them refused to move out. The art school never came to fruition but Van der Burch knew a good thing when he saw one: a 600 square metre property with six bedrooms and its own sizeable garden.

The squatters barricaded themselves into the property. They refused to pay any utility bills, so had their services cut off. They got water from anyone who would give it to them. A neighbour described them as "like hermits" who were "always begging and borrowing". Inevitably the house and gardens began to deteriorate but despite attempts by the Junta de Andalucía's culture department to have them evicted, the squatters successfully appealed all the court rulings until late 2015, when the new administration in Cuevas del Almanzora town hall decided enough was enough. They took the squatters to court again and this time they were finally granted an eviction order. The Guardia Civil arrived with a locksmith to enforce the eviction but when the squatters saw the game was up they let them in and agreed to leave quietly.

A few weeks later a deputation visited the site: the Junta de Andalucía's culture representative Alfredo Valdivia, Cuevas mayor Antonio Fernández and his tourism councillor Indalecio Modesto. They were inspecting it to see what needed doing before it could re-open. They decided it was basically sound but would need a thorough clean and some improvements. Might this signal a new lease of life for the unusual and historic Casa Siret?

Meanwhile, after that digression, back in the main part of the settlement an imposing white house, apparently abandoned, stood on the high ground near the chimney. There seemed no way to get near it but the rocks below it, some dark brown and some like obsidian, black and glassy, suggested the spoil from a foundry. This would make sense of the chimney, with the railway taking the part-processed iron the few kilometres to the coast for export. As we passed a house called El Milagro, The Miracle, a *señora* of advancing years came out to quieten her two dogs who were taking their guard duties seriously. I asked her: This is Las Herrerías, isn't it?" "No," she said, "it's Las Rozas! Herrerías is along there." She waved her arm vaguely further inland. Las Rozas wasn't even marked on the road map I had; I'd never heard of it until this moment.

I walked in the direction she'd indicated, not planning to get to Herrerías, but because there was a large building set back from the road which looked intriguing. The gates in its tall front wall had gone, though a wrought iron arch over one of them still held a coat of arms. The building was enormous but ruined, with rubble and roof-beams everywhere and what would once have been a dramatic atrium in the centre of the house. My companions had come in through a different gateway where they'd seen, painted on the wall, 'CAMPING LAS ROZAS'. They'd been exploring behind the house, finding over 40 camping pitches and a swimming pool, also full of rubble. So at some point this had been used as a campsite but, before that, it seemed, this building had once been an impressive mansion, no doubt one of the several colonial style houses lived in by the highly paid French and Belgian engineers who benefited from the great wealth generated by the mines. The plot thickened.

Trying to get a view of the big white house by the chimney, we took what we thought was the line of the old railway in the opposite direction, towards a bluff where the dark red colouring and the outline of one or two ruins again suggested iron. In a couple of hundred metres the track fizzled out in a large, bare flat area, a hollow bounded on three sides by higher ground, definitely not a natural feature. By now my companions were champing at the bit to get to the beach for some sun and snorkelling, so for now further investigation would have to wait. Without the local map of the area, it had been intriguing so far, but I was feeling like a very amateur landscape detective. I couldn't wait to come back again, with more time and after more research – and hopefully with a detailed map.

Subsequent research told me that there had been feverish activity here in the 19th century, with foundries, drains, derricks and galleries, all now gone or ruined. The large, bare hollow is what remains of a huge opencast mine, originally worked for iron ore and more recently for barites, and called La Hoya de las Rozas.

Las Herrerías

I parked and set off on foot, taking a twisting road signposted up to the church. Part way up was a cave house of unusual and attractive proportions, gleaming with fresh white paint. The church, the Iglesia de la Sagrada Familia, was consecrated on Christmas Day 1905. It looks better from a distance than close-up, though the Alpine-looking spire is briefly interesting. It was Siret who had the church built, hence its north European style. The high ground outside the church is a good vantage point over the village but the view just confirms the unremarkable nature of Las Herrerías.

Back down in the village, the only clues to past industry are a couple of tall chimneys and a prominent derrick on the skyline. From below you can see a trig point by this structure and a fence of the type that suggests a recreation area. When you are directly below this you are at the northern edge of the village, close to the village sign. However, a track that seems to be heading up towards it is marked as 'private' after a few metres. My solution was simply to walk up the bleak and bare slope alongside this track, aiming for the left-hand end of the high ground. It wasn't fenced off and it simply looked abandoned. The going wasn't difficult until I came on a sort of terrace in the landscape where a series of interlinked caves had been excavated. They are all now disused but they had had plastered, or at least painted, walls. They perhaps weren't houses, as there were no signs of chimneys, so maybe just storerooms. The ground though, had gullies and deep holes, some partly obscured by vegetation. Presumably the fact that the rock is easy to excavate also means it's soft enough to erode easily, or collapse if the excavations have been careless. However, as long as you are careful, there is no serious danger here.

Above this is the derrick. In fact, this is the metal headframe of the Alianza shaft, which gave access to a network of underground galleries linking most of the mines in the Herrerías district. There's a smart white trig pillar alongside and, sure enough, a level gravel area, four concrete benches and the aforementioned wooden fence. I've been told this was done to give it some status as a *mirador* but now it's all abandoned and overgrown, further adding to the impression that Las Herrerías is the land, or at least the village, that time forgot. There is an obvious gravel track coming up here though, from the back, as it were. I decided to follow this to see where it leads down to. Looking across to the left, I could see the old and the new contrasting: a disused stone chimney and, immediately adjacent, a modern *plastico*.

Veering right at a pylon with a concrete base (the track to the left goes in amongst the *plasticos*), I took a track towards the church. However, this petered out quite soon. Continuing ahead to a ruin on the skyline, I suddenly realised that I was looking at Las Rozas, and the flat area directly below me was the Hoya de las Rozas, the same area I'd been to earlier, where the suspected railway track had appeared to peter out. This is a striking landscape, with the flat area hemmed in by steep gullied slopes. Immediately below my feet was what appeared to be slag, glinting dark brown and purple and black in the late sun. This would suggest there was once a furnace here. Maybe that's what this ruined building had been. From below the ruin, a track skirts the near side of the flat basin. Was this the final part of the railway, or an offshoot of it, or simply something more recent?

Turning back, away from this flat basin, I took an obvious track which, in literally 40 metres, reached tarmac just by the freshly-painted cave house described earlier. (I do realise that by the time this book hits the shelves, the paint may have faded, unless they smarten the place up every year or two.) Straight on, the tarmac leads down to the main road through the village. Off my own bat, wandering around and following up other leads, I'd discovered a fair bit about the place but certainly the powers in Cuevas del Almanzora haven't seen fit to put up any kind of information board telling of the village's industrial past and the fact that a key figure in the world of archaeology once lived nearby. It was time to leave Herrerías, albeit with a nagging feeling that I was being unfair to the place and should go back again at some stage to hopefully have my view of it modified.

Louis Siret

It was Henri, the elder of the two Siret brothers, who arrived first in Cuevas del Almanzora from Belgium, in 1878. He worked initially for the French firm Compagnie Minière de la Province d'Almería and then, at the end of 1879, was given a contract by the Residents' Association of Cuevas to design a drinking water supply for the town. His younger brother Louis came to join him, having finished his studies in Louvain. In Spain, the brothers were generally known as Enrique and Luis rather than Henri and Louis. Both had already had an interest in all things historic and archaeological instilled in them by their father. In the process of researching the setting up of Cuevas del Almanzora's water supply, the brothers went to Fuente Álamo, which was used by many of the local water sellers because of the pure quality of the spring there.

At Fuente Álamo they heard that a hill near the spring was called El Cabezo de los Muertos, The Hill of the Dead, a name that led them to explore and come across Bronze Age remains (see below). Through their work on the water supply, they met and struck up a good relationship with Pedro Flores. He became responsible for managing Louis Siret's archaeological fieldwork for the rest of his life.

The water supply work was concluded by July 1882 and it was soon after this that Pedro Flores told them he had heard rumours about archaeological remains at Antas. They excavated the site, discovering the features that lent their name to the entire Argar Bronze Age culture across this corner of Spain (see below for more on this too).

At this stage both brothers were dividing their time between Spain and Belgium and in fact in the mid 1880s, Henri moved back to Belgium permanently. In 1888 the Sirets published their book, *The First Metal Ages in the South-east of Spain,* the first significant account of Spanish prehistory. In the same year, after the death of his father, Louis Siret took up permanent residence in Spain. 1890 saw him begin the excavation of the Phoenician necropolis at Villaricos.

Louis left Spain briefly in March 1891 to marry Maria Belpaire, who was also Belgian. Tragedy struck in 1895 when Maria died whilst giving birth to their son. This terrible blow only drove Siret to work even more intensively on both his industrial enterprises and his archaeological projects. By 1900 he had set up the Société Minière d'Almagrera in Paris to begin carrying out extensive drainage works for the numerous mines in the area where he was working. As well as his continual activity as a professional engineer, he also worked without cease on his archaeological projects, including those at Baria (Villaricos), the Chalcolithic village at Almizaraque (near Cuevas del Almanzora) and at Cueva de la Zájara (also known as the Cave of the Orcas, in Sevilla). During the early part of the 20th century, Louis documented a series of Chalcolithic and Bronze Age remains at Las Herrerías that were discovered, and subsequently destroyed, by the mining operations of the time. Today his notes constitute the only evidence for what once must have been a rich archaeological locality.

The two brothers, though primarily Louis, between them excavated more sites than all of the Spanish archaeologists of the time put together. But Louis Siret had a bee in his bonnet that pretty much everything that he had found was the work of the Phoenicians, a theory that was not accepted by most other archaeologists of the day. "It's not a science, archaeology, it's a fight to the death," said Siret. Louis Siret retired from his business activities in 1926 but his interest in archaeology continued unabated.

It was to Casa Siret that Gerald Brenan and his wife Gamel Woolsey, keen to visit the archaeologist, came in 1933. Brenan describes the approach as leading through a dreary region of red and yellow earth, scarred by the long effects of mining, and says that Siret's house was set in "a solitary grove of eucalyptus trees in which all the sparrows of the neighbourhood had collected and set up a deafening chirping". Siret's house was full of piles of books and papers, with rock samples everywhere. The man himself resembled the archetypal mad professor with long silver hair and an untrimmed white beard and moustache, who spoke enthusiastically in French about his many findings.

At that stage Siret had lived in the house for over 50 years: with his brother Henri for the first 25, and subsequently alone. "Fifty years at Herrerías! This took some imagining!" said Brenan. Brenan goes on to describe returning a year later (this would have been on 8th June 1934) to see Siret again, only to be halted by a funeral procession as he drove into the main street of Las Herrerías. Sadly, Siret had died the previous day.

11: Ancient cultures

'There was a time when our ancestors read the lines on the land as clearly as any text.'
(Dominick Tyler)

Fuente Álamo

On a Sunday morning in late November, a small group of us meets outside the castle in Cuevas del Almanzora. There's a distinctly icy wind blowing and I strategically change from my optimistic shorts into long trousers and add a windproof jacket over my fleece. From the *castillo*, led by Javier Rodríguez, we are setting off on foot for the Bronze Age site at Fuente Álamo. Almost immediately we lose height steeply through the streets of the town. Soon we cross the broad, channelled *rambla* of the Río Almanzora. For such a little guy (he's only about five feet tall in his stockinged feet), Javi keeps up an impressive pace. We turn off the tarmac onto a track that threads its way between fields of broad beans and artichokes, past the occasional compound with a barking dog, and an elegant curve-fronted cave house with CUEVA MARAZUL EL MINUTO 1992 spelled out in tiles above its door.

Before I left home I searched for a detailed map of the area, fairly sure I had one, but apparently not; there's no sign of it. So I decide to try to memorise the route to write it up accurately later but eventually realise there have been too many twists and turns. The notebook and pen I've brought as an aid to this have stayed in the rucksack, though I've managed a few photos. And in fact, it isn't a particularly attractive walk: it's the destination rather than the journey which is the focus. Really, for most people, it would make sense to drive to Fuente Álamo, or at least as close as you can get.

Finally, after about an hour and a half of brisk walking, we reach a valley with fairly steep sides. By now we are in the foothills of the Sierra de Almagro and we soon get to a place that looks as if it received considerable attention from the authorities perhaps ten years ago but not since. There are wooden handrails, now in a state of disrepair, and an information board on which it's very hard to make out the faded words. There's a general air of neglect, with bits of rubbish here and there. The track ends at a large brick arch built into the base of a hillside, with steps down inside it to a tap, and on the front wall alongside the arch, painted in black, AGUA POTABLE. This is the ages-old spring, Fuente Álamo itself.

Javi announces, to general approval, that we will have a short break for a drink and a bite to eat here before we climb up to the Bronze Age remains. Then, after a few minutes, he's off again, clambering up the rocky hillside apparently at random, until a thin white metal post with a red top becomes visible. When we get close, we see it has ZONA ARQUEOLOGICA written vertically on it, and there's another similar post ahead, higher up. Gradually we are on a path of sorts but the way to go wouldn't be clear were it not for the posts. And then, after a brief climb, we are suddenly there.

In front of us are the archaeological remains of the Fuente Álamo site, discovered and investigated in the late 19th century by the Siret brothers, with further work done much later by others, in 1977 and 1979. What the Sirets found was a settlement apparently dating from the second half of the third millennium BC and subsequently abandoned after a few hundred years. Archaeologists consider that at that time there were six distinct Bronze Age cultures in different parts of the Iberian Peninsula. The one in eastern Almería was the Argar culture, named after a site at El Argar near Antas, of which, more below.

The remains at Fuente Álamo are not extensive but include a round cistern for collecting rainwater, several covered circular constructions thought to have been grain stores, and a couple of 'cist burial' graves. The cists are small box-shaped tombs consisting of four sandstone slabs, half sunken into the ground. There is also a rectangular structure with thick walls which dates from the later Romano-Iberian period. The Argar civilisation was highly stratified, literally, with the nobles living at the top of the hill in an area surrounded by a wall and the workers – farmers, builders, miners – further down the slopes. The lower parts of the buildings' walls were of stone, with the upper parts and roofs thought to have been of wood and clay. Evidence has been found that there was mining in this area in Bronze Age times, though no suggestion that any minerals were actually processed here. In the museum in the Castillo in Cuevas del Almanzora, there's a room dedicated to the Fuente Álamo site, showing various artefacts found there and relating, among other things, that the people grew barley, wheat and broad beans and kept sheep, goats and pigs.

What can be seen today at Fuente Álamo is not all original. It's evident that some over-enthusiastic renovation took place a while ago; at the time of the excavations in the late 1970s, I guess. I'm not an archaeologist but my sense is that this has obscured the genuine remains and was probably not a wise move. What is very obvious though, is that this was a good defensive position. From the site you can look out across present-day Cuevas del Almanzora, a few kilometres away, to the sea. In the distance the white splash of Mojácar *pueblo*, another ancient defensive site, is visible on its hilltop.

The *fuente*, the permanent water supply at the base of the hill, was the reason it was possible to live here, of course. The site was occupied again in Romano-Iberian times and then also more recently. There are the crumbling ruins of a substantial building close to the *fuente* itself.

We teeter back down the slope, follow Javi as he fights through some undergrowth near the spring, angle up the hillside opposite, and slide down a shale bank to gain a wide track along the edge of a massive orange plantation. Our route back passes through more extensive groves of lemons and oranges with, as we get nearer the town, an unusual cave house with a modern patterned stone front.

The highlight of our return walk is an act of random kindness, when a local guy in one of those ubiquitous small vans (the resonant Spanish word for such a vehicle is *furgoneta*) screeches to a halt alongside us, pulls a large black bucket from the back of it, and says: "Here. Help yourselves. Take a few each." We thank him, reach in and take a couple of the *mandarinas* on offer. "No. Take more!" he insists. We each take one or two more. "Come on! There are still some left," he continues, taking the remaining fruits out of the bucket himself and trying to slot them into our pockets. One of our party, Horst, who has no rucksack, looks set to do the last kilometre of the walk precariously juggling an armful of bright orange mandarins.

El Argar

To return to El Argar culture in general, it takes its name from a settlement at what is now Antas. The Argaric culture flourished across Almería and into surrounding provinces between about 4200 BP (Before Present) and 3500 BP, so it was at its height after the Los Millares Copper Age culture (mentioned below) had declined. It seems that the Argar people's use of bronze allowed them to gain dominance over other tribes who were still using copper. The Argars (can we call them that, just for short?) were also noted for mining, for working silver and gold for jewellery, and for producing sophisticated ceramics.

The Antas settlement was one of about ten Argar sites explored by Louis Siret. In addition, he listed a number of others and, in total, 15 or so significant Argar locations are now known. At El Argar itself, by the Río Antas, Siret and his foreman Pedro Flores found over 1,000 graves. The majority had space for just one person though there were some for two or even three people. In the Argaric culture the dead were always buried in a foetal position. Most common were individual cist burials that were very close to the houses. These, it seems, from the evidence of the funerary goods found in them, were for the ruling classes. Other burials used pithoi, large earthenware urns, which were usually actually underneath the houses. Whilst this all sounds very interesting, as far as I am aware there is nothing to be seen above ground at El Argar nowadays.

As for where the El Argar site is, coming off the motorway at exit 534 and taking the road past the El Real industrial estate in towards Vera, after a few hundred metres, on the left, set slightly back from the road, there's a big building with 'Argar' emblazoned on it. In the interests of research I drove in to have a look, clocked that it had the appearance of a rather seedy hotel, though without further evidence I wouldn't like to say more, and drove out again. Wishing to be more precise, I checked on my copy of the Mapa Topográfico Nacional de España, sheet 1014-IV Vera, and found that in grid square 596123, on the true left bank of the Río Antas and about 500 metres from the village of Antas, is the symbol for *'restos arqueológicos'*, archaeological remains, a triangle of three black dots. However, it is labelled *'Necrópolis Fenicia'*, Phoenician necropolis, with no mention of a Bronze Age settlement. Maybe this is a hangover from Louis Siret's belief that everything had a Phoenician connection. It certainly suggests that the Spanish national mapping agency doesn't have an archaeologist on its staff, or at least didn't in 1998 when this map was published. I haven't been to that exact spot though, as I mentioned above, I understand that there are no visible remains at the site.

And on the day of the walk, after I arrived home and checked again, I found the map I'd been looking for: sheet 1014-II Cuevas del Almanzora. I had, of course, put it 'somewhere safe'. It showed the route we had taken, basically north from the town, past the scattered buildings of Las Cupillas and along a wavering black line labelled 'Camino de la Fuente del Álamo' leading to grid square 601132,

116

where the spring is named, Fuente del Álamo and, alongside it, the Cortijo del Álamo (*ruinas*). So the relatively modern but abandoned farmhouse is named but, of the Bronze Age site, there's no indication at all on the map. Strange priorities!

Los Millares and the Museo de Almería

The most extensive prehistoric remains in the whole of Andalucía lie 15 or so kilometres north of Almería, near Santa Fe de Mondújar. This is the Copper Age site at Los Millares, described by Michael Jacobs as 'memorably located in the middle of a sinister, eroded landscape'. Here, on a triangular rocky prow about 50 metres above the confluence of two dry riverbeds, the Río Andarax and the Rambla de Huéchar, one of Europe's major archaeological settlements was revealed by chance in 1891 during the construction of the railway line from Almería to the mining centre of Linares near Bailén that passes adjacent to the site.

The first excavations at Los Millares were carried out, predictably, by the Siret brothers, who funded their excavations from their salaries as engineers. Their work gradually revealed a vast Chalcolithic or Copper Age fortified settlement covering some six hectares. This was the period between the Neolithic and Bronze Ages, when both stone and copper but not bronze were being used for tools and weapons. Current techniques date the Copper Age from about 5200BP to 4200BP.

There's an excellent visual display in the entrance building at Los Millares now but it wasn't always so. An article in the newspaper *Ideal*, dated 3rd January 1993, describes Los Millares as one of the key sites in the birth of Spanish archaeology and talks of emergency work being done, at a cost of three million pesetas, to protect the site. In his book *Andalucía*, published a few years later in 1998, Michael Jacobs says: 'The site is not officially open to the public, nor in any way promoted, and the passing motorist might well think that a military rather than archaeological site lies beyond the fence. This encouraging evidence that steps are being taken to protect Andalucía's archaeological past is somewhat weakened when you discover that the key to this – one of the world's outstanding archaeological sites – hangs above the bar in the nearby village of Santa Fe de Mondújar, and can be had just for the asking.'

Now the site is open all year apart from official holidays, from Wednesdays to Sundays between 10.00 and 14.00, and entry is free. It's worth checking the opening details online before setting off for a visit, though, just to be sure. And a word of warning: it takes a while to walk round and do the site justice. There isn't much shade, so unless you are a real sun-fiend, don't go in the height of summer or indeed on any particularly hot day.

In the comprehensive display in the reception building an artist's impression, in aerial view, gives a very good sense of what the whole site might have looked like at the height of its use. The settlement is still remarkable, consisting of a village with an adjacent necropolis (cemetery), defended by four lines of walls, with several small forts beyond these. The village consisted of many round huts with diameters varying between 2.5 and 6.5 metres. They had stone footings and, it is assumed, wattle and daub walls. Nothing remains of the roofs but intelligent speculation suggests they would have been made of branches covered with mud, with a hole to allow smoke to escape. Among the huts at the furthest end of the spur are the remains of a square, fortified keep, within which is a large hollow that Siret suggested might be a water tank.

Protecting this area, a 400 metre long wall, the fourth or 'latest' wall, which has been fully investigated, ran across the spur. It was about two metres thick and had, at regular intervals, 17 semi-circular bastions and oval towers. There were also two fortified gateways (barbicans) and an impressive pear-shaped tower guarding the main gate. The remains of three much smaller walls, built successively further east and further back in time, can also be seen.

The necropolis, or cemetery, consists of about 80 multiple burials, each containing the remains of from 20 to over 100 individuals, together with their funeral offerings. Most of the tombs are in the form of a tumulus containing an entrance passageway at the end of which is a circular dry-stone chamber. The chambers are covered by a conical mound of earth and stone surrounded by a circle of masonry slabs. One group of tombs has been restored to show more clearly how they were constructed, and it's possible to go in, stooped, through the passageway to the central chamber. Similarly, reconstructed huts and a section of defensive wall, with fireplaces, pots, and weavings on a loom, give a clear sense of Copper Age life.

To the south the whole site is overlooked by several lines of hills on which 13 forts have been found. Six of these have been excavated and, again, full details are given in the visitors' display. Towards the end of the Copper Age, around 4200BP, Los Millares was abandoned. It is thought that this was either due to a period of increasing violence, reflected in the increased appearance of copper daggers and arrowheads, or as a result of an earthquake affecting the outcrops that supplied the village with water.

To make even more sense of Los Millares, you should go also to the Museo de Almería (Museum of Almería), where many of the best finds from the site are displayed. The Museum of Almería, which moved to highly-acclaimed new premises on the Carretera de Ronda in Almería city in 2006, is worth a visit in any event. It is basically a three-floor archaeological museum, welcoming and imaginatively done, with the first two floors focussing on the societies at Los Millares and El Argar. A dramatic stratigraphic column rises through the centre of the three floors almost to the top of the building. As well as the artefacts mentioned above, there is more to see, including Roman and other Andalucian remains. At the time of writing, the opening hours are: Monday, closed; Tuesday 14.30 – 20.30; Wednesday – Saturday 09.00 – 20.30 and Sunday 09.00 – 14.30. Again, things can change. It seems remarkably difficult to find these opening hours online but if you wish to check you could ring the museum on (+34) 950 175 510. Then again, phone numbers can change too. As with the Los Millares site, entry is free for EU citizens.

12. Almería

"I came to know Almería pretty well. It was so easy to reach –
a mere nine or ten hours away..."
(Gerald Brenan)

People of many cultures

Whilst we are in Almería, let's have a closer look at the place. These days Almería is a modern city but it retains an air of somewhere that might as easily be in North Africa as southern Spain. Michael Jacobs called it: 'The most African of Spanish towns.' People of many cultures have passed this way. Archaeological remains not far away mark the former presence of people of the Argar culture, as described above. Then came the Phoenicians, Carthaginians and Greeks, who settled, mined and traded along the coasts. The Romans established a presence here in the 3rd century BC and were dominant until the arrival of the Visigoths in the 7th century AD. The Moors though, under Abd al-Rahman, were in possession of Almería by 773. They ruled Almería, and indeed much of the Iberian Peninsula, for almost 800 years, apart from a decade after the Christians regained the city under Alfonso VII in 1147, only to lose it again ten years later, so it is not surprising that the influence of the Moors is strongly evident.

One of the gems of Almería, the Alcazaba is generally considered second only to Granada's Alhambra amongst Spain's Moorish fortresses, although Nina Epton wrote in the 1960s that it was: '...the most typical and best preserved Arab fortress in Spain'. The original building was begun in 955 AD, when Abd al-Rahman III, the Caliph of Córdoba, had the fortress and an arsenal built on a high rocky outcrop overlooking the sea. The project included city walls and a great mosque. The building stone came from the Canteras Califales, the quarries in the adjacent La Chanca neighbourhood. Within the *medina* (walled city) there were extensive gardens, palaces, and a population of about 20,000.

During the 11th century, after the fall of the Cordoban Caliphate, the city was more independent. It became the most important maritime town in Moorish al-Andalus, with vessels arriving from Syria, Egypt and Byzantium. According to Al-Idrisi, there were 970 inns and hostelries in the city, which was prospering because of its ceramics industry and particularly because of its silk looms, supplied by the 6,000 or so mulberry trees that had been planted both within the city and in the many nearby *huertas*.

After the city fell to the forces of the Catholic Monarchs Ferdinand and Isabella during the Reconquest in the 1480s, a long period of decline began. Every mulberry bush in Almería was destroyed in order to prevent the remaining Moors (known as Moriscos) from re-establishing their economy. The decline was also hastened by the effects of a series of earthquakes. There was a major one in 1522 and after another particularly devastating one in 1658 Almería's population stood at just 500.

A detailed chronology of the city's history is beyond the scope of this book and is widely available elsewhere. Suffice it to say that things gradually improved and the population increased particularly, if we leap ahead, after the arrival of the railway and the building of a new port in the 19th century. Today it has reached almost 200,000. Nevertheless, Almería is still the most isolated major city in Spain. Hence the continuing frustration over the fact that it takes six hours to go to Madrid by train and there is still no real sign of progress with the AVE link (see chapter 28).

As for the Alcazaba, restoration efforts over recent years have gone some way towards reversing the steady decay of centuries. Work was completed in October 2015 to repair a section of wall that had collapsed five months earlier, sending masonry into the street below. Despite what has been done, the Alcazaba must be a shadow of its former self, when the vast gardens filled with trees, aloes and flowers, and many pools and cascades, rivalled Granada's Alhambra. In 975 it was said to be 'an academy of learned men'. Its decoration in 1016 was overseen by the architect Abdala Ben Hussein el Gabali, under the first independent king of Almería, El Jairan. During the reign of Almotacin in the 1060s poets and scholars from across the Arab world assembled here.

Nowadays, entry to the Alcazaba is free to EU citizens on production of their passport. It is constructed on three levels. The lowest of these is entered through a big square tower and has water channels in a parkland setting. It has also the Tower of the Mirrors, where there was once a clever system of magnifying mirrors that allowed the lookouts to see approaching ships a long way off.

The middle area contains the remains of a mosque, converted into a chapel by the Catholic Monarchs, still with a horseshoe arch. This level also has the Tower of the Odalisque. In 1070 a Moorish slave-girl called Galiana, the favourite of the emir, fell in love with a Christian prisoner, so the story goes, and helped him try to escape. The attempt was foiled by guards, the prisoner threw himself from the Tower into the valley of La Hoya below and Galiana died of grief as a result.

The third level contains the Tower of Homage, which has a Gothic facade and the arms of Charles V with, at the furthest end, a massive tower facing west. From here a line of towers, of which almost nothing remains, strode across La Chanca and down to the sea. Over the walls of the fortress, to the west you look down on one of the city's poorest districts, the traditional area of *gitanos* (gypsies) and poor fishermen, the Barrio de La Chanca.

In *South from Granada*, Gerald Brenan vividly describes his first visit to the city in February 1920. Amongst other things (many other things...), he says: 'Almería is like a bucket of whitewash thrown down at the foot of a bare, grayish mountain.' Later, in the 1950s, the

Catalan traveller and writer Juan Goytisolo highlighted the la Chanca neighbourhood within the city in his book of the same name: *La Chanca*. A decade later Nina Epton described La Chanca as '...an inferior but more colourful Sacro Monte, whose cave-dwellings are painted in pale blue, madder, cadmium and apple green.' To clarify, Sacro Monte is the gypsy quarter of Granada, famous for its flamenco. Going on to talk about the light of southern Spain, she continued: 'Almería's luminosity has an extra quality, an extra magic which is not found elsewhere.' There are still some cave dwellings occupied in this area but guidebooks, such as *The Rough Guide to Andalucía*, warn that 'it's not a place to visit alone at night'.

The Almariya

On a large roundabout in front of the Maestro Padilla auditorium at the seaward end of Avenida del Mediterráneo stands a large boat. It's a modern version of a dhow of the type that would typically have been used by the Moors sailing between North Africa and Spain. It was built in 2005 as part of an initiative to celebrate the Mediterranean Games. Initially moored (no pun intended) at the Club de Mar, it was later moved to its present location.

A somewhat secret dimension to its presence is that it has become a favoured trysting place for courting couples, a kind of earthly version of the Mile High Club. The local council has blocked access to the boat's interior at least 20 times but has failed to deter lovers determined to enjoy the privacy it affords.

Miguel Cazorla, who was Almería's councillor for tourism at the time the boat was constructed, defends the boat as a link to the days when seafaring Moors held sway here: "I'm not going to discuss its use by couples, but taking it out of the water, moving it from the Club de Mar and letting it deteriorate is a disgrace."

Lennon remembered

There's a rather good bronze statue of John Lennon in Almería. He's on a bench, life-size, sitting with one leg bent and tucked up under the other, and playing a guitar. He has his trademark wire-rimmed spectacles and it's a decent likeness. Should you come across it by chance you might be puzzled as to why it's there, especially given that he is wearing a British Army World War II uniform.

The answer is that it commemorates the six weeks he spent in Almería between September and November 1966 whilst filming *How I Won the War*. Notably, he wrote, or finished writing – accounts vary – the iconic song *Strawberry Fields Forever* during his stay. The work, by sculptor Carmen Mudarra, cost €36,000. Incidentally, the same sculptor also made the statue of Lawrence of Arabia that adorns the sea-front at Carboneras.

The Lennon statue, commissioned by the city council in 2006 to mark the fortieth anniversary of the musician's stay in the area, was unveiled in March 2007. Since then it has had a chequered history. Initially located in the town's main *rambla,* it was vandalised and moved to what was considered a safer location outside the Molly Malone pub on the Paseo de Almería. Repeated acts of vandalism – at least seven - followed, though these, according to city councillor Lola de Haro, were not thought to be directed against Lennon or his memory. A spokesman for Almería city's cultural department, Gregorio Casanova, suggested the trouble was simply caused by "empty-headed individuals with nothing better to do". They included snapping the guitar's neck, no mean feat as it is made of bronze a couple of inches thick. This cost €5,000 to repair. On other occasions the guitar's pegs and Lennon's glasses were snapped off and the statue was spray painted in the red and yellow colours of the Spanish flag.

In 2010, after assorted repairs had cumulatively cost more than the original price of the work, the sculptor re-cast the statue from the original mould at a workshop in Antequera. It was then sited in its current (at the time of writing, at least) location, the Plaza de las Flores, hopefully safe at last from the attentions of the 'empty-heads'.

A stamp too late

In January 2016 the Spanish post office issued 220,000 copies of a new 57-cent stamp to commemorate the 1,000th anniversary of the founding of the city of Almería in 1014. I haven't made a mistake; those dates are correct. It appeared two years late.

In 2013 the Almería Millennium Friends' Association (AMRA) proposed the idea of a special stamp as one of many suggestions to herald the city's millennium. However, central government wheels ground slowly and it was not until 2015 that a model stamp was finally produced. There was a snag though; rather than showing Almería's Alcazaba, it carried a picture of the Bisagra Gate in Toledo. Alfonso Rubí, the president of AMRA, said: "Imagine our horror when we saw the stamp had completely the wrong image on it." As to the delay in producing the stamp, he commented with a wry smile: "That is how things are done here."

The design went back to the drawing board and was finally printed and distributed with two images of the Alcazaba, a 19th century etching by Nicolás Chapuy and a contemporary photo by Pako Manzano, along with the logo: 1014-2014 MILENIO REINO DE ALMERÍA. When the stamp was finally launched, with great ceremony and fanfare, by the regional head of the post office in front of an array of dignitaries, the fact that all this was happening two years after the event was diplomatically not mentioned.

Chapter 13: The Civil War tunnels

'Coming fresh from the Civil War with my mind still overshadowed by its horrors...'

(Gamel Woolsey)

Los refugios

The factory sirens were incredibly loud. They could be heard all over the city. Everyone knew the regular times for clocking on and clocking off. If the sirens went off at any other time, the first blast meant that you had just five or at the most ten minutes to get to the *refugios*. That was the time-lag between the radio reports from the lookouts on the mountains at Cabo de Gata and high in the Sierra de Gádor behind the city, and the arrival of the German bombers. The second blast meant that the bombs were imminent and you should take shelter wherever you could; if the worst came to the worst, under a table would be better than nothing.

The *refugios*, the underground bunkers, did their job; throughout the Civil War, no-one died in the tunnels. Quite a few though, were crushed to death in the mad panic to reach the entrances - there were 67 of them - when the sirens sounded. And with so many people crammed together underground, with children crying and hanging on to their mothers and the mothers terrified, there had to be rules. You had to bring a pot with you because there were no toilets. Sometimes people were in too much of a rush or simply forgot. By design the *refugios* had earth floors so pee, at least, would soak in. But it meant there was a high risk of infection.

Lamps were forbidden because they would use precious oxygen and because most of the air raids were carried out at night, so the slightest glimmer of light would give the bombers a target. And of course, there was no smoking.

The Civil War brought to the fore the vicious divisions in Spanish society. For this reason, no-one was allowed to discuss politics or religion in the tunnels. Their sole function was to be a safe refuge for everyone, regardless of their viewpoint.

In the 1930s Almería, partly due to the decline of the mining industry, was one of Spain's poorest provinces, and when the Spanish Civil War broke out in July 1936, conditions were desperate. The city had a population of about 50,000 but there was little money and very little food. You would never see an orange rind on the ground; they'd all been eaten. You would have to queue at the bakery for hours for the chance to buy a single loaf.

Almería was strongly Republican but with no defences of any kind against the right-wing forces of General Franco who was determined to overthrow the democratically elected government. Squeezed in between the mountains of the Sierra de Gádor and the Mediterranean Sea, the city was extremely vulnerable to attack. Franco's Nationalists, supported by the Germans and the Italians, were in a position to bombard Almería from both the air and the sea and didn't hesitate to do so. Citizens who could, went to their home villages for safety but this still left many remaining in the city in great danger.

The cruiser Canarias had been built during the early 1930s for the Spanish navy at Ferrol in northern Spain, to a British design incidentally, and was undergoing its final sea trials when it was seized by Franco's forces and became the flagship of the Nationalist navy. It was brought south into the Mediterranean and on 8th September 1936 it shelled the fuel depot at the port of Almería, creating a toxic cloud that cloaked the city for a week. Ageing residents, recalling those days, remember that for seven days there was no sign of the sun. After this, the Cueva de la Campsa, a large artificial cave dating from medieval times, was used for fuel storage.

Bombs from the sea

There was also the horrendous episode when the German navy bombarded Almería. The background to this is as follows. In 1937 Franco's Nationalists controlled the Balearic Islands of Majorca and Ibiza. Under a Non-intervention Agreement that they had signed, the German navy were not allowed to use the harbours there, but they did so. When Spanish government (i.e. Republican) planes flew over the Bay of Ibiza on May 30th, reconnoitring, the German cruiser Deutschland opened fire on them. In response, the planes bombed the Deutschland, causing some deaths and significant damage.

As a reprisal, the Germans decided to go for a defenceless target: Almería. The result was that at dawn on 31st May 1937 five warships came towards Almería from the direction of Cartagena. When 12 kilometres away, without warning, they began to shell the city, continuing the bombardment for an hour. This left 40 people dead, 150 wounded, and 200 buildings destroyed.

A despatch from the Spanish correspondent of the *Daily Telegraph*, published a few days later, on 5th June, described the scene: "The destruction caused last Monday in Almería in one hour by the German 'pocket battleship' Admiral Scheer is greater than that wrought by any single bombardment during the Spanish war, with the possible exception of the bombing of Guernica. I have spent two days touring the ruins and examining the havoc done....when for sixty minutes the Admiral Scheer and her escort of four destroyers shelled this old white-washed town.

"In that period 200 shells were fired. At least 40 of them were from the six 11 inch guns of the Admiral Scheer. These shells stand nearly a yard high. Three of them alone smashed 25 houses in the Majadores and Cucarra streets. It is amazing what an 11 inch shell will do to cheap lath-and-plaster dwellings such as those in the poor quarters of Almería.

"I have seen Madrid and other Spanish towns bombed from the air again and again, but never have I seen anything to equal this bombardment. During half of the time the five German ships were firing from behind a smoke screen. Throughout they were under the direct observation of a British destroyer.

"The horror of that hour, during which Almería practically disappeared under a cloud of smoke and dust, which arose from every quarter of the town, is indelibly imprinted on the minds of the inhabitants. Each night, as the sun goes down, a sad trek starts out towards the parched hills which surround the town.

"About 50 per cent of Almeria's population sleep outside the town every night....in the open. Even the wounded now in hospitals prefer to leave them rather than stay in the town.

"I have seen at least three entire streets silent and abandoned, with no inhabitants left. At a very moderate estimate, 7,000 or 8,000 people have lost their homes. No corner of the town has escaped, except for the districts surrounding the Fort, which would, logically, appear to be the only strictly military objective."

Digging the tunnels

Earlier than this though, the city authorities had begun taking steps to defend the civilian population. In February 1937 work had begun on a system of underground bunkers or *refugios*, designed by the municipal architect Guillermo Langle, with the assistance of the canal engineer José Fornieles and the mining engineer Carlos Fernández. 400 workers were assigned to the task, though the whole population helped as and when they could. The basic plan was to build a long tunnel deep under the Paseo de Almería, the wide boulevard that is one of the striking features of the town. This was so that the foundations of buildings wouldn't cause any problems as they dug the tunnels.

They started simply by digging holes into the ground and constructing steps down to a depth of about nine metres. Nowadays, that doesn't sound much but it was deep enough to provide protection from the bombs in use at that time. From the bottom of the steps, they dug the tunnels with picks and shovels, a metre at a time, putting up wooden shuttering and filling in behind it with concrete. The imprint of the wooden planks can still easily be seen on the arched roofs of the tunnels. Speed was of the essence but the tunnels were used during their construction if air raids happened. At such times when people were taking refuge in there, near to the 'working face', they could smell the still-damp concrete.

Langle had thought his design through very carefully. Some of the tunnels were 1.3 metres wide, with concrete benches along one side. The main tunnel was 2 metres wide, with benches on both sides. Baffles jutted out at intervals across the passages, like half a wall, to restrict the impact of shockwaves, should bombs explode at the entrances. In some Spanish cities, where *refugios* were built without such attention to detail, many people died from the effects of just such blasts. The baffles also slowed people down and prevented stampedes that might crush the most vulnerable.

By the spring of 1938 the *refugios* were completed and in full use; 4.5 kilometres of tunnels that could shelter 36,000 people. With the addition of the caves in the La Chanca district of the city, huddled below the Alcazaba, which could hold 9,000 at a push, and the silos of the Mineral de Hierro de la Compañía Andaluza de Minas near the port, with capacity for another 3,000, everyone in the city had shelter, in theory at least.

Two copper wires ran along the centre of the tunnel roof with a light every five metres. These were linked to the city's ordinary lighting system but were turned off whenever there was a raid. In addition, there were ventilation galleries with pipes of 100 mm diameter to bring in fresh air. These were separate from the main tunnel, built into narrower side tunnels with changes of direction, again to minimise the risk from bomb blasts and even hand-grenades.

There was also a storeroom for supplies under the main market but food was so scarce that there was little to put in it.

Some of the richer families had air-raid shelters under their own houses but this was only allowed on two conditions. They had to be connected to the main system, so that, should their house be destroyed, they could escape via the municipal tunnel system. Additionally, the public were to have access to the main system via these private bunkers. The more entrances there were, the quicker people could reach safety and the less chance there was of injuries through crushing. Anywhere that had an entrance to the system had a notice announcing REFUGIOS and also a black ribbon, this latter used as a marker easily recognised by those in the city who were illiterate.

Some shelters were made under other buildings; burnt out-churches were used, for example, because they had strong walls. Under the Iglesia de San Pedro there was room for 200 people, with a narrow passage connecting into the main system. There was an entrance to the tunnels under the Cervantes Theatre too.

Carretera de la Muerte

Further west along the coast, in early February 1937 a massive offensive by a combined force of Nationalists, Italian 'Blackshirts' with tanks, and Moroccan regulars brought about the capitulation of the Republicans at Málaga. Male Republicans who were not able to escape the city were shot; 4,000 were executed. About 50,000 refugees fled eastwards along the coast road towards Almería. In one of the most infamous episodes of the Civil War, this column of terrified humanity was attacked by the Nationalists and their allies. The historian Paul Preston wrote: "The crowds of refugees who blocked the road out of Málaga had been in an inferno. They were shelled from the sea, bombed from the air and then machine-gunned. The scale of the repression inside the fallen city explained why they were ready to run the gauntlet." German planes strafed the refugees, killing and injuring hundreds. The Carretera de la Costa became known as the Carretera de la Muerte. This inhuman massacre, known as La Desbanda, is still commemorated in Almería each February.

When the survivors reached Almería, they doubled its population. This put incredible strain on the city's resources but they were welcomed and given shelter. The *refugios* became even more crowded. Towards the end of the Civil War an underground operating theatre was built. For cleanliness, it was lined with marble tiles. It's one of the most striking features you see on a visit, with equipment from the time, now seeming astonishingly ancient and it's one of the things that makes a visit to the tunnels such a powerful experience.

Visiting the tunnels

The guide who takes you round tells of an elderly lady becoming quite emotional during a visit. When asked if she was alright she explained that her mother had always told her that she had been born in a hospital underground and now she was finally seeing the place where she came into the world. Two other old ladies on a visit cried when they reached the operating theatre, explaining that they had worked here as very young nurses. Their return opened the floodgates on their memories of those terrifying times. The tunnels seem bleak and basic now but there are occasional touches that bring them to life. Low on one of the walls, scratched into the plaster, is a poignant reminder, a child's drawing of a twin-propeller plane seen from underneath.

Almería was the last city to fall to the Nationalists, on 29th March 1939. Three days later, on 1st April, the Civil War ended. In total there had been 52 aerial attacks on the city, with 754 bombs dropped. After the end of the war the *refugios* were kept open in case they were needed during World War II. As it turned out, they were not needed. Kids went down there to play and people began to throw their rubbish down them. As seems to be the way with places like this, they were used as toilets and gradually they became a risk to health.

A decision was made to close them. The strategy used for this was to build either a bandstand or a newsagent's kiosk above each entrance. All of the bandstands have now gone and only three of the original small kiosks remain: in the Plaza Urrutia, the Plaza Conde Ofalia and the Plaza Virgen del Mar. The others, mainly along the Paseo de Almería, have been replaced by larger, distinctive black newsstands. To this day some of the news vendors use the steps below their kiosks for storage.

The authorities finally decided, in the early years of this century, to restore part of the system and in 2006 it opened to the public. Some modern-day visitors arrive in the Plaza Manuel Pérez García, near the Puerta de Purchena, knowing the entrance to the *refugios* is there but not immediately able to find it. The clue is to look for a modern but otherwise rather insignificant glass structure. The name is not there in bright lights but on closer inspection it is apparent that this is the entrance to the bunkers. Close to where you come out at the end of the visit, incidentally, there is one of the three remaining original news kiosks, still in use.

As more and more people have become aware of the existence of the *refugios*, visits have become extremely popular, so you have to book in advance. In summer in particular you should aim to book a couple of months ahead. A visit involves going as part of a guided group, with a maximum 25 people due to space constraints underground. The tours are in Spanish, though the guides do speak some English. But don't let this put you off. If your Spanish is limited, do try to team up with a Spanish-speaking friend who can translate for you. And even without understanding everything, you will find a visit to the *refugios* a moving and fascinating experience.

14: The exotics

'As for hoopoes, their gypsy plumage made them every artist's favourite. One watercolour by Michael Warren was like a piece of magic realism by Rousseau. The hoopoe sits heraldic in a fig tree, against a *dehesa* changed in the sunset to the same russet and cinnamon tones.'

(Richard Mabey)

Hoopoes

One of the birds that most grabs the attention of visitors to Almería province is the hoopoe, a classic Mediterranean species. In fact, in *Birds Britannica*, Mark Cocker writes: 'Most Britons first encounter the species during Mediterranean holidays, where hoopoes are routinely seen in hotel grounds." Its call is a triple note, a soft, far-carrying 'hoo hoo hoo' or 'oop oop oop', hence its name. Its Spanish name, *abubilla,* is similarly onomatopoeic, as is its Latin name Upupa epops. It is at the same time amusing and beautiful. Together with the roller and the bee-eater, it forms a trio sometimes known as 'the exotics'.

Incidentally, the word can be pronounced either 'hoo-poo' or 'hoo-poh'. Both are correct. My sense is that 'hoo-poh' was favoured in the past and it's what I remember hearing in the UK when I was young, but now 'hoo-poo' seems more popular, certainly amongst English-speaking birders in this area of Spain.

Hoopoes visit the UK in small numbers, about 100 per year, and there have been only about 40 nesting attempts, so it's not a bird most people will have encountered there. I recall there was great excitement when I was a kid growing up in Grimsby in the late 1950s and a hoopoe was reported in Weelsby Woods in the town. Then much later, when I was teaching in Sheffield, my colleague Pete Brown, an avid birder, persuaded me out one lunch-hour to try to find a hoopoe that had been seen fairly close by in the south of the city. We found it easily enough but it looked strangely out of place on a manicured lawn in a modern English suburb under grey skies.

The hoopoe's striking shape and features attracted the ancient Egyptians, on whose murals it regularly appeared as a hieroglyph. And in modern times this heraldic bird tops the ornithological charts for appearing on stamps, with at least 43 countries, at the last count, appreciating its almost magical graphic qualities.

Hoopoes like open, cultivated land such as olive groves but have also taken to golf courses. Spain's hoopoe population is partly migratory but here in Almería they are present all year round. They are not so common that you'll see one every day though, so each sighting is a little bit special. It's one of those birds you can't mistake too, like a magpie or a kingfisher: unique enough to be easily identifiable. It's somewhere between beige and pink and pale orange, with broadly barred black-and-white wings, a long, slightly down-curved bill and a striking crest. The crest normally points backwards but when the bird alights, the crest, fringed with black and white, is raised. In flight it's like a huge moth, with broad, rounded, pied wings. It's such an improbable bird that it's likely to make you smile.

Bee-eaters

Having written about bee-eaters in *Flamingos in the Desert,* I feel somewhat constrained here. I don't want people complaining of repetition and asking for a refund, so what more can I say about these remarkable bright yellow, red-brown and green birds? Bee-eaters (Merops apiaster in Latin, *abejaruco* in Spanish) have traditionally tended to breed no further north than Paris but they do occur occasionally in the UK and have even bred there. This happened famously in 2002, when a pair nested in an old quarry in County Durham. 'BEE-EATERS' road signs helped direct the thousands of visitors who wanted to see them to a temporary centre where, as well as seeing the nest-site at a distance, they were able to watch the domestic life of the birds in real time, relayed from a nest-cam. Further nesting took place in Herefordshire in 2005, the Isle of Wight in 2014 (two pairs) and Cumbria in 2015 (again, two pairs). Mark Thomas of the RSPB commented: "Pushed northwards by climate change, it is highly likely that these exotic birds will soon become established visitors to our shores."

In eastern Almería they are common summer visitors, nesting in colonies in long burrows in river banks or soft cliffs. They can often be seen soaring high, with stiff-winged glides, their presence betrayed by their bubbling calls as they hawk for insects. The colours, distinctive sound, and conspicuous habits of this iconic species means that it is not easily overlooked.

Rollers

Less common than the hoopoe, and challenging the bee-eater for top spot in the tropical colour stakes, is the roller (Coracias garrulus). Rollers are heavy birds, jackdaw-sized and, when perching, pale blue with a tan-brown back and a hefty bill. Only in flight is the full nature of the plumage revealed, with dramatic contrasting patches of darker ultramarine blue and black.

Like bee-eaters, rollers are summer visitors to Spain, arriving about late April and staying until the end of August. They spend the winter in sub-Saharan Africa. I'm writing this at the beginning of June 2015 and so far this year I've seen just one roller. They often perch on wires or the dead branches of trees, scanning the ground below for lizards or other tasty morsels. The name 'roller' comes from the spectacular courtship display which features mid-air somersaults accompanied by its harsh and raucous call. This call lies behind its Spanish name, *carraca*.

Rollers nest in holes, usually in trees, but as large trees are relatively scarce in Almería, they also take to holes in cliffs, buildings and riverbanks. I remember, soon after discovering this area, seeing rollers at their nest holes in the rocky cliffs of the gorge called El Afa which almost surrounds the small town of Sorbas. Like the other birds mentioned here, the roller is a bird you can't mistake.

And so it was on 1st July 2015 when I just happened to look across the valley from the terrace outside our house and saw a largish bird, flying fast and flashing vivid blue. In less than ten seconds it was out of sight but it was a roller, no doubt about it; the first I've seen in our valley in the ten years we've had the house here. A memorable and colourful moment.

Golden orioles

In 2014 Chris Stewart published *Last Days of the Bus Club*, billed as the fourth volume in his *Driving Over Lemons* trilogy. Following his lead, I'm now declaring golden oriole (Oriolus oriolus in Latin, *oropéndola* in Spanish) to be the fourth member of the 'exotics' trio.

I'm down on our bottom terrace, tinkering about with the fairly primitive irrigation system. A beautiful fluting call and I spin round, just in time to see a thrush-sized shape flying along the valley, with hints of yellow and black. It's against the sun, so the colours are not too obvious, but the package – song, size, hints of colour, mode of flight; what birders call the 'jizz', can only say 'golden oriole'. We've heard them here occasionally and guess they like the tall eucalyptus trees below the abandoned hamlet of Los Garcías, at the end of the valley and near the *fuente*, about 300 metres away. I'm just absorbing the pleasure this moment has given me, when back it comes, in swooping flight, fluting as it goes, this time with the sun on it, leaving no doubt that it is a male oriole, a superb addition to the mix of local species.

You'd think that a 24 cm (= about 10 inches) long bright yellow bird with black wings and a pink beak would be easy enough to see but they're not. They spend most of their time in the canopy of high

138

trees and are surprisingly well camouflaged. The females, olive-green above and paler below, are even harder to spot. The giveaway is the call. *Collins Bird Guide* makes its best attempt to transliterate it like this: 'Song a beautiful, loud, fluting, confusable only (at distance) with Blackbird song, e.g. '**foh**-flüo-**fih**-fioo' or shorter 'fo**flüh**-füo' or just 'fiooh', the details varied'. A brave effort. Google golden oriole and you can see and hear video and audio clips so you'll know what you're listening for. I've had several conversations with friends and acquaintances who have waxed eloquent about the joy they've had from oriole encounters, one of whom, Fred Smithers, captured it perfectly: "Seeing the oriole is like having a fleeting side glance through to another world."

Dupont's lark

I'm cheating again now. Dupont's lark is not a colourful bird at all; it's a typical lark, brown and streaky, but it can claim to be exotic in a sense because it is very rare. I mentioned in *Flamingos* that I'd never seen a Dupont's lark. I still haven't. Not many people have, in fact, and if current trends continue, then soon no-one will have the chance to see this bird, a speciality in our part of Spain, with its upright stance and distinctively curved bill. In the summer of 2015 the environmental association SERBAL (Sociedad para el Estudio y Recuperación de la Biodiversidad Almeriense) estimated the remaining population in Almería province to be only about 25 birds. These are spread between the Sorbas area, the Sierra de Gádor and the steppes of Cabo de Gata. Emilio González, a spokesman for SERBAL, explained: "It's a very select species that only lives in plains, and in Almería these are disappearing due to greenhouses." The *Collins Bird Guide* clarifies the bird's habitat requirements: 'Breeds on dry, sandy soil with tufts of grass, on natural steppe or in semi-desert and flatter mountainsides, high plateaux as well as low plains by the sea.'

SERBAL has called for the Department of the Environment to support a captive breeding programme which will, in due course, allow releases to replenish the wild population. There are colonies in other parts of Spain, mainly Castilla y Leon and Aragón, though they number only in the hundreds, and in North Africa. The problem with releasing captive-bred birds into the wild, though, is that if the habitat they need is disappearing, how will they survive? Sadly, maybe Dupont's lark is a species that most of us will never see or hear in Almería.

Bird art with a difference

The flamingo, in flight, neck extended and legs trailing, is enormous. Behind it, a storm sky threatens and is reflected, yellow and black, in the waters of a lagoon. In the distance, to the left, lie the mountains of Cabo de Gata. To the right, equally distant, the tower of the Iglesia de las Salinas, the Church of the Saltpans, spears into the sky.

I move along and come to a roller, also in flight and seen from below, against an archetypal Almería landscape: dried grasses, the crumbling ruin of an abandoned *cortijo* and the dramatic flower spikes of two agaves, afire with the glow of their seed-pods.

Next, three red-rumped swallows flying against a wall richly lit with late afternoon light, and with a repetitive pattern of red arched tiles behind the birds. The attention to detail is superb and the compositions are dramatic yet entirely realistic. You can imagine that you might see any of these situations, if you struck lucky, whilst out there birding.

This is the work of Finn Campbell-Notman and these paintings are three amongst the fifteen that he completed during 2015 for an exhibition he calls *The Immigrants*. Finn is English but has lived in Spain for many years and has spent long periods in Almería province during that time. Walking the landscape, sitting and watching, searching out or coming by chance across a certain combination of features - tumbledown beams in an old house, a particular tree in a cluster of rocks, a quirky configuration of stone buildings, evening light slanting across water - he takes photographs and finds ideas for his bird paintings. He tells me, for example, of the time he spent thinking through the way in which the strong light reflected from the wall and the red of the arched tiles would affect the colouring of the red-rumped swallows mentioned above, bringing richer tones to their plumage.

He is not trying to be a field-guide illustrator. He has a fine art background and he also knows his birds but he puts them in a context, so you can sense that this is the dry south-eastern corner of Spain. He wants to have his birds in real places. In his work the landscape and the birds complement each other. His birds are life size and the paintings tend to reflect that: the flamingo canvas is 2.1 x 1.6 metres, for example. It also means that if the birds are relatively small in real life, then they remain small, but still significant, as in his large canvas called *Welcome?*, where two black wheatears and a hoopoe are dwarfed by the swelling green architecture of a clump of prickly pear cactus against a sky of the deepest blue.

On a simple level these are just striking images of birds including, as well as those mentioned above, Dartford warbler, Scops owl, bee-eaters, black redstarts, golden orioles, short-toed eagle and others, but there is more to it than that. They are not all migrants but the title of the exhibition, *The Immigrants*, is designed to get the viewer thinking. Campbell-Notman plays on words, so the red-rumped swallow painting referred to above is entitled *Arcos de la Frontera*; not just an actual town where the birds might be seen but a reference to the 'arches' in the picture and with the 'frontier' hinting at their migration.

Another painting is of two spent cartridge cases, finely detailed and entitled *Customs & Excise*. The viewer cannot avoid reflecting on the 'custom' of shooting migrating birds and the possibility of them being 'excised' from the list of common species.

One of the most powerful pieces is the large canvas of the roller and the flowering agaves referred to above. If you weren't aware of the title, you would take this to be simply a fine image of a typical Almerian scene. But behind this, there is more. An extract (which I have edited, with permission) from the prospectus Finn wrote for *The Immigrants* series, explains: 'While this cycle of fourteen paintings seems a straightforward, representational depiction of the bird and plant species of Andalucía, it is however the pretext for a deeply considered inquiry into contemporary human population movements and migrations, the underlying drives and motivations for this, and about boundaries as a purely human construct, and those without a passport being mere flotsam and jetsam.

'It is also an examination of humanity's conception of flight itself and the privileges and possibilities afforded by our ability to fly. We have, however, lost the sense of awe in regard to the ability to fly. It has become so commonplace as to be almost meaningless while at the same time the miracle of flight has become forever tainted. The myriad hijackings, crashes, disappearances and downing of planes mean that flight itself as a means of escape has been forever undermined and we have, as evinced by 9/11, turned our means of flight against ourselves. We have, all of us, become Icarus.' The title of the roller/agaves painting is *Icarus - 9/11*. Now it becomes clear; the roller is a plane, the tall verticals of the agaves are the Twin Towers and the ruined *cortijo* is the ensuing devastation. Art as allegory, a picture to provoke thought.

Finn knows his art history. He points to one of his pictures and mentions "a bit of Caravaggio light". He talks about the visceral fury of Francis Bacon and tells me of Sánchez Cotán, a pioneer of Spanish Baroque realism, one of his inspirations but a painter of whom I hadn't heard. I subsequently check out Sánchez Cotán and am intrigued by his vivid and powerful still lifes (that is the plural: I looked it up) painted at the turn of the 17th century.

Working on *Border Patrol*, his painting of a black redstart in a ruin, Finn was thinking of the abstract impressionists. Shadows of fallen roof-beams are imprinted black against a bright wall which has faint suggestions of yellow. There's a vivid blue sky and a tiny flash of red from the bird. This is clearly a homage to the blocky, colourful work of Mondrian, or so I think until Finn refers to Robert Motherwell and Pierre Soulages, whose work he says informs his own. So it's back to Google for me and I soon see what he's referring to.

Finn aims to capture the character of the birds he sees. He describes to me how on one occasion he was watching a pair of black wheatears for half an hour, and was intrigued by their behaviour: "They're shifty and boisterous, nervous and aggressive," he says. Sometimes he'll make thumbnail sketches in the field, and will often take many photos of features he wants to use as possible settings for his birds.

When he is working through his ideas, having absorbed the birds and the landscapes, and with a thorough knowledge of painters, he finds that a moment arrives when he can synthesise all of these things to come up with a unique and original idea. There is a very distinctive artistic vision in Finn Campbell-Notman's work. *The Immigrants* was initially exhibited in the gallery space at Albar restaurant in El Pilar in late 2015 and early 2016 and was subsequently shown in Mojácar. As I check through this section of my writing, I hear that some of the paintings in *The Immigrants* series have just been crated and have taken flight, to be shown over the winter of 2016 / 2017 in Berlin and then Beijing in Spring 2017. If you see an exhibition of *The Immigrants* advertised near you, be sure to catch it if you possibly can. Failing that, check it out on Finn's website via this link: www.finncampbellnotman.com/birds/

15. Three books

'Books mattered because they led readers to places they would not otherwise have dreamed of going, not only geographical places, but also places of the spirit and emotions.'

(Hugh Thomson)

South from Granada by Gerald Brenan

Gerald Brenan (1894-1987) is one of the best-known and most accomplished British writers on Spain. Brenan lived in the small village of Yegen in the Alpujarras for a total of about seven years between 1920 and 1934. From the viewpoint of those of us in Almería province, his most significant book is *South from Granada* which, despite not being published until 1957, gives an intriguing portrait of rural Spanish life before the Civil War.

At the front of the book is a simple map showing the roads that existed in the area up to 1925. There are not many of them. Only two main roads reach Almería city: one from the west, coming across the Campo de Dalías, one of the areas which is today a sea of *plasticos*, to the south of the Sierra de Gádor, and the other striking north from Almería before forking, north-west towards Guadix and north-east then east via Tabernas, Sorbas, Los Gallardos and Huércal-Overa to Puerto Lumbreras. This latter road, now the N-340a, was built in 1890 and for a long time was called the 'new road'.

One of the engaging things about Brenan's approach to life is the way he just gets stuck in and does what is necessary. He says, matter-of-factly: 'The nearest town of any size to Yegen was Almería. Its distance by road was fifty-seven miles, and one could either walk or take the bus.' He first went to Almería in February 1920 to buy furniture and walked there. By the first evening he had arrived at Berja and the following morning, after walking a further ten miles, he reached the coast road, which he describes as a depressing sight: 'For fifteen miles the road ran in a perfectly straight line across a stony desert without, so far as I could make out, passing a single tree or house on the way.' He finally came round a hill and saw the flat, white-roofed city of Almería, having covered almost 60 miles in two days. Elsewhere he says: 'I came to know Almería pretty well. It was so easy to reach – a mere nine or ten hours away – that I used to visit it whenever I wanted a change from village life'.

The main Almería interest in *South from Granada* comes in a chapter entitled *Almería and Archaeology*. He writes vividly and perceptively about the vibrant life of the city, saying he always had a feeling of excitement when he came there. He was able to capture the flavour of the place in a few words: 'Certainly it seemed that the sea was doubly Mediterranean here, and that the city, spread out in the bright coloured light, contained within it echoes of distant civilisations.'

He also has a somewhat bizarre chapter entitled *Almería and its brothels* in which he embarks on a tour of several such establishments in the company of an odd character called Agustín Pardo. Assuming Brenan's account is accurate, he merely visits the brothels as an observer, without sampling the services on offer. It may not be accurate though. Phil Maillard, a writer who has spent much time studying British writers in Andalucía, says of Brenan: 'His format is flexible enough to include some fictional insertions, including the chapter on the brothels of Almería and his sex-obsessed but impotent guide to them, Agustín.' Although *South from Granada* has only a couple of chapters about Almería, the whole of it is well worth reading. Phil Maillard considers it: '... in my view the best English-language book ever written on Andalusia.' On publication it was widely acclaimed as a masterpiece and it has retained that status.

Campos de Níjar by Juan Goytisolo

Campos de Níjar was originally published in 1960 but I have a more recent edition which came out from the Instituto de Estudios Almerienses in 2010. Juan Goytisolo was in his twenties when he first visited Almería in the 1950s. He was an interested and open-minded traveller. "The past is a foreign country; they do things differently there," said L. P. Hartley in the first sentence of his iconic novel *The Go-Between,* and so it was in the Almería of the 1950s. It was the time of the *dictadura franquista*, the Francoist dictatorship. Much of Almería province had supported the Republicans against the Fascists, so once he held power, Franco had little interest in alleviating the harsh living conditions of this remote semi-desert in the south-east of the country.

Not only is *Campos de Níjar* in Spanish but Goytisolo transliterates speech as he hears it, with thick rural Andaluz dialect and all. I was well into the book, struggling because of my far-less-than-fluent Spanish and looking up words frequently in my hefty Collins dictionary and not finding them, when I finally realised what was going on. So, for example, Goytisolo reports someone saying: "Cá día va peó." The penny dropped and I suddenly saw that this was: "Cada día va peor." 'Each day she's getting worse.' If the level of your Spanish is like mine, *Campos de Níjar* is thus not an easy read but if you are sufficiently determined, Goytisolo will take you on a fascinating historical journey. At the very final moment before this book was published, I read the sad news of Goytisolo's death at the age of 86. *Campos de Níjar* does not generally feature among his most celebrated works but for those of us in Almería it is a striking reminder of his talents as a writer.

Having searched for a translation and failed to find one, I managed to get through the book in Spanish but then, a couple of years later, I discovered that there *was* an English version available, **Níjar Country** by **Peter Bush**. In fact it's an American translation, which can be mildly irritating at times if you are used to English

English but which ultimately doesn't detract from the narrative. It's only 100 pages long but after finishing *Níjar Country*, I sat back, stunned again by the power of Goytisolo's writing.

This celebrated travelogue pulls no punches in describing the relentless, grinding poverty and bleak, forgotten landscapes of Almería province in the 1950s. This was before the first *plasticos* had appeared, before even the most adventurous tourists had come this way. Goytisolo walked, took battered buses, and hitched lifts, which was illegal under Franco.

On a single page, chosen at random, I find adjectives like 'barren', 'ruined', 'abandoned', 'cracked', 'unpaved', 'ugly', 'deserted' and more. At the Rodalquilar gold mines, where 'the silence is excruciating', the 'waste has invaded the valley beyond the ponds and created a vast, cracked yellow sea of mud'. The descriptions are straightforward but, piled one on another, they paint a picture of people ground down by their existence in a lost corner of Spain, beset by dust-storms, failing crops, drought and neglect. 'We reach the men and join the circle. There are eight or nine of them, dirty and badly shaven, in threadbare shirts and patched trousers. One points his toes out the end of his sandals; another uses rope for a belt. The sun is still blistering.' The people are 'skinny', have 'big rotten teeth', a boy 'looks like a wild pup', the 'kids around here start working at the age of seven'. There's Filomena with a gangrenous leg and Feliciano Gil Yagüe, a roadmender who has trachoma and whose 'eyes are like two buttonholes'.

Though the image Goytisolo presents of the Níjar area is relentlessly grim, it's also clear that, the more he sees, the more he becomes frustrated at the state of the people and their acceptance of the hand they have been dealt. He still describes them and their lives with dignity though. It's not overtly stated but there is a strong sense that his real anger is reserved for the rich landowners and the authorities who do nothing to change the situation. It's no surprise that Goytisolo made few friends amongst the influential people of the area and that the then mayor of Níjar said he wanted to string him up by the balls. On the back cover of the modern English edition, there's this: 'Born in Barcelona (1931), Juan Goytisolo is Spain's greatest living writer. A bitter opponent of the Franco regime, his early novels were banned. With *Níjar Country* (1960), he was declared persona non grata, his name better known in police stations than literary circles.' That seems to me like a pretty good recommendation to read the book.

David Lean's Dedicated Maniac: Memoirs of a Film Specialist by Eddie Fowlie and Richard Torné

Eddie Fowlie worked for over 40 years in the film industry and is particularly known for the work he did with David Lean, not least on *Lawrence of Arabia*. It's not easy to describe exactly what Fowlie did. In the preamble to this book he says: 'Nowadays, they have all sorts of fancy names to describe what I did: you can be a Production Designer, an Art Director, an Assistant Art Director, a Buyer or whatever else the film unions and accountants can come up with.' As a shorthand for the many different ways in which Fowlie smoothed the way with endless ingenious solutions to film-making problems, he became known by David Lean as his 'dedicated maniac'.

Local author and journalist Richard Torné spent several years cajoling Fowlie, a long time resident of Carboneras, to talk about his own life in the film industry rather than what he seemed to want to talk about, which was the technicalities of film-making during the years, from about 1950 to the early 1990s, when he was involved in the business. He succeeded in doing so and consequently produced a book that tells the tale of a one-off, a maverick all-round trouble-shooter in a time before computer-aided special effects were available. Fowlie comes over as something of a loner, opinionated and sometimes difficult, and yet an intriguing and largely likeable character.

Richard Torné says: 'He approached life in the same way he did making films; he was a very pragmatic man who wasn't into overanalysing things, consequently it was hard for me to delve deeper. He wasn't a sentimental man and had no time for those who mulled over emotions; that wasn't necessarily a fault, especially in his line of work, he was really just a product of his generation. I suspect that in different circumstances we may not have got on at all, but in truth I was really fond of him and still miss him a lot. He was quite an extraordinary man.'

Eddie Fowlie spent two and a half years at the beginning of the 1960s working with David Lean on *Lawrence of Arabia*. A lot of the initial work was done in Jordan but due to soaring costs it was decided to move the film to somewhere cheaper and where shooting would be easier. A scout, working in Spain for Columbia films, had assured Lean that there was a genuine desert there, in Almería.

Fowlie oversaw the unloading of a mass of equipment that had been shipped from Jordan to Almería. Seeing the pile of equipment mount and being concerned for its safety, he asked a couple of Guardia Civil officers if it would be safe. 'They looked surprised. I was told we needn't worry as no-one was about to steal anything with the Guardia Civil around; this was Franco's Spain, after all.'

Fowlie describes how he has to search for a location where he can build a facsimile of the town of Aqaba. 'We were in a very dry and poor part of Spain but it was blessed with some incredible scenery, including an arid desert and small volcanic hills. These had been weathered to form astonishing shapes, interspersed with deep ravines and dry riverbeds, called *ramblas* in Spanish, which had been formed by storm rain. It was along these that we drove, looking for locations which might be suitable for shooting some scenes. We didn't know it at the time but we were the first of many film crews to land in Almería and much later others would follow our lead, mostly to shoot westerns.'

Fowlie goes on to say: 'The province of Almería has come a long way since then, attracting many retired Brits looking for a quiet life under the sun and developers keen to exploit the situation by clogging much of the coastline with luxury hotels. When we arrived there were none and the roads were mostly dirt tracks, but most importantly I learned that Almería has the most hours of sunshine on the continent. There were also impressive sand dunes located on the extreme south-eastern tip of the Iberian Peninsula, at a place called Cabo de Gata. There, we built a railway track for Lawrence to blow up. At a small fishing village to the east was a broad, dry riverbed coursing down between barren hills to end on a wide beach (Playa de Algarrobico). We decided that this would be the perfect spot to build the town of Aqaba. The village was called Carboneras, and I was so impressed by it that I finally decided to settle down here. Between the village and the set I saw a strip of land covered in little blue flowers along the edge of a beach. On the headland beyond it, the rock formation on a hill – at least in profile – looked exactly like MGM's lion. I interpreted this as another good omen, so I bought the land shortly afterwards. Forty-eight years later I am still here, so it can't have been that bad a choice.'

Talking of the time when they made *Lawrence*, he says: 'We couldn't find a single hotel anywhere, not even in the capital, so I made do with a Bedouin tent, which I moved to wherever we worked. On one occasion, we were shooting in a dry river bed between hills. Unbeknown to us there was a heavy rainstorm, but the first thing I knew about it was when a wall of water rushed in. Within seconds we were five feet deep in water. There was a mad scramble to save everything and we almost drowned in the process, but it taught us a lesson not to be fooled into thinking that it was safe to camp in the *ramblas.'*

Fowlie has some intriguing memories too, of working with John Lennon on Richard Lester's film *How I Won the War*, including the time when Ringo Starr came out to visit John. Sometime later Fowlie had a small hotel, the El Dorado, built on the land he had bought at Carboneras. It still displays mementos from some of the films he worked on. Eddie Fowlie died peacefully at his home in Carboneras on January 22nd 2011 and is commemorated in the town on Calle Sorbas, where a bronze bust of him by the sculptor Roberto Manzano was unveiled in early 2015.

16. More Almería books and writers

'In fact, all our English writers on Andalucía are restless souls investigating the nature and meaning of happiness. Most of them think a traditional Spanish provincial or rural environment is a good place to achieve whatever happiness may come a person's way.'
(Phil Maillard)

Non-fiction

In this chapter (and occasionally elsewhere...), I'm breaking with my general convention throughout the book and highlighting authors and book titles in bold, just to make them stand out a little more.

Don Gaunt is an enthusiast for old railways but his ***Almería and The Great Southern of Spain Railway (The GSSR)***is much more than just an account of a long-disused railway line. It is based on a prodigious amount of research and includes initial chapters covering the basic geography of Almería and its history.

The bulk of the book is an exhaustive study of the GSSR, which was primarily a goods line. Its fortunes were closely linked to the ups and downs of the mines it served. Many of the technical details in the book will be mainly of interest to railway buffs but for the reader whose interest is more general, these sections are easily skipped. The text and photos are thorough and open an intriguing window onto a fascinating time in Almería's past. Don Gaunt's research was done mainly between 1995 and 2001, at which time much of the infrastructure was still in situ. Since then a lot has changed but there is still plenty to see. Don's book was one of my main sources during my explorations of the Almanzora Valley, described in chapters 34 to 36.

Checking out the books in charity shops is one of my habits when I'm in the UK, and in February 2016, as occasionally happens, I struck gold; an almost perfect hardback copy of ***Andalusia*** by **Nina Epton**, complete with original dust-jacket, for £2.99. I'd come across various references to her book and was delighted to finally have a copy. It ranges widely across Andalucía but there is enough about Almería to make it worth tracking down, if you are interested in how things were here half a century ago.

Nina Consuela Epton (1913-2010) was English, but had a Spanish mother, hence her middle name. She graduated from the Sorbonne in Paris and became a radio producer, broadcaster and travel writer. Her Wikipedia entry has this: 'As a travel writer she was considered something of a novelty in the early 1950s as a good-looking woman who travelled alone and engaged deeply and critically with local conditions.' Check out the footnotes and you find that that sentence is based on a piece in the *Sunday Herald* of Sydney, dated July 1953 and entitled, in a sexist way that was typical of the time, 'A Pretty Explorer Will Set Off Again'.

She travelled through Andalucía at the height of Franco's dictatorship and given the stranglehold the Guardia Civil had on the population, that was probably a particularly safe time for a woman to be travelling alone. The 'Acknowledgments' in her book show that she moved in somewhat rarefied circles, her passage smoothed by mayors, landowners, city archivists, museum curators and regional tourism delegates. Her observations and her writing were very much her own though and her chapters on Almería provide an intriguing picture of the place in the 1960s. The interest she has in the areas where she's travelling shines through her writing.

Written in Spanish, *Mojaqueros de hecho* by **Francisco Haro Pérez** is an affectionate homage to the outsiders who came to Mojácar in the 1960s and helped alter the place forever. The title might be translated as something like 'De facto Mojaqueros', to indicate that, although the people in question were incomers, they were a key ingredient of the village. The author, Francisco 'Paco' Haro, was born in the 1950s. His father founded and ran the original Indalo Hotel, so Paco Haro grew up right in the midst of the dramatic changes that affected the village at that time. His book paints a vivid picture, in words and with a liberal scattering of photos, of the Mojácar of half a century ago. For one element of his book, the author enlisted the help of various others who were here at the time, to compile pen portraits of almost 30 of the key Mojácar characters who are no longer with us. Immediately popular when it was published in 2014, the book sold out very quickly and is now hard to find. Or so I thought until, late in 2016, I happened upon two copies at the Cepsa *gasolinera* in Mojácar and snapped one of them up. When I searched for it online just before this book went to press, amazon.es told me there was a used hardback copy available for €359.84, so a second printing would no doubt be well received.

Noted local resident Ric Polansky, who came in 1969 as one of the first foreigners to settle in Mojácar, filled one of his regular columns in a local newspaper a couple of years ago with effusive praise for *A Year in Andalucía: An American's Point of View* by **Bud Suiter.** The author had spent a year in Mojácar and writing this book was one of his projects during that time. On Amazon it had just two reviews, a one-star and a four-star. I read them, accepted the screen's offer to 'Look Inside', and was sufficiently interested to take the plunge and buy a Kindle version of the book.

Bud Suiter's work rate certainly can't be faulted and he's a great enthusiast for all things Spanish. He covers a huge amount of ground, not all of it within Andalucía and at times his text seems to leap from one topic to another without any apparent link; chapter 12 is a case in point, where he covers road works, the monarchy, energy generation, illegal immigrants and university education. He also has chapters on food, drink, and bullfighting. These are all Spain-wide, rather than being about Andalucía and certainly mostly not about Almería, though he does go into great detail concerning a bullfight he attends in Vera. On the up-side, the author covers a lot of very interesting material on Spanish prehistory and history, from an American perspective.

He takes a while to get into his stride, first going into a blow-by-blow account of how he spent much time and $2,000 applying for a visa, only to finally discover he didn't need one. If you are American and know literally nothing about Spain but want to come here, Bud has certainly done the groundwork. He hires an apartment and a car, buys a mobile phone and signs up for a pottery class.

He makes a rather unusual claim though, suggesting that foreign writers are on 'vacation' when they are in Spain. He includes in this Gerald Brenan, who lived here for many years and is universally accepted as one of the great Hispanophiles. This is a big book and, given the time he had available (though he did stay for 18 months in the end), Bud had to write it quickly, which might explain the fact that a few errors have crept in. He says, for example, that Castilian Spanish is enriched by 80,000 Moorish or Arabic words (the true number is about 4,000); he reports a sighting of an Iberian lynx near Bédar (extremely unlikely as there are none anywhere remotely near); he says it was the Río de Aguas that caused the terrible Vera Playa floods in 2012 (it was the Río Antas), and so on.

Those small issues apart, I found much of interest in this book, not least the historical sections, his passage on the Palomares Incident and the rollicking final chapter where he goes off on a road trip with the late lamented Tito del Amo.

Another insight into life in Almería comes from local pianist **Jim Mackie,** who takes a humorous look at his many musical adventures across the province in *Boogieman (and his cat) in Andalucía*.

For residents of or visitors to the town in question, *Turre* by **David Jackson** should be required reading. The author is a local writer and historian and his deep knowledge of the area comes through in this book. He has done his research amongst Spanish sources and tells a vivid tale of grinding poverty, cholera, murder, civil war and political change. The book is available on Kindle and also as a printed copy; I have the latter. One slight oddity worth a mention is this: though the Contents page lists page numbers, the printed book (my copy at least) doesn't have any. This is easily remedied by pencilling the numbers in at the page corners. If you do this, everything tallies. David Jackson is also the author of two further essays about the area, both available in Kindle format. They are *The Birth of Los Gallardos 1924-1927* and *A Brief History of the First Road between Los Gallardos and Garrucha.*

There are many other books that touch on Almería province and are well worth reading anyway for the insight they give into things Spanish. One such is *Andalus: Unlocking the Secrets of Moorish Spain* by **Jason Webster** to which I refer in more detail in chapter 29. Another is *Ghosts of Spain: Travels Through a Country's Hidden Past* by **Giles Tremlett**. Almería gets just a couple of passing mentions but this book combines history, travel and enquiry in an informative and enlightening way, though it is rather dense in places. The author was for many years the *Guardian's* Madrid correspondent and his knowledge of, and affection for, Spain shows through the pages.

Of the 'We came to Spain and these are the amusing things that happened' genre, perhaps the best known books are those by **Chris Stewart**. Again, he is not writing about Almería but I'm allowing myself to stretch a point as his books are set not far away, near Órgiva in the Alpujarras. To date, he has written four volumes: *Driving Over Lemons, A Parrot in the Pepper Tree, The Almond Blossom Appreciation Society* and *The Last Days of the Bus Club.* Together they form an ongoing narrative about the author and his family making their home at a *cortijo* in the mountains. Stewart writes without condescension about his neighbours; he's trying to make a living and he relates to them as an equal. He is also interested in the history and landscape and the issues of local importance in the place where he has come to live and his writing is all the better for that. His books are enjoyable, humorous and informative, though to my mind the first and third ones are the strongest.

Guidebooks

Where to start? And indeed, where to end? There are, after all, stacks of small guidebooks and pamphlets covering Almería and especially Cabo de Gata, suggesting what to see and where to go. They are easily available so I've excluded them and am instead going to mention just a few of the ones giving detailed background, that I've found interesting and helpful.

The most accessible book in English about the complex and intriguing geology of the province is *Geology of the Arid Zone of Almería: an educational field guide* by **Miguel Villalobos Megía** and others, published in 2003. It's ring-bound, in horizontal format, and its text, diagrams and photos form a winning combination. My copy came via the Amigos de Sorbas and I'm not sure how available it is nowadays but if you chance upon a copy, be sure to grab it. Aimed at the interested general reader, *Classic Geology in Europe 12: Almería* by **Adrian Harvey and Anne Mather** is nevertheless rather heavy on the technical language. Again though, the many diagrams, maps and photos help with an understanding of the landscape and its evolution.

For anyone interested in getting to grips with Almeria's distinctive flora, *Wild Flowers of Eastern Andalucía: a field guide to the flowering plants of Almeria and the Sierra de los Filabres region* by **Sarah Ball** is the book to have. Photos illustrate all the flowers, the text gives Spanish, Latin and English names and includes notes on traditional local uses of the plants for food and medicinal purposes.

Of the many Spanish guides available, in my opinion the *Guías de Almería: Territorio, Cultura y Arte* series is head and shoulders above the rest. The series, which now runs to a dozen or so separate books, is co-ordinated by **Alfonso Ruiz García.** The volumes I've particularly used as references are listed in the bibliography towards the end of this book. They are superbly produced and give a rich insight into many aspects of the province.

Guía de Fauna y Flora: Desert Springs Resort & Golf Course by **Joël Lodé** and **Andrés Soler Navarro** is a detailed one-off guide in Spanish, English and French, to the wildlife of the Desert Springs Resort near Cuevas del Almanzora. It includes not only birds, mammals, flowers and amphibians but also grasses, lichens and dragonflies. Over 1,000 photos illustrate all the species, with flowers colour-keyed for easy reference.

Fiction

Scarecrow by **Matthew Pritchard** is very gruesome from the off and instantly hooks the reader (well, it did this one, anyway). It's a fluently-written crime thriller with a journalist, Danny Sánchez, as the protagonist, convincingly set in eastern Almería and the UK by a writer who spent time as a journalist in this area before turning his hand to this excellent novel. The narrative is shocking yet credible, sinister, well-paced and definitely worth a read unless you are of a nervous disposition.

The second book in **Matthew Pritchard's** 'Danny Sánchez' crime series, *Broken Arrow,* again uses real Almería locations, beginning with the discovery of a corpse at one of the Western film sets near Tabernas and centring around the 1966 nuclear accident at Palomares. Pritchard weaves a tale involving radioactive contamination, corrupt construction deals and a man out for revenge. The novel was published in late 2015, not long before the 50th anniversary of the Palomares incident. The author commented: "I tried to be as accurate as I could in the book, consulting forensic science and radiation experts, as well as drawing on my own journalistic experience."

In *Murder under the Sun* by **Struan Robertson & Anne Harling**, the action takes place mostly amongst the expatriate community in the Mojácar area, so this book is ideal if you want a locally-set page-turner. I think it's unlikely that you will warm to any of the main characters though, as they are entirely devoid of positive human qualities. Nevertheless, the plot's twists and turns will keep you involved until the last page. Robertson, a Scotsman who ran a bar in Mojácar some years ago but now spends most of his time in London, returned to his old haunts here to give a very individual and amusing presentation when he launched this book, saying: "It's interesting when you stop drinking. There are acres of afternoons with nothing to do." This seemed to be his explanation for how he'd had time, again in collaboration with Anne Harling, to write his more recent and shorter thriller *Double Duplicity*, also set in Mojácar and in the UK Lake District.

A police thriller, *Flamingo Summer* by **Steve Wilkinson** is of interest because the action takes place around Roquetas de Mar and the adjacent 'Salinas', the salt pans. I enjoyed the neat plot but my Kindle edition had so many typos and misspellings that it spoilt my enjoyment of the story. Sadly, this was a tale let down by its need of a good proof-reader.

I haven't read *Hot Milk* by **Deborah Levy** but it was shortlisted for the Man Booker Prize 2016. Online reviewers have conflicting opinions about it but those who give it five stars wax eloquent about its 'woozy, intoxicating layers' and 'dreamlike, almost hallucinatory' qualities. It's the story of a mother and daughter who come to Carboneras to seek treatment for the mother's mystery ailment. 'A richly mythic, colour-saturated tale,' says the publicity blurb.

Film director and writer **James Smith's** thriller *Andaluz Blood*, which I must also confess I haven't yet read, is set partly in Almerimar. A dark story of criminals and drug-running, it has also attracted some very positive reviews of the gripping and unputdownable kind.

The novelist **Christiane Gohl** had been living near Mojácar for a decade when she was named as a recipient of the 2015 Golden Indalo award, which is presented by Mojácar council to entities or people 'who have contributed to the good of the municipality'. Her book *Indalo*, published in Spanish is: "An atmospheric novel set in Mojácar during the Reconquest." This author is the odd one out in this chapter, because the books for which she is best known are not set in Almería. Initially making a name for herself in her native Germany with over 50 books about horses – she admits to being mad about the animals and has set up a horse sanctuary on the land she owns near Turre – she chose the international-sounding pen-name **Sarah Lark** when she switched away from non-fiction and began to write novels.

In a fascinating local 'Lunch and Listen' talk she gave at the Albar restaurant in El Pilar not long after receiving her award, she told the intriguing tale of how she moved to Spain and felt she had to change the name under which she wrote because in Germany she was so closely associated with books about horses. Her early forays into fiction didn't sell well because her 'horsy' followers wouldn't take her change of direction seriously. As Sarah Lark though, selling to a worldwide audience, her 'White Cloud' historical romance trilogy, set in New Zealand, has sold over six million copies. One of the things she told her astonished audience is that she writes up to 10,000 words per day. Having heard that, after her talk I had to go home for a lie down.

17. Of plants

'Some of the villagers collect wild herbs from their surroundings and they have a deep-seated knowledge of the many plants that they use.'

(Sarah Ball)

In the company of enthusiastic experts

In early 2015 I was contacted by Sarah Ball, who had come across my book *Flamingos in the Desert* on one of her regular trips with students to eastern Almería. Sarah, a botanist associated with the University of Reading, is the author of *Wild Flowers of Eastern Andalucía*. We arranged to meet up and, one day in early April, after lunch at a Sorbas bar, we headed off to a site on the gypsum karst area nearby, where long-term research is being carried out. The aim is to determine the effect of climate change on the vegetation, including the sensitive lichens which form ground cover and are critical for retaining water after rainfall and letting it seep slowly into the ground. A large series of metal and plastic structures allow the researchers connected to this ongoing programme - from several different universities - to monitor exactly what is happening to the plants over a lengthy period. Some of the structures limit the amount of rainwater reaching the plants underneath so that the researchers are able to study the effects of prolonged drought upon a number of key plant species.

Along with Sarah were her colleagues Ronnie Rutherford, Richard Carter and Trevor Pitman of the University of Reading's 'Spain team'. Sarah described Ronnie and Richard as 'walking encyclopaedias' when it came to the local plants, though as the author of the definitive field guide to the area she was clearly being modest. Trevor was an expert at spotting unusual plants in what to the untutored eye appeared to be a largely greenish-grey area of scrub. We only had an hour or two together but in that time I learned a lot about the distinctive assemblage of plants on the gypsum.

There was the 'brown bluebell' (Dipcadi serotinum in Latin, *jacinto bastardo* or *jacinto leonado* in Spanish), 'invisible but everywhere', which looks exactly as its English name suggests, and Helianthemum alypoides, shrubby rockrose, a rare gypsum specialist with attractive yellow flowers. Its local Spanish name, *perdiguera de los yesos*, rather oddly means 'gundog of the gypsum'. Sarah tells me that a very knowledgeable friend of hers says this probably refers to the fact that the plant is found in areas that are favoured by partridges (*perdices* in Spanish). We came across the vivid green strap-like leaves of sea squill (Urginea maritima), whose Spanish name is *cebolla albarrana.* However, those who assume from the word *cebolla* that it is an onion and therefore edible should beware. Its bulbs are toxic and a subspecies of the plant is the source of rotenone which is used to make rat poison. We found Lomelosia stellata too, a small rose-purple scabious called colloquially in Spanish *botón de soldado*, soldier's button.

As we passed a tall, elegantly thin, yellow-flowered plant, Richard said: "We call this funky mignonette." It was Reseda stricta subspecies funkii, which is related to weld or dyer's rocket. This, as the name suggests, was formerly used as the source of an intense yellow dye. A minute later I looked round and Richard had apparently vanished, until I realised he was full length on the ground, camera homing in on a plant that had grabbed his attention. It was easy to see why many of the photos in Sarah's field guide came from his lens.

There was a lot to take in: Latin and English names (the Spanish names and the extra information could be looked up later), as well as taking photos and trying to keep up, scribbling cryptic and wobbly entries into a notebook whilst walking and absorbing as much detail as possible. At the end of the session, after mutual promises that we would meet up with Sarah and her colleagues again, we set off home clutching a copy of *Wild Flowers of Eastern Andalucía.*

A year later, Sarah and her colleagues were in eastern Almería with their latest batch of students. Sunday morning was their only day off, so we dangled the bait of coffee and croissants to persuade them to our house, together with the chance to botanise a bit of the Sierra Cabrera that they didn't know. They happily accepted. Coffee and croissants duly demolished, we set out onto the abandoned ridge just across from our front gate. It has a few scattered and ancient carob trees but other than that, as the local goats munch their way across it regularly, I assumed there wouldn't be much of particular botanical interest.

Happily, I was proved wrong. Progress was slow, because there was a lot to see. In a rather strange small chasm in the ground, we saw Mediterranean buckthorn (Rhamnus alaternus in Latin and *aladierno* in Spanish) and there was shrubby violet (Viola arborescens in Latin, *violeta* in Spanish) with pale whitish-violet flowers. To introduce a little confusion, we then found a blue form of scarlet pimpernel (Anagallis arvensis, *murajes* in Spanish), which can come in several colours. It was hard keeping up with these botanists who were in their element, announcing new species with bewildering regularity; in fact, at one point I simply wrote: 'Quite a lot of gypsum-y things', which pretty much sums up my scientific credentials. It was, though, great to be in the company both of such knowledgeable people and the gypsum-y things. Upright spears of white flowers proved to be those of Reseda undata, another relative of mignonette and weld (no common English name, but *jopillo de zorro* or *rabillo de gato* in Spanish, these latter meaning fox's little tail or cat's little tail respectively).

We found Thymelaea hirsuta too, a shrubby evergreen with graceful drooping branches. It has no common English name but one of its Spanish names is *probayernos*, 'test son-in-law'. This comes from its long roots which are very difficult to pull out of the ground. According to Andalucian folklore, a family would use it to test the strength of any potential suitors of their daughters. Limonium echioides (*limonio enano espinosa*), small and initially hard to see, proved very common once we'd 'got our eyes in'. Finally, there was Astragalus alopecuroides, which Sarah said they previously knew only from Gafares, where there was a 'hillside flowering yellow' with it.

The verdict was that, although there were few very unusual plants, what was unique was the specific assemblage that had evolved on this hillside, a result of the particular combination of many factors including soil, altitude, aspect and history of land-use. And there were surprises: Sarah explained, for example, that a specific bush (I forget its name, if I ever knew) was of a species she had only seen twice before. After just an hour or so, Richard had compiled a list of about 140 species. We were astonished and delighted to realise that, only a few paces from our house, we had such botanical riches. All that remains for us now is to learn how to identify more of them.

Prickly pears

We don't have a lot of land; only about 2,000 square metres, and a fair proportion of that is very steeply sloping. When we bought the plot, the steepest part was occupied by a head-high and impenetrable tangle of mature prickly pear (Opuntia ficus-indica in Latin, *chumbera* in Spanish). Apart from the fact that we couldn't realistically tackle this fierce jungle, the slope was too steep to use anyway, even had we cleared it. And to be honest, we quite liked having a totally wild patch. It did have its uses, too; we were pretty sure that Sardinian warblers nested somewhere in this secret world, and possibly other birds as well. In addition, around the fringes of their flat, fleshy, paddle-shaped leaves, the prickly pears produced an annual crop of fruits, initially jade green, turning gradually to an orangey-red, and we harvested the most accessible ones to eat fresh or to make into jam. On the down side though, one of our cats would occasionally bring us a present of a rat. My belief that the rats lived in this spiky lair was confirmed one day when, working on the lowest of our three terraces, I happened to look up at the mass of *chumbera* towering sharply above me, only to find a large, beady-eyed rodent peering back.

Chumbera was first brought back from Mexico by the *conquistadores* between 1548 and 1570. Initially they were taken to the Canary Islands. It was one of the first American plant species introduced to Europe and became important, particularly in the 19th century, for stock-proof fencing, to stabilise slopes, and for the vivid cochineal dye that could be made from the dried bodies of the tiny Dactylopius coccus insects (*cochinilla del carmin* in Spanish) that parasitize the plant. The female cochineal beetles produce carminic acid as a defence against predators and it is this that produces the dye called carmine, known in modern times as E-120. About 15% of the female insect's dried body is carminic acid.

Over time prickly pear became a significant feature of many parts of the Mediterranean coast. In Almería province it was planted on a huge scale during the 1950s and 1960s as part of a re-vegetation initiative aimed at bringing jobs to the unproductive dry lands and stemming the emigration that was taking place. The intention was to plant 20,000 hectares per year for five years. Even though prickly pear is very resistant to drought, for a good yield of fruit it needs between 400mm and 600mm of rain annually. Much of the province doesn't have this much. The yields were not forthcoming and the plan was abandoned after only about 10,000 hectares had been planted. In 2013 production of prickly pear fruit in Almería amounted to just 166,000 kilograms with an average price at the markets of €1 per kilo.

My previous book, published in the spring of 2014 and with the writing completed late the previous year, had a section about prickly pears. At that stage nothing had reached my eyes or ears to suggest they were under threat. Perhaps I hadn't been paying sufficient attention because problems were first detected in Murcia province in 2007. At about the time the book finally came out, we were noticing a few fluffy white patches, like cotton wool, on the pads of the *chumbera* in our garden. Reports began to appear in the local media with headlines like: 'A prickly problem', 'Insect invasion' and, abandoning the alliteration for something more prosaic, 'White-fly plague hits the coast'. At first we had just the odd patch of 'cotton wool' so I set to with rubber gloves, a scrubbing pad and a bucket of soapy water to clean the pads. By now I knew that the fluffy white patches were evidence of the presence of Dactylopius opuntiae, a related but different beetle to the one used for cochineal production. As I carefully scrubbed the pads of the plant, the white patches released a reddish-purple dye: cochineal. To clarify, I understand that both the Dactylopius coccus and the Dactylopius opuntiae insects produce cochineal, but the former produce more and so were used commercially. It wasn't too difficult to keep on top of the problem at first, but as summer set in and the temperatures rose, the plague took hold. I knew that once it got into the big no-go *chumbera* jungle on the slope, I would have lost the battle, and that's exactly what happened. The problem is that although D. opuntiae is smaller than D. coccus, it has a great capacity to colonise and easily overwhelms the latter species. The females and nymphs of opuntiae are dispersed by the wind, hence their rapid spread. In addition, they can have five generations per annum: three during the summer, one in the autumn and one in the winter. Each female can lay well over 100 eggs, so they reproduce at a phenomenal rate.

The opuntiae insects feed on the sap from the cactus, leaving it shrivelled and unable to survive. The local papers explained that a year earlier, in the summer of 2013, a similar infestation had wiped out hundreds of thousands of prickly pear plants in Murcia. The environmental group Ecologistas en Acción warned then that if the problem was not dealt with, the cactus would disappear within 10 years, changing the landscape of Spain's drier areas.

The *chumbera* plague was now being reported throughout eastern Almería: in Huércal-Overa, Albox, Mojácar and Sorbas. As well as killing the plants, there was another problem. The male of Dactylopius opuntiae, much smaller than the female, has wings and is, in effect, a very small white fly. It isn't dangerous to humans but it does have a mildly irritating bite and, worse still, it can pass through normal mosquito netting. A friend who maintains a swimming pool for his neighbours whilst they are away in the UK was despairing of preparing it for their return, with thousands of the insects landing on the water every day. The insects take flight towards dusk, as the heat diminishes, making sitting outside in the evening something of a trial, or even an impossibility, as many summer holidaymakers were finding to their cost.

Huércal-Overa council launched a campaign against the infestation but this amounted to simply advising farmers and other landowners with badly affected plants to cut, burn and bury them; not an option for most people, given the scale of the problem, the tricky matter of handling the spiny plants, and the ban on fires for much of the year. A couple of homeowners in Los Gallardos were reported to have paid someone €1,000 to remove and destroy their affected *chumbera*, only to find the problem returning soon afterwards. Other councils, for example in Níjar and Zurgena, also said that dealing with the plague was the responsibility of the landowners with affected plants. The regional government, the Junta de Andalucía, responding to a petition from the pressure group 'Chumbos enfurecidos', claimed it had no responsibility in the matter. 'Chumbos enfurecidos' is not easily translatable but carries the sense of: 'I'm furious about the prickly pear situation' or, at the risk of a terrible pun: 'This plague is really bugging me'.

The newspaper *La Voz de Almería* carried a report in October 2014 about a forthcoming conference at which various botanical and technical experts would present papers about the issue. The conference came up with no magic bullet. No chemical treatment works effectively and some of those available damage other elements of the environment. Biological controls exist but these and the natural predators of the D. opuntiae beetle can't cope with the speed and strength of the plague's spread.

On our slopes, meanwhile, as the prickly pear pads have withered and fallen, the underlying bedrock of the hillside has begun to appear, for the first time in many years, and we are wondering what we might do with it, if anything, in a post-prickly pear situation. The remaining *chumbera* are putting out a few new bright green pads but it's hard to avoid the feeling that they will suffer the same fate as the rest. It seems that Ecologistas en Acción may be right and the prickly pears of Almería will soon be consigned to history.

Pitas si o pitas no?

Agaves, generally known as *pitas* in Spanish, are not native to Almería, so should they be allowed to remain? The above title, 'Agaves, yes or no?', was used by the respected conservation organisation SERBAL in a thoughtful response to this question, which was raised in 2015 when the Junta de Andalucía proposed removing some of them.

Between 1956 and 1958 almost three million agaves were planted on 1,288 hectares between San Miguel de Cabo de Gata village and El Toyo, not far to the east of Almería city. This area was subsequently included in the Cabo de Gata-Níjar Natural Park when it was founded in 1997. These agaves were of two species: Agave sisalana (*sisal* in both Spanish and English) and Agave fourcroydes (*henequén* in Spanish and the same in English, though without the accent). The intention was to produce fibres and obtain some value from what was perceived in the 1950s as unproductive land. However, the scheme was an economic failure and was abandoned, though the agaves remained. They can still be seen in serried rows in the steppe area around the Las Amoladeras Visitor Centre, just off the road between Retamar and San Miguel de Cabo de Gata. The visitor centre itself is well worth a visit, by the way.

In the 70 years since the agaves were planted, many residents and tourists have come to see these spiky plants as a unique part of the scenery, not realising that they are an imposition on the natural local vegetation and that they are very invasive.

And there lies the rub. In 2015 the Junta de Andalucía announced its intention to eradicate the *pitas* of these two species, an initiative that immediately led to a backlash on social media and a petition with over a thousand signatures against the plan. People living in El Alquián and El Toyo, two of the main areas affected, were particularly vocal in their opposition. The Junta's plan was perhaps not fully explained at first, so they belatedly organised seminars to 'educate residents' about their intention, which was to restore the original habitat that was destroyed when the plantations were created. This original habitat was a plant community dominated by a distinctive spiny shrub called *azufaifa* in Spanish (Ziziphus lotus in Latin, jujube in English). SERBAL describes *azufaifa* as 'a true botanical jewel and an Iberian-North-African endemic which, in Europe, can only be seen in the south-east of the Iberian Peninsula. In addition, it has great ecological importance, being 'our arid woodland', and it 'could be considered of equal value to a beech wood or an oak wood'.

Nowadays this distinctive *azufaifa* habitat is also under threat from the expansion of both urban development and intensive agriculture under plastic. For these reasons, SERBAL supports the removal of these specific species of agaves, at least in part. Studies have shown that some of the characteristic bird species of the Cabo de Gata steppes, such as the black-bellied sandgrouse (Pterocles orientalis in Latin, *ortega* in Spanish), which SERBAL says is down to barely 60 individuals, the stone curlew (Burhinus oedicnemus, *alcaraván*) and the golden plover (Pluvialis apicaria, *chorlito dorado*) all avoid the areas with agaves and prefer their natural *azufaifa* surroundings. Taking into account the strength of opposition to its initiative, the Junta rowed back and agreed to clear just some of the plantations but this should, in time, help these birds, as the natural plant community gradually reasserts itself.

The situation was clarified further in October 2016 when the Junta announced that it would be clearing just 16 hectares of *pitas* in the El Toyo area and pointed out that this will affect only one per cent of *pitas* in the province. Ecological groups such as Grupo Ecologista del Mediterráneo and the Friends of Cabo de Gata continued to back the plans, whilst Salvemos las Pitas and SOS Pitas y Chumberos maintained their fight to save the plants. Unfortunately, the debate may soon become academic as the following passage explains.

Agave americana

I was pottering about early one evening on our lower terrace in October 2015 when I heard the distinct sound of rockfall from close by. I peered over the wooden fence and down the steep slope to the narrow road that runs below, some five metres down. On that steep slope, the lower boundary of our land, self-seeded agaves (Agave americana) grow. One of them, with its flower spike partly developed, had collapsed and fallen into the road. Its base and the lower parts of its leaves were discoloured, having become dark brown. Some of the leaves had shrivelled and a smell of cloying putrefaction hung on the air. It wasn't the first agave we've lost.

I went down to clear the corpse of the huge plant as it was blocking the road which, fortunately, carries almost no traffic. The stricken plant weighed too much to shift, so I began to dismantle it leaf by leaf. Even the individual leaves, up to two metres long and mostly still full of moisture, were heavy. Pulling the leaves off was not too difficult though, because the bases had rotted. I could see, close-up, the black beetles and fat white grubs that had reduced the rich flesh at the centre of the plant's base to a rotting and seething brown mass. Finally, it was reduced sufficiently that I could pull it off the road on to the disused land sloping away below.

The gruesome fate described above is the work of the agave weevil (Scyphophorus acupunctatus in Latin, *el picudo del agave* or *picudo negro* in Spanish), which is a species of beetle. Like the plants themselves, the weevil is a native of Mexico and adjacent parts of the USA. As agaves have been introduced to other parts of the world, so the weevils have, sooner or later, tracked them down. The adult beetle is black and 28 mm long, including its long down-curved 'beak', with which it perforates the agave leaves to lay its eggs, 300-500 from each female, in the centre of the succulent rosette. When the female weevil bores into the plant its saliva introduces a bacterium called Erwinia carotovora which quickly rots the agave, making it easier for the grubs to digest. The larvae, born within a few days of the egg-laying, feed on the soft tissues inside the plant. Between them, the bacteria and the larvae totally destroy the agave.

As an aside, in Mexico, although the practice is relatively recent, the larva of the agave weevil, known as the 'red worm' or 'maguey worm', is used to flavour mescal. A whole larva is put into each bottle, usually after being pre-cured in pure spirit.

The agave weevil was first detected in Spain in the Barcelona area in 2007. By 2012 it had reached Jávea and Alicante and in August 2014 it was found in Almería province. We first realised in the spring of 2015 that we had it in our garden too. The problem is that you don't see any symptoms of the presence of the weevils until it's too late. By the time the huge strap-like leaves of the agaves begin to turn brown and wilt, the damage has been done and the plant is finished. The weevil attacks aloe and yucca plants, as well as agaves. We have aloes and yuccas too, so I fear the worst.

As I described in *Flamingos in the Desert*, in Los Molinos, near Sorbas, the Pita-Escuela (Agave School), run by Tim Bernhardt (known to everyone as Timbe) disseminates the knowledge and skills of how to make all manner of useful and decorative items from agave trunks, the trunks in question being the flower spikes thrown skywards by the plant. Researching agaves also led me (though not literally) to Thomas Scott, who lives in Rio de Janeiro and who makes beautiful surfboards from Brazilian agave wood. Sometime after writing this I see, online, that Timbe has made one too; it looks superb.

In North America, control of the agave weevil has been effectively achieved by trapping the insects but, as far as I'm aware, this is not happening in Spain. There are various strong chemicals that can be used to combat the weevils but they are very aggressive in the environment and may enter the water table, so they are not a good solution. For what it's worth, SERBAL sees Agave americana (as opposed to the other agave species mentioned in the previous section) as having a valid place in the landscape, having long been planted to mark old routeways and boundaries. However, as it seems that there is no co-ordinated official action being taken here against agave weevils, this distinctive and versatile plant may be living on borrowed time in Almería.

A tip for caper collectors

To finish this chapter, something a bit more positive. You have to be fairly dedicated to pick capers. What you are collecting are the buds of the flowers and they are small, so it takes some time to collect a decent amount, and there are also the vicious spines of the bushes to contend with. One afternoon towards the end of May I'd gone up the local hills for my regular exercise, to discover that the caper bushes were flowering. This always seems to happen suddenly: the plant

172

spends all winter looking dead, then suddenly the leaves burst forth and buds and flowers begin to appear. The fortuitous discovery on this occasion was that I was on my mountain bike and wearing cycling gloves, well-padded to protect the main part of the hand, whilst leaving the fingers free. This proved ideal for collecting capers. Suddenly the activity was no longer fraught with the possibility of regular stabs from unseen backward-curving barbs hidden among the leaves.

I've just weighed the capers collected in three stints totalling maybe two hours of collecting. It's about 330 gm, or 12 oz. That doesn't sound like much but, once processed, they are piquant and you only need to use them sparingly, by sprinkling a few in a salad for example, so I'm already well on the way to having enough to last us for the next year. (See *Flamingos in the Desert* for more on capers, including how to process them.)

18. Here comes the desert

'Our grandchildren, if they come from Almería, will have to emigrate because the desertification process is not going to stop."
(Miguel Arias Cañete)

Rainfall

Parts of Almería province are the driest places in Europe, with less than 200 l/m$_2$ of rain annually. (l/m$_2$ means 'litres per square metre', which equates to the British terminology 200mm, meaning a cumulative 200 millimetre depth of water, if none had soaked in or flowed away). In reality though, the average rainfall varies dramatically from one part of the province to another. Generally speaking, the amount of rainfall is lowest in the coastal areas, and increases with distance inland and with altitude. The areas around Garrucha and Vera, and the lowlands around the Salinas de Cabo de Gata, for example, typically have less than 150mm of rain per year (or 150 litres per square metre). In effect, that means a total depth of about 6 inches of rain annually. This is well within the official definition of a desert, which is anywhere averaging less than 250mm per year. In the higher mountains though, such as the Sierra de Gádor and the Sierra de los Filabres there is, on average, over 700mm of rain per year.

Data in the *Atlas de Almería*, collected at Almería airport for the period 1970-2000, shows the way in which rainfall varies during the year too. Traditionally, October and November are the wettest months, with December and January not far behind. At the other extreme, July and August are by far the driest months.

A further characteristic of Almería's rainfall is that it varies dramatically from one year to the next. For example, the total annual rainfall in our small valley in the Sierra Cabrera over recent years looks like this: 2009, 588mm; 2010, 876mm; 2011, 472mm; 2012, 642mm; 2013, 394mm; 2014, 272mm; 2015, 615mm and 2016,

609mm. Over those eight years, we averaged 559mm per annum. A semi-desert is anywhere having between 250mm and 500mm. So we are slightly moister than a semi-desert, though no meteorologist worth their salt would base conclusions on just eight years' worth of data. As for the variation, 2010 saw over three times as much rain as 2014. One characteristic of our weather in Almería is the *gota fría*. The literal translation however, 'cold drop', makes no sense. What the term refers to is sudden heavy rain, often bringing the risk of flooding, and the phrase also carries with it a sense of unpredictability.

When we first had a house here, our neighbour Pedro took it upon himself to impart his local knowledge to us, much to our delight. One thing I recall him saying was that November and February were traditionally the months when a decent quantity of rain could be expected. This was based on his experience of having grown up here in the 1940s and having lived most of his life here. Now, though, with clear evidence that the older patterns are breaking down as climate change takes hold, the rainfall is becoming much more unpredictable. It seems definite that the climate here was wetter 70 years ago. Anecdotal evidence tells that the *ramblas* used to run much more frequently, and the number of threshing circles attests to the fact that the moister conditions needed to grow cereals prevailed within living memory.

In 2016 representatives of AVIAL, an organisation of Almerían landowners and farmers, met with Colonel Francisco Jiménez, provincial head of the Guardia Civil, to express their concerns that aircraft were being used to prevent rainfall in the province. The suspicion is that planes are seeding the atmosphere with chemicals that cause clouds to dissipate, thus diminishing the chance of rain. This, says AVIAL, is an attempt by large farms and insurance companies to get the rain to fall in particular areas such as Murcia instead. Colonel Jiménez pointed out that such activity would be illegal. The Junta de Andalucía, the regional government, denies that any authorisation for cloud-seeding has ever been sought or given. Meanwhile, AVIAL hopes to find concrete evidence that this is happening, and Colonel Jiménez waits to see it.

Longer summers

Back in February 1995 David Carson of the Hadley Centre for Climate Prediction and Research warned that average temperatures in Spain would rise by between two and four degrees Centigrade and rainfall would be 17% lower by 2030. In the same year, the Minister for Tourism, Javier Gomez Navarro, suggested that coastal resorts would need to be supplied with drinking water from floating water tankers.

Coming up to date, Jorge Olcina, a climatology specialist at Alicante University, has highlighted the challenging impact of climate change on south-eastern Spain. Whilst longer summers might initially sound great, he points out that for the economy of the area, it's not that simple. Northern Europeans, both residents and visitors, tend to avoid the hottest months on the Costa Almería. Sr Olcina suggests that, without a concerted effort to combat the continual rise of CO_2 emissions, southern Spain will gradually find itself with maybe five months each year in which daytime temperatures exceed 30°C and night-time temperatures rarely fall below 23°C, making sleep difficult without air-conditioning. That might mean that people who have the luxury of choice spend more time in Almería during the winter, spring and autumn. Studies by climatologists also indicate that the rain that does fall will tend to be in the coastal areas, rather than inland, where it is needed for agriculture and to replenish reservoirs. Sudden heavy downpours, *gotas frías*, will become more frequent and, inevitably, water will become more expensive.

Miguel Arias Cañete, a former Spanish Minister of Agriculture who, if my memory is correct, paid little heed to environmental issues whilst in that post, had by 2016 reinvented himself as the European

Commissioner for Climate Action and Energy. In his new role, he speaks rather differently, arguing that policies to cut carbon emissions must be adopted immediately. He admits that Spanish farmers know that rainfall patterns have changed and weather conditions are more intense. "They know the calibre of flash floods in the Levante area is unlike anything ever known historically and that the summer heat dries up their crops." He adds though, that explaining the importance of reducing greenhouse gases to a Spanish person is not easy, which sounds very condescending. We must limit temperature rises, he says, otherwise Almería will become a more and more difficult place in which to live.

Ernesto Rodríguez of AEMET, the state meteorological agency, announced that the winter of 2015-16 was the warmest since 1960-61 and this fits forecasts of more extreme climatic conditions. He predicts that southern Spain will be receiving between 10% and 30% less rainfall by the end of the century than it is now. He suggests that all products should be labelled with their carbon footprint to make consumers aware of their impact on climate change.

Desalination confusion

In the last ten years or so €620 million has been spent on building five desalination plants in Almería province. Despite this, estimates in the Plan Hídrico de Demarcación (the Water Strategy Plan) for 2016 suggested a shortage of 73 billion litres in that year. The problem is that farmers are refusing to buy the desalinated water because it is too expensive. A spokesman for farmers at Cuevas del Almanzora, Matías Gómez, explained: "A cubic litre of desalinated water is being sold to us for 50 cents, making it uneconomic to use for watering crops." The desalination plants can easily produce the extra amount of water required but there seems to be a Catch 22 situation: the desalination plants cannot drop their prices until they are running at full capacity, which they can only do if the farmers promise to buy the water. The farmers, meanwhile, refuse to make a commitment until the price of the water has come down. Incidentally, over 84% of water used in Spain goes for agriculture.

While this dispute grinds on, the Carboneras desalination plant, which could produce 42 billion litres of fresh water per year, is operating at just 20% capacity. Another plant, in Cuevas del Almanzora, has been closed since it was damaged in the floods of 2012, with money yet to be found for repairs.

Sahara dust

For a few days in February 2016 and coincidentally, again in February 2017, high altitude winds blew strongly from the south and the skies over Almería turned hazy and dense with fine sand blown from North Africa. This phenomenon happens from time to time but not usually in such a dramatic way. Driving north towards Lubrín one day, it suddenly occurred to me that the Sierra de los Filabres, usually prominently on view, was entirely invisible in the murk. A day later, arriving in Sorbas for a Spanish lesson, I realised that the strange appearance of all the parked cars was due to a coating of red dust.

This dust cloud effect is known in Castellano as *la Calima*. If it rains during such an event, *lluvia de barro* (mud rain) is the result as the sand is washed out of the sky. However, on this occasion, there was no rain. Francisco Gímenez, a meteorologist from the Barcelona Dust Forecast Centre, said: "We are not expecting any significant rainfall with the exception of scattered showers, so it will take a while for the *Calima* to disperse."

As might be expected with a wind from that direction, the temperatures rose too and this was especially noticeable because it happened during an otherwise very cold spell. The *Calima* can reduce air quality and trap contaminants over major cities, increasing the danger to health. On the other hand, once the Saharan sand has fallen to earth, as it does sooner or later, either due to the simple effects of gravity or hastened by a spell of 'red rain', it provides valuable nutrients to the soil. And the *Calima* has no specific link to climate change or desertification; it has been happening since time immemorial.

Desertification

Desertification is a term to describe the degradation of land in areas that are already dry, so that they gradually become more desert-like. Almería has been affected by desertification for a long while and awareness of the problem is not new. On 10th February 1994 *La Voz de Almería* reported on a conference about the subject. The same issue of the newspaper also reported that 6,000 million pesetas (about €36 million) was to be spent on reforestation projects across Almería, so even then the issue was being taken seriously.

Desertification results from a whole range of factors including climate change and human activities, the latter particularly in relation to land use. Historically, for example, when esparto was gathered on a large scale (see *Flamingos in the Desert*, Pp 128-129) the land was stripped of its protection and erosion speeded up.

There are other risks too. Over-exploitation of water resources is one of the most important. The issue of the super-intensive olive groves in the Tabernas - Sorbas area and the impact that is having on water resources is covered elsewhere in these pages. Going further back, small Spanish farmers have traditionally used flood irrigation on their fields, a very wasteful technique where water is in short supply. Larger agricultural enterprises and most of the modern *plasticos* use drip irrigation, a much more targeted and efficient way of watering the crops. However, there are also thousands of illegal wells in the province, depleting underground water supplies without official permission.

As far back as 2006, the then Environment Minister Cristina Narbona accused politicians in south-eastern Spain of being more concerned with building villas, hotels and golf courses than with managing their water supplies efficiently. At about the same time, Spain was named in a report by the Worldwide Fund for Nature as being at the bottom of the league table amongst developed countries for its water management, because of the amount of leakage from old rusty pipes.

Wildfires (see *Flamingos in the Desert*, Pp 138-141) also decrease the soil's protection and lead to faster runoff, so that rain flows away rather than soaking in to the ground to top up the aquifers. On page 79 in the Atlas de Almería there's a 'Map of the Risk of Desertification'. The authors are careful to say that it doesn't necessarily show the reality of the future situation, but it is their best model based on combining studies from the past 30 years of important contributory factors, namely erosion, wildfires, and over-exploitation of aquifers. The areas of 'high risk', in bright red, are to the north of Almería, along much of the coast between Cabo de Gata and the border with Murcia, and inland around Antas, Bédar, Los Gallardos, Cuevas del Almanzora and Huércal-Overa.

Golfing choices evaporate

As Almería dries up, so does the range of choice for golfers. Golf is an important part of the province's tourism strategy but unsuspecting tourists may not realise until too late that the authorities are continuing to advertise golf courses that are no longer operating. Official tourist websites for both Andalucía and for Almería province are, at the time of writing in June 2016, promoting courses that closed some time ago, such as those at Cortijo Grande and Macenas. The course at Cortijo Grande near Turre has been closed since 2014 when its water supply was cut off. A typical golf course uses as much water in a year as a town of 5,000 people. The relatively new course at Macenas was seized by the state after its operating company proved unable to pay the taxes and social security costs it owed.

Wells running dry

In the summer of 2016, as the long drought continued, further evidence of a crisis in water supply emerged, after decades of over-exploitation of underground water and a dismal lack of commitment to renew the ancient infrastructure that distributes water. It transpired that since the beginning of the year, the small mountain village of Olula de Castro in the Sierra de los Filabres, with a population of 146, had had its water delivered by lorry. The village's wells had been closed because the groundwater level was so low. In Turrillas in the Sierra Alhamilla, water was only provided between 1 pm and 9 pm. Senés and Tahal were facing similar problems and there was even talk of water rationing in larger places such as Vélez Blanco.

Estimates reckon that over 50% of the province's water is lost to leaks in the decrepit system but the water company Galasa, which supplies the north and east of the area, refuses to fix the leaks in urban areas, claiming it is the responsibility of the local councils. Galasa meanwhile is €37 million in debt, largely because of all the water wasted through leakage, and it wants to increase its prices, not to pay for improvements to the infrastructure and reduce the leaks but simply to get itself out of the red. Meanwhile, to the west of Almería, Roquetas de Mar increased its water bills by 53%. The shortage across the province in 2016 of 73 billion litres of water may prove, at the risk of an odd metaphor in the desert, to be just the tip of the iceberg as water issues bite more and more deeply across the south-eastern corner of Spain.

19. Badlands

'There is no more dramatic landscape, of a dead and dusty lunar type, then the 'badlands' between Almería and Sorbas. Ranges of bare grey eroded hills, thickly crumpled into deep folds falling into dusty riverbeds ... the landscape is fascinating. It is unique.'

(Nina Epton)

The Tabernas Desert

The Desierto de Tabernas is unique in Europe. Technically it is a semi-desert, of particular interest to geologists, film-makers and curious tourists for its unique landscapes. Back in 2000 plans were first announced to declare an area of 24,822 hectares, most of it within the municipal boundaries of Tabernas, a national park. The regional government, the Junta de Andalucía, said at the time that the area fulfilled all the necessary criteria for national park status. Since then, however, nothing significant has happened, causing Dr Hermelindo Castro of Almería University's Department of Biology and Geology to lament: "Years have passed and we have not been able to protect and launch the Tabernas Desert as it deserves." In the meantime the European Commission has begun an enquiry into the absence of conservation measures for this area on the part of the Junta de Andalucía, prompting the Junta to award the area ZEC (Zona Especial de Conservación) status.

However, in a hard-hitting article entitled 'Spain's unprotected protected parks', the journalist Roy Wickman pointed out that although about 30% of Spain's land area is listed in the Red Natura 2000, the Europe-wide network of protected natural areas, only 10% of Spain's supposedly protected areas have specific management plans, something which is obligatory under the Red Natura scheme. Wickman adds: 'And Spain being Spain, authorities have learned how to side-step all the strict rules of what can and can't be built or dug out of these 'protected' areas.' He cites several examples where protected area status has apparently made no difference to development, including the infamous case of the Algarrobico Hotel in the Cabo de Gata-Níjar National Park. This suggests that even with protected area status, the Tabernas Desert would not be immune from damaging initiatives. On the other hand, its popularity with film-makers and the huge income this brings to the area may serve as an alternative but effective form of protection, for now.

Badlands

It's mid-September. The main heat of the summer is past and, fortuitously, there is partial cloud cover too, giving further relief from the sun. We set off from the front of Oasys, once known as Mini-Hollywood, the former film-set near Tabernas. We haven't come today for Wild West re-enactments though. Facing the front of the place, we stay on the same side of the road and head off to the right, taking a track more or less parallel to the road and aiming towards a tall wooden structure about three or four hundred metres away. When we reach it, we see a guardrail nearby and find we are peering down into a steep-sided *rambla*, immediately beyond which is a grey-blue slope, bare of vegetation and seamed with many gullies.

We are about five kilometres south-west of Tabernas town and as I look at the 1:25,000 scale map of the area (Sheet 1030-III Tabernas) all I see is a convoluted maze of squiggly brown contours, indicating a deeply dissected landscape. We are in the Badlands. In the popular imagination the term is inextricably linked with westerns, with enigmatic characters acting out violent tales in stark and dusty locations. But google 'Badlands' and you get something more prosaic: 'They are characterized by steep slopes, minimal vegetation, lack of a substantial regolith, and high drainage density.' That sums it up pretty well. 'Regolith' is a name for the loose layer, including soil, that normally covers bedrock, and high drainage density means you can see the pattern of channels in which water will flow when it rains, and that there are lots of these channels. Actually, the term 'Badlands' comes from early French explorers in Dakota. They described the landforms as "terres mauvaises a traverser", bad lands to cross. The word also has an economic implication; such terrain is useless for any kind of agriculture. In rather more vivid terms, Juan Goytisolo described it 60 years ago like this: '... the harsh lunar sierra around Tabernas, scorched by the sun, shaped by hammer blows, and eaten by erosion.'

I've been invited to join Roy Alexander, known to friends as 'Alex' who, with three colleagues, has brought a group of about 20 of his students from the University of Chester for a week's fieldwork. Alex is Professor of Environmental Sustainability at the University but the particular students on this trip are third year undergraduates focusing on the physical geography of the area. So it's the geomorphology we are looking at, the processes that have created the present-day landscape. And there could be no-one better than Alex to explain it; he's been bringing students and carrying out his own detailed research here for over 20 years.

From the overlook we go to the right where a path with a wooden handrail twists down into the *rambla*. It once had steps, each formed by a log held into the ground with wooden pegs but the passage of many feet, the ravages of weather and a lack of maintenance have all taken their toll. Getting down is easy enough though. Once in the *rambla* we have a close-up view of the grey-blue slope. In technical terms it is an extensive deposit of Tortonian marl, a fine-grained material washed down some 17 million years ago from the Sierra de los Filabres to the north. In practical terms this means it is soft and easily eroded. The whole face is patterned with small gullies, joining to form tree-like patterns of mini-drainage. The main road is not far away but we could be on the Moon.

Alex directs our gaze over to the right and points a few hundred metres away to where we can see yellow sediments which have infilled above the grey deposits. These, he says, were laid down on the bed of an ancient lake about 14,000 years ago. That sounds like a long time but it's only yesterday in geological terms. One of the great skills geomorphologists have is to be able to envisage the landscape in four dimensions - the usual three, plus a huge expanse of time - and explain its slow and often complex development. This is what Alex is doing now.

The area around the modern town of Tabernas is known to geologists as the Tabernas Basin. 14,000 years ago it was a low area, trapped between the Sierra de los Filabres to the north and the Sierra Alhamilla to the south. These mountain ranges were rising due to subterranean forces created by the convergence of the Eurasian and African tectonic plates, a process which is continuing. Material eroded from these mountains was sluiced by rivers into a lake in this basin. The lake gradually filled the basin until it reached a level where it began to spill out at the lowest point of the brim. Once this happened it soon cut down through the soft material which had been damming it and drained away south-westwards towards what is now Almería city, via what is now the Rambla de Tabernas. The water rapidly disappeared but left enduring evidence of the lake's existence in the form of the sediments we were now seeing.

Badlands are landscapes that are still evolving quickly, which is one of the reasons that geographers are so keen to study them. In simple terms, badlands are likely to occur if the following three key factors are present: a dry climate with occasional fierce downpours, soft rocks that are easily eroded, and slopes that allow fast flow of water over the surface. It's typical of badlands that they have relatively little vegetation cover and also that the ground surface is covered with a crust, both of which characteristics mean that water struggles to soak in and is more likely to run off, increasing erosion as it does so.

Meanwhile, back in the here and now, Alex is talking about the plants in the *rambla*. *Ramblas*, of course, are the parts of the landscape where plants have the most access to water. We've already pushed our way through a thicket of giant cane (Arundo donax or *caña*) and now we're peering down at false esparto (Lygeum spartum or *albardín*) and saltwort (Salsola genistoides or *escobilla*). Tamarisk (Tamarix africana or *taraje*), with its feathery foliage, is common too. There's also a specialist called Moricandia foetida (no common English name, *collejón* in Spanish) which, if it rains at the right time, say in January, will burst into life and produce a carpet of pink flowers in March and April. It tends to appear in great quantities every four or five years.

We head on along the *rambla* to the right. If I am reading the map correctly, this is the Barranco del Grillo, Ravine of the Cricket, which brings us pretty soon into the bigger Rambla de Tabernas. Alex takes us to one of the many research sites that dot this area and explains what the ongoing experiments are about. He's feeding information and suggestions to the students who will, later, be given some time to make their own measurements and observations and test their own ideas as to what is happening here.

Once we have followed the *rambla* under the A-92 motorway, we eat our packed lunches in the less than salubrious surroundings of the Alfaro petrol station, where a minor tragedy unfolds when we discover that the garage shop only had two ice-creams left and the students got there first. On again, to the west now, Alex brings us to another area he knows well from his research.

One noticeable feature of the badland slopes is what geomorphologists call aspect control. 'Aspect' means the direction that something faces; 'aspect control' therefore means the effect this might have on other features, such as plant cover. Here, for example, the south-west facing slopes are almost bare, whilst the north-east facing slopes are much more vegetated. This must relate to subtle micro-climatic differences in such factors as the temperatures and the rates of evaporation; presumably the south-west facing slopes have more direct and fiercer exposure to the sun. In turn the vegetation will give the slopes more protection from erosion, so that when heavy rain comes, the bare slopes will be scoured. Does this mean those slopes will be a few degrees steeper than the vegetated ones?

We take the track west and in just a few minutes come upon a beautiful tufa curtain, like a petrified waterfall, spilling over above us. Tufa (also called travertine) is a form of redeposited calcium carbonate and in this instance it has precipitated out of carbonate-rich spring water issuing from a fault above and behind the tufa curtain. Natural awe would alert you to treat this astonishing place with reverence but there are no notices in situ to advise care or to inform you as to what you are seeing. However, the geology text to the area (*Classic Geology in Europe 12: Almería* by Adrian Harvey and Anne Mather) does say, in capital letters: THIS IS A PROTECTED SITE - DO NOT HAMMER OR ATTEMPT TO REMOVE ANY TRAVERTINE.

Above the travertine curtain there is more to see, including a flat area that has the feel of an old salt lake and which is actually an abandoned course of the Rambla Lanujar, with tilted strata poking in lines out of the ground as if in suspended animation, and crumbling exposures of rock in contorted, wafer-thin layers. Geomorphology and geology, like all disciplines and special interests, have their own language. So it is that the text book says of this area: 'A range of travertine morphologies are (sic) exposed on the valley floor and along the trace of the fault, including barrages, pressure ridges and spring pipes, some of which are still active.' For most of us, to whom that won't mean a great deal, it's enough simply to explore the area with a sense of wonder, and to know there are specialists out there to whom we can refer, should we wish to, for further understanding of this unique place.

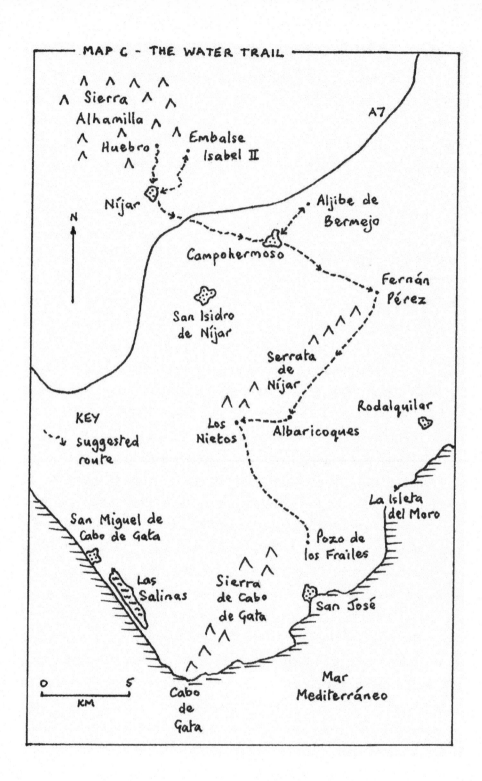

MAP C - THE WATER TRAIL

Sierra Alhamilla
Huebro
Embalse Isabel II
Níjar
N
A7
Aljibe de Bermejo
Campohermoso
Fernán Pérez
San Isidro de Níjar
Serrata de Níjar
Rodalquilar
Los Nietos
Albaricoques
La Isleta del Moro

KEY
suggested route

San Miguel de Cabo de Gata
Las Salinas
Sierra de Cabo de Gata
Pozo de los Frailes
San José

0   5
KM

Cabo de Gata
Mar Mediterráneo

20. Water in the landscape

'And the south-eastern quadrant of the Peninsula, which includes
Almería...is probably the driest part of Europe, with a rainfall not
much greater than that of the Sahara Desert.'
(Chris Stewart)

Being careful with water

In times past, the extent of human presence in this arid south-eastern
corner of Spain was determined by two things: the existence of a
water source with a reliable flow and the amount of fertile land near
that water source. Huge efforts were made to find and manage water
and a range of ingenious devices were used to do so. Evidence of its
capture, storage and distribution in the past is still widespread.

An immediate example: today, 30th December 2015, half a
dozen of us were cycling along the Lucainena *Vía Verde* and as I
glanced over at the almost entirely depopulated village of El Saltador
(apparently one house is occupied, according to friends who live
nearby), I saw the remains of a barrier across the *rambla* that passes
immediately below the old settlement. This would have been to
collect and divert water to the nearby fields. Adjacent, by the Cortijo
de las Tejas, is a well-preserved circular structure, with a water
channel leading to it, the whole thing given an exotic air by a grove of
palm trees. It would have been used to irrigate the terraces that
surround it on all sides. Not far away is a small viaduct that was also
used to move water for irrigation.

Then, as now, water could be captured either from surface
run-off or from underground aquifers. During and after a downpour,
the simplest method of using water was to divert it from the *ramblas*
where it briefly flowed either to where it could be stored or on to
cropland where it was needed. To do this a weir, called in this area in
the past an *azud*, would be built across a *rambla*. The word *azud* is
derived from Arabic, though you won't find it even in hefty tomes like

189

the Oxford Spanish Dictionary (which, I have just discovered, weighs 2.9 kg). The *azud* would go down below surface level, through the loose sandy bed to the bedrock, to trap run-off for use on nearby fields. In conjunction with the *azud*, a *corta* would be made. A *corta* was a very small-scale way of diverting water via a simple channel or furrow. Check *corta* in the dictionary and you find only the meaning 'fag end or cigarette butt', but in this instance it's obviously a word taken locally from the verb *cortar*, to cut.

We're talking here about the days before modern pipes, electric pumps, deep boreholes and the heavy machinery necessary to excavate huge water tanks (*balsas*). All of these things have blurred the former environmental limitations on economic development, though I suspect it's too early to say that the environment won't ultimately have the last laugh.

As good a way as any to appreciate some of these things is to follow a route of about 60 km that links an intriguing range of them. There is an official 'Ruta del Agua', Water Route, linking various sites across this part of the province. The route I'm suggesting coincides with this to some extent but not entirely, so I'll refer to mine as the Water Trail. Unless you are a very keen cyclist it requires a vehicle, with short excursions on foot. It would also be ambitious to try to see all of this in a single day, so it could just as easily be explored as a series of separate visits if you have the time.

Following the Water Trail
The route begins in the archetypal hill village of Huebro which nestles in the folds of the Sierra Alhamilla a few kilometres north-west of Níjar. Huebro's spring provided a reliable flow and a good head of water, to the extent that there were an astonishing 22 watermills, many of which were the work of a builder called Tío Solis Carmona, along the Barranco de Huebro between the eponymous village and Níjar. That is a mere three and a half kilometres, though the water

falls 400 vertical metres in that short distance. More astonishing still, almost all of the 22 mills were actually concentrated along a two kilometre stretch, if measured as the raven flies. Alongside this length, on the Junta de Andalucía's Cabo de Gata-Níjar map, is printed 'La Ribera de los Molinos', the Riverbank of the Mills. This location had one of the greatest concentrations of small-scale hydro-power in the whole of the Mediterranean basin.

Initially the system of farming at Huebro involved small terraced fields in the immediate area but in the 18th century the Reglamento de Defensa del Reino de Granada (the Regulations for the Defence of the Kingdom of Granada) came into effect under Carlos III. This led to a much more reliable system of coastal defence against the continual incursions of pirates from North Africa, so the local population was more secure. Cereal production rose dramatically and this led in turn to an increase in the number of mills at Huebro. Then, towards the end of the 19th century a number of windmills were built in what is now the Cabo de Gata-Níjar Natural Park to the south and the milling industry of Huebro settled back to its modest origins until finally, in 1970, the last mill closed.

The best way to see what remains is to walk from Huebro to Níjar. This is most painlessly achieved by having two vehicles, leaving one at Níjar, then driving up to Huebro and walking down. The first time I did it I was alone so, having walked down from Huebro, I had to retrace my steps uphill to fetch the car. Recommended if you want to get fit.

These days Huebro is a quiet place with only a small permanent population. They like being here though. The proof is on a prominent rock on the slope above the village, where a local patriot has painted VIVA HUEBRO in big white letters. By the church with its brickwork tower of *mudéjar* origin, there is a paved square with fabulous views south, past Níjar and the glittering sea of *plasticos* to the real sea, the Mediterranean, about 25 km away beyond the low mountains of the Sierra de Cabo de Gata.

A few metres beyond the church, just off the Calle Lejido Alto, is an information pillar and a waymark, 'Níjar 3.5 km GR 140'. The GR 140 is a 180 km long walking route between the Puerto de la Ragua, high in the Sierra Nevada, and the coastal village of San Miguel de Cabo de Gata. It just happens to come this way and it's this that we follow to see the remains of Huebro's mills. Right by the waymark is a *balsa*, the village water tank with the spring spilling strongly into it. As the information board explains, this water source, which does literally spring from the mountain, was the sole supply of water for all of the mills and the farmed terraces in the valley below the village. The village tank is 18 metres square and two metres deep. A sluice-gate at its lower end is opened by hand each morning to release the flow into the *acequias*, the channels which take it to all the houses and fields that still rely on it.

Adjacent to the tank is a small washing area (*lavadero*) and a trough from which animals can drink (*abrevadero*). What is most striking is how loud the water sounds: there is a really powerful flow here. A twisting concrete track drops away with a water channel alongside. To the right is a masonry wall with a channel on top. Immediately below this are the remains of a mill with an old circular stone still inside it. These elegant masonry structures were built out, where the land fell away steeply, to carry a water channel at just a very gentle angle, maintaining the flow but also creating a tall head of water that would fall down a vertical shaft at the far end to power machinery in the mill below. The shaft gives the structure its name, a *pozo*, a word that is perhaps familiar in a different but related context as it also commonly means 'a well'. Because the mills are no longer operating, most of the *pozos* aren't either, but the water still flows, nowadays frequently diverted into plastic pipes.

Soon, on the left, there is a hugely tall and prominent *pozo*, with a restored house, painted cream, below it. Everywhere there is evidence of the old mills, their *pozos* and the water channels. The official waymark for a GR, and indeed many other footpaths too, consists of a pair of parallel painted lines, one red and one white. There are some of these on this route but there are also bright blue painted arrows and intermittent red splodges on the ground. Sometimes the waymarks are where you don't need them, where there is no potential confusion. At other times, when you might appreciate clarification of the route, there are no clues, so on occasion a bit of intelligent guesswork is required.

Most impressive and photogenic of all is a sequence of five *pozos*, raked steeply down the side of the valley, one below another. Opposite these, on the true right bank of the valley, is a large area of terraced fields, each edged with a neatly made stone retaining wall. These now look to be mostly disused though once, irrigated by the trusty waters of the Huebro spring, they must have produced substantial yields.

The main point at which I was confused was where the path reached a terrace edge with a large red mark on the ground but no clear way forward. The answer was to go a few metres right to pick up the path again. It then zigzags down and crosses to the far bank. The stream bed here generally has no water as it is all channelled off higher up the system. Shortly after going through an arch in a *pozo* wall, the path crosses back to the left bank. Soon, where it reaches a broken wall, the path has a waymark at a fork. The official route goes right, following just inside the wall to pass a goose-pen and then bear left on a track just before some houses. Alternatively, at the confusing waymark you could go straight on, contouring along what seems to be a shallow *acequia*, as this brings you out on the same track, which is then followed to a concrete access road. This in turn reaches the tarmac road which you drove up earlier to Huebro. Here, waymarks say 'Huebro 2.3 km GR 140 Níjar 0.7 km'. From there it's a matter of following the road, which has very little traffic, down into Níjar, which you enter via the predictably named Camino de Huebro.

Boqueras

A prominent feature of the Moorish 'water culture' in this corner of Spain was a *boquera*. This was a system designed to capture the maximum possible amount of water during a cloudburst in order to saturate the adjacent fields.

A *boquera* consisted of an excavated side-channel, called a *cañon*, running more or less parallel to a *rambla*, and into which the water flow was diverted by an angled dike built out into the *rambla*. Between the *rambla* and the *cañon* would be a series of terraced fields, each slightly lower than the one before and each having a side-channel leading into it from the *cañon*. Each part of the system had a name: the initial diversionary dike and inlet to the *cañon* was the *cola* and the point where the *cañon* came back to join the *rambla* further downstream was the *boca* or mouth.

Amongst the houses in Níjar there are still many small *huertas* (vegetable gardens) which would have originally been watered by such traditional methods. In fact, I have read that there was a sizeable *boquera* in Níjar but having been to where I thought it ought to be, according to what I'd read, I couldn't find any convincing remains of it. Nevertheless, the soil in Níjar is particularly fertile and produces superb crops, including a local speciality called *patatas de ojo de perdiz*, which does not even feature in the exhaustive dictionaries to be found online but which translates literally as 'partridge's eye potatoes'.

Preparing such a *boquera* was a communal task undertaken by the local farmers and their draught animals. In addition to the arrangement described above, there would be a drystone wall at the lower edge of each of the terraced fields, and a *sangrador*, a small spillway, in each of these walls. All of these had to be maintained to ensure they would not be suddenly damaged by water pressure when the rains came.

And when the rains did come it was a matter of 'all hands to the pumps' to ensure that not only was the water being used to best effect but also that the carefully made infrastructure was holding against the flow. Water flowing down the *rambla* would divert into the *cañon* and via a side-channel, into the first or 'top' field. Once that had had a dose of flood irrigation, the water would spill from its *sangrador* on to the next terrace down, and so on. Any surplus water would finally flow back into the *rambla* via the *boca* at the lower end of the system, quite possibly to be used in another *boquera* just downstream.

In addition to the water, silt and organic matter would be deposited on the riverside fields, replenishing their fertility, exactly as the Nile floods did annually in Egypt before the Aswan Dam was built. *Boqueras* were found throughout Almería province but particularly on the large flat plains such as the Campo de Dalías, Campo de Tabernas, Campo de Níjar and Bajo Almanzora, as well as along the middle and lower courses of most of the big *ramblas*, to provide sustenance for the so-called 'Mediterranean trilogy' of cereals, vines and olives which, in Almería's harshly dry climate, could not thrive without irrigation.

A *boquera* could be anything from a few tens of metres long, feeding just a field or two, to the major systems on the lower course of the Río Andarax near Almería city. The biggest *boqueras* there, which irrigated all the cultivated land along the banks of the Bajo Andarax, were several km long. The use of the water thus distributed along the Bajo Andarax was overseen in a complex but highly organised way by a body called the Sindicato de Riegos de la Vega de Almería y Siete Pueblos de su Río, the Irrigation Union of the Cultivated Plain of Almería and the Seven Towns of its River. The seven towns were Santa Fe de Mondújar, Gádor, Rioja, Benahadux, Pechina, Huércal and Viator.

Just before this book went to press I heard from Andrés Pérez about a newly established walking route, Los Caminos del Agua, linking a number of traditional water features such as *acequias* and the San Indalecio canal, between Santa Fe de Mondújar and Almería city. I look forward to checking it out.

In the second half of the 20th century the use of tractors consigned the traditional communal tasks associated with *boqueras* to the past, changing it to a mere mechanised job that could be done in advance by fewer people.

The Isabel II Dam

The next stop on the Water Trail is along the twisty mountain road that climbs north from Níjar over the Sierra Alhamilla towards Lucainena de las Torres. Soon after leaving Níjar on this road you have the feeling of being somewhere quite remote, amongst wild scrubby mountains with only the very occasional building to be seen.

After a few kilometres, on the right, there's a sign indicating 'embalse Isabel II' with, below it and almost entirely faded by the sun, another sign pointing the same way: 'Ruta del Agua'. This is a track, not a surfaced road. A 4WD would be ideal but it is usually passable in ordinary vehicles with care, unless it has rained recently, when there is the chance of bogging down in one or two places. For the ultra-cautious, it's maybe 1.5 fairly level kilometres from the road to the dam, so you could walk it in less than half an hour if you'd rather not risk your car. There are more 'Ruta del Agua' signs and when you come through a pair of red and white metal posts to a small modern information pillar, you should be able to make out the top of the dam ahead and slightly to the right, a few hundred metres away.

As you approach the dam, you are in the area where the reservoir was once impounded. In dry conditions, you can drive up to within a few metres of the dam. Once out of your car you will see a way to walk up to the left, which brings you on to the top of the long-abandoned structure. If you have parked behind the dam, your car is on the 30 metre deep bed of silt that accumulated in the reservoir to within a few metres of its top. Consequently, once you are on the dam and able to see down the front of it, it comes as a shock to see how big it actually is. The stone construction curves across the valley, its face falling away almost sheer in several tiered steps.

On top of the dam, at one point there is a large circular hole covered with heavy-duty metal mesh. Looking down through this, you can see a set of spiral steps, with some missing, leading down into the gloom. This mesh apart, there are few concessions to health and safety. A good dose of care and common sense is required as you explore these remains, particularly if you pass the 'Prohibido el paso' notice in order to go and have a look at the prominent square building on the high ground above the dam. This presumably was the place where the offices were and where the dam manager lived, if such a position existed. The hefty timbers of the front door are mostly still intact (or were in November 2015). The two storeys of windows are now just sightless holes. The roof is largely open to the sky, beams dangle, damaged masonry has crumbled, and animals have left signs of having sheltered here. Also, the floor has given way in places to reveal cellars beneath, so do take care, and remember that I am not advising you to go into this building.

Positioned between this ruin and the dam is a small conical stone hut, presumably some kind of guard-house. From alongside this, there are extensive views down onto the dam and, in the opposite direction, south, down-valley to the extensive flatter terrain that was once irrigated by the waters stored here. The dam, 44 metres long and 35 metres high, was built at a place called the Cerrada de los Tristanes, a natural narrowing of the Rambla del

Carrizal, where the local geology provided a firm foundation, and in a strategic location above the flat plains around Campohermoso.

In 1841, with backing from the huge profits of the mines of Hiendelaencina in Ciudad Real (much further north) and the Sierra Almagrera to the east, a society was founded to raise the necessary finance. An office was opened in Madrid and soon there were over a thousand shareholders and a fund of 10 million *reales*. The architect Jerónimo Ros directed the project, which began in 1842 and was completed by 1850. As well as the dam and related buildings, the work included a spillway and channels to take the water 25 kilometres from the reservoir to the lands it was to irrigate. For the mid-19th century, this was a huge scheme, intended to release the agricultural potential of the extensive flat lands to the south. It was estimated that 84,000 hectares of land could be irrigated. It must have seemed like a sure-fire investment.

However, the Isabel II Dam soon became a classic example of how, by ignoring climatic conditions and hydrological processes, a major civil engineering project can be a financial disaster. As soon as it was inaugurated in 1850 the reservoir began to fill, but only very slowly. At the best of times there was only limited rainfall in the area but to exacerbate the situation, there was a prolonged drought between 1848 and 1854. It became apparent that the scheme had been founded on little more than optimism. Worse still, when there was a downpour the inflow of water brought with it huge amounts of sediment, and the basin behind the dam was small, so its capacity to store water was limited. Over the next 20 years, the investors must have received, with horror, bulletins of what was happening. By 1870 the reservoir was almost entirely silted up and the dam was useless.

Modern researchers have studied the Isabel II Dam as an example of 'how not to do it', using the original plans for the dam together with old maps of the area, so they have an accurate idea of how the landscape looked before the dam was built. Combining this historical information with modern GIS (Geographical Information System) techniques and fieldwork, it is possible to achieve a good understanding of why the reservoir silted up so quickly and how much sediment the dam now holds. By recreating in 3D what the area was like 160 years ago and comparing it to how it is now, research has provided answers to some of these questions.

The only two, very small, compensations that might have come out of this debacle are first, that farmers have a ready source of fertile silt, which from time to time is excavated to be used in the modern *invernaderos* that cover the Campohermoso area, and second, that some sections of the old distribution channel are currently used to conduct water to the greenhouses. Plus, I suppose, the stark remains of the dam and related works provide an intriguing destination for a certain sort of inquisitive modern visitor.

21. Water ways

'Every time I come here, I am shocked by the harsh, unforgiving nature of the landscape.'
(Giles Tremlett)

Excuse the following slight digression. The story of the Water Trail is taken up again in the second section of this chapter.

Underground water

Rain in Almería province has always been scarce and unpredictable, so a lot of attention has always centred on underground water supplies. In rural areas there were many *pozos* (wells), serving either an individual *cortijo* or a small community. At its simplest, water would be manually hauled up in a bucket over a pulley. Wells like this were also located along the old *caminos* and drove routes that threaded the countryside. A slightly more advanced design was the *pozo en escalera*, a covered well built with a flight of steps down to the water level.

Horizontal wells called *qanats* or *galerías de captación* were a different take on the same theme. They originated over 2,000 years ago. A virtually horizontal tunnel, with just a very slight gradient, would be driven into a hill slope, reaching as far as the water table, with its outlet a little lower down the slope at the ground surface. Water would flow through the tunnel by gravity. A series of vertical shafts (*lumbreras*) were made from above into the horizontal tunnel to allow for ventilation and also the occasional clearing of blockages. Below the mouth of the well, water could be stored in *balsas* (open tanks). A *qanat* could provide a year round supply of water with no need for mechanical, animal or human power but of course it was dependent on the water table being recharged by rainfall. A system of *qanats* was still used to irrigate the local agricultural land in the Campo de Tabernas into the late 20th century.

On a much larger scale were the *galerías kilométricas*, the 'endless tunnels' of the Bajo Andarax, north of Almería city. These were dug by miners and lined with masonry. They were up to 13 kilometres long and were generally made on the surface then covered, either with large slates or by a more sophisticated vaulted construction. In effect they were just very long *acequias*, big enough for people to pass along them for the annual cleaning that was required, with regular access points to facilitate this, as in the Rambla de Chirivel.

Aljibes

Storing water was as important as capturing it in the first place, and in the hot temperatures of Almería, simply keeping it in an open tank would lead to major losses through evaporation. *Aljibes,* covered cisterns, were the solution. The Aljibe of Bermejo, a couple of kilometres north-east of Campohermoso, is the next stop on the Water Trail after the Isabel II Dam, and is not difficult to find. From Níjar, go briefly eastwards on the motorway (towards Murcia) then take exit 479, passing the big car showroom called Ciudad del Motor on your left and continuing into Campohermoso. At the roundabout in the centre of the town, with the yellow post-box by it, go left, following signs to Murcia and Saladar y Leche. At the next roundabout, which comes up very soon, go straight on, on the 'Camino de Vera', surely a clue to a very ancient routeway. Continue straight on at a large yellow and white striped roundabout, out into flat, scrubby countryside. Entering an area of *plasticos*, you pass a small sign indicating that this is the Cordel de Almería, an ancient livestock-droving route that was important for centuries.

In a few minutes, watch out for a compound on the left bounded by low white walls topped with wire mesh. It's next to a recycling plant and surrounded by plastic greenhouses but there, behind the fence, is the Aljibe de Bermejo. The original Roman *aljibe* at Bermejo was rebuilt in the 18th century but because of its antiquity, its size - 23 metres long and 4.6 metres wide - and its ashlar masonry construction, it is one of the most significant water features in Andalucía. It was an important resting and watering place for livestock being taken along the Cordel de Almería. Above ground it is a long low barrel-vaulted structure but, like an iceberg, what you cannot see is more significant. Most of its volume is below ground. It has openings for the extraction of water and in one end wall, an entrance with steps leading down to allow cleaning and maintenance of the interior.

You'll have to take my word for this though because, although you can see the *aljibe* clearly enough, you can't get into the compound, which is padlocked. Worse, it's unkempt and litter-strewn. There's a fading sign on a post several metres inside the fence which I managed to decipher only by taking a photo on a long lens and then blowing it up at home on the laptop. It turns out not to be about the *aljibe* but simply announcing that this was the site of a small-scale reforestation project under the 'Medioambiente en la Ciudad', 'Environment in the City', initiative in April 2009. Quite what they planted is unclear and it seems there was no after-care because there appear to be no trees in the compound. All in all, this is no way to treat an important monument. As so often with historic and prehistoric sites in Almería (Fuente Álamo is another case in point, described earlier in these pages), it seems that at some stage, the site was brought into good condition but then simply left without maintenance.

The word *aljibe* comes from the Arabic 'al-jubb' but such covered cisterns were made long before the Moors ever came to Spain. When the Romans were here, with their salt factory at Torre García and their mining enterprises (gold at Rodalquilar and lead and silver at Baria, now Villaricos), they needed water. They built water storage facilities for their settlements and along their routeways, not least at Bermejo.

Aljibes are particularly common in some of the flatter areas. The Junta de Andalucía's 1:45,000 scale map of the Parque Natural Cabo de Gata-Níjar has distinctive blue symbols for *aljibes* and other water features in the key. It's easy to pick these out. There are, for example, clusters of such features at Fernán Pérez, at Cortijada el Higo Seco just three kilometres south-west of there, at the Cortijo El Campillo de Doña Francisca five kilometres south again, and at Pozo de los Frailes. So far so good, but then it struck me that the *aljibe* at Bermejo and the mills of Huebro are not marked. Suddenly I twigged that the symbols for these features are only shown *within* the boundaries of the Natural Park. Bermejo and Huebro are outside the boundaries, so the old water features there and elsewhere, such as at Albaricoques, don't make the cut. In this respect I'd say the mapmakers have sold their public short. As you drive around this part of Almería province you can't avoid seeing *aljibes*, assuming you are looking out for them, that is.

A key factor in the location of *aljibes* was that they had to be close to houses if they were for domestic water supply or convenient for watering livestock if that was their prime purpose. *Aljibes* tend to have a small settling tank on the outside of the main structure to ensure unwanted material did not get in, and those intended for watering animals would have drinking troughs alongside too. However, as to their location, they also had to be filled and this meant constructing them where they would fill by gentle gravity flow from nearby slopes or hills a little distance away. It's for this reason that the *aljibe* sitting on high ground at the *mirador* above Los Molinos del Río de Aguas, looking towards Sorbas and beyond, can instantly be seen to be nothing more than a whim of the local council. It's in a place where it could never naturally be filled and has been put there just as a feature of interest for passers-by. Lindy Walsh, who gave the council the land where the *mirador* now stands, assures me that this is the case.

Pasturing animals in the flat lands of southern Almería such as the Campo de Níjar was made possible in times past only by the stocks of water held in the *aljibes*. Up to the late 1980s as many as 18,000 head of livestock would spend their winter and spring there, grazing the natural vegetation before being taken to the mountain areas further north like the Sierra de Segura for summer and autumn. There is more about this pattern of transhumance and the routes that were used for it in *Flamingos in the Desert*.

Fernán Pérez

If you are following the Water Trail and your last stop was the *aljibe* at Bermejo, return from there as far as the main roundabout in the centre of Campohermoso and this time turn left. You should now be going east south-east on the AL-3106. In about five km the road rises gently over La Serrata, a low mountain range marking one part of the Carboneras Fault, the complex boundary between two of the Earth's tectonic plates. On the south-eastern side of La Serrata lies Fernán Pérez, a small village, centuries old, at a crossroads where the main route linking Las Negras to the interior met a series of other *caminos*. The village is in a sheltered basin, protected by the hills of Jayón, Los Mamones, Tortola and Las Bichas. It hasn't been ruined by modern expansion and with its small white houses and church with a neat bell-tower, it has an air of timelessness. It developed in the 18th century after the building of the Castillo de San Ramón on the coast, which brought more security to the area and a time of good harvests and relative prosperity.

Just before you reach the village, there is a large area on the left where you can easily pull off the road. On a slight rise immediately adjacent is the stump of a ruined windmill. More interesting though, further across to the left, is an aqueduct. An information pillar gives details relating to it, under the emblazoned heading: 'Ruta Etnográfica: Para los más curiosos', an 'Ethnographic Route for the more curious'. Quite why this is part of the Ruta Etnográfica rather than the Ruta del Agua is a mystery that can only be answered by the officials that came up with these constructs in the first place.

You can walk through a wide gap in the wall nearby and go across to the aqueduct. The channel along the top is still there and the whole structure is generally in good condition apart from one short stretch which is missing. It's really quite an impressive feature. It was built in the early years of the 20th century to solve the problem of getting water across a riverbed to increase the area under irrigation. This was at a time when the large amount of water available and the low cost of labour were such that the finances of the project made sense.

Prominent across the road is a restored windmill. This is in the grounds of the Casa Rural Molino Fernán Pérez but access is allowed and you can just walk up to the mill. It has a conical wooden cap and wooden arms for the eight sails which, when it was working, would have had cloth attached to catch the wind. On the ground alongside are some of the mill's former timbers, long since replaced, their huge size a testament to the scale of even such a relatively simple structure as this.

At the south-east end of the village, just off the main road at the start of the Camino del Mosto, is the public washing place, the *lavadero*. It was restored in 2003 and looks as if it should all be working but when I turned the tap, nothing happened. The walls and modern roof, the latter of long thin bricks and already damaged, seem somewhat out of keeping with how I suspect it would have originally looked.

Before describing the next water features at Fernán Pérez, a little more background might be useful. Where a large volume of water was needed, say for irrigation or the watering of stock rather than just for domestic use, more complex arrangements were made, such as the building of a *noria*, a waterwheel. Often these would be called a *noria de sangre*, the *sangre*, meaning blood, referring to the motive power which was usually a donkey plodding round and round. (See below for full details of how *norias* worked.) This was simple technology, used over many centuries around the Mediterranean basin since the time of the Ancient Greeks and Romans, and labour-saving, unless you happened to be the donkey involved. When the Moors arrived in Spain they continued the use of these devices, even installing a *noria* in the Alcazaba in Almería.

Waterwheels worked in areas where the water table was not too far below the ground. There were once literally hundreds in the province. "*Donde anda noria no anda el hambre,*" was the phrase, meaning something like: "Where there's a waterwheel working, there won't be hunger." The wheels were made by master carpenters, traditionally using wood that was resistant to water such as olive. During the 20th century the details of waterwheels evolved, with iron used instead of wood and a chain and metal buckets replacing the old ropes and ceramic containers. This made the wheels more efficient but, paradoxically, it was just at this time that motorised pumps were becoming more widespread.

At Fernán Pérez, there are two of these waterwheel sites, very close together and easily accessible. On the opposite side of the main road from the *lavadero*, there is a track labelled to a 'Reserva Natural'. Just a hundred metres along there, on the left, is a tall curved wall with buttresses. This is the remains of a *noria de sangre*. There's room to park on the wide track and you can walk up on to the platform where the waterwheel was. The wheels have gone but the pit where the vertical wheel would have been is still there, covered with a metal mesh. Peering down, I guessed it was about 20 metres deep. There are lots of holes in the walls of the pit and it's now a favoured roosting place for pigeons. Close by are buildings associated with the wheel and a large empty tank, which would have been a *balsa* to store the water brought up by the *noria*.

60 metres across the field is another empty water tank and another *noria*. The pit on this one, also protected by heavy-duty mesh, seems even deeper. The channel that fed water into the tank is clearly visible. There's also a sunken path that leads down, through an open blue door, to a vaulted passage underneath the *noria*. I'm not recommending that *you* do this, but in the interests of research and curiosity I cautiously went down it. At its far end it reaches the pit and you can look down to the bottom but it's entirely unprotected, so if you ignore my recommendation, do take care. Pigeons roost in this pit too and the stench of their guano is pretty powerful, so you may decide discretion is the better part of valour.

On a small conical rise above these two waterwheels is a cluster of abandoned buildings. I went to investigate. Skilfully built into the slope is a threshing circle with, on its upper side, a neat cobbled slope leading up to the *cortijada*. The buildings are locked but if you walk around the hillside, below the fringe of prickly pears, you will find an entrance cut into the slope that leads into a vaulted cellar that seems to have been, and possibly still is, used for quartering animals. As for the buildings themselves, this seems to have been a substantial complex, with a set of external steps, hefty buttressed walls and metal *rejas* on the windows. There's also a small *aljibe* with water still in it. In a tiny outhouse, there even appears to be a toilet made from gypsum. A nearby lintel carries a faint inscription giving the date 1955.

El Pozo de los Frailes

The final stop on the Water Trail provides a chance to see what a working *noria de sangre* looks like. To get there, take the road south-west from Fernán Pérez, passing close to the Cortijada el Higo Seco, then through Los Martínez and on to Albaricoques. If you are a film buff, you may easily be tempted by the spaghetti western legacy here, but save that for another time and continue, turning right by the large black metal cowboy figure, to take the road westwards through more *plasticos*. After almost four kilometres you reach a roundabout. This is Los Nietos. Immediately before the roundabout, on the right at the side of the road, are two barrel-vaulted *aljibes*. Peer in through the end door of either and you can see the size of the underground water-storage chamber. These *aljibes* used to be in open countryside but during the writing of this book, new *plasticos* were built, hemming them in. At the roundabout, go left, heading towards San José, and continue for another seven kilometres or so.

This brings you to Pozo de los Frailes where, right by the road in the centre of the village, is a restored *noria de sangre*. This makes sense of the ruined *norias* seen at Fernán Pérez and shows clearly how they used to work. Information panels explain it all. The two masonry pillars at either side of the circular platform held a hefty wooden crossbeam, used to stabilise the *maza*, the big wooden post to which the *arbolete* or horizontal wheel was fixed. The vertical wheel, the *rueda de agua*, had 32 wooden teeth to gear it in to the horizontal wheel. Thick ropes, *maromas*, went over the *rueda de agua* and into the pit where the water nowadays appears to be about eight metres down. From the central *maza* a suitably-shaped branch about 4.5 metres long, called a *mayal*, would reach out to beyond the *arbolete*. This would be of olive or eucalyptus and it was to this that the donkey would be attached, to plod endlessly in circles and power the whole arrangement. The only things missing today, apart from the donkey, are the *arcaduces*, the 18 ceramic pots that would have been attached to the rope for lifting the water.

There's a wooden trough into which the water would tip, with a spout at 90° to pour it down into the channel leading to the adjacent *lavadero*. Beyond that, the *acequia* continues and you can make out a tank a couple of fields away that would have stored the water for irrigation. This *noria* was working until 1983, after which a period of neglect followed until its restoration a decade later. A wooden plaque records that the restoration was done in 1994 by *'Manuel 'El Carpintero' en honor a su padre'*. Perhaps it was Manuel the Carpenter's dad who taught him his woodworking skills.

22. The death of the Río de Aguas

"You don't often get to document extinction."
(Ion Holban)

The spring at El Nacimiento

Not far upstream from the off-grid village of Los Molinos del Río de Aguas is El Nacimiento, the spring that, for centuries, has provided an unfailing water supply to the people living and farming in Los Molinos and in other settlements further downstream such as Los Perales, La Huelga and La Herrería. The walk from Los Molinos upstream to the spring is superb, with spectacular outcrops of crystalline gypsum rock, dense thickets of *caña* and dramatic cliffs looking down over the valley. In addition to creating a reliable water supply for people, the permanent water in the valley of the Río Aguas has created a unique ecosystem in the protected area called the Paraje Natural Karst en Yesos de Sorbas (the Natural Landscape of the Gypsum Karst of Sorbas).

The water feeding the spring comes from an aquifer extending to over 150 square kilometres, the largest aquifer in Almería province. Water has gushed out of the spring for hundreds of years at a rate of over 40 litres per second.

But in January 2013 locals began to notice a significant reduction in the flow of water at a time of year when that would not be expected. When this continued, investigations were carried out by Professor José María Calaforra of Almería University, who specialises in the study of hydro-geology and underground water sources. He installed measuring devices which established that the water flow had diminished drastically to 3.17 litres per second. He predicted that, if nothing was done, the spring at El Nacimiento would dry up entirely within two or three years. This resulted in an outcry as local residents realised that their only water supply was under serious threat.

The threat to the spring comes from massive new plantations of olive trees in the relatively flat and extensive tract of land between Sorbas and Tabernas, where two million new trees had been planted by late 2015, with the permission of the Department of the Environment. All of these are using massive amounts of irrigation water from deep new boreholes pumping millions of litres up from the aquifer. It is estimated that since 1998, due to over-exploitation, the water table has been dropping by at least 3.3 metres per year, producing a total lowering of the water table by some 50 metres over 15 years. However, it is only relatively recently that this has become apparent through its impact on the spring.

Campaigning against ecocide

Apart from the residents' fears for their water supply, environmentalists also expressed major concerns that the distinctive wetland ecosystem would be destroyed. By July 2014, Ecologistas en Acción and Grupo Ecologistas del Mediterráneo had made an official complaint, a *denuncia*, to the environment department of the regional government, the Junta de Andalucía.

At a well-attended meeting in Sorbas a few months later, Professor Calaforra described the situation: "The Los Molinos spring is unique in Europe. Its environmental value is of the highest, supporting indigenous protected species that are at risk of disappearing. It has never before dried up and now it is practically on the point of extinction". He added: "The regional government has granted many permissions for intensive olive farms, knowing that the spring is being over-exploited".

Meanwhile, David Dene of Los Molinos has headed a campaign against what he terms the 'ecocide' of the Rio de Aguas. Ecocide is defined as 'the extensive damage to, destruction of or loss of an ecosystem, whether by human agency or by other causes, to such an extent that peaceful enjoyment by the inhabitants of that territory has been or will be severely diminished'. He took the issue to the EU, which acknowledged that the owners of the new olive plantations are breaking the law but placed the issue in with a portfolio of other complaints against Spain to be dealt with together at some future date.

Also in 2015 Ecologistas en Acción (EA) reacted with a damning response to the publication of the latest Plan Hidrológico, the Junta de Andalucía's water management plan for the six-year period 2015-2021, saying that it failed to tackle the 'excessive water extraction' that is threatening to extinguish the Río de Aguas. EA asserted that water licences granted by the Junta allowed the industrial olive plantations to extract 66,000 cubic metres of water per year, compared to 7,000 cubic metres per year for the notorious *plasticos*, the large-scale greenhouses.

Re-charge of the aquifer is reckoned to be about 260 mm per year but the rate of evapotranspiration, estimated at about 1,000 mm per year, is four times as much. Because of this the role of the river as an ecological corridor and a site of increased humidity is very important. In 2015 the European Commission launched a 'systemic infringement procedure' against Spain for over-exploitation of water on a widespread basis. Despite this, water over-exploitation is still occurring, there is no monitoring of extraction, and intensive plantations are still expanding.

The 2015 Management Plan from the Junta mentions an average flow in the river of 75 litres/second but it is not clear what this is based on. Back in 2011 the Junta's own Hydrological Plan gave a flow of 40 litres/second but this was based on drastically outdated data from 1980-2001. That plan said that by 2015 the over-exploitation of water would be reduced by 200%. Not only has this not happened, it has been totally ignored to the extent that the over-exploitation is now estimated at 500%. The recently observed rate of flow of the Río de Aguas at Los Perales, Los Canales and Los Molinos suggests that in the near future these villages will lose their flowing water, which they rely on for subsistence agriculture.

The issue received further exposure when a half-hour documentary entitled *The Last Oasis* was screened on Spanish television in late 2015 as part of the environmental series *El Escarabo Verde*, The Green Beetle. In the programme the Junta's agriculture department called for measures to be taken "to overcome the water shortage and exploitation of natural water courses" in the province, whilst at the same time the Junta's environment department was saying there was "little that could be done" about the intensive olive plantations. Agriculture councillor Carmen Ortiz pointed out that "underutilised" desalination plants in the province could solve the problem. The response of Ecologistas en Acción to this was: "Desalinated water is too expensive for farmers. The only solution is to reduce the cultivated surface area and encourage more sustainable use".

A front-page article in the *Costa Almería News* in January 2017 reported that the plight of the villagers in Los Molinos had been raised by David Dene at a UN 'Earth Jurisprudence' conference. The Junta de Andalucía's environment department meanwhile said it was taking steps to "reverse the negative effects of irrigated intensive olive farming" in the area. In the six months from June 2016 it inspected 37 out of 42 olive farms and found some illegal water supplies, with proceedings started in 13 cases. Mr Dene said there seemed to be a "genuine desire" on the part of the Junta "to alleviate this catastrophic situation" but it may not be enough. However, despite taking action against illegal groundwater extraction, the Junta reiterated that the solution to the problem was to bring desalinated water from Carboneras and said that providing the infrastructure to achieve this was the responsibility of the Spanish government.

Vivid photos

At an eco-market in Lucainena in the autumn of 2015, I saw an exhibition of photos taken along the Río de Aguas. The colours were vivid and the compositions striking: a delicately poised swallowtail butterfly; an improbably patterned bright green-and-black chameleon looking straight at the camera; an elegant praying mantis; a turtle, mid-swim, in a deep green pool; an ibex with its head lowered, proffering its horns. Then I realised the photographer, Ion Holban, was actually there. I asked him about his work and mentioned that I'd walked the length of the river, recording the journey in my book *Flamingos in the Desert*. We talked for a few minutes, long enough to make a connection.

Fast forward to 2016. I contacted Ion and asked if it would be possible to go out with him one day, to learn more about his ongoing project to document the state of the Río de Aguas and the vulnerable species that depend on it. He said yes, he'd be happy to take me, and mentioned that, in addition, there were some orchids just flowering that he'd like to show me.

On a warm early March day, we meet up. Ion gets his cameras together, fills a water bottle, and we set off. Soon we are threading our way amongst *caña*, tiptoeing across wet mud, balancing on rocks in shallow water, and then clambering higher, onto a huge outcrop of crystalline gypsum. The A7 motorway passes high above, on soaring concrete pillars. Ion warns me to stop, just as we are about to look over the edge of the outcrop. It's a place where he knows freshwater turtles like to haul out of the water and bask in the sun, but if we suddenly appear on their skyline, they'll plop into the water before we have a chance to see them properly, and certainly before we can take photos. We move slowly to the edge and look over, down into a deep green pool. There they are, about twenty of them, lined up along the water's edge. These are Spanish pond turtles (Mauremys leprosa in Latin, *galápago leprosa* in Spanish). We take photos, retreat for a minute or two, then carefully look again. Most of the

214

turtles have noiselessly disappeared. But there are other shots to be taken; other pools, deep blue with silent water in eroded mini-canyons in the bright cream rocks, and the crumbling geometry of a huge old mill, the Molino de la Cerrá del Tesoro. It is a wonderful place, despite the huge concrete pillars and the sun-blocking carriageways of the motorway as it sweeps above us.

We leave the turtles in peace, cross the trickle of water under the motorway viaduct and are soon scrambling over more gypsum bedrock, angling across the slopes near the abandoned village of El Tesoro. Ion wants to take me to a spring he found some months earlier above the ruins. He wants to check whether it's still flowing, as part of a report he is compiling to catalogue the state of the Río de Aguas and the threats it is facing.

Ion is good at reading the landscape. He looks ahead to a dense area of vegetation and says we won't be able to get through it because there are no goat tracks. If goats had been through, we'd be able to follow the path they'd made but if just a few random animals have passed this way, we'll struggle to force a passage. We do find a way, by diverting up over some rocks on our right and easing past a few brambles. At the spring there is a hint of water but no evident flow. Kneeling by a low damp rock, Ion points out Cratoneuron moss, happy here but generally a very rare species in south-east Spain. It's not tolerant of changes in the water level though, so he fears for its future.

He's not optimistic about the Río de Aguas and its tributaries. Referring to the current concerns about how rapidly the river's flow appears to be diminishing and to his expanding portfolio of pictures - he has over 20,000 - he says at one point: "You don't often get to document extinction". But then, not wanting to be too pessimistic, he eases off, suggesting just that: "By next year it might be different".

He talks about the ecological mesh of the place: how the health of the *caña*, for example, depends on the water levels, and

215

how that in turn affects insect numbers, which determine the success of some bird species, and then also how the *caña* provides not just food for birds and mammals but also shelter and breeding places. At another point he's talking about how we take rabbits for granted and yet how critical they are as a prey for raptors such as eagle owls and mammals such as foxes. We see no foxes but we do find the distinctive pointed scat that gives away their presence.

We clamber back up from the spring. On one large rock, a tiny mauve flower is nodding gently. By chance, because of the steep and broken nature of the ground, it's at head height; otherwise we almost certainly wouldn't have noticed it. He tells me it's called Chaenorhinum grandiflorum. It's a gypsophyte, a plant that thrives on gypsum. He changes the lens on his camera, leans in close and takes half a dozen shots.

I wonder where his interest in nature stems from and he tells me that although he grew up in a Romanian city, his grandparents lived out in the countryside, in the hills by a big river in the north-east of the country. In the city, he went to an arts high school and studied sculpture and graphics. Then he moved to London and became involved with photography. At the same time he began studying environmental management and conservation. He spent some time on a Masters' degree in climate change management but left that to start an NGO with a group of like-minded others. The NGO, New Environmentalist, focused on ecotourism and encouraged tourists to do conservation work as part of a holiday. Part of this involves linking in to expertise that already exists on the ground, using guides who really know an area and so supporting small-scale local enterprises.

In the UK he met his partner, who is English and has family connections on the banks of the Río de Aguas. So it was that in 2010 he began to come here. As an ecologist and photographer he was intrigued to find a wetland ecosystem in one of the driest corners of Europe. In mid-2015, with his partner and their young twin daughters, he moved here, and it was then that he began his project to record the unique details of the Río de Aguas.

After we get back to our starting point, there's one more thing Ion wants to show me. We drive up a steep, twisting road and pull off. Ion leads a little way down a slope, tells me to watch where I'm putting my feet, and there, all around us, are tiny pale green spikes, no more than 15 cm high, with flowers of maroon and yellow around a large, reflective blue patch. The bright blue patch gives this flower its popular name, mirror orchid (Ophrys speculum in Latin). On a European level mirror orchids are abundant, but here they are less common. Ion explains their requirements. They like some shade - he indicates where the sun goes up and sets behind the rocks above us, giving shade for part of the day; some altitude - I guess we are at about 350 metres; some grazing to keep competing vegetation down; and finally, they are pollinated by a single species of insect. Those things have come together in this patch of just a few square metres. The more we look, the more mirror orchids we see. Ion gets out his macro lens and sets to with his camera. I do likewise with my more run-of-the-mill, ages old but faithful Olympus. How he found this tiny patch of orchids on this vast arid hillside is astonishing. He says he was actually looking for something else.

We look and look but after all, apart from being beautiful, orchids don't actually *do* much, so we are finally sated and head back to our cars. Ion promises to send me his report, which he says is almost complete. Whatever the fate of the Río de Aguas, I drive off knowing that, if the worst happens, its rich variety has at least been thoroughly documented and this might at least help to prevent the same environmental disaster being perpetrated elsewhere.

Reporting on the river

The report, by Ion Holban and his colleagues at New Environmentalist, was published in March 2016. Its title is a mouthful but sets out clearly what it is about: *Paraje Natural Karst en Yesos de*

Sorbas: A Report on the River Aguas, Priority Habitats and Vulnerable Species with a Summary of the Main Threats and Recommendations in line with Natura 2000 guidelines. (This link will take you to the full report: www.newenvironmentalist.co.uk/riodeaguas/)

It is based on the 2015 Management Plan for the area published by the Junta de Andalucía, together with observations made and data collected between November 2014 and March 2016. *'Yeso'* is Spanish for gypsum. The report notes that the Paraje Natural Karst en Yesos de Sorbas (PNKYS, referred to subsequently in this section as 'the park') is the second largest gypsum karst area in the world and Spain's most important gypsum karst landscape. This is a key area through which the Río de Aguas runs and which provides the river with much of its water. It includes 17 different protected habitats and many endemic and rare species. As a consequence, the 2015 Management Plan (MP) from the Junta de Andalucía classes it as a 'biodiversity hotspot'. However, despite its importance, it is only a *Paraje Natural*, a designation that brings with it one of Spain's lowest levels of protection.

The 'Natura 2000' referred to in the report's title is the largest coordinated network of protected areas in the world. Its main objective is the maintenance or restoration of natural habitats and the species they contain. The 'Habitats and Birds Directives' from Natura 2000 were incorporated into Spanish law in 2007 but, of the nine specific requirements that follow from this, it seems that none at all have been implemented in the park. In addition, the report found the environmental section of the Junta de Andalucía's website so difficult to use, through poor design and lack of information, as to be effectively useless.

Specific vulnerable species covered in the report include spur-thighed tortoise, Bonelli's eagle, European pond terrapin and endemic gypsum-loving plants such as Teucrium turredanum. The main threats are from intensive agriculture, infrastructure such as the

AVE railway, water over-exploitation, gypsum quarrying, overgrazing by goats, wildfires, pollution from agricultural runoff and sewage plants, hunting and climate change. To take just the last two items in that list, many hunting dogs are abandoned at the end of the season and become feral if they survive, adding further pressure to species such as tortoises and terrapins. Lindy Walsh tells me she has also been told by local people that young hunting dogs are left out in the *campo* and if they manage to survive on their instincts for two or three months, will be considered worth using for hunting, so are collected again. As for climate change, maximum temperatures are predicted by reliable sources to rise by between 2°C and 4°C by 2050. A study in the Doñana National Park in southwest Spain has shown that higher temperatures during April - July can prevent the eggs of spur-thighed tortoises from hatching, thus making breeding unsuccessful.

The park is 100% privately owned. For the report 20 landowners were interviewed, owning between them an estimated 200 hectares, almost 10% of the park. They have all been resident for over 10 years and represent all the significant settlements in the park. 17 were affected by water shortages, 19 thought the river and its springs were not sufficiently protected and 16 considered the habitats and species within the park lacked adequate protection. 19 had never been consulted by authorities over any management decisions and 18 agreed with the park's proposed designation as a Zona Especial de Conservación.

The report uses measured language but its conclusion is inescapable: 'It is very likely that priority habitats and species are declining rapidly inside the park'. It recommends an urgent investigation by the European Commission into the situation, the implementation of measures to control and reduce water extraction and a change of designation from 'Paraje' to 'Parque' to boost the level of protection the area has. The report's authors clearly have no confidence in the way the Junta de Andalucía has managed, or rather failed to manage, the park and say: 'The only viable action to restore these habitats and species is via a direct intervention from the EC'.

Barely had the New Environmentalist report been published when another came hot on its heels. This was a 10-page report from experts at the Spanish National Research Council (CSIC). It concluded that water-intensive crops such as olives which rely on groundwater exploitation are largely responsible for causing desertification. The report's release coincided with a warning from local mayors about the imminent demise of the Río de Aguas spring. The mayors were meeting in Sorbas and appealed to the Junta de Andalucía to act. Deputy mayor of Uleila del Campo, María Rosa López was quoted in the Spanish press as saying that the Junta "should not allow olive farming". The Junta's response? They did not send a representative to the meeting and their environment delegate, Antonio Martínez Rodríguez, was not available for comment.

Very shortly before publication of this book I read that by July 2017 the number of new olive trees in the Sorbas - Tabernas area had risen to an estimated six million. More depressing still, a piece by local journalist Emma Randle reported that the Spanish parliament had announced that it has no plans to take action regarding the over-exploitation of the water resources until at least 2022. The government said there was no agreement between the central, regional and provincial authorities to "provide urgent solutions" thus, it seems, leaving the affected communities and the ecosystem of the Río de Aguas to an entirely avoidable fate.

23. Under plastic

'The heat under the sheeting was tremendous. We were in a
tunnelled underworld stretching for acres over the landscape.'
(Jason Webster)

Invernaderos

In 1963 the first large-scale plastic greenhouses (*invernaderos* in
Spanish) appeared in Almería province. It soon became apparent
that, in the controlled climate which these made possible, and with
irrigation, a huge amount of produce could be grown in what had
been a barren area. Unsurprisingly, the number of *invernaderos*
steadily increased but this brought problems. A front page headline in
the newspaper *La Voz de Almería* on 9th December 2000 announced
an initiative to increase vigilance to detect whether greenhouses
were taking water illegally and pointed out that it was necessary to
have a permit from the Junta de Andalucía to drill a well. Then in June
2001 the paper *Levante Información* reported that two farmers, a
father and son, had been jailed for a year for the construction of
illegal *invernaderos* near Fernán Perez. They had been warned about
the offence in May 1999 and ignored the warning. At the time of their
sentence, they were given two weeks to dismantle the greenhouses,
otherwise the authorities would do it and charge the cost to the two
men. This was just the first court case of many relating to
greenhouses put up without authorisation within the boundaries of
the Cabo de Gata-Níjar Natural Park.

It used to be said that the Great Wall of China was the only
human-made feature visible from space. The same is now being said
of the huge semi-circular wedge of reflective white plastic that
occupies the coastal bulge to the west of Almería city. An aerial study
carried out by SIGPAC, the cartography department of the Junta de
Andalucía, revealed that 3.4 % of the province's total area is covered

by *invernaderos*. By April 2016 the area under plastic amounted to over 30,000 hectares, with further developments continuing apace.

So, 2013 marked the 50th anniversary of the first appearance of the *plasticos*. There is no denying that the industry has brought huge wealth to some; annual revenue is around €2 billion, so it is no surprise that the anniversary was marked by a conference of the major producers and associated politicians.

Notes of concern were sounded though. The Agriculture Secretary of the Junta de Andalucía, Jerónimo Pérez, said that many of the older greenhouses are in a poor state of repair and need to be upgraded and made more energy efficient. Environmentalists believe that careless waste management of the old plastic is a major factor in marine pollution citing, for example, the 2013 death of a sperm whale on the Almería coast which was found to have 16 kg of plastic in its stomach.

In 2015 the UK's Channel 4 TV showed a documentary highlighting the plight of workers in the *invernaderos*. This suggested that little had changed since a decade or so earlier, when Jason Webster wrote about the same thing. I refer to his book *Andalus* in chapter 29 but it's worth mentioning here his first chapter, in which Webster and a Moroccan friend escape, under threat of serious physical abuse, from an *invernadero* where the workers are being treated very badly.

A few weeks after the Channel 4 documentary, a pictorial report in *The Independent* newspaper in the UK included the *plasticos* of Almería as one of the most striking ways in which humans have impacted on the world's landscapes. The report was compiled by The Foundation for Deep Ecology and was intended to draw attention to what it called 'humanity's devastating effect on the planet'.

However, in these times of human-induced climate change, a study undertaken at Almería University has shown that over a 25-year period, the average air temperature in the province has dropped by 0.25%. This is thought to be because the insolation, the incoming heat from the sun, is reflected back by the light-coloured roofs of the greenhouses.

In the USA, scientists at the University of California at Berkeley have been analysing the benefits of the cooling effects of the greenhouses. Meanwhile, their colleagues at the University of Arizona have warned that reflecting the sun's heat in this way might actually change weather patterns sufficiently to reduce rainfall and make drought conditions worse.

Shanties

One of the downsides of the huge boom in this type of farming is felt by some of the workers who toiled in the *invernaderos*. Many of them are immigrants from North Africa, some of whom have lost their jobs since the dramatic downturn, *la Crisis*, in the Spanish economy over recent years. An estimated 4,000 people are now living in conditions of absolute poverty across the province of Almería, mainly in shanty towns in the Níjar-Campohermoso area and around El Ejido. Two charities, Médicos del Mundo and Almería Acoge, which work to help the residents of such places gain access to basic services, reckon that there are 63 shanties in the Campohermoso area alone. Níjar council, responsible for the area, says it knows of only 15 but does not have the resources to keep track of all of the people living below the radar. Areas like Níjar have come under extra pressure as councils in western Almería, led by El Ejido, have demolished shanty towns and driven homeless immigrants away.

A very obvious shanty that brings home the reality of the situation to me is the one at the ruined settlement by the roundabout where the ALP-206, going south from exit 479 on the A-7 motorway, meets the ALP-824 between El Barranquete and Los Albaricoques. On one of the maps I have this place is marked as Los Nietos. It seems as if a lot of people live there. There are always people around, and several cars, amongst the old stone *cortijada* and the makeshift extensions built with whatever cheap materials have come to hand.

Some shanties are 'home' to illegal immigrants. Wladimir Morante of Médicos del Mundo says, of the people who live in these unofficial settlements: "We see on a daily basis horrific and complicated scenes because people think they will be arrested if they go to a doctor. But worse is the state of helplessness these people are in. Many have never got over the trauma of reaching us. They come with high hopes, leaving everything and everyone they love behind, and the grim reality they are faced with breaks them."

A spokesperson for the farmers' union COAG tried to distance farmers from the issue, pointing out: "No farmer will offer work to an illegal immigrant, because the fines make the risk impossible. An employer can be fined up to €60,000 per undocumented worker found on the premises." Gracia Fernández, speaking for the central government, shifted responsibility to the regional government by saying: "Across Andalucía there are 670,000 immigrants, and the entire housing budgest is just €500,000 - not enough to solve the housing problems of a single council." It's the usual story: everyone thinks it's up to someone else to tackle the issue and no-one takes the responsibility for doing so, except for the charities and voluntary bodies.

Poniente

I wrote a short paragraph about Chus Gutierrez's 2002 film *Poniente* in *'Flamingos in the Desert'*. I now confess I was winging it as, at that point, I hadn't seen the film. Now I have - it was shown to us by our Spanish teacher as an end of term lesson - and happily, what I wrote then was accurate enough, but in the context of the *invernaderos*, it's worth saying more about it. First, it is in Spanish but there are English subtitles. Second, although it was made some time ago, it deals with what are still very live issues. And third, in my opinion it's definitely worth watching. Those of us in the Spanish class all enjoyed it and not only because it meant 90 minutes off from 'proper work'.

The plot involves a schoolteacher, Lucia who, after her father dies, returns to the village in Almería where he owned *invernaderos* in which he employs some illegal immigrants. Lucia decides to take over her father's business, upsetting her cousin Miguel, who believes that the land is rightfully his. Lucia falls for Curro, her father's accountant, who sympathizes with the mainly North African workers. He's also a friend of one of the immigrants, Adbembi, with whom he's saving to open a beach-bar called Poniente. Lucia's sympathy for the workers is not shared by the Spaniards, particularly by the racist foreman Paquito. There is rising tension with authentic details such as the workers striking to receive extra pay for extra work.

The film juggles a range of plotlines with considerable success, and brings its ideas alive through interesting characters. It perhaps oversimplifies the Spaniards / immigrants dynamic but is nevertheless absorbing and illuminating. Those who know Cabo de Gata will also recognise the starkly beautiful scenery in many of the shots.

King Tomato

In the areas where the *plasticos* proliferate, it's hard to miss huge billboards proclaiming the wonderful attributes of particular types of tomatoes. They tend to first give the name and follow that with a snappy phrase about its attributes, such as: **Bysonte**, *'larga vida con sabor y color'*, long life with taste and colour; **Poesia**, *'el Raf de calidad con resistencias'*, the Raf (itself a well-known type of tomato) of quality with resistances, presumably against disease; and the rather scientific sounding **74-336 RZ**, *'calibre constante'*, where consistent size appears to be the main attribute. It's interesting that only one of the three gives flavour a mention. Obviously these billboards are aimed at the growers rather than the consumers.

After all, tomatoes are big business in Almería. The province produces over a million tonnes every year, with 9,000 hectares devoted to the crop. Over 60% of the crop is exported, with a market value of more than €500 million. During the growing season, between September and May, over 13,000 seasonal jobs are generated.

It's not entirely surprising then, that Almería has taken to celebrating World Tomato Day on February 13th by holding a Tomato Festival and proclaiming itself 'World Tomato Capital'. One year recently, a photo in the media showed Agriculture Minister Carmen Ortiz looking faintly bemused as she stood alongside a large mascot called 'Tomatal', which is basically a man in a large tomato outfit. The sub-heading for the article was: 'Thousands turn out to celebrate the popular red fruit'. The many people who attended could taste different varieties and buy bags of tomatoes at €1. I'm sorry I missed it!

For all the issues associated with the *plasticos*, including water use and poor working conditions, the industry is making positive strides. Almería is a leading area for the development of organic bio-control solutions for plagues affecting crops. Some would argue that if there were no monocultures, there would be less likelihood of plagues. Nevertheless, the province breeds and exports hundreds of millions of insects annually to help farmers fight crop predators. And Almería itself now has over 13,000 farms using biological pest-control methods.

Organic tomatoes

As an example, let's take an organic tomato producer called Francisco, who is an acquaintance of my editor Helen Evans. Helen runs the blog ECO LOCAL ALMERÍA and what follows is based, with her permission, on a report she wrote in 2016 after a visit to see just what goes on in Francisco's *invernadero*.

Francisco and his father have been growing organic tomatoes near La Cañada between Almería and the airport for about 6 years. They have an *invernadero* with about 2,000 plants, each with two branches. These are trained up raffia strings to 2 metres and then allowed to grow down again almost to ground level. Then they are pinched out to encourage ripening of the final trusses.

The lower leaves are removed as the plant grows taller and they are placed in a large container to make compost. The composting process creates heat which destroys the pests and diseases in the leaves. Liquid drains out of the bottom of this container and is then matured for 6 months in a closed container before being diluted for use as a liquid fertiliser for the growing plants.

The growing season is during the winter, between early September and April. A type of tomato called *Ramily* is grown, chosen for its resistance to attack by the tomato yellow leaf curl virus. When the plants are small, *Nesidiocoris tenuis* flies are released into the greenhouse. These are the natural predators of whitefly and *Tuta absoluta*, the tomato borer, which are the worst pests.

The plants are watered every two to four days, depending on the temperature in the greenhouse, with water that comes from two wells, one of which is slightly saline. Tomatoes are more tolerant of saline water than many other plants. Reputedly the salt water gives the tomatoes a sweeter taste as it contains many extra minerals not available in fresh water.

When the tomatoes flower they are pollinated by bumble bees (*Bombus terrestris*). A number of colonies of bees are brought into the greenhouse in small cardboard box hives, complete with living quarters and a substitute food supply, so that they can continue their development whilst feeding on the pollen and nectar supplied by the tomato flowers. Each hive is able to pollinate an area of 2,000 square metres and has a life span of about 2 months.

Francisco and his father supply a wholesaler in Campohermoso who requires tomatoes to be harvested on the truss. The trusses are cut when there are 5 or 6 ripe tomatoes on them. The remaining 25% of the crop, which does not ripen, is removed and given to a friend nearby who feeds them to his sheep and goats. In cooler weather the tomatoes ripen more evenly and 7 or 8 tomatoes can be harvested on each truss. However during the 2015/2016 season the temperatures remained high and Francisco says he has noticed that the trend is towards a warmer growing season each year, he thinks due to climate change.

A special mix of sulphur and quicklime is used as a spray to manage fungal disease, tomato borer and spider infestation. No chemical fungicides or pesticides are used. With the increasing heat in the spring, the management of the insects and fungi becomes much more difficult, so in April the irrigation is turned off. The last tomatoes are harvested then cut in half and dried in the sun. A week later the plants are removed and taken away for commercial composting.

To prepare the ground for the next crop, the surface mulch of sand is pulled back from the planting lines and organic compost and manure are spread before the sand is replaced. With this minimal disturbance, the natural microbial life within the soil is maintained and this feeds the roots of the plants. During the summer most pests and diseases within the greenhouse are killed by the intense heat. Then, in September, it's time to plant again.

24. Níjar

'Glazed and hand-painted in bright colours, its pots and plates are sold in Madrid, Barcelona and Valencia for prices that would surprise their humble creators.'
(Juan Goytisolo, in the 1950s)

Níjar: a short circuit

Níjar lies on the lower southern slopes of the Sierra Alhamilla. It has expanded from its original tightly-packed nucleus but is still of a manageable size to be explored on foot. It's a working town, one of its main sources of employment being to cater for visitors and in particular to sell them its distinctively colourful pottery and rugs.

To reach the start of this circuit, you need to find the west side of town, that is the left-hand side as you look north towards the mountains. This is easy enough and once at this part of the town, take the road with a big arrow and a sign to the Barrio Alfarero (Pottery Quarter). A short way along here, on the right, is a shiny modern building, described on a stone pillar outside as a 'centro de artes escénicas', a Centre for Arts of the Stage. At the front is a metal statue of Don Quixote and round the back is the local Music School. Opposite the front is a large black metal statue of a potter as well as a stone carving of something similar, labelled as a 'Monumento a Los Artesanos' and a ceramic tableau announcing 'Bienvenido a la Villa Artesana de Níjar'.

At the downhill side of the building, take the road that dips down and crosses the *rambla*, passing a set of red and yellow exercise equipment on the right. The location of this suddenly makes sense when this is revealed as the Calle del Jubilado, the Street of the Retired Person. And then, at the corner on the right as we reach the main street is the Centro de Día Personas Mayores, the Day Centre for Older People. Opposite this is a *carnicería/jamonería*. Go uphill here, on the main street, which has a number of shops selling pottery and *jarapas*, the rag rugs for which the town is known. Recycled cotton fabric is one of the materials used for these literally cheap and cheerful rugs. Visiting in the 1960s, Nina Epton referred to 'the coloured strips of cotton (bought in sackloads from Barcelona) tied and woven together on an archaic 'wood and string' machine in tiny workshops up cobbled lanes'. I am not on commission from the shops of Níjar but these rugs are ideal to warm the bare floor tiles of a Spanish house or flat in the winter. We even bought a couple, striped in various blues, for a few euros, to use as throws to protect the cream cushions of our IKEA armchairs; perfect.

Watch for the Bar La Parada on the right as you get towards the top of the main street, just a few metres past the Cajamar bank. Go right here, by the sign indicating 'Salon de Belleza 200m', along Calle Lomas del Pilar. This residential street climbs steadily then curves left (don't take the sharp left at Calle Sierra de Gata). By the way, if all these route details seem rather complex on the page, I think you'll find that in reality, on the ground, they are easy to follow. At the T-junction at the top, go right, then left. In a few metres you will come out opposite what claims to be the Oficina de Turismo. In fact it is just a souvenir shop called Níjarte with a rack of leaflets from the Junta de Andalucía, not the official tourist office for the town.

Signs to the right of it point to the Oficina Municipal de Información Turística, the Atalaya and the Museo de Agua. A few metres along here is the town's main square. On the near side is the town hall, on which it says 'Plaza de la Constitución 1880'. However, on the far side of the square is the church, with a plaque giving the alternative name 'Plaza de la Glorieta'. The adjacent Cafe-bar La Glorieta favours the latter.

The church of Santa María de la Anunciación was built between the 16th and 18th centuries elements. On the tower is a two-headed eagle, which is the crest of Carlos I and inside, within a glass case, is the old municipal clock, a large device of cogs, wheels, spindles and paddles. Two separate pieces of paper stuck onto the case give its date as *'principios del siglo XVIII'* (the turn of the 18th century) and '1880'; take your pick.

Climbing to the tower

Continue past the church to the Plaza Granero where there are more arrows and a sign indicating the old quarter, with narrow streets: *'Casco antiguo. Calles muy estrechos.>2m<'*. Only the visitor who likes a challenge would venture up here in a car. A short way up Calle Colón is the Plaza del Mercado. As the name suggests, this is the traditional market place and it's here that you'll find the municipal tourist office, combined with the Museo de Agua, the Water Museum. It has a large aerial photo showing the walking route from Huebro to Níjar past the mills (see chapter 20), a small mock-up of a *noria*, and other displays based on the theme of water.

Outside is the town fountain, an impressive ceramic affair with a crest announcing: 'Fuente de la Villa de Níjar. 2 octubre 1859'. There are three taps emerging from the mouths of sea monsters, all of which worked when I was there, though a notice warns: 'Agua no clorada', water not chlorinated. Very near the fountain there's a huge old tree. I couldn't identify what it was, so went back into the museum and asked. A guy came out, looked, pondered for a while, and said he thought it might be an elm. I thought he might be correct.

Continue up the street at the top edge of the market square, passing La Tienda de los Milagros, the Shop of Miracles, and through an arch. Beyond this, an arrow points rightwards to the Atalaya (Lookout) along Calle San Anton. In a few metres, go left along Calle Cuesta de la Atalaya, gaining height and following clues to the lookout tower. It's obvious enough.

During 2015 €200,000 was spent restoring the tower, which had become so neglected there was concern that it would totally collapse. The restoration used traditional materials, aiming to retain the original appearance of the tower. Close to where the houses peter out below the tower, there are new steps up the last part of the hill. These are somewhat overdone, I would say, with hefty handrails and extensive use of concrete but no doubt they are better than a steep slope with loose stones. Part way up is the Mirador del Cerro de la Atalaya (Viewpoint of the Hill of the Lookout), with superb views over the town and away to the sea, beyond the sea of *plasticos* intruding into the middle distance.

Sightlines

Modern cast-iron steps lead up to the tower entrance which, as with all of these defensive towers, was two thirds of the way up the structure. However, frustratingly, a slatted metal screen prevents access to the interior platform of the tower. At both the *mirador* and the tower there is no shortage of information provided, about the structure and purpose of the tower and the network of warning beacons of which it was a part. This tower at Níjar was linked to a beacon at Cerro del Hacho to the south on La Serrata, a low ridge of hills. Watchers at Cerro del Hacho could in turn see the Torre de Cala Higuera, near San José on the coast. The Torre de Cala Higuera was part of the Kingdom of Granada's Coastal Defence system organised in the middle of the 18th century during the reign of Carlos III. Eastwards from Cala Higuera, there was the Torre de los Lobos, then the tower on Mesa Roldán and the Torre del Rayo, these latter two being on either side of Carboneras. In the other direction, the coastal signals went via the Torre de Vela Blanca, high on the coastal cliffs, then to Torre García and so to the Alcazaba de Almeria.

When the lookouts at the Torre de la Atalaya saw the beacon alight to the south, not only could they alert the locally stationed Compañia de Milicia Urbana, but they could also relay the warning uphill to the watchers at the Castillo de Huebro, of which nowadays only ruined walls remain.

When you've absorbed the wonderful views from the tower for long enough, it's time to head back down, either the way you came or preferably just by guessing your way downhill through the streets. You may well come out, as I did, near the main square and alongside the Níjarte shop about which I was mildly negative previously. I'm sure they are lovely people, so I take back my earlier thoughts.

Go downhill now on Calle Andalucía, past the local police station. When I passed at 2.30 in the afternoon, there were six official vehicles in a line outside so I guess it's a very large station or all the police have their lunch at the same time. This road goes down and to the left. By the Hostal Asensio (coincidentally opposite the Bar La Parada, where this route turned off the main street earlier), turn right past the Pescadería La Melliza, on to Calle Las Eras.

You are now on the main street through the potters' quarter, where rustic pottery has been hand-made for centuries. One of the styles particular to Níjar is glazed ware patterned with concentric circles, often in blue and green. Níjar's pottery is still hand-finished and is typically fired for about six hours at 900ºC. In the bigger kilns, apparently, up to 5,000 pieces can be fired at one time.

A little way down here there's a ceramic tableau on the right, by another *fuente* and there are pottery workshops here, such as the Alfarería Angel y Loli on the left, and another beyond a small courtyard on the right. Further down, just off the street but clearly visible is another Tienda de los Milagros with external artwork. We're almost back at the starting point now but completists may wish to go on past where we began for a hundred metres or so and make the small ascent to the Mirador del Cerrico Redondo, a low hill that has benches, a marble cross and the usual trio of flags: Andalucía, Spain and the EU. It may be a *mirador* but the view isn't a patch on the one from the Torre de la Atalaya.

Cactus Níjar

It would be a pity to leave Níjar without seeing one more thing. Cactus Níjar, more or less at the edge of town, close to the cemetery, on the road out to junction 481 of the motorway is, on the surface, just a plant nursery that specialises, as the name indicates, in a huge range of cacti and succulents. Owner Toni Brugger formerly had a nursery in Austria but moved to Níjar because he wanted to develop a new nursery that he could live in and have a place from which he could not only sell plants but also develop a garden. If you want to buy cacti and receive top notch advice, this is the place, but as the previous sentence suggests, there is rather more to it than that.

On a series of terraces, Toni Brugger is overseeing an impressive and ongoing landscape project, with a series of 'rooms', featuring thousands of dry-land plants among many mature olives in gardens that swoop and curve, shaped with hundreds of tonnes of slate and other local rocks, down towards the *rambla*. The project began more than a decade ago but Toni told me it had really only taken off about six years ago, "when we got water". It's a fascinating place for a wander, and was the location for an exhibition of sculptures in 2016 by Anne Kampschulte, some of whose larger pieces have remained in situ. Later in 2016 a new venture was launched by Toni and Anne, a cultural association called 'Cactus Níjar es Cultura'. This coincided with the opening of a multi-purpose venue to be used for regular music evenings and other cultural events. For contact details, opening hours, and other information, just google Cactus Níjar or check out their Facebook page, and do make sure you go for a visit .

25. Sorbas

'What many of us are hopeful of now, it seems, is being able to gain - or regain - a sense of allegiance with our chosen places, and along with that a sense of affirmation with our neighbours that the place we've chosen is beautiful, subtle, profound, worthy of our lives.'

(Barry Lopez)

Sorbas: a short circuit

In general, Sorbas gets a poor press. Nina Epton, arriving fifty years ago, thought that 'seen from a distance, or from the ashen gorge at its feet; the string of white houses built on an escarpment look terribly gaunt when one gets closer to them'. A decade earlier, Juan Goytisolo was more neutral: 'From a roadside bend I surveyed the incredible houses suspended above the abyss in Sorbas'.

If you're driving from the east, approaching uphill on the N-340a, with this 'string of white houses', the 'hanging houses' of Sorbas teetering on the cliff-edge to your right, you're nearly there. You'll see restaurant/bars on either side of the road: El Fogón on your left and the Sol de Andalucía on your right. Immediately after this, turn right and in 50 metres there are parking spaces on the left.

A few metres away is the Centro de Visitantes Los Yesares. It's free and certainly worth a visit. It has a mock-up of an underground gypsum cavern and you can learn all you could want to know about the distinctive nearby landscape, the Karst en Yesos de Sorbas. It's also a good place to buy books about the local region.

Now, a suggested stroll which will take about an hour. It's not far but there's plenty to see so if you are feeling inquisitive, allow longer. From the parking area, take the road opposite which rises gently uphill passing, on the right, the former Oficina Municipal de Turismo. The Visitors' Centre mentioned above now fulfils this function. Just before you reach a mini-roundabout with a quadruple lamp-standard on it, you can see over the railings on the right, down to the main road below. At the lamp-standard, continue ahead on an unnamed road, past a green and white 'Saneamientos' sign. In a few metres, go straight across Calle Calvario and down a short concrete slope to reach the Mirador-Paseo de las Casas Colgantes, the Viewpoint-Walkway of the Hanging Houses. There are great views of the cliffs with buildings, high above, right on the edge. It must be dizzying being on the balconies of those houses.

A wide footpath with a stone-and-wooden balustrade leads across the lower part of the cliffs, steeply at first, before levelling out. To the right of the path and lower still, are terraced fields, mainly of olive trees, embanked with stone walls. Look up and the houses are right above you. They are not particularly distinguished architecturally; more of a modern hotchpotch, but impressively sited nevertheless. As I peered up, earlier on the same day when I wrote this, a kestrel was patrolling the sky, twisting to and fro along the line of houses.

In a few minutes you are down, on the level, and close to the end of the walkway, which comes to the main road opposite a *carpintería*. Nearby, just across the road, is the tiny chapel of Nuestra Señora de Fátima. You can peer in through the grille in the door. This building, just four metres by four, commemorates a miracle, the Milagro de la Virgen de Fátima, which reputedly happened in Sorbas, as reported in the daily *El Yugo* on 5th August 1948. Juana Hernández García, a woman of 70, blind due to cataracts, suddenly regained her sight when the statue of the Virgin was brought into the church. The small building which is now the chapel formerly housed an electricity transformer and was donated to the church in 1950 as a result of the miracle.

The chequered story of Bar Fátima

Opposite the chapel is a squat, sprawling building with a chequered history. At the time of writing it is closed and up for sale, as it has been for several years. But to go back a while, the best part of a century in fact, to the 1920s, it began life as a shack by the side of the 'New Road', the N-340a which had been built in the 1890s to link Almería and Puerto Lumbreras, bypassing the narrow streets of the towns along the way. At some unrecorded point it took on the name Bar Fátima, after the chapel across the road. By the 1970s it was being run by a local character called Cojo Juan, who had one leg, or at least was lame. There is a rumour that he had been a bullfighter, which might tie in with the injured or missing leg. Cojo Juan died in the 1980s so sadly cannot clarify these details. He appeared as an extra in films, and film crews seemed to be attracted to his bar. Members of one crew, working with Michelangelo Antonioni, were even banned from Juan's bar for their excessive behaviour.

This suggests that the standards at Cojo Juan's were high. Maybe, but some of the evidence suggests otherwise. Juan dealt in *jamón* and the entire ceiling of his bar was festooned with hams, each with a little cup attached below it to catch the fat that dripped down. This arrangement didn't always work effectively and Lindy Walsh tells me she recalls being in there, this must have been in 1987 or '88, and having fat dripping down on to the back of her neck from the serried ranks above. The *tapas* were free in Cojo Juan's but the only *tapa* was *jamón*. That might be *jamón y habas*, ham with broad beans, which Karin S. de Boer remembers. Cojo Juan sold the best hams whole though, so the *jamón* in the *tapas* tended to be just the scrag ends, the fatty bits trimmed off around the edges. So much for Juan's food, but Karin also recalls that his home-made wine, which he distributed generously, was pretty much undrinkable too.

When Cojo Juan died at the end of the 1980s, Bar Fátima was taken over by José and Aurora. The standard of the *tapas* improved immediately and they did well for a little while, but then in 1992 the motorway, the A7 Autovía del Mediterráneo, opened and took away all the through traffic at a stroke. The motorway had barely opened, however, when it closed again due to a massive rockfall at Peñas Negras which showered the carriageway with car-sized boulders. It took a few months to clear the problem and ensure there wouldn't be a repeat, before it reopened in 1993.

Bar Fátima was struggling and nearly closed but at this exact time, Lindy and Bill Walsh were establishing their Field Centre at Urrá and they promised José and Aurora that they would bring them customers in the form of groups of thirsty geology undergraduates from British universities. This was enough of a lifeline to save Bar Fátima. In addition, the bar attracted new customers as word spread that you could go there without the risk of fat dripping down your neck.

Susanna Notman tells me she used to go to Bar Fátima when she first lived in the area: "It was our link to the outside world, one of the two places that you could phone the UK from. (The other was Chachos, nowadays called Un Sitio.) The phone was on the wall. You had to give them the number, they'd lift the receiver and make the request (presumably to the local exchange), replace the receiver and then once the connection was made, the phone would ring. There was a ticking mechanism that would time your call. You paid at the end, in pesetas. All the young people from Sunseed at Los Molinos came there to ring home. This would have been about 1999 or 2000. It was a very friendly place and the food was good too."

Aurora and José retired in 2008 and the owner of Bar Fátima found a new tenant, who opened the place as a bar/disco and had a lot of building work done. New parking spaces were made around the back and local rumours of prostitution and drugs circulated, but who knows? Suffice it to say that, if there was a brothel round the back, this was very bad planning because everyone in the casas colgantes looked directly down on any cars that might be parked there. Whatever the truth, Bar Fátima in its disco incarnation didn't last long. It soon closed and has remained shuttered ever since.

In fact, the coming of the motorway affected many businesses, and not just in the town of Sorbas. Many of the old *ventas*, what might once have been called the 'coaching inns', along the Sorbas to Tabernas stretch of the N-340a, succumbed to commercial pressures. The Venta del Compadre is a notable example of a wayside inn that bucked the trend.

After which diversion, it's time to continue the walk. If you pass in front of Bar Fátima, behind a large rock that separates its parking area from the road, you reach a stretch of pavement which will take you all the way back up to your starting point. However, for most of the way this is close to the main road, and also it means that you miss the details of the town, so here's a better idea.

At the base of the Paseo de las Casas Colgantes, opposite the *carpintería*, go immediately left, gently uphill, leaving the main road on your right. Continue left after 60 metres, passing signs to the 'Barrio de las Alfarerías' (Pottery Quarter) and *'cerámica artesanal'* (craft pottery). Opposite here, there is a white-painted private house. On the end wall facing you, almost hidden by the paint, you can just make out the lettering:

A VERA 36 K 200 MS

A LOS CASTANOS 10 K 830 MS

AL CAMINO DE LUBRIN 500 MS

On an inset panel on the front of the house it says PEONES CAMINEROS, solving the puzzle: this was formerly the house of the local road mender.

Continue ahead along Calle Sacerdoté Paco Ayala and just beyond the old folks' keep-fit apparatus, nattily decked-out in red and yellow and usually standing idle, you reach the Ermita de San Roque, dating from the 18th - 19th centuries. A ceramic map outside indicates that behind the church lies the Pottery Quarter. (See the following section for more on this. I have put it there so as not to disrupt the flow of the walk description too much.)

Go down to the right of the church and immediately beyond the Meson La Almazara, an old mill converted into a restaurant that flourished briefly before closing up, is one of the last surviving potteries of Sorbas, the Taller de Cerámica y Alfarería Juan Simón, with its wares on display. Beyond this, on the left, in a short street without a name, is another ceramic panel showing the 'Historia y Tradición' of the pottery quarter. Adjacent is a huge ancient kiln with steps up the outside of it and a plaque announcing that it is a *'Horno Alfarero de origen árabe'*. This is the kiln formerly used by the Simón family. They recall that it was last used in 2005 or 2006. A few steps away are low-walled tanks, about 50 cm deep, stained rich red, where the clay was traditionally prepared prior to being worked.

Retrace your steps back to the Ermita de San Roque and go ahead, uphill, passing a tap set into the wall at the bottom of the slope, hence the name Calle Fuente. This twists steeply up, taking you towards the left side of the post office on Calle Tomas Valera. In a few metres more, look over the black metal railings on the left and there, way down, are the Paseo, the chapel and the main road.

The street immediately behind this view brings you in a couple of minutes to the shade trees and ceramic benches of the town square, the Plaza de la Constitución. The Neo-classical Casa del Duque de Alba was built here in the 18th century. With its current burgundy facade, it is an impressively ornate house, latterly owned by the Valls family, most of whom live elsewhere. Consequently it maintains a silent presence overlooking the square. At right angles to it is another *casa señorial*, with a date panel showing 1893. This building, with an entirely modified interior, is now the light and airy town hall.

Between these two buildings, the Duke of Alba's house and the town hall, there's a small corner with a yellow post-box visible from the main square; here, a scene featuring Jack Nicholson in

Michelangelo Antonioni's film *The Passenger* was shot in 1975. Strange to think that the iconic actor with his distinctive eyebrows and demonic stare was once in this small sleepy town.

The town's church, the Iglesia de Santa Maria, faces the Duke of Alba's house across the square and is a mixture of styles, with *mudéjar* elements from the 16th century, Baroque from the 18th and Neo-classical from the 19th. Take Calle Andalucía, in front of the church, and you will soon pass the indoor Mercado Municipal on the left (the outdoor market here fills the street on Thursdays) and before long be back at the mini roundabout with the lamp-standard. Go right, downhill, to regain the starting point of the circuit.

Barrio de las Alfarerías

The Barrio de las Alfarerías is the Pottery Quarter. The historian Antonio Gil Albarracín has suggested that pottery making in the Sorbas area may date as far back as Neolithic times because of the supplies of excellent clay. However, no archaeological remains have yet been found to prove this. Then we hear nothing until the Catastro de la Ensenada, a survey published in 1752, in which Sorbas had '*seis maestros de alfarero*', six master potters. Confusingly, it then goes on to give details of seven potters, two of whom have the family name Mañas, with two others called Requena, of which more later.

The traveller Simón de Rojas Clemente Rubio, visiting Sorbas in 1805, mentioned that the potters brought their clay from about 15 minutes away, to the right-hand side of the road to Lubrín. At that time there were 24 potteries in the town, and their products had enough of a reputation to be sold as far away as Málaga, Baza and Guadix. By the middle of the 19th century, still with 24 potteries, Sorbas was the major centre for *alfarería* in Almería province, followed by Almería city and Cuevas del Almanzora with ten potteries each, Vera with eight, Níjar with five and Albox with four.

The early years of the 20th century saw the zenith of the pottery trade in Sorbas, with 13 potteries and seven businesses making *objetos refractarios,* such things as firebricks and ovenproof items, listed in the Anuario Riera of 1901, a guide to local industry. In this list of 20 businesses, just six family names appear. Most of these are still very familiar in the local area and, just on a whim, to see how common they are over a century later, I've counted up how many of each are listed under 'Sorbas' in the modern telephone directory. Here are the six family names: Ayala (three businesses in 1901, four in the phone book now), Lario (four in 1901, none now), Mañas (two then, 37 now), Requena (six in 1901, 19 now), Sánchez (two then, 12 now) and finally, Simón (two then, none now).

Hang on a minute, you may well be saying, this proves nothing very much. And you are right: this is a flawed idea for several reasons. First, in 1901, some of the people listed doubled up, making both pottery and refractory goods, so for example, there was only one Sánchez and one Simón, not two of each as the list suggests. More significantly, the totals from the current phone-book are based only on the first family name, and because in the Spanish system each person has two family names, the modern totals may be dramatically skewed, depending on who is the father and who is the mother of the people in the list. Additionally, the phone list for Sorbas is for the whole municipality and not just the town, so it includes folk living in Gacía Alto, Los Castaños, La Mela, Peñas Negras and so on.

And then, even further, more and more people now rely simply on their mobiles and have given up, Telefónica permitting, their landlines. So yes, it's a daft idea and if you haven't followed it, good for you. Nevertheless, I'm inclined to leave it in. And you certainly can't go far in Sorbas in 2016 without seeing the name Mañas. It's on the big forge at the edge of town, on the bus that has the contract for the school run and on the bakery near the post office, for starters.

Going back to the potters, the *alfareros*, there are 21 of them listed in the 1908 census. Amongst the data, there is a column headed: *¿Sabe leer y escribir?* Can he read and write? For eight, the answer was 'Si' and for the others 'No'. So 13 were illiterate, or in the eloquent Spanish word *analfabeto*. By 1930, the situation had improved. Of the ten potters listed, only one was *analfabeto*.

As well as the potters themselves, there were other people whose jobs depended on them. There were families of *carreros*, carriers or carters, who brought firewood, clay and water to the potteries. There were even specialists who packed the finished pots into carts for transport and sale.

Clay was obviously the key factor in the Sorbas pottery industry. There were two types of *arcilla* (clay) found locally, though it tended to be colloquially called *tierra* (earth) rather than *arcilla*. One type was known as *blanca* even though it was light brown rather than white. The other, called *roja* or *rubial*, was 'red earth'. The potters had permission from the landowners to dig it up, obviously, and paid for doing so. Way back it was dug up by hand but now the process, like many others, has been mechanised.

The *tierra blanca* came mostly from Cañada Siscar, very close to the town. It's not named on the local 1:25,000 scale map but the clue is there: a symbol of crossed shovels and the word *arcilla* at grid reference 57861066, close to where the road to Lubrín strikes north. This was used for jugs, jars, bowls, plates, pots and tiles. To give it sufficient strength it is mixed with up to 25% of 'red earth'.

This 'red earth', *tierra roja*, came mainly from La Mojonera, about seven kilometres away. It was used primarily for heat-resistant items like casseroles and oven pots. Before use, the earth was cleaned with plenty of water, to remove impurities, though a certain amount of very fine sand and very fine clay are both needed to make workable clay. It then went into the tanks, like the ones mentioned near the big kiln in the previous section. Here it stayed for between

15 and 25 days, depending on the time of year, for the water to evaporate until it reached the right level of plasticity to be worked. The potters amongst you may well by now have realised that I am not one of you, but I am doing my best.

In recent times the kilns in Sorbas have been fired by oil but for centuries they used fuel collected from the local area. *Aliaga* ('small-flowered gorse' in English) was favoured by the potters as it produced very little ash and dust, but they also used *retama*, *albaida*, thyme, and olive branches. I sent my friend Pete Adeline, an accomplished potter, this section for comment and amongst his feedback was this: 'Country pottery kilns would have been fired with anything combustible available locally, and a lot of it. In the absence of large amounts of wood (or coal) then gorse would have been perfect, as would olive tree prunings or what have you. A fast blaze is ideal; sticks are better than logs, even though a firing can take up to 36 hours. The ash and dust is sucked through the kiln and gets deposited advantageously on the surface of the pots, partially glazing the surface exposed to the flow.' Until relatively recently, but pre-2002 when Spain adopted the euro, Juan Mañas used to buy *retama* from a man from Turrillas for 160 pesetas per sheaf. This, and most of the rest of what I have written here, was gleaned from a series of articles in the journal *El Afa*, N° 10 (2004), a special number focussing on the *Alfarería de Sorbas*. If you read Spanish or are sufficiently interested to work at it, you can find the journal online.

The Sorbas potters left some of their work plain, but increasingly, as tourists became interested, glazed it in a range of distinctive patterns. The Sorbas pottery industry has declined for a number of predictable reasons: the widespread use of plastic, the depopulation of the countryside, and changes in peoples' shopping habits, for example. There is no longer a demand for many of the specialised items the potters used to produce: churns for goat milk, chamber pots, the ceramic jugs attached to waterwheels, 'pigeon pots' in which the birds would roost and nest in the many lofts (*palomares*) in the local countryside and, in November, big jars and bowls for the *matanza*, the annual ritual of pig-killing and processing.

Another factor was the arrival of piped water in houses. Prior to that, large pottery water jars were used and some people even had a full-time job going to the spring, the *fuente*, to collect water for others. Many of the old products of the potters are now items of decoration or curiosity. Tourists remain a significant source of income for the local potteries but sadly, it is clear that the heyday of the Barrio de las Alfarerías is long gone.

Sorbas Canyons

Sorbas Canyons was the name given in 2008 to a project to develop a large classy golf resort close to Sorbas. When the economic crisis hit, no more was heard of the scheme until 2016, when it raised its head again. The plans, which envisage an 80-hectare, 18-hole golf course, with a luxury hotel, holiday apartments, a sports club and 500 detached villas, received approval as part of the town plan. Given existing concerns about water shortages in the area, and the fact that two other local golf courses, Cortijo Grande and Macenas, have been abandoned after becoming insolvent, many people would struggle to agree with the local council's view that this would be a 'very important development' for the town.

Environmentalist Ion Holban, whose survey work on the threatened Río de Aguas is described earlier in these pages, said: "It's very worrying indeed. Golf courses require huge volumes of water and are not considered sustainable even in parts of Spain that still have some water, never mind in Sorbas-Tabernas, right next to the only desert of Western Europe." Sorbas mayor José Fernández Amador says that it would be possible for the scheme to use recycled water: "Sorbas produces enough waste water, which currently discharges into the *rambla* via the water treatment plant, to irrigate the golf course."

Meanwhile, the Irish-Spanish partnership behind the idea, the Sorbas Land Development Company, awaits support from the Junta de Andalucía before proceeding to more detailed planning. The development would no doubt provide some employment for the area but it is hard to see, given the background facts, that this is a viable scheme in such a sensitive environment. Time will tell.

26. Vera

'I remember particularly the sombre, baked and almost organically formed towns of Sorbas and Vera.'
(Christopher North)

A distinctive hill

Dominating the flat lands around Vera is the distinctive conical hill known nowadays as the Cerro del Espíritu Santo (Hill of the Holy Spirit). It's a place with a long history. Working from several different Spanish sources, which in places conflict with each other, this is my attempt to piece together a potted version of that story.

Archaeologists believe that humans have occupied this hill, as a stronghold and refuge, for at least 5,000 years. Remains dating from the Culture of Los Millares (Copper Age, about 3,200 - 2,200 BC) and the Argar civilisation, centred where Antas is now, (Bronze Age, about 2,200 - 1,400 BC) have certainly been found. Other artefacts suggest both Byzantine and Roman occupation of the site. The Moorish settlement of Bayra (the spelling varies: either Bayra or Baira) was built on the ruins left by these older cultures.

In the words of an anonymous medieval traveller, the Hispano-Muslim Vera of many centuries ago looked like this: 'On the eastern coast of the Cora de Bayyana, which had its head at the city of Almería, close to the mouth of the river that the Arabs called Wadi Bair or the Río de Vaira (nowadays called the Río Antas), lies the population and castle of Vaira, built on a mountain and dominating the sea'. In 1243, under the Treaty of Alcaraz, the Río Almanzora became the hypothetical frontier between the Cora de Tudmir and the Cora de Elvira. 'Cora' might be translated as 'County', so for example the Cora de Tudmir was the County of Teodorimo, who was a local bigwig at the time. The fortified settlement at Bayra was the headquarters of one of the 17 agricultural districts into which the Cora de Tudmir was divided. With the frontier nearby, Bayra had important political and defensive functions for the Kingdom of Granada.

A castle or *alcazaba* formed part of the medieval Hispano-Muslim frontier town on the hill during the last centuries of the Nasrid rulers of Granada. Over time it was modified by both Arabs and Christians. The elevated and imposing site controlled both the coast and the network of routes that went inland. The castle was 25 m by 18 m in area with a tall tower. A zigzag path led up to the entrance, a narrow corridor no more than 90 cm wide, in the western flank. In a 1912 study, Paz y Espejo referred to the tower as having the capacity for a garrison of just three or four men.

Archaeological evidence has shown there were several water cisterns in the fortified settlement, of which the largest, an underground tank called the *aljibe-ermita*, was 12.48 m long by 3.40 m wide and 5.23 m high. The four main cisterns could hold 650,000 litres which, in ideal conditions, could supply a population of 600 with about three litres of water each per day for a year.

But conditions were rarely ideal. Unless there had been heavy rain or dew, water supplies had to be brought from elsewhere and then, if it was in the *aljibes* for months on end, problems would arise. Ib-al-Jatib reported that many people had ailments because of the scarcity and poor quality of the water, which became stagnant as it sat in the tanks.

Bayra came under the control of Fernando el Católico, the Catholic monarch Ferdinand, when the Moorish town capitulated on 10th June 1488. It was immediately repopulated with 'old Christians' and six years later, on 16th October 1494, when the German traveller Jerónimo Münzer arrived at Vera, he confirmed that there were only Christians living there. He also said that most of the town was in ruins. It had the feel of a frontier zone because there was the constant risk of attacks from the Moors who had been ejected from the area. Münzer's description shows what Vera was like in the early years after the Christian Reconquest. He mentioned also *'varias fuentes'*, several springs, at the base of the hill, no doubt including the Fuente Chica del Algarrobo, nowadays dry.

Under the Catholic Monarchs, the former mosque had been consecrated and dedicated to Santa María. There was also a castle, and, according to Münzer, around the base of the hill were about 600 houses, evidence that the river, despite being small, was adequate to irrigate the fertile surrounding land. By comparison, Lorca at this time had about 800 houses. In the Archivo Histórico Municipal de Vera there is a document dated 1503, referring to the repair of an inn in the town square, presumably the same one that Münzer had stayed in nine years earlier. In 1505 the Queen of Castilla, 'Juana La Loca', set up a primary school and another school teaching Latin, on behalf of the State.

The 1518 earthquake

Between 11 pm and midnight on 9th November 1518, only about 30 years after Vera had been repopulated by Christians, a devastating earthquake hit the town. We have no way of knowing how it would have registered on the modern Richter scale but it left the town totally ruined. Definitive records show that there were about 600 inhabitants at the time. 150 of them, one in four, were killed and many more crippled. Only the side-chapel of the first Christian church remained standing amid the rubble. Documents from the Biblioteca Nacional de Madrid and the Archivo General de Simancas include the testimonies of seven survivors, written down on 26th November, about two weeks after the event, in front of the mayor, Yñigo de Guevara. These eye-witness accounts paint a vivid picture of the aftermath of the disaster. One of the survivors lived in Huéscar and was visiting his parents when the earthquake struck, killing his parents and burying him. He was pulled from the rubble and lived to tell his tale.

The authorities did everything in their power to sort out the situation, to repopulate the town and bring military forces there because, with the town in ruins, the way was open for the Moors to invade and attack Baza and Lorca. To reconstruct and defend Vera was an urgent matter of national security.

In the Vera archives are two letters from Carlos I to Pope Clemente X requesting help. The key person in the reconstruction efforts was Alonso Fajardo, cousin of the Marqués de los Vélez. He was Vera's town clerk, an educated man of great ability and with good connections. He pushed the Marqués, the Field Marshal of the Kingdom and the King's Mayor, to act quickly, realising that the town had to be rebuilt, whatever the cost. Trenches were dug high on the slopes of the hill known today as Cerro del Espíritu Santo and an invading Moorish force 1,500 strong was stopped with rocks and crossbows in 1523.

With the old town in ruins, a new town was built 'un tiro de ballesta', a crossbow shot, away from the hill on the plain, largely using material from the ruins. The layout was planned in a square pattern, allowing space for 140 houses. The church and public buildings were in the central square, where they are today. There were defensive walls with eight towers and several gateways: the Puerta de Arriba, where the Plaza del Mercado is today, coinciding with the old route to Baza and Granada, and the Puerta de Abajo, now the Plaza del Sol, on the old way to the coast. In addition there was a small gateway by the Convento de San Agustín which linked to the old camino to Almería. Through a further gate led the traditional route to Pulpí and here, in 1605, the Convento de la Orden de Los Mínimos was established.

The church was like a central fort with a tower at each of its four corners. On its facade are three shields: those of Bishop Villalán of Almería, Carlos I and Pope Clemente X, the three people responsible for funding the reconstruction.

Sacred connotations

The 11th century chronicler Al-Humaydi referred to Vera's hill, long before it was known as the Cerro del Espíritu Santo, in his discussions about 'the original mountain' which, in eastern tradition, was a brightly coloured mountain rising from a green sea, with shimmering clarity at its summit. So the notion of this hill having sacred connotations goes back a long way.

Owing to its altitude, just 80 metres above sea level but seeming higher in contrast to the flat plain around it, the hill was once a superb spot for astronomical observations of the night sky and gained a reputation as such. Sadly, this no longer applies because of the light pollution from the widespread settlements on the plain and the night-time illumination of the religious statue on the summit.

Leaping forward to the 20th century, during the Civil War the zone around Vera was Republican and the hill was inevitably converted into a fortified point to defend access to the town from the N-340a, the main road. More or less following the line of the medieval city wall of Bayra, a large trench was excavated halfway up the hill, with a cave dug out as a munitions store.

On 17th July 1949 the image of the Sagrado Corazón de Jesús was unveiled on the summit of the Cerro del Espíritu Santo. The tall, slender statue of Christ, arms spread wide in benediction, now dominates the top of the hill and can be seen from miles around. It has come to be known colloquially as 'El Santo', which some take as a reference to the patron saint of the town, San Cleofas.

More recently, during the project to adapt the hill as a *mirador* (viewpoint) for tourists, information boards were put in place to explain and illustrate various aspects of Bayra's history. There is a wealth of detail, added to which superb sketches by Emilio Sánchez Guillermo give a real sense of how the place must have looked. Budget constraints meant that the second phase of the project never happened and already time and vandalism are taking their toll on the installations, with portions of the wooden guardrails having collapsed and the information boards having been graffitied.

Nevertheless, it's definitely worth taking the well-graded and paved walkway that angles up the hill. It begins opposite the Pabellón Polideportivo Blas Infante, the municipal sports pavilion. Across the road with the black metal railings, the Carretera Almería, and a few metres along, you will see where the path starts. Halfway up is *la ermita,* the Hermitage of the Holy Spirit. It's stone built with an arched roof and tucked into the hillside but unfortunately locked. At the summit, if you are religious, you can have a close-up look at El Santo and, that apart, there is a view in every direction over the plain that stretches away. The immediate foothills are not particularly attractive, with light industrial units and undistinguished modern buildings, but the scale of the panorama is impressive.

On 9th November 2016, for the third consecutive year a group of people who are followers of the 'No Eres de Vera si...' ('You're Not From Vera Unless...') Facebook group, held a commemorative walk up the Espíritu Santo hill. Several were in medieval dress in honour of the 150 victims of the earthquake of 1518. Juan Antonio Soler, suitably attired, played the part of Don Yñigo de Guevara, mayor at the time of the disaster, and read in ancient Castilian from a scroll to mark the event and remember the 150 victims.

Vera now

In his book *Andalucía*, the late Michael Jacobs, writing in the late 1990s, barely mentioned Vera but he did say this: 'One of Vera's very few attractive buildings, a late 18th century warehouse, was recently pulled down to make way for a modern bank'. I think he's being a little hard on the place.

I've been to Vera probably hundreds of times as most Saturdays we go to the market there, and over time I've wandered many of the streets and been to concerts, events and exhibitions. But

I certainly don't claim that I really know the place so, in an attempt to rectify this, in late 2016 I called in to the Tourist Information office in the town hall and asked if they had a town map. "Yes, there's one in the yellow leaflet," said the polite woman behind the counter. I like maps. I'm a geographer and I've been reading and making maps for 50 years. So I can't pull my punches here: as an example of the cartographer's art, the Vera map in the yellow leaflet is dreadful.

It's small and cramped and the print quality is poor, so that even back at home with a magnifying glass I was only just able to make out the detail. According to the key, a pale green line shows the *'ruta turística recomendada'*, a recommended walking route for tourists, but it took me five minutes to even find the cunningly pale green line on the map. There's a dashed line also, more or less forming a square, but there's no mention of this in the key. I'm pretty sure it delineates the bounds of the 'new' town established after the 1518 earthquake. There's no scale on the map either, so you can't get a sense of how long it might take to walk the tourist circuit. The recommended route links some of the town's main features but not all of them and there's no explanation of its rationale. My eyes aren't so great these days but I think most people will struggle with this map. Let's hope that by the time you read this a new and improved version will have appeared

As a consequence, I'm inclined to abandon the map for now, and just mention a few features of the town that I think are worth seeing. I'm no fan of bullfights, so I won't be visiting it but in the interests of completeness, I should record that, in the southeast of the town, Vera has the oldest bullring in Almería province with, inside it, a Museum of Bullfighting. Heading along Calle Mayor from the bullring will bring you into the old centre of the town. In the Plaza Mayor are the Town Hall and the church referred to above, the Iglesia-fortaleza de Nuestra Señora de la Encarnación. The 'fortaleza' part of the name reflects the fortified nature of the church. When it was built it was constantly under threat from Berber pirates.

Just a few metres downhill from the main square is the Convento de Nuestra Señora de la Victoria. It was founded at the beginning of the 17th century by the Minimi order and inhabited by them until 1823. Nowadays, usually just referred to as the Convento, it's a venue for small-scale music events and exhibitions. Further in the same direction, past the Casa Palaciega, one of Vera's few fine buildings, is the Fuente de los Cuatros Caños, the water supply used by the original Moorish inhabitants centuries ago when they still lived on the hill. The public wash-place there has now been converted into a Museum of Water Culture.

In the northwest part of the town, adjacent to the bus station, is the superb, recently opened Teatro Auditorio Municipal, a state-of-the-art venue with superb acoustics. The local council seems keen to make effective use of it, as a consequence of which entry prices are kept low. Check out forthcoming events there and go. I'd be surprised if you are disappointed. Between this new auditorium and the Repsol *gasolinera* at the roundabout, unmentioned in the local tourist literature, is the dramatic Gaudíesque 'Juzgados', the court building. Adjacent, and presumably designed by the same disciple of the unique architect, is another building with similar flourishes. Its ground floor, once home to the Las Candelas Cafeteria Restaurante is, rather sadly, disused at the time of writing.

Back in the town itself, in the Cervecería de las Cañas, a popular watering hole in the warren of streets where the Saturday market is held, there are some photos of old Vera, including a large sepia aerial view of the town in 1950, showing it as a much more compact settlement than it is today. And somewhat bizarrely, the Cervecería de las Cañas has, ranged in a line above the bar, over 20 British beer pump plaques. So, fans of Ruddles County, Spitfire, London Pride and Flowers IPA, amongst others, this might remind you of your local back in the UK apart from the small detail that the beers in question are not actually sold here.

27. Wild visitors

'Miracles happen in nature every day, we just don't pay attention.'
(Rob Cowen)

This chapter begins in our garden, and quite possibly yours too, but I found it gradually drew me further afield, whilst still being entirely grounded in eastern Almería. Here is just a selection of the wild creatures we may encounter.

Common wall lizard

Late one afternoon at the end of May I just happened to see, on the tiled floor in the corner of our living room, a lizard. It wasn't moving and was obviously doing no harm but I realised I had to catch it and take it outside before our cat discovered there was a new toy in the house. I put a large transparent plastic food box over it without incident, then carefully slid one of those thin flexible chopping sheets from the kitchen underneath it. This produced some frantic activity. I took the whole thing outside onto the terrace, put the bright blue chopping sheet on the ground and lifted the box off it. The lizard simply sat there, which was great, as it gave me time to fetch the camera and take a few shots against a dramatic background colour.

Finally, the lizard scuttled off but subsequently the photos allowed me to identify it as a female common wall lizard (Podarcis muralis in Latin, *lagartija roquera* in Spanish). It was only when I looked closely at the pictures that I realised the tail was more than twice as long as the body and the fourth 'toes' on the hind feet were incredibly long, five or six times the length of the inner toes. What an amazing piece of natural engineering. It got me thinking about some of the other wildlife that has graced our house, garden and the nearby *campo* from time to time.

Ocellated lizard

The ocellated or eyed lizard (Lacerta lepida, *lagarto ocelado*) is big enough to be impressive; it is commonly 45 cm long, a foot and a half, including its tail. We used to have them in the garden fairly often but I hadn't seen one here for a year or two until recently, when a young one appeared several times. I had been thinking that, as the garden has developed and the habitat has steadily changed, it no longer suits them, or it might be that they are simply better hidden now there is more vegetation cover. They are definitely still around nearby though: we see them from time to time on the local roads, standing in their characteristic way with the front part of the body raised, as if they are checking out their surroundings, which I guess they are.

The adults are green with hints of yellow, and blue spots along the flanks. Males in particular have a large head with a serrated collar. The young are different but equally distinctive: olive-greenish, patterned with many dark circles with pale centres. When disturbed, they lift themselves onto the full extent of their legs and run off at high speed. They will always tend to avoid humans but can apparently give a nasty bite if cornered.

In Extremadura, ocellated lizards were traditionally considered a culinary delicacy. They would be skinned, sliced thinly, fried in olive oil, mixed with tomatoes, onion and garlic and cooked over a slow fire. This dish, *lagarto con tomate*, seems a terrible end for such a fine creature.

Geckos

We have geckos in and around the house, though I've no idea how many. They secrete themselves away in any number of places, though behind pictures, air conditioning units and external wooden shutters seem to be favourite hideouts. These are mainly Turkish geckos (Hemidactylus turcicus), which doesn't mean they have come from Turkey: it's just their name. They are found widely across the Mediterranean and are sometimes known also as the Mediterranean house gecko. Their wonderful Spanish name is *salamanquesa rosada*. They're pale, with a slightly pink translucent skin and a body covered in many small bumps and speckled with brown patches. The scientific name, Hemidactylus, meaning 'half-finger' in Latin, refers to the fact that the adhesive pads on their feet, uniquely among geckos, do not extend to the ends of the toes. Turkish geckos are mainly nocturnal, hence their prominent dark eyes.

In our wooden shed there is also a substantial colony of geckos. It's not a large shed but it is definitely to the taste of the geckos. These though seem to be mostly Moorish geckos, aka common wall geckos (Tarentola mauritanica, *salamanquesa común*), generally plumper and larger than their Turkish cousins. The common wall gecko has specialised microscopic suction pads known as 'setae', which go right to the end of its toes, allowing it to climb totally upside down on flat ceilings.

The droppings, which are small, dry pellets, are the main disadvantage of having geckos live with you: a small price to pay for the entertainment they provide, I'd say. And of course geckos help to keep the number of irritating insects down. They win every time over a chemical spray in my book.

Scorpions

The *Wildlife Travelling Companion: Spain* says: 'Snakes and scorpions are around, but the possibility of being bitten or stung is very slight'. I was somewhat unfortunate then, to be on the receiving end of a scorpion's sting some time ago. Rather stupidly, I was gathering the fallen leaf-litter from below one of our ficus trees without wearing gardening gloves and I paid the price: a sudden sharp pain on my hand. The offending creature was carefully gathered and thrown across the road into an olive grove. I didn't want to kill it: after all, it was only doing what scorpions do to defend themselves. The pain wasn't actually too bad so, as the nearest medical centre and *farmacia* are both in a town half an hour's drive away, I decided to put up with it and monitor the situation. I should say that this is not the recommended course of action, so 'don't do this at home' as they say, but in my case, after about six hours, the throbbing ache subsided and all was well.

Just to clarify that point, if you *are* stung by a scorpion, this is what you *should* do. First, don't panic. Very few deaths actually occur from such stings. The scorpions found in Almería province, in terms of risk to humans, can generally be put on a par with bees or wasps. Don't try to make the stung area bleed, as this will make things worse. Don't drink anything, especially alcohol, so a stiff brandy is out of the question. Wrap a bandage firmly over the area of the sting, and restrict the movement of the area that was stung. This will keep the venom localised for many hours. Seek medical attention as soon as possible. In other words, to be on the safe side, don't do as I did and just tough it out.

The scorpion that stung me was only about three centimetres long and was the commonest one in Spain, the Mediterranean scorpion (Buthus occitanus), known as *alacrán* in Castellano. They're pale brown or even slightly yellowish (another Spanish name is *escorpión amarillo*). The males can be up to five centimetres long and the females up to seven centimetres. I guess these larger ones might pack more of a punch than the individual that stung me.

There are many scorpions out there but they are nocturnal and usually hide under stones during the day, so they are not normally seen. A wise precaution to take if you are moving stones in your garden is to wear good thick gloves. Rest assured that I learnt my lesson.

Chameleon

When we first bought a house here in 2005 there was no garden to speak of. Slowly, starting from little more than rock and dust on a steep slope, a green oasis of sorts has evolved, with trees, shrubs, flowers and vegetables. We first found a chameleon (Chamaeleo chamaeleon, and *camaleón* in Spanish) in the garden in 2012. Now, over the last year or two, we've seen several or, possibly, the same one on several occasions. But you have to be lucky to spot a chameleon as the camouflage is as effective as it's rumoured to be. If it stays still you almost certainly won't notice it.

On one occasion my wife Troy saw one walking across the gravel, in which situation it's camouflage was no use at all. It carried on, unhurriedly, towards a small fig tree which it slowly climbed. They move deliberately, as if ancient, keeping an eye on you. If they are in a tree or a bush and you are trying to get a decent photo, they seem intent on foiling you, sidling in an apparently clumsy but very effective way behind stems or leaves. A chameleon is basically leaf green but its patterning might involve yellow or brown or black too, to dapple and break up its outline. Where chameleons are to be found, it's entirely possible to walk right by one and not realise it. But this small armoured creature is a treat to see; a chameleon day is a day when you will definitely smile.

Mosquitoes

Common or garden mosquitoes are bad enough, especially if, like me, you are one of those people who react strongly to their bites. The name mosquito (the noun is the same in English and Spanish) comes from the Spanish *mosca* (fly) plus the diminutive '*ito*', hence 'little fly'. There are thousands of species of mosquito in the family Culicidae and, for the record, it is the females that bite.

In the late summer of 2015, councils across eastern Almería received a deluge of complaints about the insects. This followed a period of rain and warm weather in early September which swelled the number of mosquitoes, but a bigger concern was that the Tiger mosquito was identified for the first time in the province, with confirmed reports in several places including Vera and Mojácar. The Tiger mosquito is an invasive south-east Asian species and has white stripes on its head, legs and thorax. More significantly, it is more aggressive than the 'ordinary' mosquitoes that occur naturally in this area.

The damp areas where mosquitoes breed in eastern Almería are sprayed annually by a specialist company using helicopters to deliver a natural biological agent called Bacillus thurigensis, which attacks mosquito larvae. Normally this spraying occurs later in the autumn but the unexpectedly damp weather in September 2015 caught councils on the hop.

Should you be the unhappy victim of the attention of Tiger mosquitoes and you are not totally occupied with trying to avoid or kill them, you can contribute to the advance of science by taking a photo of the offending insect and sending it to www.atrapaeltigre.com, a website set up by ICREA (the Catalan Institution for Research and Advanced Studies), which is tracking the movements of Tiger mosquitoes in Spain.

Pine processionary caterpillars

On the twisty mountain road we have to take every time we go out, there are a few pine trees adding a dash of green to the superficially drab landscape. We have three in the garden too. For several years these looked puny and we weren't convinced that they were going to survive but now, presumably having established a good root network, they are finally putting on height and bulk and looking like real trees. And along with their new status has come an occasional problem: pine processionary caterpillars.

The pine processionary (Thaumetopoea pityocampa) is a silvery-grey moth with black markings, harmless as an adult but potentially dangerous to humans and particularly animals at the larval stage of its life-cycle, in other words, as a caterpillar. The female moth lays its eggs in late summer or autumn, high amongst the branches of pine trees. When the eggs hatch, the larvae (caterpillars) make quite large white silken cocoons technically called 'tents'. These are usually very easy to see in trees that are infected. The caterpillars overwinter in these cocoons, coming out after dusk each night in single file, nose to tail, to feed on pine needles, and returning to their nests before dawn. The cocoons do not have any obvious openings; the caterpillars simply force their way out through the layers of the shelter.

As the caterpillars advance, they lay down a pheromone trail from the tip of their abdomen. Trail marking allows them to cluster at the best feeding sites and also find their way back to their nests. Whilst in the trees the caterpillars are not a danger but when they are ready to pupate, usually in March, they leave their cocoons and move down the trees in their characteristic procession. At this stage they are coming to the ground in order to find soft soil where they can bury themselves in order to pupate. It is during this phase that they can be seen in long lines on the ground. Groups of up to 300 individuals may be found, marching in search of the ideal place to bury themselves.

In 1916 the entomologist Jean Henri Fabre conducted an experiment in which he set a group of pine processionary caterpillars marching around the edge of a pot, in single file, with food just outside the circle. They continued marching in a circle for a week. I have seen mention in one local magazine that, in this situation, the caterpillars will literally go round and round until they starve to death but I haven't found any scientific confirmation that this is true.

The caterpillars have hairs on their bodies which cause extreme irritation to the skin. In their fifth stage (the technical term would be their fifth 'instar') the caterpillars can even eject hairs when threatened or stressed. The hairs are like little harpoons and can penetrate and irritate all areas of exposed skin nearby. Contact with the hairs causes allergic reactions such as skin rashes and eye irritations.

This can be serious for some humans but much more so for dogs. When the paws or other body parts of a dog come into contact with the caterpillars' hairs, they will become severely irritated. The dog's response will be to lick the affected area so, in turn, its tongue will become severely irritated. The tongue may become necrotic, and it may be necessary to amputate the tongue to prevent sepsis and spread of necrosis. Severe reactions to the hairs may also cause kidney failure in the dog, and death may occur. So, don't take your dog for a walk in the pine woods in March, or anywhere where you know or suspect there may be pine processionary caterpillars.

Giving another perspective, the director of the Sierra de Baza Natural Park explained his decision not to treat the pine trees in his area in 2015: "The plague of processionary caterpillars is a natural cycle that comes and goes without harming the trees. Although spraying the trees eliminates the caterpillars in the short term, it also affects other insects and birds. Given that the forest is not near populated areas it is not necessary to control the caterpillars here".

We've had processionary nests in our pines on a few occasions. Our response has been to get suitably geared up (long sleeves, thick gloves, a dust mask), then very carefully cut the affected branches out of the tree, with nests attached, and either dispose of them in a sealed bag or, if the woodstove is on, in go the offending nests. I only recommend you do this if you are confident about your ability to do it, though, and if the nests are easily accessible.

On the positive side, pine processionaries do have natural predators. Ephippigers (bright green bush crickets) eat the eggs, birds such as great tits and great spotted cuckoos eat the caterpillars, hoopoes eat the pupae and bats eat the adults but for humans and their dogs the best advice is: when you see these caterpillars, avoid them.

Wild boar

Just below the summit of the lowest of the three hills that flank our valley, there's an almond plantation. I was up there one summer's evening, contouring across between the trees on my way towards the drystone column that marks the top of the hill when I came across a huge area of newly-turned rich red earth. It's often evident that wild boar (Sus scrofa in Latin, *jabalí* in Spanish) are present in an area not from sightings of the animals themselves but from clues like this that they leave behind, patches of disturbed ground where they have been digging for roots. I've found such diggings within 50 metres of our front gate on some occasions. My editor Helen Evans, when she saw this, said: "We have a family of wild boar who come past our house regularly at about 1a.m. during the height of summer, scrumping the low hanging almonds as they ripen on the trees."

There are reckoned to be about half a million wild boar in Spain and some 60,000 – 100,000 are killed by hunters each year. In the dry south-east of Spain they are considered to be scarcer than in other areas because boars don't have sweat glands to cool themselves and so they rely on wallowing in areas of wet mud, not a common feature in eastern Almería.

Hunting wild boar can involve unexpected hazards though. In 2006 a hunter died near the historic Cortijo del Fraile by falling down an uncovered well, nearly 3 metres in diameter but hidden by vegetation. He was on an authorised night-time hunt, with two companions, looking for wild boar, when the incident occurred. The company that owns the *cortijo* had granted permission for the hunt. Nine years after the fatal accident, a court found the owners of the *cortijo* and one of their employees guilty of negligence for not having covered or marked the position of the well, despite knowing that

264

nocturnal hunting was taking place there. Both defendants were given a one-year suspended sentence and ordered to pay compensation of 150,000 euros to the victim's family.

As the previous paragraph indicates, wild boar are nocturnal, spending the day hiding in cover, so your likeliest chance of seeing them is at night. This might lead to a problem when you're driving home in the dark because a change to the traffic laws in 2014 means that in many instances when a car and an animal collide, the driver is responsible. The wild boar mating season begins in November and December. At this time males will search for a receptive female and will become more active and aggressive.

In twelve years in Spain I've seen wild boars on average maybe once a year. Several of these were whilst I was on foot and the others whilst I was driving. I've been lucky because sometimes a boar will run right out in front of a car. In the five years up to 2013, according to the traffic police, the DGT, there were 673 accidents in Spain involving wild boar, which led to 58 human fatalities.

In certain circumstances drivers are not considered responsible for such collisions: if the wild boar is being hunted at the time, if the road is fenced but the fence has been damaged so that animals can get on to the road, or if there are no signs indicating the possibility of wild animals crossing. Other than that, if you hit a wild boar, it's your fault. Some insurance policies don't cover you for such collisions either, and as a wild boar is big enough to cause serious damage to your car, it might be worth checking your policy. It's a slim chance that this will happen to you though; it is more likely that you will have a fleeting view of a wild boar in the headlights or glimpse one trotting across a hillside just before dusk and feel privileged at seeing such a fine creature.

Having written all of that, perhaps I was feeling complacent. 16th March 2017, I'm driving home on a sunny afternoon. I've just come off the motorway and am heading downhill towards Peñas

Negras, doing about 70 kph, which is normal for that stretch of road. One second, there's an open road; the next second, there's an enormous boar running into the road, right to left, just a few metres ahead of me. I jam on the brakes, swerve and hit the animal with a solid thud. It seems at the same time as if the incident has been slowed down and yet is over almost before I've realised what is happening. The car continues to skid round and ends up facing back uphill, off the road and on the sloping gravel verge. For a moment I'm convinced it's going to roll. I get out, heart pounding. Of the boar, there is no sign. As for the car, part of the plastic housing near the front grille is cracked and the number-plate is rather battered, but otherwise it seems okay. I drive home, slowly and carefully, my brain trying to compute that, in broad daylight, this has really happened, and given that it has, all parties involved, hopefully, have been lucky and have escaped unhurt.

Ibex

The Spanish ibex (Capra hircus in Latin) is, as the Spanish name *cabra montés* indicates, a mountain goat. Thinking to write something about ibexes (the plural ibices is also correct if you prefer it), I confidently looked it up in *Collins Complete Mediterranean Wildlife* only to find it's not mentioned. Next stop the *Travelling Wildlife Companion: Spain*, which says this: 'Rare, confined to summits of high sierras where it shows amazing ability to maintain footing on precipitous mountainsides. Almost extinct until King Alfonso XIII controlled hunting in 1905'. So perhaps it is this supposed rarity that kept the ibex from inclusion in the Collins book.

This is rather a surprise, as ibexes, whilst not being common, are definitely not rare here, though their preferred habitat is steep slopes and cliffs in hilly areas. I've seen groups of them near Polopos, in the El Nacimiento area upstream from Los Molinos del Río de Aguas and on the slopes above Rambla Honda near Lubrín.

The fact that they are not rare in our area was confirmed by an unfortunate incident at the latter location in the summer of 2014, when three ibexes were killed by hunters in full view of children. Local farmers had applied to the department of the environment for, and subsequently been granted, a temporary licence for one month, to cull ibexes which they said were damaging their almonds and olives.

One Saturday evening that August, Rambla Honda resident Karen O'Hagan heard shots nearby, went outside, and found half a dozen hunters dragging a dead ibex down the hill very close to her house. The hunters were in fact the same farmers who had applied for the licence. On being asked what was happening, they responded aggressively, saying: "This is what we do, this is our sport". The hunters did have the licence and were not doing anything illegal but their answer suggested their motive was not primarily a concern for the wellbeing of their crops. Their attitude is a common one amongst hunters in the country areas of Almería. They brazenly go wherever they wish to, taking no account of private land or other people's opinions. I've had conversations with several people who have had altercations with hunters who have come right up to and past their houses in pursuit of their quarry with no thought of seeking permission first.

Ms O'Hagan and her two young daughters had, prior to this, been following the progress of a female ibex and its two young. She said: "They used to come right up to our house in the mornings. We would see them every time I took the girls to school." In fact the girls had seen the shooting from their bedroom window and were, according to their mother, "inconsolable". The hunters claimed there were up to 40 ibexes in the area but Ms O'Hagan said she estimated that there were about 16. On the occasion I saw ibex there, before this incident took place, there was a group of about eight moving elegantly across the rocky slopes high above the houses, pausing briefly in silhouette on the skyline, and then gone.

I contacted Karen O'Hagan when I was finalising this chapter in early 2017 and she added to my account, saying:"I raised a petition in the village and the support from locals both native and foreign was quite extraordinary." No further culls have taken place since 2014, and Karen goes on to say: "It's good to see the ibex around here again and looking healthy with all the greenery sprouting everywhere. They are still hanging around and rubbernecking us from the top of the mountain as to our comings and goings...good times again."

Monk parakeets

A survey by the organisation SERBAL in March 2016 found over 50 monk parakeet nests in Almería province and estimated a population of about 120 birds, at sites including Almería city, Aguadulce, El Toyo, Mojácar, Puerto Rey and Huércal-Overa. Gilly Elliott-Binns also told me a while ago about a small flock that was resident in a *rambla* near Urcal, north of Huércal-Overa, though I don't know if the birds are still there. Monk parakeets (Myiopsitta monachus) are bright green with soft grey underparts and a hooked orange bill. A couple of years earlier the newspaper *El País* announced that monk parakeets were being seen as a plague in many Spanish towns, with about 20,000 in the country as a whole. They were first detected in the wild in Spain in Barcelona in 1975 and now they are considered a major environmental problem.

It all started when people began to keep them as pets. Over time some escaped or were deliberately released and they gradually established viable feral populations, to the extent that they are now found in about 450 Spanish locations mainly, though not entirely, in towns and cities. They are native to the subtropical parts of Argentina (in Spanish they are known as the 'Argentinean parrot') and have adapted easily to the similar climate found particularly in southern

Spain. They prefer urban areas, rather as the colonies of rose-ringed parakeets do that are now living happily in various British cities. They are typically found in highly visible and very loud groups. I recall seeing a screaming flock of them hurtling across the sky in Málaga a few years ago.

In 2013 monk parakeets were included on a list of destructive species but according to Juan Carlos del Moral of the SEO (the Spanish equivalent of the UK's Royal Society for the Protection of Birds) it would cost an awful lot of public money to eliminate them. Even though they look attractive, del Moral says this exotic species is causing "a negative impact on Spain's natural fauna and flora." For example, they disturb the nests of other birds and have been blamed for damaging trees because they eat their shoots and buds.

A SERBAL spokesman says the population has grown steadily since they were first seen in Almería province in the 1990s. So should you see a bright green bird that screeches, or more likely a flock of them, they'll almost certainly be monk parakeets. And it seems they are here to stay.

28. This one will run and run

"The real problem is that the Almería AVE was a mere election pledge, not a serious project ever intended to bear fruit." (Manuel Jiménez Barrios)

The Algarrobico Hotel

As I check through this chapter in early 2017 a monstrous, disused white ziggurat still stands immediately behind the Playa del Algarrobico near Carboneras where, in 1962, a replica of the Jordanian town of Aqaba was built for the film *Lawrence of Arabia* on what was then an unspoilt stretch of coastline. But more recently a dispute has rumbled on for over a decade about the legality of the incomplete and infamous Algarrobico hotel. Permission was given in 1988 to build a hotel here but at that stage nothing was done. Then in 1997 the site was included in the newly-established Cabo de Gata-Níjar Natural Park. Only in 2003 did the developers, Azata del Sol, decide to go ahead with the construction. The project was then halted in 2006, with the hotel virtually finished, when the Junta de Andalucía revoked the building licence, and it has remained paralysed ever since. (For a fuller version of the saga, see *Flamingos in the Desert*.)

Meanwhile, a long sequence of court cases has come and gone involving, variously, Carboneras Town Hall, the developers, the Junta de Andalucía, the central government, and environmental groups such as Greenpeace. One of the key legal decisions came in March 2012, when the Andalucían high court (the TSJA) ruled that the hotel broke the Ley de Costas, the Law of the Coasts, which in simple terms deems that building within 100 metres of the high tide line is illegal. At its closest the hotel is just 14 metres from the sea. Following this the central government and the regional government (the Junta de Andalucía) agreed to split the cost of demolishing the hotel and restoring the site.

It was a massive surprise to everyone when, in March 2014, this same body, the TSJA, inexplicably ruled that the land occupied by the hotel is 'zoned for building'. This decision was in response to an appeal by Azata del Sol against the land having been classified as 'protected' in 2008. The press described the new ruling as a 'bombshell verdict' and 'a disgrace'. One newspaper set out the history of the case under the headline 'Timeline to a travesty'. Law suits were filed by three environmental groups – Ecologistas en Acción, Salvemos Mojácar and Levante Almeriense - against the three judges involved for 'issuing an unjust sentence in contradiction to preceding decisions'. These law suits were subsequently thrown out.

Then in September 2014 Azata del Sol failed to turn up for a meeting at which it had been due to sign over the deeds for the land on which the disputed 400-room hotel stands. The Junta de Andalucía's environment ministry had been led to believe that the developers were going to agree to the Junta repurchasing the land for €2.3 million. Azata is holding out for €70 million in compensation. For the Junta, environment minister María Jesús Serrano said it would use "all administrative and judicial avenues at its disposal" to prevent Azata from restarting construction work. In a move that muddied the waters still further, Azata then produced documents showing that the company that had originally sold it the land was Parque Club El Algarrobico, a company whose major shareholder was called the Society for the Economic Advancement and Modernising of Andalucía (Soprea), in which the Junta had an interest.

July 2015 saw Supreme Court judge Rafael Fernández Valverde announce, with reference to outstanding actions on the hotel, that he would be able to "issue all four sentences at the same time" and "make a final ruling as to whether the hotel would be demolished or opened to the public" in September. The Algarrobico hotel meanwhile featured in a list published in the UK by the *Daily Telegraph* of 23 of the world's ugliest hotels. The pictorial feature in the *Telegraph*'s travel section described the hotel as "a white eyesore" and suggested its "sheer ugliness" should have been enough to qualify it as illegal.

September 2015 came and went without a final court ruling but then eventually, on 10th February 2016, a definitive judgement was handed down by the Supreme Court. The Algarrobico hotel was at last determined to have been built on land that could not be urbanised, meaning that it must be demolished. The Supreme Court also concluded that the building stood on land owned by the Junta de Andalucía, which had exercised a contractual right to buy back the land from Azata del Sol for €2.3 million.

The Supreme Court did not pronounce on the €70 million compensation claim brought by the developers against the Spanish government, the regional government and Carboneras council. This matter was left to be dealt with by the regional high court. The Supreme Court's ruling also did not cover the timing and method of demolition of the hotel. The Junta de Andalucía said it will finalise its €2.3 million buy-back option for the land, then liaise with the environment ministry of the central government to carry out the demolition, which estimates suggest will cost about €7 million.

Predictably, Greenpeace celebrated the decision as "an historic day for the fight to save the environment". Equally predictably, the mayor of Carboneras, Salvador Hernández, said his council "regretted the waste of time and loss of employment opportunities" on a project that "could have benefitted the whole area."

In a bizarre twist, just a couple of weeks before the Supreme Court made its ruling, Carboneras council presented a promotional video at the annual *Fitur* tourism fair in Madrid, in which the Algarrobico hotel seems to have been airbrushed out of existence. In the four-minute video, which includes aerial footage, there are several views of the Algarrobico area but the camera angles are such that there is no sign of the unfinished concrete monstrosity.

In March 2016 the first meeting took place of a new board, consisting of members of both the national government and the Junta de Andalucía, that was set up to take care of the necessary procedures for demolition. The board confirmed there would be "no turning back" on the demolition and said that the Madrid government would pay half of all the costs involved. A year later, nothing concrete (pun intended) has happened.

The AVE

Work on the long-awaited high speed rail (AVE) line from Murcia to Almería had gone dormant by the summer of 2013. The link will be 184 kilometres long, of which 108 are in Almería province, assuming it comes to fruition. (See *Flamingos in the Desert* for the back story.) In 2013 no money was available for further work and nothing was happening. Then in May 2014 the public rail infrastructure company ADIF sealed the two parallel 7.6 kilometre long Sorbas tunnels on safety grounds. The tunnels had already been completed at a cost of €291 million and formed the most complex of the four finished sections of the line within Almería province. They hit the news again in late 2016 when a man was arrested after being caught red-handed by security guards in one of the tunnels, in possession of a circular saw and a generator, in the process of stealing copper and other materials.

At a conference in September 2014 the chairman of the Almería Chamber of Commerce, Diego Martínez Cano, complained angrily that since 2009 neither ADIF nor the Spanish Ministry of Transport had shown anything other than complete indifference to the project, part of the overall Corredor Mediterráneo linking France and Algeciras. Only 27% of the works had been completed.

Late 2014 also saw the central government announcing that the link would be reduced from a double to a single line, only to cave in to huge pressure from the business community a few weeks later and agree that the AVE would have provision for a double track. The government's delegate in Almería, Carmen Crespo, said however that the final decision would be subject to "reasonable criteria in the use of public funds and service efficiency". This was interpreted as saying that the project might still revert to single track, with the double track stretches that had already been built being used for overtaking to increase capacity.

In March 2015 the government invited tenders for the 12.5 kilometre section of track between Pulpí and Cuevas del Almanzora. The expected cost was €86 million, with a build time of two years. The new stretch of line was to include a 420 metre long viaduct over the Canalejas *rambla* and a 180 metre long 'false tunnel' to allow the crossing of animals. A double track width was promised but, initially at least, with just one line. This section would not be connecting to other sections at either end but at least it would signal renewed intent on the part of the government. The contract was subsequently awarded.

Some thought that this new initiative was not unconnected with the national elections, due towards the end of 2015, and the wish by the Spanish Minister of Transport, Ana Pastor, to be photographed alongside a JCB as the new works began, to keep her name in the public eye in the run-up to voting.

In a further twist also linked to the elections, Rafael Hernando, the Partido Popular (right-wing) government delegate for Almería, claimed that the first AVE trains could arrive in Almería in 2018, but only if people "concerned about rail travel" voted for his party in the December 2015 general election. Sr Hernando did not explain why there had been so little AVE progress during his party's current term in power. Responding to his claim, rail experts consulted by the Spanish newspaper *Ideal* dismissed his suggestion as impossible, given the amount of infrastructure still to be built, and said the earliest realistic date "would be 2024 and more likely the late 20s". As if to back this up, in February 2016 work stopped on the stretch between Pulpí and Cuevas del Almanzora.

Another blow came in November 2016 when the construction company Sacyr announced that it wanted to break the contract it had won in September 2015 to build the stretch of line through the Cuevas del Almanzora area on the grounds that the national government had still not completed the expropriation process and that the terms of the agreement had changed in the meantime. This led to a predictable outburst of bickering amongst politicians, producing the quote shown at the beginning of this chapter.

In early 2017, it was revealed that five companies awarded contracts to build sections of the Almería - Murcia line had rescinded their tenders, saying that they are losing money because of the abandoned contracts. It also emerged that ADIF had reassigned over €150 million allocated for the coastal AVE to pay for extensions to two of Madrid's main railway stations.

When the Murcia – Almería AVE might be up and running is one question. Whether there will then ever be a link onwards from Almería to Granada is another. Maps of the projected national AVE network show this as an intention for the future but meanwhile, to switch modes of transport for a moment, the final 10.5 kilometre piece of the A7 motorway jigsaw slotted into place on the coast of Granada province in October 2015.

The motorway along the Granada coast, a particularly rugged and difficult challenge for the engineers, took many years to complete. In Granada province alone, the A7 has viaducts totalling about seven kilometres and tunnels covering ten kilometres. The final section cost €113.5 million, some three times as much per kilometre as the cost of a motorway in more conventional terrain. The main significance of the new link for residents of Almería is perhaps that it opens up access to Málaga airport as a possible option for flights.

Tortoise chaos

What have tortoises to do with a high-speed rail line? Read on and all will become clear. In 1995 a law was passed to give protection to spur-thighed tortoises (Testudo graeca in Latin, *tortuga mora* in Spanish). This specified a fine for keeping a tortoise as a pet, but on 1st July 2015 an amendment to this law came into effect, prohibiting the keeping of such tortoises on pain of a prison sentence of between six months and two years, in addition to a substantial fine. Some weeks prior to this an amnesty had been announced. The tortoises in question are classified as 'vulnerable' under the IUCN Red List of threatened species and 'in danger of extinction' in Andalucía. The result of the amendment to the law was that, across Almería province, some 2,000 tortoises were handed in through Seprona, the wildlife protection section of the Guardia Civil. In Turre alone 250 tortoises were brought in. Environment councillor Martin Fuentes said they would be given a check up and then be released into the nearby Sierra Cabrera mountain range.

Generally, all tortoises handed in in Almería go to CREA (a wildlife rehabilitation centre) in Vélez Blanco. Here they undergo a health check and are kept in quarantine for a while before being released back into their natural habitat. According to CREA, tortoises that have been pets will easily adapt to life in the wild. However, according to the provincial agriculture ministry in Murcia, only healthy tortoises kept in captivity for less than a fortnight and whose genes can be verified, should be released back into the wild. It is not clear which of these standpoints is correct.

Hermann Schleich, who runs the Arco tortoise sanctuary in Tabernas, reported a significant increase in tortoises being handed in and added: "This is making things quite difficult as we receive no government funding and have to pay for transport to take the creatures to the centre in Vélez Blanco".

In a linked development, at more or less the same time, the central government published plans to expropriate a swathe of land for the construction of the 12.5 kilometre stretch of the AVE railway between Cuevas del Almanzora and Pulpí. This was to involve the demolition of many properties. A key issue was that some of these properties were on 500 hectares of land designated as a spur-thighed tortoise reserve which would compensate for areas of natural tortoise habitat which would be lost to the AVE line. The intention was that this new reserve would link two areas of prime tortoise habitat in the Sierras of Aguilón and Almagrera already owned by the government. The Ministry of the Environment had apparently allocated €20 million for this.

Not surprisingly, uproar resulted. 'Are tortoises more important than people?' was the cry. Mayor of Cuevas del Almanzora, Antonio Fernández totally rejected the government's plans and said the council would propose an alternative that would not affect residents but would still protect the tortoises' habitat. A group of property owners met with the government secretary general for infrastructure, Manuel Niño, in Madrid, after which the government agreed to look at the alternative proposals. The issue continued to rumble on though. Locals in the Los Lobos area, where the compulsory purchase of 200 properties had raised its head again, staged a protest in the autumn of 2016, blocking a major road with 50 tractors and 20 lorries. At the time of writing the issue remains unresolved.

An entirely different tortoise tale concerns the €600,000 spent back in 2008 by the Junta de Andalucía constructing the Casa de las Tortugas (House of the Tortoises) near Bédar. This was intended to support the 'conservation, rescue and breeding' of spur-thighed tortoises. The premises, which include extensive gardens and tortoise enclosures, together with a vet's surgery, store room, conference room, reception area and restaurant, were completed in 2011 and handed over to Bédar council for them to run but by then neither the council nor the Junta had funds to cover the ongoing costs.

In late 2015, it transpired that about 50 spur-thighed tortoises were living at the Casa de las Tortugas and were being looked after on an informal basis by a town hall employee. The mayor of Bédar, Angel Collado Fernández, explained that people had handed them in since the new law had come into force. They were being cared for temporarily at the Casa de las Tortugas until they could be taken to the Vélez Blanco rescue centre. He did not know when that would happen but he did confirm that the current state of the finances mean that the Casa de las Tortugas is still not viable, so there are no plans to open it officially at present.

The first local criminal prosecution under the new law occurred in early 2016 when, acting on a tip-off, police seized 16 spur-thighed tortoises that were being kept in the front garden of a house on the outskirts of Turre. The animals were sent to CREA and the individual who lived in the property, and who did not have a permit to keep the tortoises, was charged with environmental crimes.

Proyecto Testudo is an annual census of tortoises in 12 breeding areas across the south-east of Spain. It is co-ordinated by Elche University. The 2016 census reported that spur-thighed tortoises seemed to be thriving. In fact, tortoise numbers in the Sierra Cabrera around Turre had more than doubled since the previous year. A spokesperson for SERBAL, which conducted the Turre survey said: "We came across many released pets. It is easy to tell they were kept at home, as many have shell defects that come from poor nutrition caused by too much lettuce and tomato. The good news is that the animals appear to be doing well."

29. The Moorish influence

'To me, Almería felt almost like an extension of Morocco, a foothold across the Mediterranean.'

(Jason Webster)

Mesón Gitano

16th June 2016. It's my wife Troy's birthday. For the evening she's spotted a couple of things in Almería that sound interesting. The first is the opening of an exhibition of paintings by Manu Muñoz at the Galería Acanto at 9 p.m. and then a free concert by the Tetuán Asmir Ensemble at the Mesón Gitano at 10 p.m. We have rustled up some friends who are interested and we meet up for *tapas* before searching out the gallery. It proves easy enough to find and we get there just about 9 p.m., which is a good strategy as the gallery space is tiny. The free drinks are being poured and the nibbles have just appeared; even better. We manage to see Muñoz's dreamlike birds - ibises, roseate spoonbills and swans - reflected in water with swirls of dusk clouds before the room is so full that it's time to squeeze out.

We know the Mesón Gitano is somewhere near the Alcazaba so we walk that way, cutting through the streets. As we get closer and turn a corner I see a couple just behind us and tell them we're looking for the Mesón Gitano. The guy enthusiastically takes my arm and says: "We're going there. We'll take you." He says we need to go up a gear as the concert will be starting, so we walk faster. I tell him it's Troy's birthday and he's delighted. He talks of champagne, his wife kisses Troy on the cheeks. I'm wondering if we'll get in. We've never been to Mesón Gitano but it means something like 'Gipsy Inn' and the publicity says *'Entrada libre hasta completar aforo'*, free entry until the limit has been reached. Will there still be room for us? By now we are walking along a new stretch of road with the floodlit walls of the Alcazaba towering above us to the right. We can hear the strains of Arabic music above us too; they *have* already started.

Finally we get to the correct set of steps, several flights, which lead up to a huge flat area with a stage a hundred metres away. On the left, in the bedrock of the cliff on which the Alcazaba was built, is a line of old caves. Ahead, there are endless rows of white plastic chairs. The front rows are occupied but there's loads of room. I later discover that this huge development, in which both Almería city council and the Junta de Andalucía were involved, not without controversy and complications, is on the site of a former bar and a warren of old caves and this is where the name Mesón Gitano comes from. The bar and caves were obliterated in the redevelopment; a fact that still rankles in some quarters.

We find places and settle in to hear the four piece band, dressed in flowing white garments and already deep into their music. Amin Chachoo is lead singer and plays the violin, holding it vertically on his thigh. The other three play oud, qanun (a traditional Middle Eastern stringed instrument related to the psaltery and dulcimer) and darbuka (a goblet-shaped single headed hand-drum) and contribute harmony vocals. In between the pieces, Amin explains that these are instrumentals and songs from the time of al-Andalus, when by and large the Muslim, Jewish and Christian communities of Spain lived in harmony, with influences of all three cultures finding their way into the music. He adds that they are just playing fragments, as in al-Andalus a song would typically last three hours. "When we listen to a song of al-Andalus, we can detect in it a strong medieval Iberian component and also an eastern Arabic component," adds Mehdi Chachoo, the oud player. Their explanations give a welcome extra dimension to the concert and it seems entirely natural to be sitting on a warm evening, under the huge walls of a Moorish fortress, listening to this music that integrates the great ancient cultures of Spain.

Two books

The subtitle of **Jason Webster's** 2004 book *Andalus* is 'Unlocking the Secrets of Moorish Spain'. Though factual, it's written in a gripping way, especially at the beginning, where the author and his Moroccan friend Zine are escaping from a seriously threatening situation in an industrial greenhouse. Webster travels around Spain, often in the company of Zine, with whom he has a complex relationship, in his 'attempt to understand Spain's unique character: a culture which appeared to have been formed by two ostensibly opposed religions.' He has a couple of chapters specifically about Almería, and his impression of it is highlighted above, at the start of this chapter.

He records that, after the Reconquest, Christian landowners had a saying: *"Quien tiene moro tiene oro."* This suggested that North Africans were good workers, more or less 'worth their weight in gold'. And watching a modern Moors and Christians pageant, he says it 'was a neat and simple story that masked the complexities of who the Spanish really were.' The whole book is worth reading as a popular attempt to give a sense of the Moorish flavour that is not always obvious but is nevertheless a key ingredient of Spain, especially in the south. Phil Maillard, in his unpublished but fascinating 16,000 word essay *English Writers on Andalucía* captures the nature of the book neatly: '*Andalus* is a road book starring Jason Webster and his shadow-mate Zine, strangers in a strange land, buddies in pursuit of the ever-receding horizon, as archetypal as Kerouac and Cassady, or Tom Sawyer and Huck Finn, the meaning residing as always in the intimacies and difficulties of the journey rather than in any possible arrival.'

There's not much about Almería in *In The Glow Of The Phantom Palace* by the late **Michael Jacobs** but he also is trying to track down Spain's Moorish past, travelling from Granada to Timbuktu as he does so. It's a mix of travelogue, history, imagination and fiction, with a lot of the author himself in the text. I like Michael Jacobs' writing and I found this book engaging. It's as if he writes well even when there seems to be very little to write about. Phil Maillard thinks: 'There's something 'On-The-Roadish' about this journey. How much is fact and how much fiction is part of Jacobs' game with us. His characters – the bitchy, keep-them-on-a-string Moorish Queen and the wildly adolescent Harry – are probably all aspects of Jacobs himself, buried but still alive beneath the respected academic.'

The Moorish influence

Muslims ruled most of the Iberian Peninsula from 711 AD until their final expulsion in 1492. That word, expulsion, sounds rather final but the Moors had been here, influencing agriculture, architecture, learning and language for almost 800 years, interbreeding with the previous population, so it is no surprise that many words in modern Spanish come from *los Moros*, as they are usually called in Spain.

The parts of Spain with the longest history of Moorish domination have a greater number of words of Arabic derivation in common use. Andalucían Arabic is recognised as rather different to classical Arabic, perhaps in the way American English differs from UK English, with words and usages having diverged over the centuries. There are estimated to be about 4,000 words in Spanish based on Arabic, some 8% of the total Spanish dictionary. The definite article, 'the', is 'al' in Arabic, and it is always attached to the noun. At least, that is my understanding, with apologies to Arabic scholars out there who may know that the reality is more complex than that. Hence we have Almería, which may have originally been 'al-Mirayah', the mirror, or 'al-Meraya', the watchtower. Experts disagree on this but whichever it is, it is definitely Arabic, as is its Moorish fortress, the Alcazaba, meaning 'palace' from 'al qasbah' meaning 'the quarter'. Straying slightly further afield, Granada's Alhambra is from 'al-hamra', meaning 'the red one'.

When you arrive in Spain you may be stopped at customs, *aduana*, from the Arabic 'diwan'. If this proves stressful, you might feel the need for a drink. *Alcohol*, the same in Spanish as in English, comes from the Arabic 'al-kahul' and after that, you may want a sleep. The pillow on which you lay your head is an *almohada*, 'al-makhada' and will almost certainly be made of cotton or *algodón*, 'al-qutun'. Or maybe you'd prefer an iced soft drink, *sorbete* in Spanish, from the Arabic 'sharba', whence also come the English words sherbet and sorbet.

The bricklayer or construction worker who built your house was an *albañil*, from 'al-banni', and that building he made nearby for storing things is an *almacén*, 'al-majzan'. The mayor in your local town hall, where you go for your building permit, is the *alcalde*, from 'al-qadi', meaning judge.

Out in the countryside the Moorish legacy is felt too. A small village or hamlet is an *aldea*, 'al-day'a'. As mentioned elsewhere in these pages, water channels are *acequias*, from 'al-saqiya' which, translated literally, means 'the irrigator'. That sandy stretch of dry riverbed which is *rambla* in Spanish is 'ramla' in Arabic. A carob tree is an *algarrobo*, 'al-kharouba', and those oleanders planted all along the central reservation of the motorway are *adelfa*, 'ad-difla'. The wild boar that might break in and trash your garden if you're unlucky is a *jabalí*, 'jebeli'. You take your olives, *aceitunas*, 'az-zeituna' to the olive press, the *almazara*, 'al-ma'sarah', for processing, and the oil you take away is *aceite*, 'az-zeit'. As for Spain's famous femme fatale, Carmen, it seems to derive from the Arabic 'carmen' meaning when you have both a garden and an orchard with your house.

Down at the coast of Cabo de Gata there are well-known salt lagoons, *albufera*, from 'al-buhaira' with alongside, the village of Almadraba de Monteleva. The cubic white houses of that village and many others nearby are very typically North African. An *almadraba* was a particular Moorish fishing technique involving trap-nets. Birders may know that the Spanish for a shrike is *alcaudon*, 'al-kaptan', and for gannet, *alcatraz*, 'al-qatras'.

283

In the restaurant your *paella* will contain rice, *arroz*, from 'ar-ruzz' and saffron, *azafrán*, 'az-za'faran'. As for those meatballs, they are *albondigas*, 'al-banadiq'. Sugar, as most people know, is *azúcar*, but that too comes from the Arabic 'sukkar'.

The market is the place you really can't escape Arabic. Here are just some examples: apricot is *albaricoque*, 'al-barqouq'; spinach is *espinacas*, 'isbinaj'; aubergine is *berenjena*, 'bidinjan'; artichokes are *alcachofas*, 'al-harshoof'; orange is *naranja*, 'nāranja'; chard is *acelgas*, 'as-silqa'; basil is *albahaca*, 'habaqah'; watermelon is *sandía*, 'sindiya'; and carrots are *zanahorias*, 'safunariyya'. There are more but that will do for now.

In the wider Spanish language common words from Arabic include *barrio* or *barriada*, meaning area or neighbourhood, from 'barri' which itself means 'outside'. *Usted*, the polite Spanish for you, is too similar to the Arabic honorific 'ustadh' for mere coincidence, surely. Zero is *cero* from 'sifr'. That marinade they use for tinned fish, *escabeche*, is from 'as-sukbaj'. A corner is a *rincón*, 'rukan'. Fruit juice is *zumo*, 'zum'. Cough syrup is *jarabe*, 'sharba'; a potter is an *alfarero*, 'al-fah har'; a rug or carpet is an *alfombra*, 'al-húmra' and a clay brick is *adobe*, 'at-tuba'. The preposition *hasta*, until, comes from 'hatta'. Then there's *ojalá*, meaning hopefully, coming from 'wa sha Allah', 'should God will it', and finally, for now at least, *olé* and, some think, also *hola* from 'wa-Allah', 'by Allah!'.

Place-names

The derivation of Almería's place-name has been mentioned above but there are plenty more places that betray their Moorish origins. Albox comes from the Arabic for tower. And if 'al' is the Arabic definite article, is it too much of a leap to imagine that most, if not all, place-names beginning 'Al' were named by the Moors? If you're still with me, then in no particular order we have Almocaizar, Alcudia de Monteagud, El Alquian, Sierra Alhamilla, Almanzora, Albarracín,

Albánchez, Alcóntar, Alfaix, Almajalejo (near Huércal-Overa), Alhama de Almería (Alhama is from 'al-ḥammām', meaning bath, by the way), La Alijambra (near Albox), El Alhanchete (near Cuevas del Almanzora) and so on. That's from just perusing a map of Almería province for five minutes. La Alfoquia comes from the Arabic 'foquia' meaning 'the higher one', in this case in relation to Zurgena, which was lower and was also populated by Moors.

Other obvious Moorish names include La Isleta del Moro in Cabo de Gata and Rambla Aljibe near Lubrín. Not so far away, the hilly region we call the Alpujarras comes from 'al-basharāt', the grasslands. All names with the prefix 'Beni' mean 'sons of' or 'descendants of' in Arabic. Local examples include Benitaglia and Benizalón. Marchal is of Arabic origin too, meaning garden. There are quite a few of these in Almería, including an El Marchal south of Macael, another between Bédar and Lubrín, El Marchal de Araoz north of Almería city and El Marchal de Enix a little further west, and the well-known abandoned village of Marchalico-Viñicas near Sorbas.

If you go north-west of Almería city, there are others: Alicún, Alboloduy, Alsolux, Alhabía, Almocíta, Benecid and Bentarique, for example. Further afield there are Alicante, Alcoy, Benicassim and not forgetting what the Moors called Beni-Darhim, now Benidorm. By this point, you'll be getting the picture so I'll leave it there but I'm sure you'll find plenty more if you look closely at a map.

30. Pig-killing and cave paintings

'La matanza del cerdo: una costumbre y un oficio casi desaparecidos.'
'The pig-killing: a custom and a trade that have almost disappeared.'
(Ana María Rodríguez Agüero)

La matanza

In the first few years that we had a house here we would see, each November, signs of lively activity in La Herradura, a tiny hamlet, usually very sleepy, that we pass to get home. There'd be a cluster of randomly parked cars and a chattering group of people gathered around a fire under a cauldron outside one of the houses. This was the *matanza*, the annual killing and processing of the pig that the family had raised over the preceding months. Relatives and friends had come to lend a hand and turn this ritual task into something of a *fiesta*. It was hard work though, and a serious business. After all, this would be the family's meat supply for the ensuing year. Usually each family would have one pig, at most two. As time went on and fewer families kept a pig, they would sometimes buy in a pig specially, to continue the tradition.

The *matanza* itself would last two days but that didn't include the preparation time; stockpiling firewood, scouring the cauldron and the killing table, making sure everything was ready to hang the *embutidos*(sausages) from the rafters, peeling and slicing the onions, frying the peppers and cracking open the almonds. Most of the preparation was done by the women, '*como siempre*', 'as always', wrote Ana María Rodríguez Agüero in a 2009 article in the Sorbas journal *El Afa*, where she reflected on the fading tradition of the *matanza*.

Ana remembered the *matanzas* at the house of her uncle Pedro Rodríguez Mañas and her aunt Manuela Roca in Los Monicos, Cariatiz. Tío Pedro and Tía Manuela had always been closely involved in the *matanza* and Ana wanted to record the tradition in detail, before it became just a distant memory. At the time Ana researched her article, Pedro was 81. He had worked the land all his life, doing a whole range of jobs, whatever was necessary: sowing, harvesting, and making and repairing tools. In addition, for 30 years, he had been the local *matarife*, the slaughterman. The role involved killing and jointing pigs for the families of the area. Pedro explained that this wasn't a full-time job. It was seasonal, so you couldn't make a living doing that alone.

In eastern Almería the *matanza* season lasted from 20th November into early January. It had to be then so that when the pig was hung up the meat would be very cold and would be easier to cut. According to Pedro, the ideal date would be 8th December, because then the *chorizos* would be in perfect condition for Christmas. Pedro had learnt how to do the job simply by watching his father, José María, do it year after year. There were no complex secrets but there was a knack to it. It was necessary to strike in exactly the right place to minimise the animal's suffering. Some slaughtermen had a range of tools but not Pedro. He just had a sharp knife and an axe. The following details are not for the squeamish, so do skip the next two sections if you think this might be you.

Day One

On day one, Pedro would be up at the crack of dawn to go off to a *cortijo*, or else he might go and sleep there the previous night, to be ready first thing. By 8 a.m., activity would be well under way. There was a lot to do. A huge cauldron would be out in the street, suspended over a wood fire, boiling water to scrub the killing table.

The pig to be killed would not have eaten the previous day, it would just have had a little water. It would be roped around a foot, then manhandled by four or five men on to the table, with its head projecting over one end. Pedro would tie its snout so it couldn't bite. It would be normal for the pig to struggle, so the men would make sure they were holding it down firmly. It was not unknown for a pig, in mid-slaughter, to break free and run off. Says Pedro, proudly: "Nunca se me ha escapado ningún chino de la mesa!", no pig on the table has ever escaped from me!

At the chosen moment he would take an ear in one hand and, with his knife in the other, slit the pig's throat. "If you are skilled enough, this isn't difficult," Pedro points out. One of the women would have already put a bowl underneath to catch the blood and would stir it constantly so it didn't clot.

After the pig had been bled, the trotters, snout and ears were thoroughly cleaned with boiling water, the trotters were cut off and the hide was scraped to remove the bristles. Then the hide was scalded with boiling water ladled over it and the tail, held with a bit of sacking to avoid burning the hands, was removed. Next, a cut was made at the anus, to find and tie up the intestines so the contents didn't leak out. Then, with steel hooks, the pig was suspended by its back legs so it could be opened more easily. With his sharp knife, Pedro opened it from top to bottom. It was kept open by pinning its hide to canes stretched across its back.

"First, we take out the innards, carefully, so they don't break. There's a membrane that doesn't come out by hand, so we cut it with a knife and the guts come out all in one. The women catch them in a sieve made of esparto so they don't fall to the floor. Also, we take out the liver and the heart." In 1990 a regulation came in stating that a vet had to verify that the pig was healthy, so it was at this stage of the process that a sample of meat was taken for the vet to analyse. For Pedro, this was his final task of the first day.

By now though, the family was busy with other aspects of the process. Making *morcilla* with the fresh blood was a key part of the first day of the *matanza*. Ana's aunt Manuela takes up the story: "In a bowl, you put onion, already peeled, chopped and cooked, cooked rice, and the blood. Then, in proportion, add aniseed, cinnamon, milled pepper and cloves. Oh, and the almonds and salt. Taste it and if it's okay, put the mixture into the casings." Traditionally these casings were natural, made from cattle intestines. The *morcillas* were then carefully boiled for three quarters of an hour or so to complete the process. Any women who were menstruating were not allowed to be involved in the making of *morcilla*.

Day Two

The pig was still almost whole, so there was more work for Pedro to do. First the ribs and steaks were cut out. These were hung on canes so the air could get to them. The head was removed and boiled. Next, the shoulder blades and the belly pork were dealt with. The backbone was cut up and finally, the hams went into salt for 15 to 20 days. When Pedro first became a slaughterman he wasn't paid in cash. The custom was to give him the pig's backbone, so the job was never going to make him rich.

For the women, day two was another busy one. There were *butifarras*(white puddings) and *chorizos*(spicy sausages) to be made. The ingredients varied but the process was fairly standard. *Chorizo* had lean meat, the flesh of red peppers, garlic, cloves, black and white pepper and salt. *Butifarra* had fattier meat. Both of these were simmered for an hour, then put on a table. The skins were pricked to ensure any trapped air could escape, then a board was put on them and weighed down with heavy, flat stones, to squeeze out any excess fat. Once this was done the *butifarras* and *chorizos* were hung up to dry.

All parts of the pig were used. There was the crackling, for example, and the *repostería*, the confectionery. This consisted of *mantecados*, as mentioned in the Turre feast later in this chapter. *Mantecados*, made with flour, lard, sugar, eggs, cinnamon and lemon, continue to be a very popular Christmas speciality. Having given you a few hints to add to your Spanish cookery repertoire, I'll finish by saying that Ana's article was illustrated by photos of *matanzas* in La Huelga in the 1960s, Los Alias (undated), Quijiliana in the 1970s and La Rellana, near Gafarillos (also undated). This tradition, which kept people close to the animals they raised and the food they were eating, is now all but gone. You would be very lucky to see a genuinely traditional *matanza* these days.

A walk and a meal

Javi Rodríguez was calling the walk he was about to lead the *'Ruta de la Matanza'*, as there was to be a meal afterwards to celebrate the *matanza*, the annual pig-killing. I figured this was the closest I would get to the tradition of the *matanza*, so I decided to go along. Some of the walkers were near the Turre town fountain, paying their money for the meal which they hoped would be a well-deserved reward for their effort. Others were hovering in the main square. Finally, once Javi had managed to round up his scattered flock, he had fifty or more people raring to go.

Never one to dawdle, Javi was off along Avenida de la Libertad at a fair lick and we were soon at the cemetery on the western edge of the town. A series of paths, *ramblas* and short stretches of tarmac followed, taking us in a big loop to the north of Turre, passing Los Jardines de Agua and the desiccated Cortijo Grande Golf Club, to a large grove of eucalyptus trees where Javi suggested a break for a snack. Most of us were saving ourselves for the *matanza* feast, so lunch was a brief affair. We were soon off again, into the dramatic valley of the Río de Aguas, where we turned right, downstream. Soon, the high arch of the Puente Vaquero came into view, towering above the valley.

The Puente Vaquero and the nearby Puente Largo, taller but much more difficult to see easily as it's in a twisting tributary valley, were built from huge blocks of rich yellow sandstone in the 1920s. Puente Vaquero takes its name from the sad fact that the only person who died during its construction was called Vaquero. The bridge was in the news in 2015 because a senior engineer in the county council's roads department alerted Turre council to the fact that it was in danger of collapsing. Heavy rains had undermined the bridge's foundations. Concern about this led, for once, to prompt action. The gaping cave that had opened up beneath the bridge was filled and local politicians turned up at the bridge to congratulate themselves.

We sped on downstream and before long were clambering out of the *rambla* to pass the former Cortijo el Gitano, now the Tío Tomas Hostal Rural, and so complete the circuit back to Turre. Once there, I stopped at the car to take my boots off and unload some gear, then made for the area by the fountain, where stalls and a bar had been set up. A couple of guys were feeding sticks and branches onto a fire under a huge *paella* pan as two old ladies in black added water to the ingredients, using a large plastic tub and seemingly judging the quantity by instinct. I was slightly puzzled though, because in the crowd of people there was no-one I recognised from the walk. Eventually, I showed one of the women the card I'd been given in the morning and asked if it was here that I could trade it in for food, presumably a plate of *paella*. She looked blank and beckoned a younger guy across. I told him I'd paid earlier that day for the walk and the *comida de matanza*. Suddenly he twigged and pointed to a door in the side of the council building across the square: "They're all eating in there. That's where you need to go."

Just inside the door I handed my ticket in at a counter and was hurriedly ushered through and shown to a seat at a table. No sooner had I sat down than a plastic plate of *migas* (fried breadcrumbs) with a couple of pieces of *morcilla* was thrust in front of me. I was hungry but the best that could be said of the *migas* was that it was filling. By chance I was sitting next to Dean and Jackie, a couple I'd met on the walk. The room was filled with large tables, as was the adjacent room, visible through double doors. There must have been well over

291

two hundred people here for the annual jamboree to celebrate the pig-killing. A swell of loud Spanish conversations bounced off the walls, making it difficult for us to hear what the old guy next to us, resplendent in a bright yellow jumper, was trying to explain as he handed round his *bota* (leather wineskin), inviting us all to an upended squirt of red wine. The gist seemed to be that he'd been drinking it since he was fourteen and, given how healthy and youthful he was, if we did the same, we would also be young forever.

On the tables there were plates of sliced radishes, chopped cabbage, various chunks of sausage and *chorizo*, and bowls of bread. We were asked if we wanted more *migas*. We had no idea what or how much was still to come. To most people there it didn't seem to matter. It was all about the occasion, the socialising, the chance for a good natter, catching up with neighbours and friends, not the fine detail of the food. No-one would be reviewing this meal on Trip Advisor.

Next, plates of potato wedges arrived, generously doused in oil, again with a few bits of pork. After this came the *paella*; not with shellfish though, just pieces of pork again. After all, this was *comida de matanza,* with each course acknowledging the bounty of the pig. It was, though, beginning to feel more like 'trial by carbohydrate'. Will there be a *postre*, we wondered? The answer was yes but, in keeping with the theme, the *postre* was *mantecados*, substantial biscuits of various shapes, in which a key ingredient is lard. They were quite good, not too heavy, with almost a shortbread consistency and a tang of lemon. So overall certainly not haute cuisine, but filling, tasty now and then, and a genuine local, seasonal experience.

Coral reefs and cave paintings

Now another walk but one rather different to the Turre circuit described above. Cariatiz is the name often loosely given to what is actually a sequence of small settlements that lie at about 400 metres above sea level at the foot of a belt of higher ground stretching east-west. Broadly speaking, this high ground is part of the Sierra de los Filabres. The settlements of Cariatiz, from east to west, are Los Ramírez, Los Martínez (which is sometimes itself referred to as Cariatiz), Los Andreses, Los Mañas, Los Monicos, Los Alías and Las Herreras. These are spring-line settlements, located where the original settlers found reliable sources of water issuing from the lower slopes.

At Las Herreras is a neatly-made stone threshing circle. From very close to this the Rambla de Castaños can be followed upstream. Wherever farming was possible, terraces were made and many of these remain, though they now seem to be mostly abandoned. The *rambla* twists westwards, and walking it involves weaving amongst thickets of *retama*, oleander, and gorse. We followed it on Boxing Day 2014, aiming to work off the excesses of the previous day. Before long, we found a net stretched across the riverbed with a male stonechat helplessly entwined in it but still alive. This was no mist net of the type genuine researchers use for bird-ringing. What was it for? Surely they don't eat small birds here? An acquaintance later suggested it might be to catch cage-birds for keeping. We suspected this was almost certainly illegal, so released the bird, with considerable difficulty, then took the two poles supporting the net out from between the large rocks holding them up and laid the whole contraption on the ground.

Two years later I saw a small item in a local paper saying that in Chirivel a motion was to be tabled prohibiting the trapping of goldfinches and other songbirds in the municipality, as this was badly affecting the numbers of such species. This would make it the first village in Almería province to ban the practice. Councillor José Ternero said that traps "are openly put and maintained in local riverbeds."

Back on our walk, at times a track followed the *rambla*, servicing the small terraced fields that are obviously still used along here. Tall eucalyptus trees dot the *rambla* in places, and we came across one that appeared to have exploded after a lightning strike. Then we came across more that looked the same, so presumably lightning was not to blame. When we were describing these trees a few days later, a friend who was part of the conversation suggested they might have been excavated by carpenter bees to such an extent that they had collapsed; an intriguing theory.

High up on the south side of the valley, we could see the line of the minor road that climbs up to join the Sorbas-Lubrín road (the AL-P 115), with just the very occasional vehicle twisting along it. The north side of the valley here is formed by what geologists call the Cariatiz Formation, which refers to fossil coral reefs. Many university geology groups come to study this notable feature. They are able to understand sentences in the International Association of Sedimentologists Field Guide to the area, such as this: 'The clasts are typical of the Nevado-Filábride basement, dominated by amphibole and chlorite mica schists.' That level of detail is lost on me, but I am very happy to learn that the slopes I'm looking at are in fact reef carbonates, which means they consist of the skeletons of corals and various other creatures such as molluscs that lived here in what was a warm open sea during the Lower Messinian period, about six million years ago.

In the *rambla*, it was slow going but not really difficult. Then after a kilometre or so, as the *rambla* curved round in a northerly direction and the valley sides steepened, a jumble of huge blocks came into view, filling the riverbed. It looked impressive, particularly when we stopped on a patch of flat ground just below it for a modest picnic. At the right hand side was a big cavern under massive fallen blocks, with light shining through in a couple of places high at the back of the gloomy cave. This might have been a way up the obstacle, but we settled for scrambling a little further left, working our way up the face of the rock-fall without too much of a problem.

One mystery is that the 1:25,000 map shows pairs of pecked lines, labelled Vereda de Lubrín, following this *rambla*. A *vereda* was a traditional livestock droving route, which in this case would have been used to move animals seasonally between the higher land to the north, where they spent the summer, and the Almerían coastal lowlands, where they would winter. It's hard to see how animals other than goats could have come down this way, given the chaos of big blocks forming such a major obstacle in the valley. This huge choke of car-sized boulders (and bigger) has clearly been here a long time, in historical terms if not on a geological time-scale.

Once above the rock-fall, we followed the *rambla* in an increasingly shallow valley, twisting northwards until we had a choice of continuing along the riverbed, which the map shows passing to the east of La Mela, or taking a track that veered off to the left, towards the main road. We opted for the latter as our next objective involved a bit of prehistory. We turned south on the road in La Mela, very briefly, before taking the surfaced turning to the right, angling away in a west south-west direction. The turning is almost opposite a small hill to the left of the road called Cerro Mandres. We now passed a few houses, one of which is named Almendra Vista, a nod to the photogenic views north across almond fields.

Not far beyond these houses the road passes to the left of a threshing circle then leads down into a shallow *rambla*. This is the Rambla de Mora and, all being well, it would lead to our goal. About eight years earlier we'd been on a walk with the Amigos de Sorbas, led by Andrés Pérez, and he'd taken us to see some cave paintings. I was pretty sure they were down this *rambla* but there was some guesswork involved. In places dense vegetation created minor problems but these were easily overcome. The *rambla* steadily became narrower and deeper, where the intermittent river had carved its way down through the old reefs, and there was some tricky going, with boulders and uneven ground. There were lots of steeply tilted strata in the looming rock walls and the cream and golden cliffs were streaked with lines of dark seepage.

"I'm sure it shouldn't be this far," said Troy, but I was pretty sure we were going the right way and that soon we would see the tall metal fence that protects the site. So it was. Up on the left, a hundred metres ahead, a line of metal posts on the cliff suddenly came into view. On the map, sheet 1031-1 Sorbas, we were in grid square 578112, more or less where the 500 metre contour crosses the constricted *rambla*.

Once there, we clambered easily up to the fence and could see fading red ochre drawings on the left-hand face of the *abrigo*, the shelter. The most obvious ones are fish skeletons (or tallies) and patterns of diamonds and zigzags. Supposedly there are also human figures with their arms in various positions but I think that seeing these requires more imagination than I appear to have. The drawings are considered to date from sometime between the Neolithic Era and the Copper Age, 6,000 to 3,000 years ago.

The rock art is interesting for itself but the position of the overhang, slightly up the cliff and with good views out along the *rambla*, is really quite dramatic. The geology and colouring of the ancient reefs are fascinating, with pockets and caves and striking slashes of angled strata. It's a place well worth seeking out, as long as you are fairly confident on awkward ground.

Vowing that one day we would follow the *rambla* further downstream to the small village of Moras, we turned to retrace the way we had come, as far as La Mela, where we had left a car before starting the walk. As is often the case, the return leg seemed much shorter than the outward walk and it was soon time for refreshments in the nearby Bar El Almendro.

31. Mixed fortunes in Cabo de Gata

'From the hide we could see many Greater Flamingos as well as Avocets, Ringed Plovers, Dunlin and the odd Little Stint, Sanderling, Kentish Plover and Redshank. There was a line of distant Black-tailed Godwits and numerous Slender-billed Gulls were feeding.'

(David Elliott-Binns)

Invisible warnings

In early October 2014, the post woman drew up outside our gate and called to me to sign for a registered letter. It had 'ACUSE DE RECIBO' stamped on it in capital letters, which means 'acknowledgement of receipt', plus, in case I should doubt where the envelope was from, in various font sizes and levels of boldness: Ministerio de Agricultura, Alimentación y Medio Ambiente, **Dirección General de Sostenibilidad de la Costa y del Mar, Demarcación de Costas en Andalucía-Mediterraneo,** Servicio Provincial de Costas en Almería, plus an address in Almería city. This had the look of bad news.

Inside, stamped with the date '22 Set 2014', were two sides of closely-typed legalese, starting with this: *'Resultando que con fecha 18/06/2014 ha sido formulado parte de denuncia por la Guardia Civil, en el que se le atribuye al Sr. Borman la infraccion de la vigente Ley 2/2013, de 29 de mayo, de protección y uso sostenible del litoral y de modificación de la Ley 22/1988, de 28 de Julio, de Costas, motivada por la realización de los siguientes hechos'.*

Those last three words, *'los siguientes hechos'* mean 'the following facts', though it took another eleven paragraphs, almost all longer than the one above, to set them out. The gist of this was that the Guardia Civil had seen my small VW campervan parked in the wrong place at La Fabriquilla, by the saltpans of Cabo de Gata at 6.25 a.m. on 18th June 2014. The letter stated that parking in this particular place is expressly prohibited by the *'colocacion de señales verticales'*, the display of vertical signs. No such signs exist there, and as far as I am aware, never have.

It's also the case that in Spain, and France also come to that, parking with consideration and sleeping overnight in a campervan is not perceived as the heinous offence that it seems to be in the UK. It is simply an unremarkable fact and, in an increasing number of places it is positively encouraged; after all, the vast majority of the occupants of campervans spend money with local businesses and treat the places where they stay with respect. I'm talking here of parking for just a night or two; not the unacceptable behaviour where a juggernaut of a motorhome stays put for a month, creating waste and blocking someone's view of the sea.

I checked back on the calendar and yes, I had been at La Fabriquilla on that date in June 2014. I'd driven down to arrive the night before a meeting of the birdwatching group which I go out with regularly, to check out the saltpans in the evening and avoid the long drive first thing in the morning. I'd parked up where campervans often do, on the seaward side of the road at the edge of the quiet village of La Fabriquilla, away from the nearest houses where, incidentally, there is no indication that parking is not permitted.

The penalty for my infringement, the letter declared, was to be *'una multa de 422,4 Euros'*. Gulp, I thought, that's a bit steep. A fine of over €400! And why the apparently random total, €422.40? How was that arrived at?

Kafka would have been proud

With the help of my Romanian friend Calin Sandru, whose Spanish is considerably better than mine, after several attempts to phone the number given on the letter we elicited the information that the fine was based on a rate of €40 per square metre of the vehicle's area. I was told to send in a copy of the van's 'Permiso de Circulación' (logbook), showing the exact dimensions of the vehicle, and then the

298

correct fine could be calculated. They also agreed that, yes, it is true that there are no signs prohibiting parking at the place in question and that is because they can't afford them. It's okay to park overnight on the inland side of the road at that location, they advised, but not on the seaward side. To point out that it's a touch unfair to fine people for such an offence, without warning them they are about to commit one, seemed superfluous. Kafka would have been proud.

I scanned the logbook and emailed it to them, with a covering letter, multiplying the length by the width of the van, and calculating that the fine should be not €422.40 but €340. However, I added, if I paid within two weeks, assuming the usual 50% discount for doing so applied, then the fine would be reduced to €170. This would at least be a little less eye-watering.

I emailed this to them on 9th October and asked them to acknowledge receipt of the information. Nothing. I sent all the same information by email again on 30th October, explaining that as I hadn't heard from them, I wasn't sure that they'd received it first time round. This time I got a reply to say, yes, they had received it and the case was being processed. Then more silence.

Until 30th December, that is, when I got a further letter to say that they had decided, in the light of the details I'd submitted, that the fine would be reduced, not to €170 as I'd suggested, but to €120. There was nothing to explain how this sum had been chosen. Hmm, I thought, this is heading the right way. This letter consisted of 18 paragraphs of legalese and, despite stating quite clearly, in bold, that the fine was now **ciento veinte euros** and that it was now in the hands of the Tesoro Público, there was no indication of actually how to pay it.

Fortuitously, a Spanish friend, Pepe Guinea, was staying with us over New Year. Unsurprisingly, we failed to make contact with the Tesoro Público by phone over the New Year period. However, Pepe said: "I work just round the corner from the Tesoro Público in Madrid.

I'll nip round in my lunch hour and pay it if I can, then you can pay me by bank transfer."

A few days later Pepe texted me to say he'd been to the Tesoro Público, with a copy of the documentation, but he hadn't been able to pay. This was because the letter in question was simply to say what the suggested fine would now be, and offering me the chance to challenge it. If I didn't wish to challenge it, I should simply do nothing and wait for a further letter to be sent, along with the necessary forms for payment. In due course, at the end of February 2015, such a letter and forms arrived and I was finally able to go to the bank and pay the €120 fine. As to the cost to the Servicio Provincial de Costas en Almería of this prolonged and bewildering administrative procedure, who knows, but it must have been somewhat more than €120.

Saltpan surprises

By the time we'd finished our coffees and tumbled out of the Barquero cafe in Pujaire with the cheery cry of the owner Manolo's: "Bye bye!" ringing in our ears, it was getting on for 10 am, which is not the best time of day for viewing the Cabo de Gata saltpans from the first watch-point. This is just before San Miguel de Cabo de Gata village, where there's a large pull-off and a small hide on the left at a bend in the road. At this time of the morning you are looking into the sun, so the birds are little more than silhouettes, chief amongst them the ever-present greater flamingos.

Nevertheless, it was immediately apparent that there was also something special here. Two huge birds were standing at the edge of the nearest lagoon, over to our right. Cranes, *gruas* in Spanish, just the same as the vehicle that tows you when your car breaks down. The supporting cast included the expected greater flamingos and avocets, together with various other waders, but the cranes moved off after about 15 minutes and we decided to do likewise.

We followed the road into Cabo de Gata village, made the usual left at the roundabout, and after a little way convoyed on to the verge behind our leader for the day, Rod. There are three hides along this stretch, between the lagoons and the sea. A scan of the sea brought views of a few gannets, far away but clearly visible folding themselves into white missiles as they plunged from height for fish.

We walked the short distance to the hide and now, with the sun in our favour, began to identify birds more easily: stonechat, greenfinch, slender-billed gull, little egret, grey plover. Richard suddenly said: "What's this?" He'd been scanning the scrubby steppe and had homed in on a great bustard, a superb find. Great bustards are huge: a metre long and with a wing-span of over two metres. They are terrestrial though and not often seen in flight, being more usually found striding around steppes and large areas of open ground, searching for seeds, plants, insects, rodents and reptiles. The definitive guide *Bird* says: 'One of the truly great birds of Europe in every sense,' adding that 'its future is deeply uncertain in the face of agricultural pressure throughout its range.' To see one in our area was a real treat.

In the process of swivelling my telescope slowly across the scrub, trying to find the bustard, I chanced on two small egg-yolk yellow marks, several hundred metres away, just to the left of a bush. There was something about them... I focussed and gradually realised these bright yellow dashes were the eye and beak-base of a motionless bird, so astonishingly well camouflaged that it's outline was virtually impossible to see, even when you were staring closely at it. "I think I've got a stone curlew," I announced. "Come and have a look. I need another opinion." Alan peered through my 'scope. "Confirmed!" he said. The bird was sitting on the ground but merged so well into its surroundings that one or two of the others in our group, even knowing it was there in the circle of the lens, could not make it out at first.

The same evening, I mentioned, via Facebook, to local wildlife guide Jesús Contreras, the presence of the cranes and the bustard. He replied: "Yes, they have arrived. The bustard will be here for some weeks. The cranes a bit less time, as is usual every year." So November is the time to hope that these wonderful creatures might be in 'our' area. A month later we were at Las Salinas again. No sign of cranes or great bustards this time but groups of 10 spoonbills and 25 shelduck and a scattered raft of over 80 black-necked grebes made up for the missing rarities.

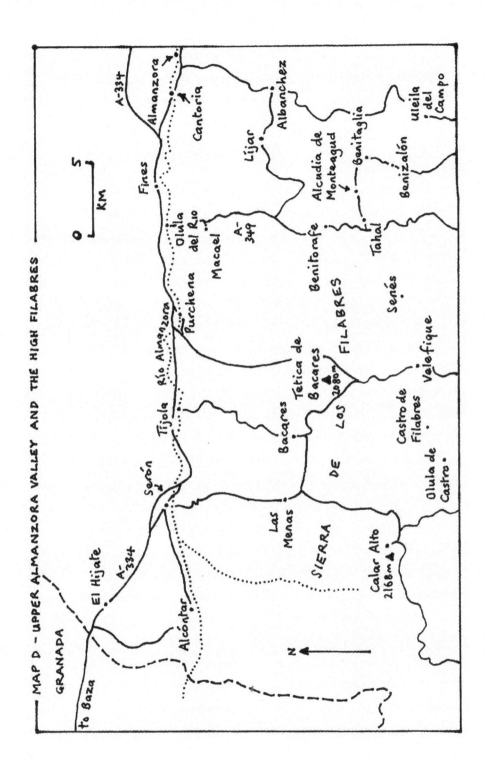

MAP D - UPPER ALMANZORA VALLEY AND THE HIGH FILABRES

303

32. The High Filabres

'The best maps are not published, but are the maps we make ourselves, about our cities, towns, villages and landscapes.'
(Alys Fowler)

Alto de Velefique

One way to reach the highest parts of the Sierra de los Filabres is to take the A-349 north from Tabernas and then, after a couple of kilometres, take the left turn to Velefique. The road climbs almost imperceptibly at first, but as you approach the village of Velefique, it begins to rise more. It becomes apparent from the architecture that you are in slate country. More obvious still, the huge dark wall of the mountain chain rears into the sky beyond the village at its foot. Velefique is famous amongst cycling enthusiasts for the Alto de Velefique. In just 13 kilometres the road twists upwards more than a vertical kilometre, taking you from 820 m to 1,860 m above sea level. The road and adjacent rocks carry the white-painted names of legendary cyclists such as Miguel Indurain who have raced this way. To mere mortals the notion of cycling up the Alto de Velefique seems an impossibility; just driving the road is dramatic enough.

It finally levels out and the top of the climb is marked by a notice announcing 'Alto de Velefique 1,860 m'. There's a puzzle here though. On the relevant 1:50,000 map, sheet 1013-III Velefique, the point where this sign stands has a spot height of only 1,791 m and the contours and lie of the land appear to show this is indeed the case.

Adjacent is a small slate structure, an open square, presumably made as a shelter. To the west, a track leads up a convex slope alongside pine forest towards Cerro de María Antonia, 1,936 m, and to the east two tracks strike off, the higher of which goes to the trig point on Portillo, visible about a kilometre away.

Just before writing this I made two visits to the Alto de Velefique. The first was early on a mid-April morning when the wind had such icy ferocity that I decided, given a miscalculation which meant I was totally under-equipped for the conditions, that to stay outside the vehicle for longer than necessary would be unwise. I drove on north and, after about a kilometre and a half, took the narrow road, optimistically advertised with a camera symbol and labelled 'Mirador La Tetica 3.3 km'. This took me up into the clouds, literally, so there was no view to be had. Back to the drawing board.

A week later, again very early in the morning, I was back at the 'Alto de Velefique 1,860 m' sign. This time it was much more promising; still cold, on account of the height, but already sunny and clear. And I had warm gear. There's plenty of parking space by the road and from there I set off for the short walk to Portillo. The track goes steadily uphill across stony ground with low scattered plants. One of these, very common in this high mountain environment, is a stemless thistle with a rosette of deeply-divided pale silvery-green leaves, a striking plant known as *cabeza de cardo* in Spanish. It has no English name but is Onopordum acaulon in Latin. There are chunks of quartz and rose quartz too.

The most widespread rock here though is slate. There are many outcrops of it and, tucked against one such, a shepherd's refuge has been built. It's a basic affair of breeze blocks with the slate bedrock forming part of the walls. There are windows and shelves, and wooden branches supporting the roof, though it's not a place you would choose to spend the night. Below it is a more substantial slate hut, built into the slope, neater and presumably older, with animal pens and a threshing circle. At about 1,840 m above sea level, I wonder if this is the highest threshing circle in Almería province? It's astonishing to think they must have grown cereals up here in the relatively recent past.

The track dips briefly then rises to reach the white concrete pillar marking the summit of Portillo at 1,868 m. This is a superb viewpoint. Nestling far below in the folds of the brown-pelted hills is the white splash of Velefique. A dozen kilometres eastwards I could just see the white domes of the observatory at Calar Alto over the intervening hilltops, with a late coating of snow on the Sierra Nevada beyond. To the north, less than three kilometres away as the raven flies, is the cluster of masts that crown the highest point in these parts, the Tetica de Bacares. Despite the intrusion of the masts, the Tetica somehow still manages to be an elegant mountain.

The view and the map showed that, from Portillo, a high-level walk onwards via Piedras Resbaladizas and Piedra de la Mujer to the next trig point, on Nacimiento (1,743 m) would be perfectly possible and undoubtedly enjoyable but despite being retired and theoretically having the time to do such a thing on a whim, I had a different agenda on this occasion so, with some reluctance, turned back. I did divert briefly to the edge of the pinewoods where I could see the trees were badly infested by processionary caterpillars. There were hundreds of nests and many parts of the trees had been very badly affected.

Tetica de Bacares

I've heard it said and seen it written that the Tetica de Bacares, at 2,080 m, is the highest point of Almería Province. It isn't: that honour goes to El Chullo, which at 2,609 m is a lot higher. El Chullo is over 40 kilometres south-west of the Tetica and lies just to the east of the Puerto de la Ragua which marks the provincial border between Almería and Granada. However, the Tetica is one of the highest points in the Sierra de los Filabres and that's surely a sufficient accolade (Calar Alto, also higher, see below, is 2,168 m high). I still find it astonishing that, eleven years into exploring this wonderful area, I can drive in an hour and a half from our house here, up to somewhere that is half as high again as anywhere in the British Isles. The sheer scale of the Filabres, the geology, the distinctive climate and flora: it's a great privilege to have this so near.

As for the Tetica, you can drive almost to the summit. Courtesy of Teléfonica and its masts, there is an access road that ends just a few metres below the top of the mountain. As mentioned above, this is indicated by a Mirador de Tetica sign. It's a narrow road, single track without obvious passing places and protected with a wood-clad crash barrier all along its outer edge. There's very little traffic but I'm sure if you met another vehicle, you would manage to find a way to pass, edging by at slow speed.

At the road end there's a board with a map commemorating the 130th anniversary of the date in 1879 when the first triangulation by surveyors was made between Europe and Africa. This was based on two mountains in southern Spain, Tetica and Mulhacén (at 3,479 m, the highest peak in the Sierra Nevada and indeed in mainland Spain) and two in Algeria, Filhaoussen and M'sabiha. As an aside, I've always been intrigued by the seeming disconnect that the country we call Algeria in English is Argelia in Spanish; a game of anagrams.

A walkway leads the final few metres up to the walled platform at the mountain summit. Here, by the concrete trig pillar, is a metal plaque with raised lettering, adding the information that the first geodesic link to Africa was achieved under the direction of Don Carlos Ibañez de Ibero, the founder of the Instituto Geográfico Nacional. The plaque was *reconstruido* in 1979 but quite a few of its letters have now gone, so it's time for a bit of further reconstruction. There are the masts of course, plus a modern trig point and the remains of a couple of older ones. There's also a 'coin-in-the-slot' telescope. The views are tremendous. You can see huge distances in every direction. Early in the day, long shadows create abstract patterns in the pinewoods on the nearby slopes. Far below, nestling about three kilometres to the west north-west in a fold of the mountains is Bacares, the village after which the Tetica is named.

Bacares

Bacares, which calls itself the 'Hidden Pearl of the Filabres' is a village built, predictably, from slate and tucked deep into the seams of the hills. Even the cemetery just outside the village is steeply terraced. I parked near the Hotel Restaurante Las Fuentes. Close by, a display panel for mountain bikers shows the six local stages (out of 24) of the BTT TransAlmería-Almanzora route that links Macael and San Miguel de Cabo de Gata. The spiky shapes of the stage profiles suggest this is a challenge for the very fit.

I spent an enjoyable hour wandering the streets, initially passing a big slate wall in the niches of which were displayed old wooden ploughs and yokes and traditional esparto items. The white tower of the Church of Santa María de Bacares, built between 1500 and 1505, spears the sky above streets neatly paved at their bends with curving patterns of slate setts. A tiny stream separates the main part of the village from the tall rock on which the castle was built many centuries ago by the Moors. Bacares has a long history connected mainly to iron mining and silk production. The latter was based on a local resource of over 180,000 mulberry trees. The castle itself was the spiritual refuge of the poet and thinker Ben Arabi (1164-1240), who is buried in Damascus.

To reach the castle ruins I walked down past the Fuente Grande, the village water supply with its three permanently flowing spouts. Right alongside it is the old *lavadero,* its washing troughs now inside a renovated, or possibly new, building which is locked and has a plaque to say it is a Museo Etnográfico. You can see in through the grilles but the locked access seems a bit over-protective. Apart from anything else, it means the rubbish inside can't easily be removed. It's a short climb up to the ruins of the castle which are sadly obscured by an excess of rusted iron and wooden walkways and barriers. It's understandable that the authorities don't want people scrambling on the ancient remains and damaging them further but the amount of iron and wood means it's very difficult to get a sense of what the place might once have felt like. Solid metal doors, all locked, block off the interior, including one that has the universal Tourist Information 'i' symbol. I peered in through the window and could see only a bare table, a pile of cushions and a stack of empty plant-pots: no sign of tourist information.

Back down in the village, at the side of a paved square opposite the church, I headed into the dim interior of the Bar Los Arcos and ordered a coffee. It was late morning and seven old boys were putting the world to rights over beer and brandy; archetypal Spain. Despite the inaccessibility at the *castillo* and the *lavadero*, and the fact that I was visiting out of season, or perhaps because of it, I liked the feel of Bacares. The terraces on the surrounding hills give a green splash, the narrow streets invite exploration and there's a serenity about the place that's attractive.

Arquitectura negra

In Bacares almost everything is built with slate. It's the ubiquitous local material and the dark nature of this rock has led to the term *arquitectura negra*, black architecture, though the slate of the village buildings is almost all painted white. A rather elegant book illustrating *arquitectura negra* came my way a couple of years ago. Called **El Paisaje Cultural de la Sierra de Filabres**, The Cultural Landscape of the Filabres Mountains, the text is limited as the book largely consists of photographs illustrating details of the villages and farming landscapes of the high mountains: walls, roofs, chimneys, street paving, animal corrals, cemeteries, terraces, mills, you name it, they are all made of slate. As far as I can gather, the book was an initiative by the town halls of four of the typical Filabres villages: Castro de Filabres, Olula de Castro, Senés and Velefique. It was published in 2009 and I suspect it may be pretty difficult to locate a copy now but if you do come across one, I'm sure you'll find it interesting.

Odd goings-on at Lijar

During a state visit to Paris in late 1883, the Spanish king, Alfonso XII, was insulted by a rowdy crowd, quite possibly because of his bizarre choice of headgear. It's difficult to describe the hat in question but a surviving photo shows it as a kind of rope affair, tilted across his forehead, with a small angled mortarboard above that, topped with what looks like a vertical doughnut. It's no wonder that the Parisians laughed.

However, in Lijar, a tiny village in the Sierra de los Filabres, the mayor, Don Miguel Garcia Saéz, was incensed by the king's reception and by the fact that the Spanish government didn't seem too concerned about it. He called a council meeting, at which the minutes recorded that: 'Our King Alfonso, when passing through Paris on the 29th day of September was stoned and offended in the most cowardly fashion by miserable hordes of the French nation.'

The mayor reminded his council and 300 villagers that when Napoleon's troops invaded Spain at the start of the 19th century: "Just one woman, who was old, wretched and bedraggled but a daughter of Spain nonetheless, had on her own cut the throat of 32 Frenchmen who were billeted in her home." He added that although Lijar was "the most insignificant of all the villages in the Sierra de los Filabres, that is no reason for inaction," and then announced: "The example of this woman is enough to let the inhabitants of France fear that this village of Lijar, although it has only 100 able men, proposes to declare war on all of France, since one man of this our village is worth 10,000 Frenchmen."

This meeting of Lijar council on 14th October 1883 unanimously passed the war motion. The declaration was sent to the President of the French Republic, with a copy to the Spanish government. A further copy of the faded hand-written document is still kept in the village's archives. In reality this declaration of war led to nothing much at all. No-one from Lijar invaded France, which was

800 kilometres away. The mayor gained some notoriety though and was nicknamed 'The Terror of the Sierras'. Despite the lack of action, the state of war continued for a century.

In 1970 the then Spanish King, Juan Carlos, received a rather more cordial reception in Paris. Lijar's socialist mayor of the time, Diego Sanchez Cortes, subsequently tried to mend fences through a formal process with the French but they seemingly had more important things on their mind and nothing initially came of it. Then, in late 1983, the French finally agreed to a peace treaty. The French ambassador ordered the consul general in Málaga, Charles Santi, to go to Lijar for a peace celebration in the appropriately named Plaza de la Paz. An official from the French Embassy in Madrid, Jean Francois Thiollier, said: "We are pleased that hostilities will come to a formal end soon. We find it all rather amusing but it's nice to have someone making peace." This somewhat bizarre ceremony even made the pages of the *Washington Post* in a report dated 20th November 1983.

Calar Alto

As you travel west along the Autovía del Mediterráneo, towards Almería airport say, your eyes may well be drawn northwards to the heights of the Sierra de los Filabres, especially if you are in the passenger seat, as in both senses you'll be on the right side of the vehicle. High on the horizon you'll see a small white sphere. This is the German-Spanish observatory at Calar Alto, a collaborative project between the German Max Planck Institute for Astronomy and the Spanish Institute of Astrophysics of Andalucía. At 2,168 metres above sea level, it's located in a remote spot which was chosen because of the clarity and darkness of the Almerían sky, with light pollution from distant urban areas not intruding on astronomical activities. It was officially opened in July 1975.

The telescopes at Calar Alto provide information to the international scientific community. The largest, at 3.5 metres (138 inches) is the biggest in Europe and of major astronomical importance, so there was widespread concern in the first half of 2013 when a cut of 75% was announced by the Spanish government as a result of its austerity measures. At that stage Calar Alto was receiving a grant of €1.5 million per year from Spain, with €2.5 million from the German government. The proposed cut from Spain would have meant a proportionate cut from Germany, reducing the annual budget from €4 million to €1.2 million.

The announcement of the cut unleashed a string of protests. The proposal was described as "drastic" by the CSIC, the Spanish Council for Scientific Investigation. The Andalucian Astrophysics Institute petitioned central government to find a solution. The president of the provincial council, Gabriel Amat, met the mayor of Gérgal, in whose municipality the observatory lies, to discuss the matter. The director of the observatory, José María Quintana, resigned, citing a lack of funding. Members of staff, faced with a 35% pay cut and redundancies, threatened strike action.

Subsequently, a less draconian budget cut was agreed and the observatory staggered on. In a neat touch, German astronomers named three new asteroids after three cooks who were made redundant at the observatory when its catering was outsourced. For the record they are Joseluiscorral (asteroid number 124143), Angelbarbero (213269) and Elviracheca (246759). Chase up the first name, for example, on Google, and you get this: 'José Luis Corral Berruezo (b. 1967) worked from 1999 until 2014 as a chef at the Spanish Calar Alto Observatory. Through his culinary skills he contributed significantly to the well-being of his fellow colleagues, visiting astronomers, and the discoverers of this asteroid. He and his food are dearly missed.'

Then in 2015 there was better news when it was announced that a new instrument called Carmenes would begin operating in January 2016. Carmenes is the acronym for 'Calar Alto high-Resolution search for M dwarfs with Exo-earths with Near-infrared and optical Echelle Spectrographs'. In simple terms, that means the device can look for Earth-like planets that are orbiting stars outside our solar system. It does this, in conjunction with the 3.5 metre telescope, by detecting speed variations in the movements of stars hundreds of billions of kilometres away to an accuracy of one metre per second.

Carmenes consists of two spectrographs, one measuring visible light and one measuring infrared, linked to the telescope with optical fibres. These 'eyes' are located inside two vacuum tanks surrounded by a radiation shield which maintains a steady temperature of about minus 160 degrees centigrade. Installation of these tanks took several months to complete during 2015. The Carmenes project is being carried out over 600 nights and is due to finish in 2018, although depending on progress, this may extend into 2020.

Back on Earth, it's possible to drive up to Calar Alto. If you are interested, visits by the public are available. These involve a guided tour lasting about one and a half hours and must be booked in advance. Go to this link to find out more about this in English: http://www.azimuthspain.com/en/calar-alto/

Even without a guided tour, it's worth going up there for the spectacular views. Perhaps the best route up to Calar Alto is from Gérgal, north via the A-1178 and then briefly west on the AL-4404. This involves climbing 1,390 metres in just 23 kilometres. Even in summer it can be cold at 2,000 metres above sea level, so make sure you have suitable clothing. Calar Alto frequently sees snow in winter so the road is not always passable, but to be up there with snow on the ground and rime on the bushes, reducing everything to an ethereal and otherworldly silent whiteness, is quite an experience to contrast with the more usual heat of the nearby Almerían lowlands.

33. Las Menas

'De las entrañas de la tierra en Las Menas de Serón, Sierra de los Filabres, hombres extraian hierro para vivir y sustantarse...'. 'From the bowels of the earth in Las Menas de Serón, Sierra de los Filabres, men extracted iron in order to live and support themselves...'
(Inscription on the Miners' Monument, Las Menas)

The iron mines

At Las Menas, high in the Sierra Filabres, lie the remains of an extensive mining enterprise. It's deep in the mountains a few kilometres above Serón, with access from the Serón-Gérgal road. Evidence shows that lead and silver were mined here as far back as Neolithic times but the real heyday of mining was based on iron ore and occurred in the latter part of the 19th century. The concessions for mining were granted to a consortium of Belgian and Spanish entrepreneurs which was registered as a Belgian company called Compania Mines et Chemin de Fer Bacares-Almería. The 'chemin de fer' bit of the title, meaning 'railway' in French, was there because of plans to build a railway over the mountains to Almería, but this came to nothing, surviving as an idea only in the outfit's name. In fact, the company was generally known as Casa de Menas.

Work began at the mines in 1885. In 1894 the GSSR (Great Southern of Spain Railway) reached Serón and by 1902-1904 the mines were developing fast. A cableway was built to take the iron down to a loading bay at Los Canos on the GSSR line. The population of Las Menas boomed, as did that of Serón, in which municipality Las Menas is situated. From 4,689 in 1900, Serón municipality's population doubled to 9,361 in 1930. This was its peak though. The stock market crash of 1929, the Civil War and the gradual exhaustion of some of the mines led to a long period of decline. There was a brief revival in the 1950s but the downward trend soon set in again and in 1968 mining finally ceased.

Many hundreds of miners had been employed at Las Menas. A remarkable complex of buildings included substantial houses for the director, the director's assistant, the doctor, the draughtsman, the workshop chief, the cashier and the head foreman. There was a hospital which had two-bedded patient rooms, treatment rooms, a surgery, an X-ray department and a kitchen. In addition there were mine offices, a food store and a bakery. A little way down a track were the Guardia Civil barracks, housing a contingent of eight guards and their commander.

Good quality accommodation for some of the miners and their families was provided free by the company. Each living area had a kitchen and fireplace, a larder, two bedrooms, a toilet, and a sitting room. There was electricity, running water, a supply of firewood and even a weekly change of linen. In 1958, when there was a temporary upsurge in the fortunes of the mines, a new dormitory for miners called the Santa Bárbara Residence was built. (Santa Bárbara is the patron saint of miners.) It was very well equipped and even had central heating.

The bizarre tale of the Hotel Las Menas de Serón
Once the mines closed in 1968 the population plummeted. Most of the buildings were abandoned and began to deteriorate. All was not lost though. Sometime later, much effort and money from the Junta de Andalucía went into turning the heart of the mining site into a tourist area. The old hospital became a campsite in 1992. Then the administration block and two long workers' dormitories were transformed into the Hotel Las Menas de Serón, which opened in 1999 after major refurbishment. It offered 11 apartments with one bedroom, 8 apartments with two bedrooms, a conference room with capacity for 80 people, a restaurant and a cafeteria-bar. Don Gaunt stayed for a night in 2003 and reported that: 'The apartments are beautifully furnished and the restaurant does a good meal.' He also

said that the woman who cooked his food told him that the day after the mines closed for good in 1968, many people came up from Serón and 'stripped the buildings of everything moveable'.

I'd been to Las Menas a couple of times previously but went again on 19th April 2016. It was a cold windy day and the place was eerily deserted, apart from a couple of cyclists who appeared briefly then vanished. I've always been intrigued by the remains of human activity in dramatic and remote landscapes: the slate mines of Honister in the Lake District, the tin mines of Cornwall and the sad remnants of villages forcibly abandoned during Scotland's Highland Clearances. Las Menas is one of these evocative places.

And what I found in April 2016 gave a further strange twist to the long history here. The hotel was clearly closed and had a definite look of disuse about it. I went up to one of the windows by the entrance, where I could see a couple of sheets of paper displayed on the inside. They turned out to be an official letter, dated just the previous day, 18th April. The day after my visit a friend, José Javier Matamala García, coincidentally posted an article online about the situation at Las Menas. From these sources I pieced together what seemed to be happening.

In early April 2016, the mayor of Serón, Juan Antonio Lorenzo, was alerted to the fact that furniture was being removed from the hotel at Las Menas. Concerned by this, he visited it on April 16th to discover that not only had furniture been removed but that fittings such as air-conditioning units, heating pipes, electrical items and plumbing systems were being stripped out of both the main building and the apartments. A legal letter of April 18th, putting a halt to this, was his response. He was concerned that the dismantling of the hotel meant that the Andalucían authorities intended to abandon it and leave it to deteriorate.

Mayor Lorenzo said he would be lodging a complaint with the Defensor del Pueblo Andaluz, an ombudsman nominated by the

Andalucían parliament to defend the rights of citizens against government maladministration. He also pointed out that the Serón town hall had publicly offered, a few months earlier, to collaborate with the Junta de Andalucía in the management of the hotel and the payment of the employees who were looking after the site, in order to maintain the facilities with a view to having them up and running again at some future date. Since then, I've come across no updates on the situation but I guess the best that may have happened is that the damage to the hotel has been arrested.

Evocative remains

I went down below the hotel, along an angled ramp, to the old Guardia Civil barracks, a two storey building with a garden at the front enclosed by a high wall. The gateway and adjacent apertures had been bricked up. On one part of the brickwork was a spray-painted, large blue interrogation mark. A good question indeed. One of the apertures had been broken through, giving access to the barracks. As I stepped through the hole, a pair of choughs flew out of the ruined building, shrieking, their curved blood-red bills prominent. The building, once quite impressive by the look of it, is now steadily falling into ruin, aided by pilferers and graffiti traffickers.

Back at the main area is the Miners' Monument, a striking feature in cast metal. Three large relief panels, designed to look like the entrances to local mines called Necesaria, Concepción and Jota, under the dates 1885-1968, list the names of hundreds of miners. The inscription at the head of this chapter is prominent on the monument and continues: '... In memory of all those families who had their roots in this ground and who keep it in their hearts.' At the bottom of the central panel Don Antonio Melanas (1885) is recorded as 'the first worker in the mines'.

On the reverse of the panels are many more names of people and places linked to the mining activity. In front of the monument on a short stretch of rails is an iron wagon, still loaded with ore, and over to one side is a huge cubic block of iron-bearing rock, taken from the Esparteña Mine in 1926. It was placed there *'como obsequio al director de la explotación Don Federico van Bererronde, holandés, hijo adoptivo de Serón'*, 'as a gift to the director of mining operations, the Dutchman Frederick van Bererronde, adopted son of Serón'.

More recently, but before the events at the hotel described above, the director's house became the Centro de Interpretación de la Minería, the Mining Industry Interpretation Centre, surrounded by a two-hectare *parque forestal*, planted with typical local trees and shrubs. This was in 2015. The Parque Forestal and the Mining Industry Interpretation Centre were closed on the day I visited, a Tuesday. A notice gave the opening times and I was unlucky to have hit on one of the days - Tuesdays and Thursdays - when that part of the site is closed. As far as I am aware, it is still operating at other times. I would hope so as there has clearly been substantial investment and it hasn't been open long.

'We've gone shopping'
Signs at the camp site suggested it was still open for business too, but it didn't seem to be when I was there. There was one closed-up caravan on the site. Umbrellas and plastic chairs at the front of the reception/bar/restaurant were scattered around haphazardly. Some were upturned. I suppose this may have been due to the strong wind at the time. However, the front door was closed and on the metal grille locked across it had been chalked: *'Abrimos a las 7 pm. Hemos ido a comprar.'* 'We're opening at 7 pm. We've gone shopping.' There was a mobile phone number and the name José. The chalk looked old though and I was not convinced that José would be back from his shopping any time soon. I may be wrong. The place to check this if you fancy a visit is at www.campinglasmenasdeseron.com

I'm not painting a very positive picture of Las Menas, I realise, but I find the whole place fascinating. And there's more. From the main site, and particularly from the old barracks, the remains of another large mining settlement at Rascador can be seen stretching across the opposite hillside. Then, if you drive on downhill from the main car park, very soon on the right you will see, below you, a huge stone-lined hopper and below that again, a photogenic iron bridge with wooden sleepers crossing a small valley. There is space to park but the remains of the hopper and bridge are in a precarious state, so do take care. There are lots of chunks of dark iron-bearing rock here too.

The road you are now on is the shortest way down to Serón and it passes many more mining remains en route. A kilometre or so beyond the iron bridge is a small chapel, the Hermitage of Santa Bárbara, built for a German director of the mines, Alfonso Sierra Joldi, between 1911 and 1918, hence, presumably, its northern European appearance. In 1959 a hurricane destroyed part of its tower but it was finally restored in 2001. Beyond the chapel the road twists down an increasingly dramatic gorge with pinewoods clothing the steep slopes in places and a lot of hairpins.

The road is narrow, too narrow to have a white line down the middle. It's spectacular but there are many blind bends. I enjoyed it thoroughly but those of a very nervous disposition might be advised to go the other way out of Las Menas to regain the wider main road between Gérgal and Serón, the A-1178. I should also say here that I have a different map on which the shorter, more exciting road described above is marked as the ALP-407 and the main road the A-339. Either way, go downhill and you will come to Serón. Would I recommend a visit to Las Menas? Well, if you have any interest in industrial archaeology, social history and intriguing landscape then absolutely, yes. In fact, go now!

34. Along the Almanzora Valley

'All rivers are stories - connecting places, carrying history...'
(Philip Marsden)

Hatching a plan

I feel I'm overdue to explore a few places that I've been to on odd occasions but don't really know, such as Serón, Purchena, Macael and Cuevas del Almanzora. As I spread out and look at a new and rather attractive map of Almería province that I've recently bought, an idea arrives in my head. The map is colour-shaded for height, with various greens for low ground and browns for the uplands; the higher the land, the darker the brown. What becomes apparent because of this arrangement, although really I already have a sense of this, is that these places that I don't know so well are all on or close to the Río Almanzora. Moreover, the valley of this river runs west to east across the whole of Almería province and pretty much bisects the northern half of it. A journey from the source to the mouth of the Almanzora would be a good way to link these places and get a feel for that region.

Time for more research. The *Atlas de Almería* proves a good place to start. I find a map of the province entitled Demarcación Hidrológica : Cuencas Hidrográficas. In other words, drainage basins, the areas drained by each river and its tributaries. This shows the rivers of Almería, which include a roll-call of 'A's from north to south: Almanzora, Antas, Aguas, Alías, Andarax. The data it gives for the Río Almanzora say that it is 105 kilometres long and drains an area of 2,611 square kilometres. Any rain falling on the northern slopes of the Sierra de los Filabres or the southern slopes of the Sierras de las Estancias, Almagro, and Almagrera will flow into the Río Almanzora. The thumbnail sketch of the river in the *Atlas de Almería* concludes by saying that it has many *'barrancos y arroyos'* (ravines and streams) in its upper course and *'ramblas de gran torrencialidad'* (more or less 'dry riverbeds prone to dramatic flooding') in its middle and lower course.

Next, it's time to decide where the source actually is. The *Atlas de Almería* doesn't give an unequivocal answer but on more than one map it suggests, with bold blue delineation, that the south-bank tributary called the Río Alcóntar is the key. At this point a slight mystery arises. The river named as the Río Alcóntar in the *Atlas de Almería* is not called that on any of the three other detailed maps that I have, two of Almería province and one of Andalucía. On these maps it is either the Río Sauco or the Rambla de Sauco. To obfuscate the situation further, the three maps have three slightly different spellings of this name: Sauco, Sáuco, and Saúco. It gets even more complex too: the atlas does have a Rio del Saúco but it's the next tributary, eastwards from and parallel to what it calls the Río Alcóntar. Also, the atlas's Río del Saúco is called, on the other maps, the Río or Rambla de las Herrerías. By this time, I've got maps strewn across the room and I suspect I've lost you. Of course, in the great scheme of things, none of this really matters.

Finally, I spot that the source is not far from a summit in the Sierra de los Filabres also called Sauco which is almost 2,000 metres high. The situation might become clearer when I get hold of a copy of the most detailed local map for that area, which I think is sheet 1012-2 of the Mapa Topográfico Nacional de España.

The *Atlas de Almería* comes with a neat transparent overlay showing all of the *municipios* (administrative districts) of the province. This allows me to work out that if I follow the Río Almanzora from source to mouth, I'll pass through 13 of these: Alcóntar, Serón, Tíjola, Armuña de Almanzora, Suflí, Purchena, Olula del Río, Fines, Cantoria, Arboleas, Zurgena, Huércal-Overa and finally Cuevas del Almanzora. Soon after this I'm casting my eye back on various newspaper cuttings; in one of them I find a quote from a government public works delegate called Felipe López referring to:

"the 70,000 people that live in the 28 towns of the Almanzora valley". Clearly, I'll have no shortage of places to explore. So far so good; I've discovered all this and barely moved from my desk. It's time to get out there and start the journey.

Headwaters

So the journey begins, though by now it's many months later and I've decided, for various reasons, that doing it all on foot is not the best idea. It won't be an exhaustive gazetteer giving details of every town and village along the way either. I'll pick and choose as whim takes me or things catch my attention.

I've driven east to west, up the Almanzora valley, and arrived in Alcóntar, a cluster of houses with sloping tiled roofs packed around short narrow streets on the northern slopes of the Filabres. The village is almost 1,000 metres above sea level and, at the end of March, the air is clear and crisp. Around the neat square are the town hall, the church (locked) and the Bar Los Tres Morales. Just off the square is the town fountain, with a couple of carved figures dated 2010, though the *fuente* is no doubt much older and comes, I've read, from the 'arroyo del Sauco' . A few metres down from there is Calle Acequia with, as the name would indicate, irrigation water audible in a culvert close by. Close by is the small village swimming pool. At this time of year it's green and uninviting. No doubt it will be sorted out before the summer.

A little way further down still is the Río Almanzora itself, little more than a trickle today. There are tall trees here, poplars and pines, and from somewhere close I can hear a great spotted woodpecker hammering loudly. There is a long walk from here of almost 18 kilometres, indicated on an information board, the Sendero de Los Rincones. This however, goes north to Hijate, in entirely the opposite direction from where I want to go, so I decide to leave that for another day. My aim for today is to head higher up into the Filabres to get a sense of the gathering grounds where the initial tributaries coalesce to form the main river.

The map of Almería province (I haven't got the detailed local map, which I've failed to get round to ordering) shows a hamlet called Los Checas up to the south, one of more than half a dozen that lie on the slopes above. That looks like the area where I want to be. Just outside the village, I find Los Checas indicated, along with Las Carrascas, Los Molinos, Las Carboneras and El Saúco. The road immediately twists past a series of numbered white pillars marking, I presume, the Stations of the Cross then, a little further, the Rambla del Sauco lies below, in a surprisingly wide and fertile looking valley, with broad terraces. Crumbling stone *palomares* (pigeon lofts) stand above the road, impressive even in ruins, recalling times past.

After a couple of kilometres I'm not at all sure I'm on the right road. It's a bit of a maze, to be honest. I arrive at a tiny place called Domenes, a dead end. Back the way I've come, and another turn. This is Amarguilla, and I'm still not right. I call out of the window to an old couple outside their house above the road, asking for Los Checas. "You have to go down into the *rambla*, then up the other side," they shout back. I find a turning which has a sign to Aldeire and other places, not including Los Checas. I have a hunch it might be the right one though and drive down it, past what appears to be a disused factory. Down in the *rambla*, there is a sign indicating that Los Checas is to the right. But that isn't going to take me up into the Filabres. Nearby though, literally just a few metres away, is a sign to Almería, pointing up a sunken track between tall trees. This is interesting, given that Almería is many kilometres away on the far side of the 2,000 metre high Filabres mountain range. This is the track I take.

Very soon the tarmac finishes but the track continues, well-graded and wide, curving up the mountain slopes, passing occasional pines and then into thicker pine woods, before coming out to more open slopes again. I drive for ten minutes, twenty, half an hour, with deep dramatic valleys falling away. At one point there's even a Junta de Andalucía sign, giving the road number of this track, but I fail to note the details. Then the white domes of the observatory at Calar Alto appear, maybe three or four kilometres away and not that far above me. These are big slopes, with summits way higher than anything in the UK, and big distances. It's difficult to judge. I drive on for another fifteen minutes until, eventually, the track levels off and begins to dip slightly. This will do for today. I'm sure I'm above the highest springs that feed into the smallest tributaries that together form the infant Río Almanzora. This is near enough for me to claim I'm somewhere near the source of that river. After all, I'm playing a game I invented, so I can make the rules. And I'm in our small VW campervan, so I can stop and make a coffee and take my time, gazing out over this huge landscape. I've passed no vehicles and no people in the 45 minutes or so that I've been driving up here. This is western Europe and I'm on a numbered road, albeit unsurfaced, wide enough for two vehicles to pass easily, but totally deserted. It's amazing.

I resolve to come again sometime soon with Troy and drive right over the Filabres, maybe go up to Calar Alto for a 2,000 metre picnic, then see where we come down on the south side of the mountain chain. But for now I turn round and retrace my route. Way down below, across the upper Almanzora, there are many wind turbines on the Sierra de las Estancias. Nearer, the slopes are patched with pines. There's an occasional structure of very dark slate. I stop at one, where the drystone walls have been fashioned around some huge boulders protruding from the ground. Part of it was once roofed, though it's now collapsed, so this was perhaps a shepherd's shelter, not just an animal pen.

The journey back down to Alcóntar seems relatively quick, past a very high turning to Aldeire and lower ones to Los Pintaos and Los Sordos. The dashboard display tells me I've just done 12 kilometres each way up and down the mountain. You could spend days exploring this network of high mountain roads that link the score or more of tiny, remote hamlets. Now there's an idea.

On your bike

Back in Alcóntar, or strictly speaking just outside it, near the cemetery, there's a turning on the left (that is, not the one towards Serón) which I hope will take me to Pilancón. There, I hope to find the *vía verde* that I know follows part of an old railway line that came down the Almanzora valley. I've seen various mentions of the *vía verde* but don't know exactly where I can access it.

For once I've guessed correctly and the road twists entertainingly, unless you are in a hurry, across the undulating foothills to Pilancón which turns out to be an almost entirely abandoned cluster of houses. The road I'm on goes over a bridge and down below it I can see the trackbed of the old railway. I push on to the main road, the A-334, and turn left. Soon I'm at Estación de Hijate, right on the Granada/Almería provincial border. The old railway station is a hundred metres or so on the Granada side of the border. By the A-334 there is a small wooden signpost, pointing into Almería, indicating the *vía verde.* By now it's 6.30 in the evening but I figure that I can at least explore a little of the old railway. I take the bike off the rack on the back of the van and gear up.

The first part of the *vía verde* is barred with red and white tape and a notice warning that lorries are working, but they clearly aren't, so I ride round the tape and set off. There's a surprising downhill gradient. To the right is a valley, shallow but bounded with low, striking cliffs, and to the left are the wind turbines I'd seen from on high earlier. A ruined way-house stands by the track at one point, flanked by two dead trees. I get down to the bridge at Pilancón, just before which is a large map and information board showing that the *vía verde* runs to (or from) the far side of Serón. There's no time to do that much, out and back, right now. It's after 7p.m., so I turn and

326

cycle back up the gradient to Estación de Hijate. This has been just a flavour of what was once known, rather convolutedly, as the Great Southern of Spain Railway. My appetite has been whetted.

The Great Southern of Spain Railway

The major authority on this railway for English speakers, Don Gaunt, says of it: 'Built on a foundation of hopes and riches, the GSSR had ambitions beyond its means, got built anyway, ran out of money, got more, made a profit for a time, then made increasing losses'.

Most of Spain was criss-crossed by railways by the middle of the 19th century. However, there were none in Almería and although 600 kilometres of new roads were built in the province between 1850 and 1900, they were not of good quality. With the mining industry expanding rapidly, there was increasing pressure for railways to be built to get minerals to the coast for export. A decision was made to link Granada and Murcia and for this line in turn to connect to the port at Águilas. Observant readers will notice that none of these places are actually in Almería province. This is true, but let me explain. The full story is long and complex but the gist is that concessions for lines between Granada and Baza and also between Murcia and Lorca were granted separately, so the GSSR, when it finally came into being, was just to have a line from Baza to Lorca, with a separate link going from this at Almendricos to Águilas on the coast. In short, most of the GSSR lay in Almería province.

Work began on the Almendricos to Águilas section in 1887, though it did not open until 1899. As for the main stretch of line all manner of complications presented themselves, largely political, though the difficult terrain through which the line was to run meant that the costs were also a lot higher than had been estimated. The problems were finally overcome though. From the Almendricos direction, the line opened to Huércal-Overa in 1891, to Zurgena by

1892, to Albox (Almanzora) by 1893, and right through to Baza by the end of 1894.

After that bit of history, I'll revert to describing the line west to east, down-valley, in the direction in which I explored it and concentrating on the section through Almería province. This direction is also the way that the minerals went, carried to the coast for export. But just before that, I should mention that the section from Baza to Hijate, where the line entered Almería, passed through largely unpopulated countryside, climbing to Hijate, which was the highest point on the entire line. There's a logic here, because the Granada/Almería border at this point, as political boundaries often do, was following a watershed; in this case, between the drainage basins of the Río Almanzora to the east and the Río Guadalentín to the west. Hijate station is at 974 metres above sea level. There was a drop from there of 710 metres down to Zurgena. This meant that gravity helped with the loaded mineral trains, but to pull the wagons back up to Hijate, they needed dual or triple traction (two or three engines). The same situation applied, in reverse, on the Granada side, where there was a significant drop to Baza.

Incidentally, in the information provided locally about the line, such as on the board mentioned in the previous section, it is not always called the GSSR. The railway is also known simply as *'la línea férrea Guadix - Almendricos'*, that is, 'the Guadix - Almendricos iron line'.

Back on the *vía verde*

A few days later I'm back at the bridge at Pilancón, with my bike, set to explore further, eastwards, down-valley, with the aid of gravity. A couple of kilometres from the Pilancón bridge, at Km 108 on the old railway, are the remains of the Cargadero del Tesorero, the Loading Bay of the Treasury. The name comes from the fact that it was where ore from the Hispano-Dutch Treasury (Tesorero) Mine was loaded on to the railway. A 15.5 kilometre long cableway (a strong moving aerial cable with wagons or very large buckets hanging from it) brought the ore from the mine which was in a remote part of the mountains. The cableway had 310 wagons, each of which carried 450 kg at a time, travelling 2.5 metres per second. This meant that 40 tonnes of ore per hour arrived at the loading bay.

The main thing to see now is a long masonry wall with many niches, inhabited by a noisy flock of jackdaws. By going a hundred metres further along the track, it's possible to scramble up to the top of the loading bay. Here, there are still piles of dark brown iron-rich rock and the toothy remnants of a building. However, an adjacent information panel, itself somewhat the worse for wear, says: 'Es el cargadero que peor a soportado el paso del tiempo', 'It is the loading bay which has least well withstood the passage of time.'

A kilometre further on, right by the old track, lies Fuencaliente, a village overlooked by the church of Santa Cruz on a small rocky hill. I push the bike part way up and walk the rest to get the wide view along the valley of the Almanzora. The fast descent back to the vía verde takes less than a minute. The next feature that catches my eye comes in the form of a little local humour. Attached to a wooden telegraph pole right by the track is a hand-painted sign announcing ESTADIO LOS DONATOS. Los Donatos is just a few houses and the stadium is a small patch of more or less level ground, struggling for a few blades of grass and bounded by rock outcrops and the odd pile of debris, with kid-sized goalposts at either end.

Aided by the gradient, I'm soon at Estación de Serón, which is a couple of kilometres out of the town of the same name. The station here was the busiest between Baza and Zurgena because in the early 1900s the iron mines to the south, around Las Menas, were the most productive in Almería province. Thousands of tonnes of ore came down out of the mountains on cableways, from mines like Manzana, La Leona, Perdigona, Ignacia and Ramalillo. The buckets on the cableway held 480 kg each and arrived at a rate of one every half minute. This amounted to about 500 tonnes in a 10-hour working day.

There is a lot to see at the old station site, all well preserved. The station building is now the Restaurante La Estación. A low terrace of cottages alongside is, predictably, Calle Estación. There's a water tower, a guardhouse and a toilet block. Opposite are the remains of a huge hopper which could hold 20,000 tonnes of ore. Just below this is the base of a turntable. This was used for turning engines until the mechanism was removed in 1976.

One of the most distinctive relics, between a short stretch of the original rails, is a metal weighbridge with the details:

GSSR

W. & T. AVERY

MAKERS

LONDON &

BIRMINGHAM

1889

This was used for checking the weight of the mineral trucks before they set off for the coast. Because this station was the nearest to many of the mines, it was the reception point for all the equipment that was brought in. It was also the arrival point for people looking for work and their families; all in all a hive of activity.

Nowadays there is play equipment for children here too and, whilst I was there, a group of school kids were piling back onto a coach after a visit to La Estación de los Cuentos, the Station of Stories. One of the large old buildings has been turned into a place that enthuses children with the world of tales and books. There are vividly painted designs, flowers, a life-size figure made from scrap wood, an old bike welded to the railway line, and huge poems and quotes on the outside walls. *'Leer es... aprender, viajar, soñar.'* 'To read is ... to learn, to travel, to dream.' The school group were being waved off by a guy with a broad-brimmed hat, a huge beard, a big smile and an orange jumper; every inch the storyteller.

35. Heading past Marbletown

'Macael tiene una vaca y la ordeñan los de Olula.' 'There's a cow in
Macael and it's being milked by that lot in Olula'.
(Local phrase)

Back on track

Pedalling on, less than a kilometre from Estación de Serón I find
further access to the *vía verde* at Los Zoilos, alongside another
children's play area. There are odd bits of old switching gear and
signals by the trackway along this stretch, and views south to Serón
perched on its prominent hill. It's April and poppies are flagging vivid
red at the sides of the track just before a small tunnel of square cross-
section that takes the green way under the A-334. Very soon after
this the *cargadero* (loading bay) at Los Canos comes into view. What
remains is an enormous and impressive hopper, once capable of
holding up to 40,000 tonnes of iron ore. The ore came down to the
loading bay at Los Canos by cableway from the mines at Las Menas,
San Miguel and Dulce María. All of the cables in the area (there were
many) were 26-27mm diameter, and made of steel by an English
company called Ropeways Ltd.

The buckets on the cableway to Los Canos each held 800 kg of
ore and the system could deliver about 1,200 tonnes to the hopper in
a normal 10 hour working day. It all worked by gravity, with the
weight of the laden buckets coming downhill being sufficient to haul
the empty buckets back up from Los Canos to the mines. At the base
of the hopper are two parallel tunnels which once had rail sidings
running into them. The rails are no longer there but the Los Canos
loading tunnels are still in good repair and are accessible. They had
multiple chutes spaced so that, when a sequence of wagons went
into the tunnels, ore would drop exactly into each of them without
any spillage or the need for shunting. Whilst the wagons were being
filled, the engine would steam the three kilometres to Estación de

Serón to use the turntable before returning to Los Canos facing in the right direction, hitching to the wagons and heading for the coast. Up to seven trains per day hauled the ore off to be loaded for export at the El Hornillo wharf at Águilas.

Very close to the hopper a wooden post indicates that this is 'Km 0' on the Camino Natural Vía Verde del Hierro, its official start/finish. The bed of the old line continues eastwards but for me and my bike, for the moment, it was time to pedal back and have a look at Serón.

Serón

I'm not sure if you'd call Serón a small town or a large village. Whichever, it's a place worthy of exploration. It's got a shop window with a combination of dresses and garish kids' footballs, a post office open for just an hour each day, and striking red and black logos indicating that hams have been made here since 1880. In one street I came on a plaque commemorating the centenary of the birth of Don Francisco Martínez García (1903-2001), 'businessman and founder of Jamones de Serón S.A.' Obviously he was the guy who put Serón hams on the map. In front of the town hall is the Plaza Nueva, an elegant expanse of marble with a fountain, trees and a cafe; a good place for a coffee.

Above the Plaza Nueva the streets such as the Calle Real are mostly narrow and cobbled. Here, dating from the 19th and early 20th centuries, the time of greatest wealth from the mines, there are casas señoriales, 'noble houses' of three storeys with ornate cast-iron balconies. Past the considerable bulk of the Church of the Annunciation, a combination of mudéjar and Christian architecture, the streets lead upwards to the remains of the castle. This was built by the Moors in the 13th century, during the Nasrid era. It has tapered stonework towers, though much of what is visible now is reconstructed. Below the main structure there's also what appears to be a performance area with cast-iron tiered seating; bring you own cushion, presumably.

At the top, there is a neo-*mudéjar* style clock tower built in the early 20th century. The other feature on the highest part of the castle is a huge cast-iron viewing platform. Admittedly it does afford superb views but it is basically a great ugly intrusion. Unless of course you perceive it as an art installation, in which case it raises questions about the juxtaposition of the modern and the ancient.

Serón goes down in history as a key place where, long after the Christian Reconquest had been finalised in 1492, the Moors rebelled in 1568. For more on this, see the section on Purchena, below.

Hopping down the line

Tíjola is the next sizeable place down the GSSR line. The town has a very long history, sustained by its extensive *vega*(area of fertile land), stretching down to the Río Almanzora and on its far bank towards Cela. Like the Estación de Serón, Tíjola's station too was some way out of the town. It's on the far side of the A-334, from where the turn-off to it is signposted. It was not a mining station and was used mainly for passengers but its importance was that it had a reliable water supply for the steam locomotives. This came from a spring about one kilometre away to the south.

A stretch of the old rail bed has been restored but as far as I can ascertain it's not an official *vía verde*. There is much to see though. The station building was for a time used as workshops for apprentices but the evidence suggests that is no longer the case. The guard hut appears to be the favoured position for an old man with a stick who likes to hail each vehicle that passes, waving it forward in case the driver can't see where he's going. There's a height gauge and a weighbridge complete with rails. Close by is an old diesel engine, number 11339, from the days when Renfe (the Spanish state railway

334

company) ran the line. The original toilet block is sealed with concrete and in some disrepair. A cylindrical metal water tank atop a stone-clad tower still has its delivery pipe, there's a further grey-painted water pipe in good condition, and a much bigger water tower, which I imagine dates from the Renfe days. This latter has a plaque above its wooden door announcing Avenida de los Ferroviarios. The platforms are still very much in evidence and, with a touch of unintended irony, the *parque infantil*, the children's playground, immediately across from the station building, contains the only train you are likely to see here nowadays. Just for the record, it's bright red, blue and yellow and isn't going anywhere.

Purchena and the Moorish Rebellion

Purchena is my next port of call. It has typically narrow streets and as proof that this stretch of the Almanzora Valley now benefits from the famous marble industry, there are striking carvings dotted around the place; a large shoe with a turned-up toe in one small town square, a nod to the Moorish influence, I guess, and a vast narrow tilted marble head outside the town hall. Other than that, there's the church of San Ginés, designed in 1550 by the architect Juan de Orea. It's built from huge blocks of warm golden stone with, just outside, a much smaller structure, temporarily empty, on the glass window of which a small handwritten notice says LA VIRGEN ESTA RESTAURANDOSE, 'the Virgin is away being restored'.

Two streets carry handmade blue and brown ceramic plaques giving their names as Calle Pablo Picasso and Calle Princesa Kristina de Noruega. There may be other similar plaques that I didn't find. I've yet to discover what the connection is between Princess Kristina of Norway or indeed Picasso and this small southern Spanish village. Purchena's streets are also enhanced by a number of colourful murals featuring the words of Ibn Battuta, José Zorrilla, Antonio Gala and Ibn Jalis. The latter was a 12th century poet who lived in Purchena.

Idealistic and presumably young inhabitants have also taken to the streets with their stencils, contributing both thought-provoking statements such as 'LA EDUCACION ES LA ARMA MAS PODEROSA QUE PUEDES USAR PARA CAMBIAR EL MUNDO', ('Education is the most powerful weapon that you can use to change the world', a quote from Nelson Mandela), and 'PURCHENA TALLER STENCILS IS AMAZING', which latter effort the average onlooker might consider open to debate.

Before this visit I didn't know Purchena at all, so the next discovery was particularly intriguing. Above the village is a small but prominent plateau. The obvious modern features here are a small chapel and a statue of Christ but it has been a defensive site for centuries. A fortress was built here in the 10th century by the Moors from Al-Mariyya (Almería).

It's very evident if you look at a relief map of south-east Spain that the Almanzora Valley is the obvious natural routeway between the coast of eastern Almería, which is often called the Levante, and the inland depressions and plateaus around Baza, then on north-west to Jaén or south-west to Guadix and Granada. Monitoring and control of movement along the valley was thus always a strategic necessity, so at various times castles (at Serón, Tíjola, Fines, Cantoria and Albox, for example), towers (at Purchena, Arboleas and Zurgena, for instance) and other fortified buildings were constructed. The fortified Alcazaba on the plateau at Purchena was a key feature too. These fortifications were built at different times; they weren't designed from scratch as a single unified system. In fact, a tower was built to the north of Purchena, across the valley from the Alcazaba, to provide sight-lines to other towers and castles so that messages, using mirrors or fire, could be relayed to the Alcazaba.

The Alcazaba on the Purchena plateau was an enclosure (*recinto* in Spanish)where the remains of 13 towers have been found. The peak of the development of these defensive systems came during the Nazarí Kingdom of Granada when the Muslims were opposing the steady Christian advance of the 13th to 15th centuries. Purchena finally fell and was incorporated into Castille after the Christians defeated the Muslims in 1489. Not much later, when Juan de Madrid visited Purchena in 1517, he reported that several of the towers were already in bad repair.

After the defeat of the Muslims, the first Christian mayor of Purchena was Don Rodrigo Manrique, who ruled under the higher power of the Duke of Medinaceli. However, the *mudéjars* (the Muslims who had agreed to remain in place under the Christians) were not treated well. Several of the conditions under which they had agreed to surrender were being breached and this led to uprisings in 1500-01 and then, more seriously, in 1568-70. This latter episode, generally known as 'the Moorish Rebellion', was initially led from Las Alpujarras by Abén Humaya, who appointed Jerónimo el Maleh commander-in-chief of the Almanzora area. El Maleh occupied the castles at Serón and Cantoria and declared a rebellious mini-state stretching from Serón to Zurgena with the Alcazaba at Purchena at its centre.

Abén Humaya immediately took the opportunity to revive traditional Islamic customs and in 1569 called people from all the towns in the old Kingdom of Granada to convene for a series of athletic, musical and dance competitions. Among the 12 athletic disciplines were the long jump, triple jump, foot races, throwing the weight, and archery, making these games very reminiscent of the original Olympics.

In 1570 El Maleh died and was succeeded by El Habaquí, who led the last phase of the rebellion. It took a campaign of almost a year, from December 1569 to August 1570, led by Don Juan of Austria, to put the rebellion down. To do this, his forces came out from Granada and went via Baza over into the Almanzora Valley. At Serón (1st - 9th March 1570) they defeated the Moorish rebels only at the second attempt, then went on to Tíjola (19th - 21st March), Purchena (25th March - 1st April) and Cantoria (2nd April), before passing via Zurgena and veering over to Sorbas, then Tabernas, Rioja just to the north of Almeria, and so back through Las Alpujarras to Granada. The Moorish uprising along the Almanzora Valley had been defeated and very soon the other Moorish redoubt, Las Alpujarras, fell too.

Meanwhile, back in modern Purchena, at the base of the plateau are the remains of the Torre del Agua and an *aljibe* which provided those in the fortified enclosure above, and those in the village below in times of peace, with a reliable water supply. At the base of the tower by the side of the *aljibe* is a hole in the wall. You can slip in through this and though there's not a lot to see, the neat brickwork of the arches and the vaulted roof is impressive.

Back on the GSSR, Purchena has a station too. Don Gaunt, in his 2006 book, says: "The station is not easy to find." That may have been true when Don was researching the line in the early 2000s but now it's not too difficult. I park opposite the cement works, just a few metres from where the road to Urrácal branches off the A-334. The old trackbed is well surfaced here and has been brought up to spec with wooden safety rails in places, though as far as I can tell this stretch is not an official *vía verde* at the time of writing (April 2016). Initially I head back in the direction of Tíjola because I can see something above the track that I want to investigate, though I can't at first see just what it is. As I get closer I see that it's a cast-iron aqueduct on neat stone piers, bringing irrigation water across the old line. Once over the line, it turns 90 degrees and the channel becomes a raised *acequia* running along the top of an arched stone structure with details picked out in brickwork. This looks to date from the same time as the original railway.

I now head back eastwards as I'm pretty sure that's where Purchena station lies, about a kilometre away. In 15 minutes I'm there. As in some other places, this station is now a restaurant called, surprise surprise, Restaurante Estación. A swish modern sign announces El Andén Cocktails but the place is closed today. The station name has gone but I can make out the distinctive standard shape of the original toilet block, or its top at least, over a high wall. At least things are better than when Don Gaunt was here. He said then: 'The station is in a poor state and cannot last too many more years'. There's nothing else to see now, except the discovery that you can more easily get here by car via an insignificant turning off the main A-334, which is not far away.

Marbletown

A few kilometres downriver lies Macael, Spain's 'Marbletown'. It provided marble for Granada's Alhambra, the Mezquita in Cordoba and the Escorial palace near Madrid. It now produces 80% of the country's output. Marble, incidentally, is a metamorphic rock, limestone or dolomite changed by incredible heat and pressure in the earth's crust. Macael was not on the GSSR line (and, strictly speaking, it's not on the Río Almanzora either but a couple of kilometres south of it). However, in the days when the railway was operating, the marble was taken as freight, mainly from Fines-Olula station. After iron ore, marble was the next most important commodity carried by the GSSR in its heyday. Nowadays, with no railway as an option, it goes by road, though there are still marble yards alongside the old line, where the stone was cut and prepared for transport.

The extent of the industry can be seen most strikingly to the south of Macael from the A-349, the road that goes over the Sierra Filabres to Tabernas. Whole mountains have been excavated, gleaming faces of white marble are exposed, and heavy vehicles are constantly on the move. The vast opencast quarries are a strangely compelling sight. In the town itself the source of its livelihood is also apparent everywhere. There's the Centro de Interpretación del

Mármol (*mármol* is marble), outside of which are displayed artefacts associated with the industry - a winch, a wagon, a marble cutter. There's also a tourist office but it's clear that the raison d'être of the place is marble rather than visitors. A fountain, a monument to the quarrymen and various statues decorate the streets. Most notable, on a roundabout, is the largest pestle and mortar in the world, weighing 32 tonnes and towering above the road signs that flank it. Traditionally, making a pestle and mortar was a task given to apprentices in the marble industry. At a single stroke this huge example declares in a quirky way what the town is about. It is, predictably, in the Guinness Book of Records and in 2016 found its way on to a list of the '15 most peculiar roundabouts in Spain' compiled by the travel website El Viajero Fisgón. A council spokesman said that before the pestle and mortar was made and displayed "visitors did not come to Macael" but now it is attracting 600 tourists per month.

On the edge of town are many processing works and storage yards and in a modern building, marble-clad of course, is the Centro Tecnológico de la Piedra, an institute concerned with the research, development and marketing of the magic stone. Although Macael is the centre of the industry, it's important in neighbouring towns such as Olula del Río, Fines and Cantoria too. Olula isn't surrounded by quarries, noise and dust but it does quite nicely out of the stone, as the quote at the head of this chapter suggests. One Spanish guidebook I've just been looking at describes marble as *oro blanco*, white gold. On my trip down the Almanzora Valley, the first traffic lights I saw were in Olula: clearly, I'd reached civilisation.

A sobering encounter

On this stretch of the GSSR the next station, midway between Olula and Fines, is called, with incontrovertible logic, Fines-Olula. I find it easily enough as it's right by the main road between the towns, though the buildings themselves are in dire need of rescue from the ravages of time, weather and vandals. An old crane that was used for loading marble on to the wagons is the main feature and a few metres away there's an original water pipe too. The line of the old railway can be seen along this stretch but it hasn't been preserved or rehabilitated in any way.

As you approach Fines from Olula you are in no doubt that marble is important here too. The town sign is mounted on a huge marble block to the right of the road, with a sculpture alongside. More striking though, above four tiered stone walls and to the left of the road, is a tall gleaming white sculpture of a woman. It's a beautiful and elegant figure, with head and arms swept back. The path up to it announces that this is the Mirador Rosa Galera, so I walk up to have a closer look and to check out the view. The sculpture is called 'Libertad' and is by Andrés García Ibáñez. When I begin to read the details though, the view out from the *mirador* becomes irrelevant and the gleaming woman takes on a new meaning.

Rosa Galera was a *'vecina del pueblo'*, a resident of the town who, on 30th May 2011, was *'brutalmente asesinada a manos de su ex pareja'*, viciously murdered by her ex-partner. So the work was made in this prominent position as a memorial to her and to record the total rejection by the town authorities of gender violence. It's a moving and powerful reminder not just of the tragic demise of Rosa Galera but also of the continuing problem of gender violence in Spain. It gives a sobering dimension to my whimsical journey down the Almanzora Valley.

In reflective mood, I walk back down from the *mirador* and cross the road to something else I've seen. This is a kind of linear park with palms, bushes, modern lights and occasional pergolas. It's like a wide central reservation between the opposite lanes of a barely-used dual carriageway. This is obviously the old railway line. I follow it eastwards through the town, coming at one point to a plinth (marble, it goes without saying) declaring that this is the Avenida Ferrocarril 1a

Fase, proof that the GSSR did come this way. Further along, beyond a *fuente*, there's an avenue of sculptures, the result of an international sculpture symposium, with work by Vasily Fedorouk (USA), Fetiye Boudevin (France), Kyoung Uk Min (South Korea), Leandro Seixas Díaz (Spain), Liliya Pabornikova (Bulgaria) and 15 others. All made of marble, naturally.

Soon after the sculpture avenue, the linear park reverts to a rough surface, with the normal road alongside for a kilometre or two before it veers away. The old railway is in a fairly unkempt state by this stage. It has been built over by marble works in at least one place as well, and so is impassable to all but the ultra-fanatical, of whom I am not one.

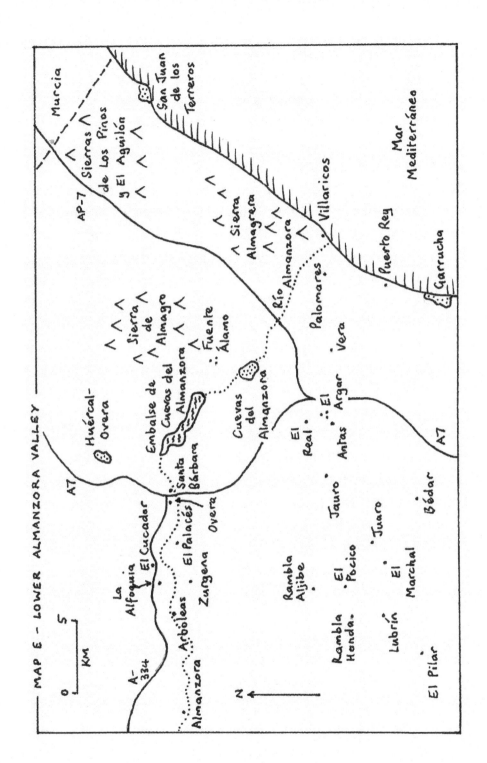

MAP E - LOWER ALMANZORA VALLEY

36. East of Fines

"The only certain thing in all this is that the future of the palace remains uncertain."
(María Dolores Carreño, talking of the Palacio del Almanzora)

The Almanzora motorway

By now I've come roughly to the mid-point, in terms of distance, in my exploration of the Almanzora Valley. From the Purchena/Macael/Olula del Río area, with all the marble traffic funnelling eastwards along it, the main road is distinctly busier than further west. Which brings us to the Almanzora motorway, a project on which work began in 2005 with the intention that it would ultimately connect the A7 near Huércal-Overa with the A92 at Baza. In April 2011, with a couple of sections completed, work was suspended when the funds ran out. Subsequently many residents and businesses, particularly those in the Albox area, were frustrated not only by the total lack of progress but also the uncertainty as to when work might restart. There were a number of high-profile demonstrations against this situation. Finally, in late 2013, the motorway received 'Gran Proyecto' (Grand Project) status from the European Union, with associated funding of about €63 million, which meant work could begin again, initially on an 8.7 kilometre section past Albox, completing the section between Fines and El Cucador. As to when the entire link from Baza to the A7 will be finished, no-one is saying.

The Pearl of the Almanzora

East of Fines, the main road veers to the north away from the course of the river while the older road, more or less close to the GSSR line, heads for Cantoria. The town is a warren of narrow streets and, having become geographically embarrassed on one visit (i.e. lost), this time I take the road that curves around to the south of the town.

This brings me to the old station. Nearby is a street plan of the town proclaiming 'Cantoria - Perla del Almanzora', the Pearl of the Almanzora. Opposite the old station buildings is a disused marble works, its entrance open and windows broken. In the yard are jibs and wagons, rollers and marble cutters, stacks of marble shards and abandoned headstones, rusty chains and tanks, with weeds and bulrushes growing around and between the abandoned debris; not a commercially vibrant scene but certainly a fascinating opportunity for a photographer.

By the station itself there's a spacious paved area with a long pergola. The main station building still has the name CANTORIA in place and is in the traditional livery with window surrounds and corner edges picked out in dark red, as is the toilet block. A decade ago Don Gaunt described new buildings being constructed in the style of the station. These fit in well and give a sense of purpose to the area. One of them is the municipal music school.

El Palacio del Almanzora

Cantoria also has a palace. Its first incarnation came in the 16th century, when a grand building was erected on the remains of a Moorish fortress. The current incarnation of the Palacio del Almanzora dates back to 1872. It's an elegant manor house in white marble, the construction of which continued through the late 18th and early 19th centuries and is considered the best example of neo-classical architecture in the province. You'd imagine it would be a cultural gem of which the locality is proud. Instead the building is crumbling and semi-ruined. Despite the best efforts of pressure groups to call for restoration work on the palace, nothing has been done, seemingly because ownership of the building is split between the council and two private owners.

In early 2016 the mayor of Cantoria, Purificación Sánchez, announced that "provisional repair works" would be carried out to the section of the building owned by the council, to prevent further structural deterioration. However, these provisional works amounted only to the installation of a flimsy roofing panel. The council admits that, even if agreement about major renovation work can be reached with the two private owners, such a project would be beyond the coffers of the town.

María Dolores Carreño, a member of an association of supporters of the palace who are pushing for renovation, Salvemos El Palacio del Almanzora, admitted there was little hope of the building ever being open to the public, pointing out that: "There is no money to put it into public ownership and carry out a proper restoration."

Arboleas

I take a road east out of Cantoria, hoping to find the next station in the sequence, Almanzora. At least, I assume that is what it was called. It's true that the map I'm using, a map of the whole province at a scale of 1: 235,000, lacks detail, but about four kilometres east of Cantoria, and on the line of the railway, is a settlement marked by a black dot and the name Almanzora. It proves easy enough to find the station, in its new incarnation as the Cafe-Bar La Estación. However, there is no name on it but I subsequently read that, even though it is four kilometres due south of Albox, this is the town it was named after, a clear clue to Albox's size and importance.

Albox itself is well north of the Río Almanzora. The town has its own wide *rambla*, the product of the confluence of the Rambla de Oria, the Arroyo de Olías and the Rambla del Saliente. The combined occasional waters of these streams form a single north-bank tributary of the Río Almanzora, feeding in roughly where the Cafe-Bar La Estación stands.

By now I'm on a twin mission, trying to keep tabs on both the railway and the river. My next tactic is to start from Arboleas, on my bike, aiming to follow the *rambla* back upstream, seeing how far I can get. It's nine o'clock on a cold February morning in 2017 as I pedal westwards on a good track, along the north bank of the *rambla*. Very soon though, the track ends. What to do? I opt to follow tractor tyre marks down into the gravelly *rambla* bed. I manage some further progress, criss-crossing shallow and narrow rivulets threading the wide river bed and passing a local tending a huge blazing pyre of olive clippings. It isn't easy though and after maybe three kilometres, I decide to bail out when I spot a strip of tarmac coming down to the north bank.

I take it and begin heading back to Arboleas, through a more or less continuous string of old settlements. In one of these, La Perla, by absolute chance I suddenly see a familiar figure in front of a house set back from the road. "Dave?" I shout. "I thought it looked like you!" comes the reply. I knew that David Elliott-Binns, a key figure in the Arboleas Birdwatching Group, lived somewhere around here but despite having stood at his shoulder, binoculars akimbo, on the lookout for bluethroats or whimbrels many times, I've never been to his house. Until now. "A drink?" asks Dave. And so, over an extremely welcome mug of tea that thaws the finger-ends poking out of my cycling gloves, he tells me that just along the road are the remains of Arboleas station.

When I set off again I'm there within two minutes, the abandoned shell of the building standing prominently above the road. It still retains its tiled name panels, ARBOLEAS, even though it's a couple of kilometres out of that village. The trackway is obvious, as are the platform edges, but the building is steadily falling into ruin. After finding this further piece of the jigsaw, I cover the short distance back to Arboleas feeling positive and, now the sun is higher, distinctly warmer.

Arboleas gets its name from the trees lining both banks of the river. It's an ancient settlement, traditionally supported by the citrus and olive groves covering the flat areas of the valley. Dominating the town is a restored octagonal tower, la Torre Vigía, built originally in the 12th century as part of the communication and defence system of the valley in response to the threat of incursions from the coast. It's easy to park in the upper part of the village by the Parque del Cerro del Torreón. Metal lettering on a wall indicates that this is also known as the Parque Alcalde Francisco Pere* **ras. This is not a mistake on my part; the unfortunate former mayor's name has lost some of its components. Stroll round through the park and you reach a rising walkway that twists up to the tower, which is surrounded by a riot of brick and stone terraces and steps. It's a great viewpoint over the town and in both directions along the valley. Also in the upper part of the village and worth a look is the Museo Pedro Gilabert, a museum dedicated to the work of an internationally known and self-taught local sculptor.

Zurgena and La Alfoquia

From Arboleas, the road via Los Menchones to Zurgena mostly follows the south bank of the river, overlooking extensive citrus groves. Prominent at the edge of Zurgena is a very tall and slender brick chimney at the end of a small building by the *rambla*. To investigate this, I have to go round behind the architecturally undistinguished modern pavilion, the Pabellon Municipal de Zurgena Pascual Martos A. Jimenez. There are no obvious clues to the chimney's former function, but alongside it, I strike gold, to my way of thinking at least; a disused mill. It's a long, low building with millstones both inside and out. Much of the workings are still in situ, with wooden hoppers, cogs, axles and belts.

It's clearly been a long time since anything was last milled here (I've subsequently heard that it processed almonds) and the whole place is, sadly, steadily collapsing. One end of the mill is perched right on the edge of the *rambla*, with stone buttresses retaining it. Below is an adit, a neat arched stone tunnel leading from under the mill, presumably to lead used water back into the riverbed. I see no sign of a waterwheel though, so I'm not sure how the whole thing was powered. I'm sure someone out there must know more about this mill. If you do, I'd love to hear about it.

Opposite the municipal pavilion is the Parque Gines Parra, named after a local painter. Go in through the arched entrance, and straight ahead is a flight of steps that takes you up to the Torre del Reloj (Clock Tower). The well-graded steps end, rather oddly, about ten metres below the octagonal tower which, sure enough, has a plain clock on one of its faces. There is no information on site about the tower which, as at Arboleas, was presumably used for early warnings against attacks. Apparently, all Zurgena's early town records have been lost.

For an old village Zurgena has unusually wide central streets and a chance conversation I had with local resident Robin Hawkins explained why this may be so. Robin told me: "A tributary used to flow through Zurgena from the hills behind it, and into the Almanzora down by the Park Bar at the ford. Before the rains of 1973, it used to flow down the wide street called Avenida 19 de Octubre where the market is currently held on a Friday. When it got to the Tobacco Bar, it flowed left into the main road through the *pueblo,* also called Avenida 19 de Octubre. That name continues through to where the road goes out of the *pueblo* to Arboleas. It makes me wonder if that was the date of the rain. The old course of the river then turned right, past the supermarket, and flowed down into the Almanzora. I'm told it washed away several houses and some people were killed. As a result, a cutting was made through the hill on the south bank of the Almanzora. A new road and bridge were built through the cutting, and across the Río Almanzora, and a culvert was dug diverting the river away from the village and this now runs parallel to the new road." Robin stressed that these details were based on what he had heard and observed, rather than necessarily being hard and fast. He urged me to check the facts as far as I could, so I'm happy to absolve Robin of any responsibility for what is written here, and I'd be delighted to hear from anyone who can clarify the details or add to Robin's account of that devastating flood. Robin also told me that there are some interesting large photos of Zurgena from the 1960s before the river was diverted: one in the town hall and another in the Hostal Marquesado on the main street. Regarding the 1973 rain, the most extreme rain recorded in Almería province was indeed in Zurgena, over the days of 18th and 19th of October, with 600 mm falling in 24 hours.

On the north side of the Río Almanzora is La Alfoquia, a large sprawling village, once considered part of Zurgena but now with its own identity. It's still in the same municipality, which explains why one of its main features, the next railway station in the sequence, is called ZURGENA. The wide track areas, platforms and a whole complex of maintained buildings are here, in good condition and still used for concerts and other purposes.

The main road east from La Alfoquia leads past a rest area with an old steamroller (why?) in a position of prominence. A turning on the right then leads to another old and scattered village: Overa. The river valley is wide here. The intermittently active *rambla* is relatively narrow and much of the rest of the flat land by the river is given over to arable land and citrus and olive groves. Overa appears to be something of a backwater, largely a haven of traditional Spanish life, despite the proximity of the A7 motorway. The road through the village leads back out to the A-334 almost at the point where the motorway cuts south through the landscape.

A little-known landscape

Tucked east of the motorway lies the small settlement of Santa Bárbara, a village that I can't think you would go to by chance. It's not on the way to anywhere; hence my suggestion that it's a little-known landscape. There's an ancient square tower on a conical hill above the village, and a picnic site with a kids' playground and a barbeque area. Close by are the broken remnants of a substantial stone bridge over the Río Almanzora. The approaches and side arches are still there but the central span has simply gone. You can walk out on the tarmac right to the brink but please take care. I imagine this was once the major road, the A-340N (the A7 motorway is just a hundred metres away and obviously replaced it) and I assume a flash-flood, quite possibly the one in October 1973, did the damage.

Keen to follow the *rambla* downstream to the head of the Almanzora Reservoir, I set off, walking along the gravelly bed, constricted here between steep rocky slopes. I'm guessing it won't be long before I see an upper arm of the lake, though again I don't have the detailed local map. I've not gone far when I meet a couple coming the other way. I ask if they've been as far as the reservoir. No, they say, they haven't. It turns out they are geocachers, Dave and Barbara Sewart, who have been to find a cache at a little-known hermitage in a side valley a few kilometres downstream. (*Geocaching* is an outdoor 'treasure hunting' game, hugely popular, in which enthusiasts navigate to a specific set of GPS coordinates and then attempt to find the *geocache,* usually a small container, hidden at that location.) They give me enough information for me to decide to return to the campervan and get my mountain bike down off its rack. It's going to be seven kilometres out-and-back to the hermitage, an uncertain distance further to the reservoir, and the *rambla* looks more or less manageable by bike. We walk back together and then, as Dave and Barbara settle in at a picnic table, I set off on my bike for all points east.

Finding La Santa

Some of the gravel in the mostly dry riverbed is small and loose, which makes the tyres sink, but in general it's okay. After about three kilometres two small yellow signs indicate 'Cuevas' to the right and 'Santa' to the left. 'Santa' sounds like the hermitage I'm looking for, so I veer that way, pass an area of striking blue and orange cliffs and then, on the left, there is an obvious valley. The geocachers told me this is the key to finding the place, though they also said you can't see the hermitage until you are some way in to the valley. At the valley entrance is a delightfully surreal installation, an ancient white-painted bicycle prominently fixed to the top of a tall pillar of stones. What appeals to me about this is that so few people will see it. It's a mysterious statement, pretty much in the middle of nowhere. Though the side-valley is narrow with steep rocky sides, the small but steady flow of water coming out of it is easily avoided. And then, very soon, after a couple of bends, there it is.

On the right, built against the valley side, are three small shrines with steps up to them and protective wooden railings. A small plaque indicates that this is 'La Santa', The (Female) Saint. The site is well cared for and alongside one of the shrines is a poem, *'A nuestra Virgen del Río'* by Josefina Egea, etched into a slate slab. There are tables here too. I guess people make a kind of pilgrimage here and bring a picnic to be eaten in the presence of their Virgin of the River. There's nothing to explain why the shrine is here and Dave the geocacher has already told me he has failed to find more information online, so for now it remains a mystery. Sites like this intrigue me, though I have to declare no particular religious interest.

From the shrine, I head back to the main *rambla* of the Río Almanzora and continue for another kilometre or so, initially by bike and then on foot, thinking 'surely over the next ridge I'll see an arm of the reservoir', but no. I reach a point at which I realise I could go on until I see the lake, but why? Well, to fill all the gaps and complete the journey from source to mouth of the Río Almanzora. But time is pressing and I've had sufficient sense of the terrain to satisfy me, so I head back upstream, intending to continue my journey at the dam that holds back the reservoir.

Below the reservoir

You might want to hop ahead to the final section of the next chapter, about the reservoir itself, which interrupts any attempt to follow the Río Almanzora downstream, before taking up the story here. No public roads or tracks follow the shores of the reservoir, so the story continues at the dam, the Embalse de Cuevas del Almanzora, where a notice by a track that appears as if it *might* follow the shoreline says: *'Camino muy peligroso. Uso restringido a personal autorizado'*, 'Very dangerous track. Use restricted to authorised personnel'.

The downstream journey therefore continues at the parking place just below the dam, which can only be accessed by going up the way you intend to come down. If you are enthusiastic you can go from here all the way to the coast along the south bank of the Río Almanzora on foot or by bike or, with care in places, by car. From the top of the dam the narrow road twists down to the base of the dam and the 'Mediterranean Games' lake. The road along the southern levee of the *rambla* is then almost flat. Every few hundred metres though, there is a weir where the bed of the *rambla* drops several metres and the road along the bank does likewise, dipping sharply before levelling out again. The banks of the riverbed are of sloping concrete and the bed itself is bare until, at Cuevas itself, there are a few football pitches set out in it. Even these though, have no blade of grass. The road jinks a few times to accommodate the points where other roads at right angles, ones that cross the riverbed, come up the slope, and just beyond the pitches it passes under the major bridge that takes the A-332, the Cuevas-Águilas road, over the *rambla*. There's a walkway by the road along this stretch, with palms and benches, and it's popular with the evening power walking fraternity.

At the edge of town the levee road becomes narrower and more functional, mainly just serving the fields and various rural enterprises. Shortly before the low bridge that carries the notoriously empty AP-7, the *peaje* (toll motorway) to Cartagena, the road becomes an unsurfaced though still passable track. It's okay but if you are very protective of your car, you may think twice about driving it. The worst that is likely to happen is that it will get covered in dust. By this stage, there are shrubs and even occasional signs of water in the *rambla*. It's not classic scenery but there is something impressive about the scale of the riverbed. Here it is, basically dry and yet, at times, it has seethed with water powering down to the sea. There's an 'edgelands' feel to the area; it doesn't exactly look like farmland, it's not quite desert, there are anonymous agricultural structures and at times there are scrappy corners with broken pallets and piles of rubbish but there's still something intriguing about the landscape.

It has character. There's a hint of a large quarry just over a low earth barrier to the right at one point. I stopped to check and sure enough, a huge hole, its base way below the level of the *rambla*, has been created, though it appears disused now and echoes with the calls of jackdaws that can be seen flying around holes high in the muddy cliffs. I surmise that it must have been sand and aggregate that were extracted here, as there's no sign of solid bedrock in the quarry walls.

I was lucky late one day towards the end of September 2016, coming this way as evening light spilled in and rare clouds massed to the north. This stretch of the *rambla* had more vegetation and several pools. Mallards and moorhens scudded about, black-winged stilts dotted the water, and a flock of 60 little egrets flew in and settled. The contrast with the stark, bare riverbed further back upstream couldn't have been greater. It was the water making the difference. A green sandpiper flew off, an unmistakable dark wader with an obvious white rump. The rich low light was doing wonders with the colours: vivid green vegetation and gleaming blue pools, with red, mauve and golden slopes beyond. Then, from just a few metres in front of me on the levee track an eagle lifted off, a real surprise. A booted eagle had been seen in the area and this was it. Then, a few seconds later, a kestrel did likewise and a hoopoe in looping flight completed an unusual trio.

Beyond the north bank of the riverbed, I recognised the church that perches on a knoll above Las Herrerías, with the desiccated outline of the Sierra Almagrera as a close backdrop. By now I could sense the sea ahead. Shortly, more familiar features on the north bank came into view: the buildings of Las Rozas and the castellated shape of Casa Siret (see chapter 10). Next, a complex of low, windowless buildings with a square pattern to the walls. This is the Bajo Almanzora desalination plant, built at a cost of €77 million but so badly damaged a year after it opened, in the floods of 2012, that it has been out of action ever since, with money yet to be found for repairs. Just beyond this, where another *rambla*, the Rambla de Canalejas, comes in from the north, huge chunks of the concrete facing have been destroyed by the same floods, and are also still awaiting repair. This is more easily seen from the north bank.

The track on the levee briefly comes out to tarmac, then is a track again as far as the main Garrucha to Villaricos road, the ALP-118. Ahead lies the estuary of the Río Almanzora, described in chapter 5. On the north bank, a cycle and pedestrian track, with a fancy wooden rail, runs inland from the ALP-118. A small sign at the seaward end of this, dated 2012, indicates that the plan was to extend it as far as Los Lobos. However, it runs for just two kilometres before literally seeming to crumble away to nothing at the point where the back road from Villaricos to Las Herrerías dips to cross the Rambla de Canalejas. Another case, no doubt, of the money running out.

It's been a long, varied and fascinating journey from the far headwaters of the Río Almanzora for more than 100 kilometres through the heart of Almería province to the Mediterranean. As always when a journey ends, there's a slight pang of regret and a question hanging: what next? In this case, a return back upstream to explore Cuevas del Almanzora in more detail.

37. Cuevas del Almanzora

'Oasis and desert, cave villages and date palms: one could suppose
oneself in Africa.'
(Gerald Brenan)

The Castillo del Marqués de los Vélez

The Castillo del Marqués de los Vélez is the cultural centre of Cuevas
del Almanzora. To find it, you basically just drive uphill once you
reach the town. Depending on the route you take, this may involve
some narrow streets. You'll get there though, and once you do, there
is generous parking in the Plaza de la Libertad at the front of the
castle.

The castle dates from 1507, when Don Pedro Fajardo y
Chacón, the first Marqués de los Vélez, decided to have a fortress-
palace built around a Roman tower that had already been modified
by the Moors. The existing tower was remodelled to become the
keep, on top of which was a smaller tower housing a bell used to
warn of pirate attacks. The Castillo includes a large open area
enclosed within tall stone walls. The single entrance once had a
drawbridge on thick chains and this was the only way to cross the
moat that surrounds the castle. Three stone coats of arms adorn the
front wall above the entrance. The central shield is that of the first
Marqués, with those of his two wives flanking it.

Through the entrance and at an angle across the courtyard is
the Tourist Information office. This is in the two-storey Casa de la
Tercia, which was originally built as a granary and warehouse to store
tithes paid to the Marqués by the townspeople. In the same building
there is the town's free Archaeological Museum, displaying a range of
Bronze Age artefacts from the Argar site at Fuente Álamo. The
museum has pots, plus hunting, mining and farming tools, and a good
section on the burial traditions of the Argar people, showing a variety
of tombs and some of the grave goods provided to accompany the

dead on their onward journey. It's very much a traditional museum, with nothing interactive, but none the worse for that.

In an adjacent small gallery, there is a collection of 24 etchings by Goya and in a much larger gallery next to it, almost 50 prints, also by Goya. These, entitled *La Tauromaquia* (Bullfighting) are illustrations that he made for a large-format book called *Los Toros de Burdeos*. What diverts the eye in this gallery, almost more than the pictures, are the many huge ceramic urns, sunk almost to their necks in textured concrete. What is that all about?

Across the courtyard of the castle is the Museo Antonio Manuel Campoy. It's really an art gallery rather than a museum, and a good one. Not too big, and with a sprinkling of famous names such as Picasso, Miró and César Manrique. What I enjoyed though, was coming across artists with whose work I wasn't familiar. I jotted down a few of their names: Luis Brihuega, García del Moral, Mariano Peláez, Rafael Amézaga (a very striking and not at all gory bullfighting scene), Enrique Padial and Nicolás Martínez Ortiz. When you visit I dare say you'll be struck by half a dozen entirely different artists. In addition there are a couple of pieces by Jesús de Perceval, including the intriguing *Orfeo en los infiernos* (Orpheus in the fires of Hell). I knew de Perceval's name from having read about him being one of the founders of *'el Movimiento Indaliano'* back in the 1940s, but this was the first time I'd seen any of his work, and I was impressed.

Campoy, for whom the museum is named, was an essayist, novelist, journalist and art critic who wrote nearly 50 books and hundreds of newspaper articles. I suppose, on second thoughts, that the Museo Antonio Manuel Campoy does qualify for its status as a museum because as well as the many artworks, Campoy's study is preserved, behind glass, but in such a way that you feel you are in it. The sense you get from seeing it is: "He must have been an interesting guy!" What I haven't said yet is that a ticket to see this museum, and the two others described below, costs just €2.50 at the time of writing, or €1.25 for concessions: staggeringly good value.

In the castle courtyard there is also an amphitheatre with modern tiered seating. This proved an excellent venue for the Festival Flamenco del Jaroso in October 2015, which superbly celebrated the local flamenco tradition from the nearby mining district in the Sierra Almagrera. At the time of the mineral rush in the first half of the 19th century, thousands of miners came from the Sierra de Gádor and brought with them their particular style of flamenco. It is this style that the Festival Flamenco del Jaroso, now an annual event, commemorates. On the basis of the one we went to, I'd definitely recommend it; a vibrant experience under the stars in a great location.

Cuevas del Almanzora: a short circuit

The next stop on an easy walk round some of the town's main features is the Cueva Museo. To get there you go across the front of the castle, turn left alongside the castle wall, then take the Cuesta del Calvario. You pass the municipal washing place, which we'll come back to on our return, but just beyond it is the Cueva Museo. Outside the neatly whitewashed facade stand a huge ceramic urn and an authentically crumbling two-wheeled cart. The cave house itself is full of old artefacts. There's an ancient weighing machine, esparto baskets and sandals, an *arado romano* (a 'Roman or traditional plough', of a style used until the mid 20th century), beautifully carved double yokes for animals, and a wooden-tined fork. The bedroom, deep in the bedrock, with no windows and no doubt an almost constant temperature, has an old double bed, a small wooden crib and a rocking horse.

The kitchen, the traditional centre of household life, has a big fireplace, a rack to hold several ceramic flagons of water (there was no running water in these houses until the middle of the 20th century) and a double sink carved out of a huge single block of marble. There is also various milling and threshing paraphernalia, for example, a small threshing board, a *trillo*, with metal inserts on its base, along with photos showing how these things were used back in the day.

What intrigued me most though, having been mildly confused when I was researching the history of milling for *Flamingos in the Desert*, was to actually see physical measures for some of the mysterious weights I'd only previously read about. Here in the Cueva Museo there is a *celemin* (a small square wooden box), which was a dry measure equal to about 4.6 litres, and two *fanegas* (much larger oblong boxes). The two *fanegas*, though, are not the same size as each other. This tallies with what I discovered a few years ago. A *fanega* of barley was 33kg, a *fanega* of millet 40kg, and a *fanega* of wheat 44 kg. These measures also varied from place to place. Why that was, well, you'll have to ask one of the old millers, if you can find one.

Returning from the Cueva Museo, you pass again by the old *lavadero*, the municipal washing place. This is the Lavadero Público del Calvario, where the women of the town would meet and natter as they washed their families' clothes. There are over twenty separate sinks (*pilas*) and they had to be paid for in advance, a week at a time. The price, according to the caption below a wonderful photo on the wall there, taken in the 1950s, and which shows every basin occupied by a busy woman, was *'una perra chica por pila'* (five centimos per sink).

Sotomayor

Back at the Castillo and opposite its front entrance, take Calle Cuesta del Castillo downhill, passing a small (triangular) square with a statue of Don Jose María Muñoz, 'Heroe de la Caridad' (Hero of Charity). This street takes you down the side of the church. Immediately after that, turn right and in a few metres, almost opposite, is the final one of our three museums: the Museo J. M. Álvarez de Sotomayor, the former house of the man of that name.

When I got there, an English couple was already being shown round by the enthusiastic guide, Ignacio. Ignacio is disabled and walks with difficulty and the aid of sticks, but he seems a perfect fit for this role. He works so hard as he takes you round, telling you snippets in heavily accented English about Sotomayor. He points into the bookcases: here is Sotomayor's copy of the Koran, and here's the handwritten manuscript of his *Collected Poems*. The tour with Ignacio lasted about 15 minutes, at the end of which he slid a visitors' book in our direction. Naturally we wrote very complimentary things about our guide and as I left I was intrigued enough to want to find out more about Sotomayor.

Sotomayor was a noted poet who wrote about the hard nature of farm-work and the social injustices visited on agricultural labourers. He was born into a middle-class family in Cuevas del Almanzora in 1880. After he left high school with good qualifications, he enrolled in a military academy in Toledo but left after a couple of months, unwilling to submit to the discipline required. Back at home with his wealthy family by 1895, he spent years indulging himself in composing and writing poetry, before marrying his first wife Isabel in 1905.

By this time he was turning out to be something of a character. He took on the persona of an Arab leader called Sidi Aben Hozmin el-Jaráx, a pseudonym under which he wrote various poems and articles. He referred to his house as the Alcazár de la Sultana (having bestowed on his wife the title of Sultana), and considered the district of Calguerín, just to the north of the town, to be a caliphal state where he ordered a summer palace built. In the court of Hozmin el-Jaráx, he declared his friends to be emirs, appointed them as ambassadors, and had currency minted.

Amid all this eccentricity, he also spent time in Madrid with a bunch of writers, actors and artists who met in a cafe called El Gato Negro. His first play, *La Seca*, was performed in 1922 and a sequence of works followed, all rural dramas that paid homage to the integrity and honesty of the agricultural workers who Sotomayor referred to as 'gentlemen of the fields'. He continued to go to Madrid each spring and autumn as his list of published works steadily expanded. Ignacio told us that Sotomayor was at odds with both sides in the Civil War. The Republicans didn't like him because he had been a member of two right-wing parties and the Nationalists didn't like him because he wrote poems about poor people. As for the latter, young falangists in Cuevas took particular exception to a poem he wrote to the Batallón Floral. The right-wing hotheads threw his portrait from the balcony of the town hall and simulated his hanging in the square there.

His wife Isabel died in 1938, and although he married for a second time two years later, in 1944 he published a collection of poems dedicated to, and entitled, *Isabel*. The poems of his later years were characterised by anxiety and anguish. In 1947, just a few days before his death, his book *Romancero del Almanzora*, dedicated to his home region, was published. On which note, our short circuit through Cuevas del Almanzora finishes simply with a stroll back up to the Plaza de la Libertad in front of the castle.

The pirate Al Dugâlî

During the 16th century, the whole coastline of Almería was on the alert for attacks by Berber pirates. There were many Moors in north Africa who had been expelled from the Almería area and they acted as informers for the Berber pirates who saw this part of Spain as a source of easy pickings. They also managed to get intelligence from Moors who still lived in the area, so they knew the weak points on the coast and the state of the defences. They knew, for example, that the Spanish navy which patrolled the coast returned to its bases in

Cartagena and Puerto de Santa María in the autumn, so they could time their incursions accordingly. For the resident side, as it were, guards kept the coast under constant surveillance and could at least try to warn the local population via messengers and signal beacons if pirate ships were approaching.

The summer of 1573 was a quiet time for the citizens of Cuevas del Almanzora. A new governor called Bonifax had been appointed to the town by the Chancery of Granada to oversee the repopulation process that was taking place at the time. Bonifax considered that the pirate alarm was being sounded too frequently and that these were usually false alarms. He thought this was creating fear and hindering the repopulation programme so he ordered that the alarms be reduced to a minimum.

On 28th November 1573, at dawn, a large number of pirates from Morocco, under the command of Al Dugâlî, landed on the unguarded beach at Granatilla. This is at the seaward end of the *rambla* coming down from Sopalmo, almost halfway between Carboneras and Mojacar. The valley just to the north of it is called Barranco de los Moros, Ravine of the Moors, which suggests that this was the way they went inland. They moved speedily, via the now deserted settlement of Teresa in the Sierra Cabrera and then north via Antas, arriving at Cuevas del Almanzora by nightfall.

The previous day the beacon on Cerro de Montroy near Villaricos had been lit to give the news that ships were coming along the coast from the Cabo de Gata direction but Bonifax was not convinced of the accuracy of this information and did nothing. The result was that the pirate forces were able to enter Cuevas without any serious opposition. Even when reinforcements arrived from Vera and Mojácar, they were no match for the well-equipped and well-organised corsairs.

A day later, Bonifax sent a report from Albox to his superiors at the Chancery of Granada, as follows: 'Yesterday morning dawn was breaking when seven or eight hundred Turkish from Algiers seized the fortress entrance to Cuevas and went into the place and sacked it for three hours and captured all the Christians that there were inside it. Fifty men who had defended themselves were found dead, shattered.

'In the sacking of Cuevas all your Majesty had of wheat and silk was lost and other things that the depository had, since the Moorish surveyors set fire to the silos as a demonstration of power.'

A few of the citizens of Cuevas were able to hide or managed to flee from the town but the majority, including women and children and the High Mayor Illescas de Castro, were made prisoner. Naked, and with their hands tied behind their backs, they were put on a galley and six galliots (a galliot is a small galley) at the river mouth near Villaricos and taken back to North Africa. It took four days, without food and in winter weather, for them to make the crossing. They were taken to Tetouan, where ransoms were demanded in order for them not to be made slaves. Four years later negotiations were still going on. By then some of the prisoners had died and others had converted to Islam in order to gain their release and begin a new life in North Africa.

The Almanzora Dam

We're jumping ahead almost 450 years now. If you drive out from Cuevas in a north-easterly or easterly direction you will reach the *rambla* of the Río Almanzora. When you reach the narrow road that runs along the nearside bank, turn left and follow it northwards. After about three kilometres you will see the dam of the Cuevas del Almanzora reservoir ahead, colourfully painted and with a huge black Indalo figure. This, together with a water treatment plant, was opened in 1993 by the then president of the Junta de Andalucía, Manuel Chaves, who drank a symbolic first glass of water from it. The distribution of water from the reservoir to 57,000 inhabitants of the region was subsequently put in the hands of Galasa (which acronym stands for Gestión de Aguas del Levante Almeriense Sociedad Anónima).

Closer to, in the *rambla* itself, is a large rectangular lake. In 1999 a delegation from Almería went to Tunisia and heard that its submission to be the venue for the rowing and canoeing events at the XV Mediterranean Games, to be held in 2005, had been successful. In 2004, nine months of frenzied work saw the lake and its associated infrastructure completed. The lake, which was filled by water transfer from the Tago and Segura rivers, was 1,200 metres long by 108 metres wide and four metres deep. The scheme envisaged the area as not only a venue for the Games, but also subsequently as a leisure area. Built into the plans too, was the notion that it could be used to alleviate flood risk after very heavy rains. Included in the sports complex were changing rooms, offices, a press room and a restaurant. There were temporary features too, such as a control tower and stands to seat spectators. Parking areas and landscaping were added, with the total cost running to almost €13 million.

Drive towards the dam and you will reach a small roundabout, from where a road leads down to the parking area and sports centre. Beware of a narrow but deep gulley across the road just near the bottom of the slope. The chances are that yours will be the only car there. Despite hopes that the Mediterranean Games sports venue would subsequently become a leisure destination, it now lies forlorn and deserted. When I visited in March 2016, the lake was full and apparently still available for use but weeds were growing in the parking area and around the sports centre building. The entrance doors were wide open, with the sign saying 'Athletes/Deportistas' and 'Judges/Jueces' still neatly displayed, but random bits of debris were scattered across the floor inside and the place had a general air of abandonment. As for the panel in the window announcing 'Zona Wifi Gratuita', I think not.

Having said that, just occasionally the lake still makes the news for positive reasons. In late 2016 a team of 84 specialist paddlers, assembled from all over Spain, broke the record for the furthest distance travelled by a Dragon Boat in 24 hours. Working in relays they managed 263.53 kilometres, breaking the record formerly held by a German team by 25 kilometres and thus ensuring their place in El Libro Guinness de los Récords, as they say round here. Early 2017 brought further hope for the lake, with a high-level meeting to discuss the idea of building an aquatic film studio there, and news that the 2019 European Rowing Championships will bring an estimated 5,000 participants from all over the continent to the Cuevas area.

Back at the small roundabout, the next exit to the right takes a winding uphill route to another parking area, which is the closest you can drive to the dam. From here, a further uphill walk of a few minutes brings you out on top of the dam. To the right, there's a dramatic view down past the sports centre, along the *rambla*, over the town of Cuevas and out to the Mediterranean. Above the spillway, you look right down on the huge painted Indalo, whose arc is about 25 metres across. Is this the largest Indalo in existence?

To the left is the reservoir (*embalse*) which the dam (*presa*) was originally built to create. On my visit the water level was way down after one of the driest winters for years. The structure of the dam itself is fully explained on information boards. These also give details of the geological considerations with which the dam-builders had to contend, including 'complex tectonic structures' and 'overthrusts'. The astonishing multi-hued rocks outcropping by the access road, plus the details given on the boards, suggest to me that engineers and geologists will have a fascinating time here. As for the rest of us, the views are worth the visit.

38. Roadworkers' houses and threshing circles

'The traveller...thinks at last that all he needs to do is to begin, that perhaps he is giving too much thought to a journey that he really wants to make a bit haphazardly, rather like a fire on a threshing floor.'

(Camilo José Cela)

Roadworkers' houses

From 1759 onwards, road maintenance workers were appointed to look after the main roads in Almería Province. The roads were very basic, as was the equipment of a typical road-worker; he had just a tool-belt and a pick. Each maintenance man worked on foot and had a 'league' of road, about 5.5 kilometres, to maintain. The job involved not just looking after the road surface but also ensuring that the white bands painted around the base of the roadside trees, usually pines, were kept up to scratch to aid night-time visibility for travellers.

In time some of these road-workers were provided with houses, *casillas*, for their families. At one stage there were over 50 such houses in Almería province, according to *La Voz de Almería* newspaper. Many have now disappeared but there are still a few remaining. They are distinctive, solid houses and they generally have, in large lettering, destinations and distances on their end walls. Most of them were built to a standard design, with shallow buttresses to strengthen the walls.

I know of a dozen or so of these houses in eastern Almería. There are, for example, four on the N-340a, to the east of Sorbas. The first is in Sorbas itself (see chapter 25). The next, further east, is at Los Castaños, above the road on a bluff, then the next is on the bank of the Río Antas, just a couple of kilometres west of Vera. If you leave the A7 motorway at junction 529 and drive in towards Vera, you will pass it. Then there is another, up a set of steps, alongside the road by a bend near the narrow bridge just to the south-west of Huércal-Overa. In many places along this road there are pines planted, I like to think, by far-sighted road engineers over a century ago to provide shade to weary travellers. Such trees are also an obvious clue to the many old stretches of the original road, which have been abandoned as the demands of modern traffic have led to the straightening of the road and the easing of bends.

As well as the large lettering on the end walls of the *casillas*, there is normally an inset panel above the front door of the building. In this panel it might say CAMINEROS, as at Los Castaños and Vera, or PEONES CAMINEROS, as at Sorbas, or even CASILLA DE PEONES CAMINEROS, as on the one near Uleila del Campo. As well as the one at Uleila, I know of others at La Alfoquia and also close to the Puente Vaquero on the old road between Turre and Los Gallardos. This latter, painted in somewhat bizarre peach and blue livery a few years ago, is used nowadays, rather appropriately, to store highway equipment. After I'd written a first draft of this section, I came across another *casilla*, by the A-352 between Cuevas del Almanzora and Vera, in good condition and now also used, it seems, as a local authority highways store.

One of the many *casillas de peones camineros* which as far as I know no longer exists was apparently at Barranco del Lobo, just to the west of Sorbas. No doubt there were several more along the road to Tabernas and on down to Almería. Similarly, I assume the sequence continued eastwards to Puerto Lumbreras, given that what is now the N-340a was built in the 1890s as 'the new road', right through from Almería to Puerto Lumbreras.

Heading in a different direction, the *casilla* in La Alfoquia suggests there might be a sequence along the Almanzora Valley, by the A334 or, more accurately, by the original line of the road along there. I should confess that I haven't made a determined search in these areas where they might be expected. Maybe readers know of roadworkers' houses I haven't mentioned or might be inclined to go and search. If you do, I look forward to hearing from you, as I did from Brian Rowlands, who alerted me to the Huércal-Overa *casilla* and Barrie Naylor, who reminded me about the one near Puente Vaquero.

In the final stages of preparing this book for publication, I came across more *casillas.* One lies just south of Vélez Rubio and is still basically sound, though somewhat dilapidated. It has clear white lettering in a blue panel on the end wall, indicating 27 km to Puerto Lumbreras and 106 km to Murcia. And there's another, not far away. I was driving from Vélez Rubio south towards Huércal-Overa on the A-327 when I saw a *casilla's* unmistakable outline, just a couple of kilometres from where the A-327 leaves the A-91 motorway. This building, surrounded by chain-link fencing, has 'CAMINEROS' over the front door but no distances and place-names on the gable ends. It is well maintained in white and orange livery and also seems to be a store of some kind. And, at the last gasp before publication, I read that a roadworker's house at Zurgena was about to be restored.

I've heard from a couple of sources that during the Franco era the roadworkers' houses were occupied by the Guardia Civil as convenient bases from which they could monitor movement along the strategic roads in the area. Lindy Walsh tells me that because of the negative connotations of this, many of the older local people still shun the *casillas* and wouldn't want to live in them.

Of the road-worker's houses that I know about, only the one in Sorbas is occupied. Apart from that and the three mentioned above being used as stores, the others are disused and falling into ruin. The one in Los Castaños, for example, has been uninhabited for over 15 years. A couple of years ago a friend who at that point was living opposite the *casilla* in Los Castaños told me there was talk of knocking it down as it was in danger of "falling down the cliff" on which it perches and into the main road.

Then, the day before writing this, I came across a post on Facebook from Marisol Campolina in Spanish suggesting demolition was imminent: '*Si nadie lo remedia el próximo lunes la casilla de peones camineros de Los Castaños va a ser derribada por el Ministerio de Fomento. Y el pino también lo quieren derribar. Los vecinos han recogido firmas, han ido a visitar al alcalde de Sorbas, han ido a ver a Andrés García Lorca, subdelegado del gobierno, pero hasta ahora nadie ha atendido sus reivindicaciones. En pocos dias una de las señas de identidad de esta barriada sorbeña desaparecerán, los vecinos perderán una sombra mejestuosa, un mirador unico y un arbol monumental de más de 100 años.*' So, the authorities were about to pull down both the roadworkers' house and the huge old pine tree.

Automatic computer translation can be an easy laugh and, despite the serious message, here's an example that's too good to omit. In spite of the mangled language in the translation, Marisol's message remains clear: 'If no one takes care of the next Monday, the box of road workers of the chestnut is going to be shot down by the ministry of encouragement. And the pine tree so they want to tear down. The neighbours have collected signatures, have been visiting the mayor of Sorbas, have gone to see Andrés García Lorca, deputy director of the government, but so far no one has attended to their demands. In a few days one of the signs of identity of this slum Sorbeña will disappear, the neighbours will lose a shadow mejestuosa, a gazebo and a tree only monumental of more than 100 years.' Understandable for the most part, but not English as we know it.

The continuation of the story was that, on Monday 13th June 2016, the day when two vehicles from the provincial roads unit, accompanied by a JCB, arrived to demolish the house, they found about 20 local people who had taken up their positions in front of the building at 7 a.m. Faced with this situation the vehicles left. The Los Castaños villagers had fond memories of the local road-worker

Francisco García bringing up his large brood in the house. One of the protesters, Paqui Pérez Codina, from nearby Cariatiz, said: "We are very happy to have been able to stop the demolition and gain more time for discussions with the authorities." Local television covered the protest and the Spanish press headlined the story of the villagers' success: *'David defeats Goliath at Los Castaños'*.

Remembering the *casilla* at Los Castaños

A timely article appeared in the Sorbas journal *El Afa* in 2016, in which María del Sol García de las Ballones García recalled her childhood memories of the roadworker's house mentioned above. María del Sol's father was from Sorbas but her mother came from Los Castaños and it was her mother's parents, Juana Mañas and Francisco (Paco) García who lived in the *casilla de peón caminero* there. It was Paco García who had responsibility for the local roads. María recalls that her grandparents spent the whole of their happy married life in that house.

María's own life took a different turn though. When she was just six, because of the dire political and economic situation in Spain at the time, her parents emigrated and took her to Brazil. Much later, when she had grown up and came back to Los Castaños for visits, her maternal grandparents' house was her only point of reference. Her paternal grandparents, who had run the small wool factory in Sorbas, had died by this time. Looking back, María recalls that her grandparents, Juana and Paco, lived for over 70 years in the house that was always called 'La Casilla'. That was where their seven children were born.

In her memory María sees the floor of large square black and white tiles and the two huge entrances that always reminded her of church doors. There were four rooms, one of which had big built-in gypsum storage bins for wheat and rye. Two of the rooms had elegant fireplaces and there was a kitchen on the patio, where Juana always had lots of colourful flowerpots. And the house had the first, or possibly the second, flushing toilet in the village, which meant it wasn't necessary to go out to the fields.

One room under the roof was used for storing all the products of the *matanza*, the annual pig-killing, as well as potatoes, onions, garlic and oil. There they salted and dried the hams. It was accessed via a ladder through a trapdoor. All the neighbours in Los Castaños and villagers from the nearby hamlets knew that the particular ventilation in that room meant the hams would be cured as in no other place. This room intrigued María when she was little; it was like nothing else she'd ever seen and it was where she hid to read books that were forbidden under Franco's dictatorship. María says: "In that marvellous house, I spent the best winter of my life, learning from my grandmother how to do cross-stitch and embroidery and things that we no longer do, because we don't need to, like darning socks. It was all accompanied by the story of everything that happened in Spain during the Civil War and in the time of Franco.

"What most intrigued me was the story of how frightened to death people were, hearing the news that came from family in Almería, the frequent bombardments, the air-raid tunnels, the misery, and the times that my aunt, still a child, had to go out in the early hours, often when it was absolutely freezing, up into the hills to buy eggs...

"The *casilla* had a privileged view over the village and surrounding fields. In front of it was an ancient and majestic pine, which provided lots of cool shade and was the place where all the villagers would meet up in summer. And it's this house that, since the death of my grandmother and aunt, they want to pull down.

"When I came back to Spain for good, exactly 13 years ago, seeing the situation with the abandoned *casilla*, I tried to buy it but I didn't have the amount they were asking. Now they haven't knocked it down and plans are being drawn up, perhaps it can be the pilot project for a network of houses for rural tourism, as I imagine there must be other similar *casillas* across Andalucía..."

The revival of threshing circles

Dotted across the rural landscapes of Almería are distinctive circular threshing floors (*eras* in Spanish), usually surfaced with stone flags. They are much more common than roadworkers' houses and I wrote about them at length in *Flamingos*, so won't say much more here, other than to record the fact that since then I've heard from several people about *eras* that have been cleaned and restored.

Mat Edwards of Bar La Montaña provided the refreshments for a team of friends who restored the *era* dating from 1942 at El Campico above Bédar. Lee Frankham is hoping to restore one at a property he has bought outside Lubrín. In fact, by now he may well have done so. Thierry Duty told me about one he has restored at his parents' house in the Rambla del Chive after what he suspects is 70 years of neglect. Andrés Pérez, as enthusiastic as ever to maintain and pass on the history of the locality, has posted pictures of a restored *era* owned by his family in the Cariatiz area. All of which is not enough evidence to suggest a major trend but it's encouraging to know that these traditional features of the landscape are being valued.

And then, one day in late 2015 I happened to be at the Urrá Field Centre, not far from Sorbas, when I saw someone cleaning the superbly made threshing circle there. I stopped, introduced myself, and we had a natter. Gregorio was the name of the guy doing the work. It's a big circle and it took him several days but when he had finished, it looked superb, with the segmented stone pattern clearly revealed and a date stone at the centre revealing the original maker as the 'Maestro de Lubrín, José Codina', and the date as 1884.

39. Moments of encounter

'I get an astonishing emotional joy out of the material aspects of the natural world. It is the colour of a feather, the sound of a song that is important to me.'
(Richard Mabey)

4th May 2015: The briefest glimpse but enough to say 'fox'.
It's been dry now for a fortnight and in the last few days the temperatures have kicked up into high summer mode; 32°C in the shade during the afternoon and staying up at 20°C at night. The garden is a riot of flowers and dense foliage: roses, geraniums, sweet peas, broad beans, lettuces, olive trees laden with understated flowers and vines showing early promise with bunches of, as yet, the tiniest grapes. Butterflies are active; whites, a painted lady, marbled whites and various brownish-orangey things that I really must learn the names of.

Meanwhile, the green *campo*, the result of a cool and wet month from mid-March to mid-April, is losing some of its vibrancy. The vegetation is still thick and tall though, by our semi-desert standards. There's still green, set off by what seems to be the best-ever flowering of *albaida*, a profusion of yellow that, whilst not exactly carpeting the landscape, is nevertheless astonishingly prolific. I go up Cerro de los Lobos, as is my recent habit, by mountain bike and foot, which means I have to push the bike on the several sections that are too steep for me to ride. It's the time of year when the local plants, the grasses in particular, produce a range of spiked, hooked and Velcro-ed seeds and fruit that stick in my socks and in the mesh of my trainers, poking through to irritate the skin.

On one such bike-push, I halt and lay the machine down, to see if I can locate the stonechat that is making its 'knocking pebbles together' song somewhere on the slope below. It proves easy to see, just 30 or 40 metres away, perched on top of a bush in its crisp livery of black head, white collar and orange breast. There's another, calling just a little further away but despite their habit of singing from a prominent position, I can't see the second one. In the process of scanning across the steep slope though, I catch a brown shape flowing just for a second, across a gap between the shrubs. It was hardly anything, the briefest glimpse, but enough to say 'fox'. I wait to see if it will emerge, way below, beyond a dense area of bushes, if it continues on the line I sensed it was taking. It doesn't.

I continue up the hill until I'm stopped again, high on the slopes, this time by a smart black wheatear. The bird is all black but for a white rump. Not that exciting a colour scheme, you'd think, but it is the breeding season, so somehow the black of the bird seems blacker than normal, the contrast with the pure white of its rump even more striking. And there's an energy to the bird as it flits and calls from the branch it's on. Then I see a woodchat shrike, also black and white but more finely patterned and with a give-away tan head, on the same branch, maybe two metres from the wheatear. Two iconic local species on one branch; excellent! Only then does the shrike go for the wheatear and the two are off, one in pursuit of the other, across the slope. The territorial imperative, alarm calls, defending the patch, of course. They weren't just posing together to give a passing writer with some knowledge of birds the opportunity to compare and contrast.

31st May 2015: Black-eared wheatear flying away
I'm pushing the mountain bike up a steep section of the track opposite the house. I can hear the soft repetitive purring of a turtle dove, a sound sadly uncommon enough to be worthy of note. I scan the hill slopes above but I can't see the bird. The song continues, a beautiful evocation of summer; it's a tragedy that these birds are still hunted in some of the countries of southern Europe. Then, right by the track, on a sharp-edged block of quartz, a painted lady alights,

closes its wings, opens them, closes them, opens them, and continues this mysterious sequence. It's as familiar a butterfly as any in Almería but that complex patterning of pinkish-orange with white and black markings never ceases to please me.

A little later, once I'm back home, I'm out on the middle terrace, dipping the watering-can into one of the *bidones* (water butts) to give some newly-planted tomatoes and aubergines a drink when, beyond the fence, I catch a movement and look up just in time to see a black-eared wheatear flying away. This is related to but different from the black wheatear mentioned above, and is one of the neatest birds we have here, a summer visitor from April to September. It has a cream body with hints of ochre wash and black wings and a black mask. Just that glimpse before it's gone.

18th June 2015: Ladder snake and smashed eggs

During the morning we notice four smashed eggs on the tiles outside our porch, greyish and marked with darker patterns. I recognise them: they are house sparrow eggs. A whole clutch, more or less, but how have they come to be here? We have several pairs of house sparrows nesting with us: one pair in a nest-box on a pillar on the front terrace, another pair in a disused red-rumped swallow's nest in the porch, several pairs in holes in the pocketed cliff behind the house, but the nearest of these is a few metres from where the smashed eggs are.

A couple of days ago I leapt into the air as I walked out into the porch. An adult ladder snake, a big one, was curled up right by the door. It was as shocked as I was, if the speed with which it shot behind the adjacent shelving was anything to go by. A minute or two later we could see it, apparently climbing the wall behind the shelves. The sense I had of it was that it was about a metre long. We decided not to disturb it further.

Yesterday I was out there again and chanced upon it, moving with astonishing speed from the porch, across the tiles and away into the nearest part of the garden. So the question is: was the ladder snake responsible for the broken sparrows' eggs? Snakes love birds' eggs and will raid nests if they have a chance, but the nearest nest, in the red-rumped swallows' old quarters, is three metres up a vertical wall. Surely not possible for a snake, even one with a ladder in its name? I suspect the crime will remain unsolved.

5th July 2015: "Do you want to sell that car?"

There's some commotion at the front gate. It's a roasting hot Sunday morning. I put on a tee-shirt and go to investigate. A stocky guy is peering through the gate, his van behind him, engine running. "Carmen said you might like some water melons," he says. Carmen is our neighbour. She lives about 100 metres away, out of immediate sight, at the end of the tarmac. "No thanks" I reply, "We've got loads of fruit. We went to the market at Vera yesterday." He brings his fingers to his mouth in the standard gesture: "They're really delicious!" "No, really, not today!" In an instant he changes tack, points over my shoulder and asks: "Do you want to sell that car?" The answer is no again. Little does he know that, two days ago, a kilometre from home, we were coming up the hill when an overenthusiastic driver had come screaming downhill, round a bend, and straight into the front of our car. We managed to limp home in it after exchanging all due details, but now it is awaiting the *grua* to take it away for repairs at 9 o'clock tomorrow morning.

4th/5th October 2015: Bee-eaters migrating

Two evenings in a row I hear bee-eaters outside. It's the time of the autumn migration and I thought maybe they'd all already gone so, as it might be my last chance for this year, I go out to watch them. There are plenty of birds scattered across the sky, all flying more or less west. This makes sense because that direction will take them along the south coast of Spain towards Gibraltar, to the shortest crossing to the African continent for their onward journey over the Sahara.

But what is strange is that I'm hearing bee-eaters but seeing swallows. I think maybe the bee-eaters are too high to make out but after a few minutes I do manage to find them, bigger and sharper-winged, in amongst the swallows. Both species are undulating and looping along, angling in striking patterns against the background clouds, and with the ululating calls of the bee-eaters, it's hard not to sense that the birds are showing exultation and excitement as they make their journey. We are told not to anthropomorphise, not to attribute human feelings to wild creatures, but there is something about this sky full of colourful and vibrant migration that conveys a shimmering delight in life and movement. Once they've finished passing on the second evening, I go back indoors, thinking I might see no more of them until next year.

25th October 2015: Toad in the road

I'm driving home alone (my wife is away) around midnight, buzzing with the delights I've just seen at the Fusion Filabres Festival in El Pilar: the traditional dances and resounding music of the Sorbas-based Cuadrilla del Maestro Gálvez, the percussive step-dancing and vibrant Appalachian tunes of the Buffalo Gals Stampede and the banjo-and-guitar interplay genius of Leon Hunt and Jason Titley. All of which is by the way.

I've negotiated the twisty hills around Los Molinos and I'm on the long downhill straight leading to where I pass under the motorway, when suddenly there's something in the headlights, crossing the road slowly. There's no time to stop so I swerve enough for the car to pass over it safely. It's been a drear day, what the Scots would call 'dreich', at any given moment either drizzling or threatening to.

That's obviously what has brought this toad out. I know it's a toad (*sapo* in Spanish and the wonderful *Bufo bufo* in Latin) rather than a frog because I get enough of a glimpse to see that it is brown and it's walking across the road, not hopping. And it's big, so probably a female. They can reach 15 centimetres (six inches) in length. I've always been surprised that toads live here, in the semi-desert, but they do, and apparently there are plenty of them. However, in dry conditions they seek out the cool and moist places and often stay buried underground, so we tend not to see them.

Ten minutes later, as I pull up to our front gate, there's another. I get out to unlock the gate and gently persuade the creature out of the path of the car. As I nudge it with my shoe it clambers through the metal bars of the gate and heads into the leaf litter below a pine tree. The drizzle continues. It occurs to me to hope that our cat doesn't find it and take an undue interest. When toads feel threatened they exude a strong toxin that can be fatal, especially if not treated quickly.

The toxin is particularly dangerous for dogs. Cats, apparently, seem to be more aware of the risks posed by toads and tend to avoid them. In fact, I have a couple of photos from several years ago, before I knew about the toxicity of toads, of our other, late lamented cat, peering at a toad which was sitting minding its own business in a large flowerpot just outside our porch. Certainly on that occasion the cat kept its distance.

14th October 2016: "Can we look round the house?"

Not all unexpected encounters in the garden involve wildlife. This evening, about an hour before dusk, Troy is shouting through to me: "There are people in the garden!" We go together to the front door. There are three of them, total strangers: a middle-aged woman and two much younger women who look like sisters.

"Are you the owner?" the elder woman asks me. "We are," I say, indicating the two of us. She says she's heard we might want to sell. We don't know where she's got that from as there's absolutely no truth to it, but we get talking nonetheless. She makes no allowance for the fact that we're *extranjeros* and it's fair to admit we're not following everything she says but she's wondering about the possibility of buying the house, maybe for her daughters. I'm not convinced that the daughters have been consulted about this.

Bit by bit we piece together what's going on. She's called Catalina and it was her father Antonio who sold this place to the couple we bought it from 11 years ago. Antonio is now 92 and is housebound. Catalina is 58 and hasn't been here for 40 years, even though she only lives a few kilometres away in Venta del Pobre. She says she remembers it well from her childhood, although it's almost entirely different now. We're still at the front door as we establish all this and the two younger women, her daughters, in their early twenties, I'd guess, are looking slightly embarrassed.

"Can we have a look round?" asks Catalina. The daughters, whose names we didn't get, look even more embarrassed. We say of course, and give them the medium version of the guided tour. They are fascinated by the books in the study, the 360° view from the terrace on the roof, even the lettuces and oranges and quinces and peppers on the middle terrace in the garden. The daughters are wide-eyed, muttering: *"Preciosa!"* at frequent intervals.

Catalina tells us her parents ran this place as a shop, and a bar, with dancing. We'd heard this when we first came here and it's good to have it confirmed from a genuine source. The village had needed a shop back then because there was no tarmac road out of the place, just tracks that people walked on or travelled with mules or horses. When we reformed the house, we made sure to keep the metal rings in the front walls where people had once tied their mules when they'd come for a wild night out.

Catalina is clearly touched to see that the house is in good heart. She invites us over for a meal in the Restaurante La Fragua that she runs in Venta del Pobre. She says that if her father could see the place now, he'd cry (she uses the verb *llorar*) with happiness, to know that there are people here looking after it, growing things, keeping it alive. We were caught on the hop by their sudden appearance but it's been wonderful to meet them, an unexpected link to the history of this house that has come to mean so much to us. We promise that if we ever decide to sell up, we'll give Catalina first refusal. It's dusk now, time for them to leave. And we promise, one day soon, we'll come to La Fragua for that meal.

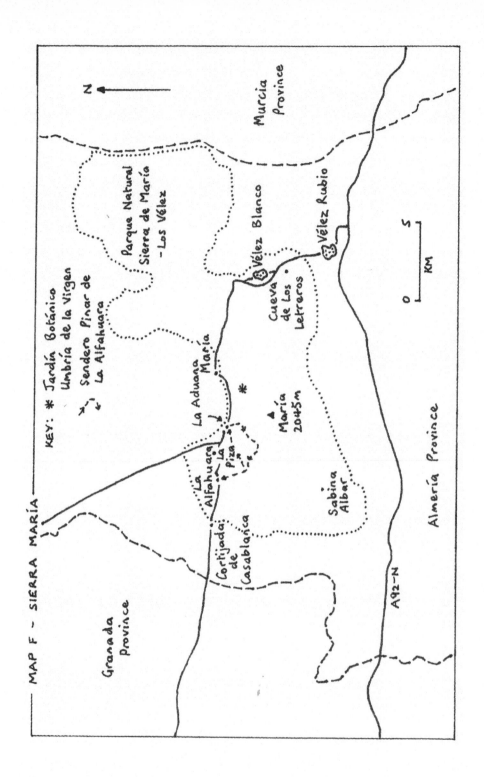

MAP F - SIERRA MARÍA

KEY: * Jardín Botánico
Umbría de la Virgen

Sendero Pinar de
La Alfahuara

Granada
Province

Cortijada
de
Casablanca

La Alfahuara

La Aduana María

La
Piza

*

María
2045m

Sabina
Albar

Parque Natural
Sierra de María
- Los Vélez

Vélez Blanco

Cueva
de Los
Letreros

Vélez Rubio

Murcia
Province

Almería Province

A92-N

0   KM   5

N

40. Sierra de María

'La sabina destaca solitaria como un punto verde en el valle.' 'The juniper stands lonely like a green dot in the valley.'
(Javier Navarro Pastor)

A walk through the pines

Just to the north of the N-342 linking Puerto Lumbreras and Baza, and just west of Vélez Rubio and Vélez Blanco lies a dramatic toothy mountain ridge, the Sierra de María. In area it's quite small but the highest summit, María, also known as Cerro Poyo (in the Atlas Almería) and La Burrica (in the leaflet put out by the local botanical garden), reaches 2,045 m. There are other impressive heights, too, such as Cabezo, 1,938m or 1,948m, depending on which source you consult, and Maimón, likewise 1,754m or 1,761m. The area is protected as the Parque Natural Sierra de María-Los Vélez and the best map of it has the same title. At a scale of 1:40,000, it's published by the Junta de Andalucía. It shows a network of footpaths threading the area, though none of them go to the summits.

The Sierra de María is as different an environment as you can imagine, compared to the desert for which Almería is better known. It is a noted haunt of griffon vultures and is also renowned for its extensive woodland. There are many holm oaks (Quercus rotundifolia in Latin, *encina* in Spanish) but the most significant tree species are pines, including Aleppo pine (Pinus halepensis, *pino carrasco*) and maritime pine (Pinus pinaster, *pino negral* or *resinero*).

A walk of about eight kilometres through the pinewoods begins at the Ruinas de la Aduana, about four kilometres west of María village on the ALP-832 road to Orce. *'Aduana'* means 'customs' as in customs and excise and its meaning here carries a similar sense. The building was the sole entrance to the extensive hunting estate of the Marques de Los Vélez and was the base for the forest guards who kept everyone else out, such as those who might be keen to pilfer firewood. It is largely due to the iron control that the landowners exercised through these guards, from the 16th century until the early 20th century, that the pinewood habitat has been protected.

The walking route is waymarked as the Pinar de la Alfahuara. A broad well-compacted track, clearly signposted, leads off from the warm stone of the tumbledown customs building through open, natural woodland with lots of junipers. It climbs steadily at first, then more steeply after a sharp right-hand bend at about 1.5 kilometres. Green and white flashes on wooden posts mean it is impossible to get lost. The track is now trending between west and south-west and still climbing. The tree-cover here is mainly shrubby holm oaks with occasional Austrian pines (Pinus nigra subsp salzmannii in Latin, known locally as *pino laricio*). Austrian pines cope well with drought and cold and some of the individual trees are thought to be up to 600 years old. By the time you reach the *mirador*(viewpoint) at Puntal del Morral you have gained about 140 metres of height and are about 1,400m up (over 5,000 ft). Here there are information boards and superb wide vistas.

The track begins to lose height into the Barranco Agrio, where there is another sharp turn on to a north-west heading. Over to the left are impressive mountain slopes and soaring, broken crags. A couple of information panels give details of some of the characteristic species, including the aforementioned Austrian pine and also *gayuba*. Gayuba is an evergreen shrub, the Latin name of which is Arctostaphylos uva-ursi. The latter part of this means 'grape of the bear' and it's one of a group of related plants called bearberry in English. The fruit is edible but has an insipid taste and is not very juicy, so let's leave it for the bears. It has other uses too: the plant's leaves have been used traditionally as an antiseptic.

After a further two kilometres, easy because downhill, the route reaches a path junction. So far, route-finding has been simple, but here there is a choice. Before making it, though, if you wish, you can explore or use the large recreational area with barbecue pits, table and toilets off to the left. This is the Area Recreativo Los Alamicos with, just beyond it, up on a knoll with further excellent views, the Los Alamicos mountain refuge. Despite what some guidebooks say, at the time of writing this is not abandoned.

Back down where the paths cross there are two options. The first is to continue on the waymarked path, passing the disused nursery of Los Alamicos, where in the past seedlings were raised to help reforest the area. The main nursery office is still in good shape, locked behind a high fence with a metal arch above the gate saying 'VIVERO del ESTADO' (basically, Government Nursery).There are red squirrels in these woods, plus there is always the chance of a glimpse of a booted eagle or a hawfinch if you are very lucky. The path leads to the Cortijo de la Alfahuara on the ALP-832. Amongst the buildings here is an abandoned resin factory, which formerly processed the resin from the Aleppo pines into varnish, disinfectant and related products, reaching its peak of production in the 1920s. To complete the circuit from here involves a three kilometre stretch uphill back along the road, unless some earlier juggling with a second vehicle or bikes has been cunningly arranged.

The second choice is to leave the 'official' route at the track junction mentioned at the start of the previous paragraph and take another broad forest track on the right which is also signposted and leads north-east, all the way back to La Aduana and the start of the walk. I opted for this, as I was alone on a December afternoon and didn't relish the final stretch on the road. The sign suggests this last leg is three kilometres but I did it in a fraction over half an hour, so I'm pretty sure it is less. In fact, this finish makes an excellent circuit of the walk without the need to touch tarmac. Apart from occasional twittering from unseen small birds, all I saw in the way of wildlife was one raven, calling as it flew high overhead. It was a superb walk though, on a cool, bright winter day and I didn't see another soul. I'd certainly do it again. And if you wish to see the remains of the resin factory, you can just drive down the road to do so.

Umbría de la Virgen Botanical Garden

Just to the west of the village of María a narrow road leads steadily uphill. There are benches spaced equidistantly along it, giving a clue to its destination, the chapel of Umbría de la Virgen. The seats are for pilgrims to rest on during their climb. There is ample parking at the chapel and the family who live in the house round the back sell jars of excellent local honey. You just have to knock at their door and ask.

A further short walk uphill from the chapel is the Jardín Botánico Umbría de la Virgen, to which entry is free. There's a visitor centre with displays and above that, the garden itself, laid out on the mountain slopes. It's a must for anyone interested in the plants of the area. May to September opening hours are Tuesday to Sunday and holidays 09.00 to 15.00; October to April, it's Tuesday to Sunday and holidays 10.00 to 16.00. To check these times or to ask about guided group tours, the number to call is 697 956 046. Quite near to the entrance are areas showing plants of particular habitats such as steppes, salty areas or rock faces, as well as beds of herbs and specifically local vegetation. There's a traditional still too, which was used to extract essential oils from many of the aromatics growing here, such as lavender and thyme.

Three circular walks have been laid out to show the plants of the area. These also give fine views of both the mountains and the plain below. The shortest, the Senda Baja (Low Path), takes about 15 minutes; the Senda Media about 50 minutes, and the Senda Alta (High Path) about 1 hour 40 minutes. All are clearly waymarked.

Back down near the entrance stands a striking bronze sculpture, Homenaje a la Sabina Milenaria by Miguel Llamas Yeste. The homage is to a particular *sabina albar* tree, a kind of juniper with the Latin name Juniperus thurifera. This one, often called La Sabina

Albar de Chirivel and estimated to be between 600 and 1,000 years old, stands alone in a remote valley (hence the quote at the head of this chapter) at the southern edge of the range for this species. In 2003 it was declared a Monumento Natural in recognition of its great size and age. It has traditionally sheltered shepherds and their flocks, and survived fires and ice, as well as the depredations of those searching for firewood or fine quality wood to work. The *sabina albar* can grow at a higher altitude than other species, and survive in areas with poor soil, growing steadily and slowly, century after century; definitely a tree deserving of a celebratory sculpture.

Looking for vultures

Four cars pulled into the parking area at the Ermita de la Virgen de la Cabeza on the northern slopes of the Sierra María at about 10 o'clock one November day. A dozen birdwatchers clambered out. Cloud was swirling over the higher slopes and obscuring the summits. The air had a chill tang of winter, a shock after the recent hot days. On the vast, steepening slopes below the cloud there was a sprinkling of new snow, caster sugar dredged over the landscape. I pulled my woolly hat down and felt in my pockets for gloves. The one member of our group who had optimistically turned up in shorts has paid me handsomely not to reveal his identity. Don't worry Richard, your secret is safe.

Despite the cold, there were already several griffon vultures circling high against the cloud. Given our good-sized group, with plenty of pairs of eyes, a fair sprinkling of expertise and no shortage of binoculars, hopefully little was going to escape our notice. We scanned the water trough by the chapel, a magnet for birds during the hot days of summer but today there was no sign of life there.

As we walked up the paved road towards the Botanical Garden several of us saw and heard them at about the same moment, and voiced our thoughts: "Aren't those ring ouzels?" Bigger than blackbirds, more upright, with a different song from a blackbird too. The *Collins Bird Guide* says it is a 'stony clicking 'tück', harder and somewhat higher pitched than a blackbird's.' But we had good views of these ouzels and the clincher was the off-white crescent-shape splashed across the upper breast. They were noisy and very active and a real treat to see. They would have just arrived from northern Europe, the avian equivalents of those humans who head south for the winter in search of sun.

The visitor centre at the Jardín Botánico Umbría de la Virgen had its woodstove roaring and a group of chilled birders was soon jostling for position around it. Once thawed, we set off again in search of more birds. On this occasion there 'wasn't much about', just the odd jay, disappearing into the pines with a flash of a white rump, a fleetingly-glimpsed green woodpecker, a circling sparrowhawk, a blackcap and a cirl bunting. I just had time to buy two tubs of the excellent local honey before our convoy headed back down to the ALP- 832 and turned left to our usual next stop, by the disused resin factory mentioned earlier. Depending on the time of year and the degree of luck, all manner of birds can be seen here. We've had rock sparrow, mistle thrush, hoopoe, raven and black wheatear, for example.

Continuing in the same direction, the road drops to a vast flat plain, a quite striking area called the Llano de la Alfahuara. The birders' cars travel along here slowly, the occupants looking out for little owls, red-billed choughs, maybe a calandra lark or a northern wheatear. A favoured stop is by a drinking trough on the left of the road by more farm buildings. This is the Cortijada de Casablanca. If goats aren't around, there is a fair chance of seeing birds attracted by the water source; a black-eared wheatear perhaps, or a flock of linnets. On again, in a short while there is another cluster of farm buildings, pale brown, as is the ground, but standing stark against the horizon in this flat landscape. This spot is referred to by the birders as 'the hamlet' and is right on the provincial boundary with Granada. It's a good place to scan for lesser kestrels and maybe a black wheatear on a barn roof. The pale dun steppe stretches away, broken by low lines of stones. It doesn't sound very dramatic but it's the now dry basin of an ancient lake and there is an other-worldly, timeless feel about the whole place. Were you to carry on, you'd reach Orce, where excavations have revealed some of the oldest stone tools found to date in Europe. Orce is in Granada province and so beyond the scope of this book but the area is well worth a visit. Just drive slowly through the area and you can sense prehistory around you.

The birders return from this point and head back east along the road, up into the pines, then turn off left to the La Piza forest cafe. This is a friendly place, open all year and with a roaring fire in winter, an absolute necessity to counter the cold. There are feeders and water here for the birds. You are almost certain to see crossbills, which are a local speciality, and a range of tits - great, crested, coal, long-tailed. Chaffinches are common here too, despite being virtually unknown in most of Almería province. The range of habitats and landscapes in this area can be relied upon to provide an excellent outing, whether you are interested in birds or not, I'm inclined to say.

Vélez Blanco

As you walk up towards the striking castle that dominates the small town of Vélez Blanco, its towers and walls and arches rise dramatically from the natural rock plinth on which it stands, soaring above you. A striking photo of it is used on the cover of Michael Jacobs' guidebook *Andalucía*, winning out over other iconic Andalucían buildings such as Granada's Alhambra and the Mezquita of Córdoba. The Vélez Blanco castle dates from the 16th century when it was built on the remains of a Moorish citadel for the first Marqués de Los Vélez. He, Don Pedro Fajardo, was governor of Murcia during the reign of Ferdinand and Isabella and helped to suppress Moorish rebellions in their lands. As a consequence he was awarded the town of Vélez Blanco by royal decree, and between 1506 and 1515 he had the castle built. Its huge tower, the Torre del Homenaje, over 20 metres high, was designed as a symbol of power over the local area. Inside the stone structure were wooden stairs which could be removed in case of danger, isolating the upper level as a last defence. Another striking feature was the central courtyard, called the *patio del honor*, embellished with Italian Renaissance ornament in local Macael marble carved by craftsmen from Lombardy.

The building is something of a shell though, as the interior was gradually stripped by its owner of its most valuable features at the beginning of the 20th century. As part of this process, the *patio del honor* was acquired by a French merchant, a specialist in interior decor, in 1904 and sold on to a banker called George Blumenthal. Blumenthal shipped the components of the patio to New York and had them reassembled at his home on Park Avenue. He was the President of the Metropolitan Museum of New York between 1934 and the year of his death, 1941. He bequeathed the patio to the Metropolitan Museum in New York, where it remains on display to this day.

In 2005 the castle became the property of the Junta de Andalucía which, in 2016, approved a budget of over €1.1 million for a project which includes recreating the original interior patio. The idea is that the work will be a showcase for the talents of both local masons and local resources, though at the time of writing no date has been set for the work to begin.

In the town itself there is a visitor centre at the old Almacén de Trigo and a four-spouted town fountain, tiled in vivid colours and which, when I was last there, had a notice stuck up alongside it warning that you are allowed to take away no more than 25 litres of water per visit. Further evidence that water is an issue here, as well as in the areas around Sorbas and Tabernas (see chapter 22) came from a huge slogan hanging vertically down a cliff-face outside the town: NO AL ROBO DE AGUA, 'No To The Theft Of Water'. I later discovered that irrigation of industrial-scale lettuce cultivation not far away is considered the main culprit in the water shortages here.

The town lies just off the A-317 and where the spur roads from the town join that main road there are imposing metal sculptures, taller than a human, of the Indalo (see chapter 2) and the Brujo (see front cover), two of the key images found amongst the cave-paintings from the Cueva de los Letreros, a kilometre or so to the south. Inscribed stones adjacent to the figures celebrate their connection with the town. The Indalo is the better known of the two but to me at least the Brujo, a shaman or wizard, is the more striking: an almost-human figure, standing tall, with big widely-splayed horns and sickle-shaped hands, one of which holds aloft what seems to be a pot of some kind. What might be in the pot? Some fiendish concoction? Why does it have sickles on the ends of its arms? At the risk of offending the sensitive, what is that hanging between its legs: a tail or something more predictable? Whatever it is, it's impressively long. And the head is wrong for a human: it's far too elongated, parallel-sided, and has an odd horizontal slit where the forehead should be. The Brujo is an intriguing figure of mystery and menace, raising more questions than it answers.

41. Still filming

'Living is easy with eyes closed...'
(John Lennon)

Film on

Almería's history as a venue for film-makers is well documented in many places (including *Flamingos in the Desert*, chapter 28) and some might think that the highlight came in the days of Sergio Leone and his spaghetti westerns. However, film fans know that in recent years Almería has seen another surge in filming activity.

2013 saw the release of *Vivir Es Facil Con Los Ojos Cerrados*, 'Living Is Easy With Eyes Closed', which won six Goya Awards and was nominated for an Oscar in the 'Foreign Films' category. The title is a line from the Beatles' song *Strawberry Fields Forever*, written by John Lennon whilst he was staying in Almería during the shooting of *How I Won The War* in 1966. *Vivir Es Facil...*, written and directed by David Trueba and starring Javier Cámara, is based on the true story of Juan Carrión, a teacher of English in Cartagena, who decided to travel to Almería to visit Lennon whilst he was filming there. Carrión was in the habit of using Beatles' lyrics in his lessons, saying they were "a very important source of vocabulary". When he met Lennon he suggested that the Beatles' song lyrics should be put on their record covers, an idea that history suggests was subsequently taken up when John Lennon returned home. Juan Carrión, aged 90 when he heard the film had been nominated for an Oscar, said: "I never imagined my story would go so far."

His story went a little further too. It was told in full, in Spanish, by journalist and Beatles fan **Javier Adolfo Iglesias** in his book *Juan & John*. This was published towards the end of 2013 and is now sadly out of print, but the internet suggests you may still be able to get a copy at Picasso bookshop in Almería city.

The 50th anniversary of John Lennon's time in Almería was marked in due style in Carboneras in October 2016. The celebration included an exhibition, a presentation by Adolfo Iglesias of his book and a concert featuring cover band Them Beatles, but pride of place went to the inauguration of a huge mural close to the main square. Vibrant and imaginative, it includes two images of Lennon, both wearing the battle fatigues that he had on in *How I Won The War*. One of the images shows Lennon sitting on the beach with a young lad in a ragged vest and shorts looking at him from a few metres away. Adolfo Iglesias, who is *the* authority on the Beatles' links to Almería, told me more about the mural. The Lennon images are both based on actual photos. Adolfo added a poignant detail: "... the one with the child is a beautiful story. That boy from Carboneras never knew who John Lennon was nor that he had been sharing a photo with such a celebrity. This man only learned this more than 40 years after, and a few days later he died in a car crash."

In 2014 *El Niño*, directed by Mallorcan-born Daniel Monzon and featuring British actor Ian McShane, used locations in the Cabo de Gata-Níjar Natural Park. The action movie, based around a tale of drug trafficking, was partly shot in San José and at the Ensenada de Media Luna. Also in 2014 *Risen*, a biblical thriller set in Roman times and directed by Kevin Reynolds, was shot at locations including Almería's Alcazaba and the Tabernas area. The film tells the story of a Roman centurion, played by British actor Joseph Fiennes, who investigates the alleged resurrection of Jesus Christ. The film continued a sequence of major recent movies, following Ridley Scott's *Exodus: Gods and Kings*, which was shot in Almería a year earlier.

As for independent movie-makers, screen-writer and producer Caroline Spence of London-based Raya Films used locations in Almerimar, Berja and Balanegra for *The Finca*, a cyber-thriller, for which shooting finished in October 2014. It's the tale of a London girl in her 20s who escapes the city only to find herself in a 'voyeuristically terrifying thriller'. The same company have another film, *Guilty in Andalucía*, which has been in development for several years and is described as 'a fast-paced comedy thriller' involving 'a deadly pursuit in the heat and dust of southern Spain'.

Tax breaks

With a budget of $20 million, Kevin Reynolds' *Risen* was, relatively speaking, a cheap movie, but during its production the issue of film finance came to the fore. The film's Spanish producer, José Luis Escolar, explained that attracting film-makers meant competing against countries such as Germany, the UK and Malta, which offer higher tax inducements. Even so, Escolar says: "Having tax incentives in Spain returns up to 20% of a producer's costs – that's about €4 million for *Risen*. Without these, producers wouldn't come here."

US producer Pete Shilaimon added that financial incentives are the most important deciding factor but said that Almería's impressive locations had been a key secondary decider. Escolar also highlighted the fact that once producers have worked in Almería, they tend to want to return. This has a knock-on effect too, he explained: "...because the more films are made here, the more trained staff you have."

The creative director of London-based advertising agency VCCP, Colin Byrne, waxed eloquent about the six days he spent in the Tabernas desert in 2015 shooting a one-minute ad to promote the launch of the 570S, a specialist British sports car by McLaren. "We needed a flat expanse of space and a long flat plain to drive at speed, with nice vistas, a nice mountain range and the sun. We had to move all the rocks out of the way and then put them back again after the shoot," he said. He was very complimentary about the "help from local guys" and said " the food was amazing," but he declined to reveal how much the ad had cost to make.

800 Bullets

We were in Cambridge, visiting Alastair Reid, a friend who's a bit of a film buff. "Here, you can have this, I've already watched it," he said, handing us a DVD. "I think you'll find the Almería connection interesting." It was *800 Bullets*, subtitled *A Wild Tale of the Way, Way, Way Out West*, with the blurb on the packaging promising that it was: 'Brilliant, wonderful ... perfection'. This seemed a rather grandiose claim. It said too: 'Calamity...and death-defying feats of stupidity and bravery are never far away in this acclaimed action comedy from one of modern cinema's unsung masters.' Hmm, an 'unsung master' sounds like a director no-one's heard of. But, particularly with the Almería setting, we thought the least we could do would be to give it a try. And so we did, with English subtitles to help.

Originally made as *800 balas*, the film was released in 2002. At the premiere, the director, Álex de la Iglesia (who is certainly not unheard of and is considered among the most innovative of Spanish directors) said that his film was not trying to emulate the spaghetti westerns but rather was to stand as a symbol of film-making in Almería in the 1960s and 70s. The star of the movie, Sancho Gracia, declared that Almería had been, at that time, one of the three most important locations for film-making, along with Hollywood and London.

800 balas was dedicated to the stuntmen, those who appeared in the spaghetti westerns in a secondary role and who, as that golden age drew to a close, found themselves scraping a living by appearing in the Wild West spectaculars that were being put on at the old film sets for tourists, whilst they waited for the next big film, ever less frequent, to come along.

The script sees Sancho Gracia as Julián, a stuntman who has worked with the best. Gracia had actually been a stuntman in the industry, and he used his experience to produce a proud performance that adds much to the film's strength. Carmen Maura makes a fine contribution and Luis Castro is superb as Carlos, Julián's grandson, who won through in a casting process of 1,500 hopefuls. The other key actors are good too, giving a comical and poignant sense of a group with a somewhat surreal existence, living in the old film set and coming over almost as a bunch of crazies.

In January 2002 the shooting made the front pages when a scene with horsemen coming down one of the main roads towards the Gran Hotel in Almería brought traffic to a halt. Scenes were shot in other places too, but the bulk of the action took place in what was then known as Texas Hollywood and is now called Fort Bravo. The director's open approach to film-making meant that the media and Almerían society in general had a lot of access as the film was shot. This in turn led to the circulation of numerous stories, such as the absolute stubbornness of Sancho Gracia, who refused to have a stunt double even in the most dangerous scenes, and the rumour surrounding the whole filming process that there was to be a cameo by Clint Eastwood. And did Clint appear? Sorry, that would be telling; you'll have to watch the film.

On the back of the DVD box, the movie is described thus: 'A gleeful, gloriously wicked blend of action, hilarity and luminous panoramic photography, *800 Bullets* is cult auteur Álex de la Iglesia's hyper-stylized tribute to the classic spaghetti westerns'. I'd pretty much go along with that summary, so I've deliberately not given away much of the plot as I'd recommend this movie to anyone who has an interest in the film history of Almería and who wants 127 minutes of good entertainment.

Walk of Fame

In November 2014 the director and star of *Risen*, Kevin Reynolds and Joseph Fiennes respectively, were each awarded a 'Walk of Fame' star for their contributions to film-making in Almería province.

According to culture councillor Ramon Fernández Pacheco, the 'Walk of Fame' is the Diputación's (the provincial government's) attempt to highlight Almeria's film heritage and, in that awful modern business-speak, 'strengthen the brand'. However, the cost of bringing film stars to the province is substantial. In September 2014, the Diputación spent €45,540 to pay for Arnold Schwarzenegger's visit to the city. The Austrian-born American actor was paid €12,600 and received his own 'Walk of Fame' star, in the hope that the frequently-flagged third instalment of his epic *Conan* series might be filmed here.

Another member of the select 'Walk of Fame' group is Terry Gilliam, director of major film hits such as *Brazil* and *Time Bandits* but also well-known as a member of the Monty Python team. Whilst attending the Almería Short Film Festival in late 2014 Gilliam received his star in recognition of having shot part of his 1988 fantasy movie *The Adventures of Baron Munchausen* on Mónsul beach in the Cabo de Gata-Níjar Natural Park. At the time the Diputación's culture deputy María Vázquez said she was hoping that Gilliam would return to the province to re-shoot his project *The Man Who Killed Don Quixote*, a film that was shelved part way through its original production a decade and a half earlier, due to financial and other problems.

American actor Patrick Wayne, son of the legendary John Wayne, was a guest at the same festival a year later. 76 at the time, he received an 'Almería Tierra de Cine award' and a 'Walk of Fame' star to commemorate the three films he made here decades earlier: Burt Kennedy's *The Deserter* in 1969, Sam Wanamaker' *Sinbad and the Eye of the Tiger* in 1977, and Hugh Wilson's *Rustler's Rhapsody* in 1984.

The only other person to receive a 'Walk of Fame' star so far is the late Omar Sharif, who was in Almeria in 2012 for the 50th anniversary of David Lean's *Lawrence of Arabia*. As for the stars, it seems that in order to get one, the person involved has to physically come to Almería to receive it, thus giving the opportunity for photos and publicity, and it helps if they might have a project in the offing that could be attracted here too. This means that if my hunch is correct, some of the notable names that have been associated with films in Almería but are no longer with us – John Lennon and Peter O'Toole spring to mind – will never have a star in the 'Walk of Fame'.

One more busy year

February 2015 saw the El Llano del Búho area of the Tabernas Desert doubling for Afghanistan, with a Danish crew shooting *A War*, directed by Tobias Lindholm and starring Dar Salim. Soon afterwards, shooting began on the German film *Der General* in Almería city. Starring Ulrich Noethen and directed by Stephan Wagner, it focuses on Fritz Bauer, the lead prosecutor during the trials in the 1960s of those accused for their roles at the Auschwitz-Birkenau death camp during the Second World War.

At the other end of the province, and the spectrum, Huércal-Overa, not normally considered one of the centres of the local film industry, was chosen in 2015 as the setting for a Swedish TV reality show. The programme, shot in the town's bullring, is called *Mastarnas Mastare*, 'Master of Masters', and is a Survivors-type show in which well-known retired sportspeople undergo a series of gruelling tests. The programme, screened in spring 2016, also featured Turre, Sorbas, Tabernas, Mojácar, Garrucha and the beaches at Cala del Plomo and Algarrobico.

About a thousand people queued outside the Moises Ruiz pavilion in Almería city in July 2015. They were hoping to be chosen as extras for the sixth series of the cult fantasy TV series *Game of Thrones*, with shooting taking place in October. Modexpor, the casting company, was looking for 2,400 extras, with the following criteria: they should be dark-skinned, tanned or black, between 18 and 65, and have "no modern hair styles or tattoos". In addition, they should live within 40 kilometres of Almería city. Extras earned €50 per day and had to sign a contract swearing themselves to absolute secrecy. If they turned up just a few seconds late for work, they could expect to be sacked.

Much of the *Game of Thrones* footage was shot at a major set at Pechina on the edge of the Sierra Alhamilla, as well as at Almería's Alcazaba, at Mesa Roldán, a dramatic high plateau overlooking the sea near Carboneras, and in the Tabernas desert. December 2015 saw the beginning of filming for *Assassin's Creed*, to turn the hit videogame into a movie, starring Michael Fassbender, Jeremy Irons, Charlotte Rampling and Javier Gutiérrez. Filming was again focussed at El Chorrillo near Pechina.

Film sets and a spa

Apart from the film sets which are open as visitor attractions (see chapter 28 in Flamingos in the Desert), there are others standing quietly in the landscape, just waiting for the interested visitor. One such location lies north of Almería city, between Pechina and the spa at Sierra Alhamilla. To find it, take the exit from the A-92 motorway signposted to Pechina and Sierra Alhamilla, about 15 kilometres north of Almería and go uphill, in the Sierra Alhamilla direction. After about 3 or 4 kilometres, look down on your right and you'll see a cluster of buildings in a large flat area. This area is called El Chorrillo and, with care, you can drive down a track to reach it.

There are actually two areas to look at. The more recent and more obvious one consists of what appear to be mud-walled buildings and was used for Ridley Scott's 2014 biblical epic *Exodus: Gods and Kings*. What you see are the remains of a much larger set but it's intriguing to see the techniques used to create authentic-looking buildings. In many cases they are just facades, constructed with the liberal use of metal frames, wire mesh and polystyrene. It seems as if thick muddy daub was sprayed on to create the walls. This set was also used for *Game of Thrones*.

A few hundred metres away is a series of older, more substantial buildings. There are clues that films were made here too, if you look closely. One or two areas of low walls, apparently of stone, have broken down to reveal polystyrene innards. Likewise a large millstone. And on the facade of one of the buildings is the faint lettering, almost faded to nothing: MENDOZA'S SALOON & TRADING POST. This site was used for the 1961 film *The Savage Guns*, directed by Michael Carreras. Released also in Spanish as *Tierra Brutal*, the film was not a commercial success but was the first western to be shot in Almería, predating Sergio Leone's much more famous 'Dollar' trilogy. An actual visit is recommended but if you are not up for that, this link takes you to a five-minute Youtube video of the sets: https://www.youtube.com/watch?v=5NIxVC89mN8

For a different experience, if you drive back up to the road and continue uphill, you soon reach the Balneario de Sierra Alhamilla, an ancient hot water spa. Water emerges from the ground here at a steady 58°C. You can see and feel it doing exactly this as it gushes from a pipe in the centre of the small settlement. The hot springs here were appreciated and used by the Phoenicians, the Romans and the Moors. Today the tradition continues at a modern hotel, with an earlier, more ornate but now ruined version up the hill behind it. You don't have to stay at the hotel to book a session in the hot baths though. And from the front of the hotel, there's a panoramic view down over date palms to the Mediterranean.

Save the cost of this book!

All year round the old western film sets put on shoot-outs in the dusty streets and can-can dances in the saloons to pull in the crowds, as well as having ancillary features, a zoo for example, or a swimming pool. All of this, if you are a visitor, and especially if you bring the family, comes at a substantial cost. However, once a year the Almería Western Film Festival takes place over a long weekend. The 6th edition of this event was from the 6th to the 9th October 2016. As well as the usual attractions at the film sets, the festival also includes the screening of a range of westerns and other linked events. The reason I mention it is this: on one day (7th Oct in 2016) entry to Oasys Mini-Hollywood was free from 3 p.m. Likewise on another day (8th Oct in 2016) entry to Fort Bravo was free from 3 p.m. If you are taking the kids, this tip alone will save you several times the cost of this book. Details of the festival can be found here: www.almeriawesternfilmfestival.es

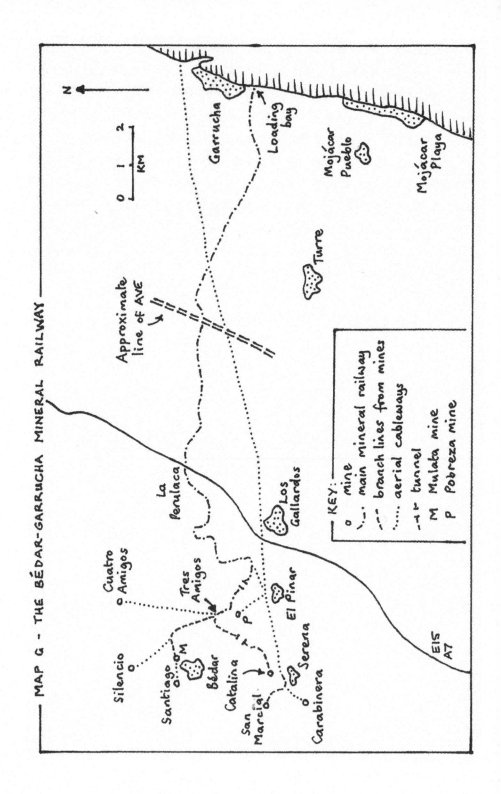

MAP G — THE BÉDAR-GARRUCHA MINERAL RAILWAY

N

0 1 2
KM

Approximate line of AVE

Garrucha

Loading bay

Mojácar Pueblo

Mojácar Playa

Turre

La Peñulaca

Cuatro Amigos

Tres Amigos

Silencio

Santiago

Bédar

Catalina

San Marcial

Serena

Carabinera

El Pinar

Los Gallardos

EIS A7

KEY:
o   mine
—·— main mineral railway
– – – branch lines from mines
······ aerial cableways
—ɪ— tunnel
M Mulata mine
P Pobreza mine

402

42. Another lost railway

"...and silent cuttings mark where a useful country line wound along..."

(W G Hoskins)

A brief history of the Bédar to Garrucha iron ore line

In the mid 19th century the industrialist Ramón Orozco came across old iron mines in the Bédar area. In 1857 he set up a company with the intention of reopening these mines, transporting the ore to Garrucha and smelting it there. However, his foundry of San Ramón, popularly known as El Martinete, didn't last long due to the high costs of importing coal from England, despite the fact that this was the cheapest coal available. The cost of transporting the ore on horseback from the mines to the coastal foundry was substantial too. Later, Holway & Bros of London, represented by the British vice-consul in Garrucha, Clifton Pecket, made a further attempt to exploit the area's iron ore, only to be defeated by high costs as well.

A further initiative began in 1885, when the Compañía de Águilas began to work the Bédar iron mines. The transport issue was tackled with a 15 kilometre aerial cableway linking Bédar and Garrucha. It was designed and built by the Garrucha-based German engineering firm Karl Bahlsen.

In 1894 the Bédar mines were bought by Víctor Chávarri, whose Chávarri, Lecoq y Compañía immediately stated its intention to build a narrow-gauge railway as the definitive solution to transporting the mineral to the coast. By 1896 Chávarri had ordered the metal bridge for the coastal loading facility at La Marina de la Torre and by the start of 1897 the line was ready for use. It ran from Tres Amigos, south-east of Bédar, to Garrucha and had a gauge of one metre, which allowed tighter curves and lower construction costs in hilly terrain. It was 17.5 kilometres long, with a vertical drop of 234 metres. Seven substantial stone maintenance huts were also built, spaced out along the main line. Hefty masonry bridges with large, well-shaped stone blocks were constructed over various obstacles such as *ramblas* and the road to Mojácar. There was also a tunnel 43 metres long near the inland terminus of the line, which was the station of Tres Amigos. Close to Tres Amigos were offices, engine sheds, workshops and a huge hopper, which is still very obvious to the left of the road as you drive up from Los Gallardos to Bédar. A short branch line ran into the base of this hopper to facilitate the loading of wagons. The hopper in turn was served from above by two branch lines, each about two kilometres long, that brought ore from the mines of Mulata and Santa Catalina.

The locomotives, five in total, were built in Belgium in 1895. Three, each weighing 30 tonnes and called Mojaquera, Garruchera and Bedareña, were used on the main line. The two others, called Mulata and Catalina, of 10 tonnes, were used on the branch lines to the eponymous mines. Each of the main line engines pulled 20 wagons and had a passenger carriage that was hitched up for use when necessary. On average each train made the return trip to and from the coast twice every day, though this depended on the demand for ore.

Víctor Chávarri died in 1900 and by 1916 the outfit operating the mines was called La Union Bedareña. It was at this stage that the aerial cableway was dismantled, leaving the railway as the sole means of getting the ore to the coast. In the early 1920s the operation was affected, like all other mineral enterprises in Spain, by an economic crisis and, in addition, by about 1923, lorries were offering a more efficient service than the railway. The rail infrastructure was abandoned but it was not until 1942 that the line was dismantled. At this point the track and metal bridges were sold for a million pesetas. One of the engines was used in the construction of the port of Garrucha and the rest were sold to other mining companies.

Serena to Tres Amigos

Serena is tucked amongst the folds of the Sierra de Bédar, a small and ancient village blessed with a good water supply. Nowadays this gushes reliably out of three spouts at the village *fuente*, set below a rock face into which, neatly carved, is the date AÑO DE 1890 and the words, above one of the washing toughs, PARA ROPAS DEL HIERRO, which is saying that the miners' iron-stained clothing should be washed there. People still come from far and wide to collect good drinking water from this *fuente*.

By the *fuente* is an information board with a map of the Ruta de Minería de Bédar SL-A 77. SL stands for Sendero Local, local footpath, and the SL-A 77 goes for 7.6 kilometres to the Tres Amigos loading bay, from where the main mineral railway ran down to the coast. It does this via a very convoluted initial loop taking in many of the mining remains in the Serena area, such as masonry towers that supported an aerial ropeway, a substantial stone bridge which is a clue to yet another narrow-gauge railway, a hopper with protruding metal ore-loading chutes, roughly-hewn tunnels and towering crags of red-brown iron-rich rock, before eventually following the trackbed of the Catalina branch line from the Santa Catalina mine to Tres Amigos.

My route is a shorter version of the SL-A 77 which omits the initial loop. So I start from the information board in Serena, pass the *fuente* and follow the narrow road into the village. Soon, on the right, there is a large, stone-built, roofless ruin, hemmed in by nearby houses. This is known as the Serena mosque and the name of the adjacent street, Calle La Mezquita, suggests that a mosque once stood here. Andrés Pérez tells me that the ruin is actually that of a church built in the 16th century after the Christian Reconquest under the Catholic Monarchs in 1488, almost certainly on the site of a mosque. It may be that the building was used again, very briefly, as a mosque, during the Moorish rebellion of 1568-70 (see chapter 35).

It's possible, just, to peer in through gaps in the huge metal-studded wooden doors and see a set of conical millstones of the kind used to process olives, testifying to its more recent use as an olive mill.

Immediately opposite the lower side of the mosque my route takes a narrow concrete track, dropping down from the road by some grey railings and passing various *huertas,* allotments. At the bottom of this path, I turn to the right and work my way along the small *rambla*, climbing slightly up to the left to walk along an irrigation channel as far as a rectangular water tank. Here I drop back to the right alongside the tank, into the *rambla* where I turn left, effectively continuing in the same direction I'd already been going. The *rambla* gets bigger and more open as it curves to the right. Before long a distinctive small stone bridge comes into view. To the left of it is another roofless stone ruin, of similar dimensions to the Serena mosque. This was the locomotive shed for the Catalina engine, named after the main mine it served.

I take the almost level track to the left and it's soon obvious that this is the line of an old railway, with gentle curves and cuttings through the hilly landscape. Small wooden posts, with what look like new (in October 2016) plastic SL-A 77 signs, complete with green and white flashes, confirm I am going the right way. These are helpful but I wonder how long the plastic will last in this unforgiving climate. A triple wooden fingerpost further confirms that this is the way to Tres Amigos and then the next cutting deepens and leads into a tunnel. It's about 300 metres long and straight, so you can easily see daylight at both ends. It's a wise precaution to have a flashlight with you though, as vehicles regularly use it.

Once out of the tunnel and through another small cutting, to the right, across a ravine-like *rambla*, a mine entrance is clearly visible, together with more ruins, areas of dark iron-rich spoil, and various levels on the hillside. This was the Pobreza mine. Scattered modern villas dot the hills here and soon the white splash of Mojácar

Pueblo and the craggy profile of the Sierra Cabrera come into distant view. Closer at hand, through a gap in the hills, there's also a glimpse of the main Bédar to Los Gallardos road, the AL-P 117.

By now the trackbed is beginning to lose more height. Where there is a tarmac drive on the left and a track twists steeply away down to the right, continue ahead, as indicated by the waymarks. The rail trackway ended here and a short inclined plane took the ore down to the flat area directly above the huge Tres Amigos hopper. You can see down into the four bays, separated by hefty stone walls that are still in solid condition. In total this hopper could hold 12,000 tonnes of iron ore. To the left you can also see what was the Catalina mines manager's house, a big square building that is now a private residence and, beyond the road, halfway left, the old station area.

A closer look at the station area is worthwhile. It's easy to get down to the left of the hopper. The ruin is of a station building and just behind that is the platform and the cutting alongside where the rails used to be. On the slope behind the rail line is where the loading bay for the ore from the Cuatro Amigos mine used to be. The ore came via an aerial cableway from Cuatro Amigos, which is two kilometres due north. It's marked clearly on the 1:25,000 scale map (sheet 1014-IV Vera) with a symbol of crossed shovels.

This station area also received ore via another branch railway that came from the Mulata mine which was less than a kilometre to the north-east of Bédar. A small 0-4-0 tank engine worked this branch line. Aerial cableways fed into this line from the mines at Silencio and Santiago. The Mulata locomotive brought the ore to an inclined plane, down which it went into the 'funnel-shaped hopper'. When I first explored this area quite a few years ago it was possible to go via the end of the railway, just beyond the platform, along a short tunnel, into the base of the funnel-shaped hopper. On my most recent visit, the tunnel was blocked and access wasn't possible. You can clamber up the slope to the left of the hopper though and see in to it. It's fenced off for obvious reasons but its size and the stone lining are impressive. When the railway was in operation, wagons were pushed in along the tunnel and filled via a chute from the funnel-shaped hopper.

Tres Amigos towards the sea

The next stage of the journey is to follow the main rail line as it leaves Tres Amigos, heading for Garrucha. From the huge hopper the first part of the line is obvious, along to the road, but then it has been obscured by tarmac. For this stage I'm cycling, so an easy kilometre of gentle downhill free-wheeling follows, as far as a sharp right bend. Here, the old line veers straight ahead into a cutting leading to the short Boliche tunnel. There's an open door in the arched entrance but the far end is blocked by a grille and rubble, so I take the track that by-passes it to the right, climbing then dropping again to regain the old trackway.

Soon there's a badly littered area of rubble, scrap plastic and general garbage with, alongside it, an ironic gem courtesy of the Ayuntamiento de Los Gallardos, a large sign announcing that the dumping of rubbish is forbidden and those responsible will be punished. Beyond here the view opens out to Mojácar Pueblo and the sea. A tarmac surface begins and in a few metres the trackbed swings left through a cutting. A waymark indicates that this is the E05, an off-road cycle route, and it's 16,770 metres to Garrucha. The ruins of one of the maintenance buildings stand on the left, then I negotiate a narrow bit of embankment where a vicious gully has removed most of the line and is fenced off with emergency tape. It's hilly along here, so the line alternates between embankments and cuttings. One dismantled bridge, its masonry walls still high, has to be skirted on rough ground.

By the next wooden signpost at an obvious junction, I continue ahead, bearing slightly right, following the direction to 'Pago de Angela Antonia 3,020 m'. The trackbed follows a big curve out to the north here to maintain its level as it negotiates a shallow valley. Soon I'm passing a large water *balsa* on the left, a *plastico* down to the right, and then another maintenance house. Just past this is a beautiful curved embankment, steeply faced with buttressed masonry.

The A7 motorway is now in sight to the south and the landscape is gentler and more obviously agricultural. After a while I reach tarmac and use it to whizz down and up, by-passing another downed bridge on the embanked trackbed alongside. Away to the left is the prominent volcanic plug of Cerro Cabezo María with the Ermita de la Virgen de la Cabeza perched on its summit. Where the tarmac sweeps up to the right, the old railway goes straight on, unsurfaced. Shortly, it crosses tarmac again and passes to the right of a small group of houses. It's narrow now and partly occupied by pylons and a fence. I can see the motorway is very close so I abandon the bike and walk the last hundred metres or so to where the stream of modern traffic is cutting clean through the old line.

South of the motorway

The next time I come out, a couple of days later, I take exit 525 from the motorway, turn back towards Los Gallardos on the N-340a, and find a place to pull in when I can see the embankments of the former line. I cross scrubby ground, little used for agriculture it seems, to the embankment and walk a short way to my right, to where the old trackway is cut by both the N-340a and the A7. At this point I am looking back to where I had to finish on my previous visit. Initially at least, here, south of the A7, the narrow embankment is walkable, so I set off to see how far I can get, having heard and read several accounts suggesting this will not be a rewarding task. One issue is that the electricity pylons on the old trackbed north of the motorway continue here. It is passable but uninspiring and in less than a kilometre the trackway loses its definition, meets fences and generally reduces to being a project that is more trouble than it's worth. I had wanted to see for myself but those who have been here before were right. It's time to retreat.

It's some months later, at the start of 2017, that I finally fill in the last piece of the jigsaw. A group of five of us have decided to cycle the route from La Perulaca to Garrucha. We park by junction 525 of the motorway, unload the bikes, pedal a couple of hundred metres towards Los Gallardos and turn left on a tarmac track, the same one described at the beginning of this section, to follow the red-flashed bike route. The waymarks are good, solid wooden posts at each change of direction. The tarmac gives out in a while and the route follows earth tracks, some of which have been badly damaged by the heavy rains of December 2016. There are new olive groves, a strange modern-looking stone tower on a low hill up to the right, and a stretch of old railway embankment to the left at one stage, with the tumbled remains of a maintenance house alongside it.

A little further on a ruined cortijo on the right, the name of which I don't know as I don't have a detailed map for this stretch, catches my eye as it has an adjacent building with a triangular opening that I know indicates a pigeon loft. As the others forge ahead I dismount and find my way into the building, the roof of which has fallen in, so that rafters are angled down to the floor amidst rubble. But the right-hand side room has walls (or at least, the remains of walls) with square pigeon niches. The main farm building is substantial but has clearly been long abandoned. A largely intact water channel leads away nearby. This was once no doubt quite a prosperous farm.

By now the others have vanished. Soon, I see the moribund line of the AVE (Alta Velocidad Española), overlain at right angles on the much older mineral line, though the AVE won't be up and running any time soon (see chapter 28). The bike route veers down alongside it to pass under it in a big square tunnel. I catch the others here and they ask if I heard them singing. I didn't but they have discovered impressive echoing acoustics in the tunnel. The bike route goes right after the tunnel before veering slightly left. Before veering left, you can go ahead briefly on another track that gains height, in order to see the high-speed trackbed itself, a pristine, wide swath of tarmac, protected by a two metre high mesh fence topped with barbed wire.

Back down at the point where we regain the red waymarks, we gain a little height, then there's a 90° left turn. Here, we rejoin the old trackbed. Ten metres to the right there are the stone revetments of a dismantled bridge to prove it. Taking the left turn, we ride the line of the trackbed before dipping down on to a parallel track to avoid a couple of points where the old railway, on another embankment, is not passable due to breaks in the line.

Before long, over to the right, are ten or so big lagoons. A ceramic tile on the gate pillar indicates that the water company Galasa owns this place and olfactory evidence confirms it's a sewage works. Probably good for birdwatching though! Even from a distance and without binoculars I can see many gulls and black-winged stilts. Beyond here, the trackbed is mostly surfaced and much easier. It passes through a deep cutting to reach a straight stretch, embanked again, above scrubby ground and olive groves. The traffic noise from the A-370, the fast Garrucha - Los Gallardos road, increases as the trackway approaches it. To the right is Garrucha Karting, a go-kart circuit, and soon enough the old railway reaches the modern road, which we join to head in to Garrucha to reward ourselves with lunch overlooking the Med.

By the sea again

For the final stage of the exploration, I'm back on my own again, on foot, at the point where the access road to the karting track leaves the A-370. From here, I head up behind the big billboard promoting

Garrucha's new Lidl supermarket. There's a kind of shelf of land here where a line might have run but I'm not convinced. I cut over the higher ridge to my left, cross the access road to the cemetery with its neatly manicured trees and then I can see the distinctive stone profile of the loading bay at the end of the line. It's not easy to access this but you can scramble up the angled masonry facing if you are so inclined. I went up right by the prominent stone feature at its seaward end. Don't tell them I suggested you can do this.

On the top there is obvious iron-rich rock and you can see the sea through a hole in the front wall. Trains coming from Bédar ran along, at a higher level than currently exists, to the top of the loading bay. An old photo shows that two tracks projected beyond where the remaining stonework is. The ore was tipped sideways out of the trucks, down into more trucks below which were pulled out on to landing stages by horses or donkeys. The ore was loaded into shallow-draught barges which went out and transferred it to bigger ships for export. 'Unlike the pier for the Agua Amarga - Lucainena line, the sea was not deep enough for the ships to moor at the pier.' This, and more, is on Don Gaunt's excellent website, including a detailed map of the area at the seaward end of the line, here: http://faydon.com/Bedar/Bedar.html.

There are deep gaps in the embankment behind the loading wall, so simply walking back inland isn't possible. Getting down the stone facing is not much more difficult than getting up. A couple had been watching my antics and the feature on which I'd been performing them. They proved to be Brits on a week's holiday. "Did that used to be a railway?" they asked. Excellent: landscape detectives in shorts and sun-cream.

Facing inland from where the embankment merges into higher ground, you can sense that the line curved to the right, almost parallel to the sea. There are linear piles of rubble here, with space for the line between them. I think this may have been the engine shed. Whatever it was, it's almost entirely ruinous, with just a few large facing stones still in situ on one wall.

But again, it wasn't clear where the line had run. Somehow the line had to pass over the ridge here and there are just no clues as to where that happened; there's no cutting, the slopes are too steep. Maybe this area has been changed too much and the clues have all gone, but back down near the karting access road, opposite the Lidl billboard and by the huge green-and-white 'Red de Carreteras de Andalucía' sign, there is a lot of iron-rich rock, spilled from the rail wagons, it would seem. Don Gaunt's map shows that the line did run across the area where I was searching but on his map he says 'Route of line here only approximate.' Writing soon after the turn of the century, Don lamented: 'This is all very sad. Ten years ago the buildings, sheds, administration, etc. were all still there, albeit in poor condition. All have now gone, swallowed up by development. The only building left is the loading bay, which so far seems to have been protected although each year I expect to see it gone.' So far Don Gaunt's fears haven't come to pass; the loading bay remains, and in pretty good condition too, a distinctive reminder of another lost railway.

About the author

Kevin Borman was born on the Lincolnshire coast in 1950. He went to Sheffield University in 1968, stayed in the city, and from 1972 until 2004 taught Geography in comprehensive schools there. Between 1989 and 2004 he also worked as a writer, photographer, reviewer and news editor for *High* magazine. In 2003 he received an Award for Excellence for his regular *Walking World* column in *High* from the Outdoor Writers' Guild. He has written several books and contributed about 400 articles to a wide range of magazines and journals. His interests include natural history, hillwalking, music, writing, dark chocolate and the occasional glass of red wine. He has been exploring Almería since buying a house there with his wife Troy Roberts in 2005.

Other books by Kevin Borman

Poetry
Lovemapping (Rivelin Press 1974)
Dust & Jungle (Rivelin Press 1976)
Seasons In A Raw Landscape (Rivelin Press 1982)
Inside The New Map (Redbeck Press 1999)
Blue Is Rare (Redbeck Press 2005)

Guidebooks
Peak District Short Walks (Jarrold 2001)
The Derwent Valley Heritage Way (Jarrold 2003)
Peak District Walks: Pathfinder Guide (joint author, Jarrold 2003)
Flamingos In The Desert: Exploring Almería (FeedARead 2014)

And contributions to these anthologies
Perspectives On Landscape (Arts Council of Great Britain 1978)
Speak To The Hills (Aberdeen University Press 1985)
Orogenic Zones (Bretton Hall 1994)
Kinder Scout, Portrait Of A Mountain (Derbyshire County Council 2002)

Acknowledgements

Enormous thanks to Helen Evans for again proving to be a thorough, supportive and very professional editor and to Pete Adeline for enthusiastic and forensic proof-reading. For any mistakes that remain, I bear the responsibility, not least because I was still tweaking the text even after final proof-reading. Gary Lincoln again gave me his time and skills to design the cover and my old fellrunning partner Tim Mackey helped me ensure the maps and general layout were as I wanted them to be. My wife Troy Roberts has provided both great support and also many thoughtful suggestions regarding the book.

Lindy Walsh has been a source of much information, not least via her collection of newspaper cuttings dating back to the mid 1980s, to which she happily gave me access. I should also record my thanks to Richard Torné, editor of Costa Almería News, where earlier versions of several passages from this book first appeared.

In addition, many people have helped me by providing information in various forms, checking sections of the text, providing photos for the online album, helping distribute this book's predecessor, and proving excellent companions during the explorations described: Catherine Arthur, Karin S.de Boer, Jackie Bragg, Charlie Brown, Pete Brown, Toni Brugger, Lawrence Burton, Finn Campbell-Notman, Jesús Contreras Torre, the late Harvey Defriend, Allen Dunning, Thierry Duty, Mat Edwards, David and Gilly Elliott-Binns, Joe Evans, Don Gaunt, Robbie Gibbins, Terry Gifford, Pepe Guinea, Robin Hawkins, Javier Adolfo Iglesias, Anne Kampschulte, Barb Knowles, Sue Macdonald, José Javier Matamala García, Hamid Mezane, Barrie Naylor, Christopher North, Susanna Notman, Karen O'Hagan, Angeli van Os, Matt Packer, Richard Pointer, Emma Randle, Alastair Reid, Francisco Javier Rodríguez Arias, Brian Rowlands, Calin Sandru, Claudia Scholler, Frank and Sheena Selkirk, Denise and Fred Smithers, Brian Taylor, Pete Thom, Steve Townsend,

John Wallis, Johnny Whelan, Gordon and Frankie Young, and members of the Arboleas Birdwatching Group.

The Sorbas journal *El Afa* is a rich seam of information on the history and culture of the local area. In the spirit of community, its editors allow the use of its articles, provided their source is acknowledged. Consequently, my sincere thanks to the following authors whose work in *El Afa* I consulted in my research for this book: Gemma María Clemente Orta, María del Sol García de las Ballones García, Antonio Gil Albarracín, Andrés Pérez Pérez, Rosa María Piqueras Valls, and Ana María Rodriguez Agüero.

Fieldwork outings with Roy Alexander and Phil Marren of the University of Chester in the 'Badlands' near Tabernas, Sarah Ball and her colleagues from the University of Reading's 'Spain team' in the Sierra Cabrera and on the Karst en Yesos plateau, and with environmentalist and photographer Ion Holban along the Río de Aguas, all proved immensely enjoyable and informative.

Flamingos in the Desert would have struggled to achieve its success without the help of the owners and managers of the 30 or so outlets in eastern Almería (garages, cafes, newsagents, bars, hotels, bike shops, camp site shops, visitor centres, a library and even a launderette) that sell or have sold copies. Hopefully they will stock *Where Hoopoes Fly* too. Thanks to all the groups, stretching from Xàbia (Jávea), way up beyond Alicante, and down to Mojácar - who invited me to talk about and read from the book. All those who bought, recommended, reviewed or otherwise helped get word out about *Flamingos in the Desert* also have my grateful thanks.

Almost last, but by no means least, I have really appreciated the positive feedback from everyone who emailed me to tell me what they thought about *Flamingos*. Those comments were a major factor in my deciding to write this book. So, similarly, please give me your feedback on *Where Hoopoes Fly*. You can reach me at kevindborman@gmail.com. Also, in case you missed it, the introduction to this book includes a link to the online photo album that accompanies this text.

Perhaps I should anticipate the question: "Will there be a third book in the series?" At this stage I think almost certainly not. I'm not sure there is enough material for another one, I have an entirely different book idea that has been on the back-burner for several years, and I need a rest! But then, after *Flamingos in the Desert*, I had no expectation of writing a follow-up, and three and a half years later here it is so, at the risk of hedging my bets, I guess we'll just have to wait and see.

Bibliography

The following list gives background reading and sources consulted:

Ball, Sarah, *Wild Flowers of Eastern Andalucía* (Gosport 2014)

Borman, Kevin, *An Artist's Eye for Almeria's Birds*, Birds of Andalucía, Vol 5, Issue 1 (Ronda 2016)

Bush, Peter (translator), *Níjar Country* (Santa Fe, New Mexico 2010) (see also Goytisolo, Juan, *Campos de Níjar*)

Cañadas Hernández, Domingo, *GR 140 Sendero Almería: Puerto de La Ragua - Cabo de* Gata (Almería, no date)

Cavanagh, Lorraine, *Mediterranean Garden Plants* (Nerja 2005)

Cela, Camilo José, *Journey to the Alcarria* (1948, English translation Wisconsin 1964)

Cifuentes Vélez, Eugenio, *El Paisaje Cultural de la Sierra de Filabres* (Almería 2009)

Clemente Orta, Gemma María, *La Cochinilla, La Plaga Que Está Acabando Con Las Chumberas*, El Afa N° 33 (Sorbas 2016)

Cocker, Mark and Richard Mabey, *Birds Britannica* (London 2005)

Epton, Nina, *Andalusia* (London 1968)

Evans, Frank 'El Inglés', *The Last British Bullfighter* (London 2009)

Fernández Bolea, Enrique, Francisco Viúdez Asensio and Jose Manuel Alarcón Soler, *A Tourist, Cultural and Hereditary Guidebook of Cuevas del Almanzora* (2nd edition, Mojácar 2005)

Finlayson, Clive, and David Tomlinson, *Birds of Iberia* (Fuengirola 2003)

Fowlie, Eddie and Richard Torné, *David Lean's Dedicated Maniac: Memoirs of a Film Specialist* (2nd edition, London 2014)

Frías, Antonio, *Guía de Especies Marinas del Parque natural y la Reserva Marina Cabo de Gata-Níjar* (Almería 2007)

García de las Ballones García, María del Sol, *Casilla de Peón Caminero: Crónica de Una Generación e Historia Perdida*, El Afa N° 33 (Sorbas 2016)

García Lorca, Andrés (Director), *Atlas Geográfico de la Provincia de Almería* (Almería, no date given but approx 2010)

Garvey, Geoff, and Mark Ellingham, *The Rough Guide to Almería* (London 2003)

Gaunt, Don, *Almería and The Great Southern of Spain Railway (The GSSR)* (Gloucestershire 2006)

Gifford, Terry, and Christopher North, *Al Otro Lado del Aguilar* (Devon 2011)

Gil Albarracín, Antonio, *La Larga Historia de la Alfarería en Sorbas*, El Afa N° 10 (Sorbas 2004)

Goytisolo, Juan, *Campos de Níjar* (Almería 2010, originally published 1960) (see also Bush, Peter, *Níjar* Country)

Grima, Juan, *"En el terremoto de Vera murió uno de cada cuatro habitants que tenía la ciudad"*, in Actualidad Almanzora (Dec 2014)

Haro Pérez, Francisco, *Mojaqueros de hecho* (Almería 2014)

Hartley, L.P. *The Go-Between* (London 1953)

Harvey, Adrian, and Anne Mather, *Classic Geology in Europe 12 Almería* (Edinburgh 2015)

Hemingway, Ernest, *Death in the Afternoon* (New York 1932)

Herrera Plaza, José, *Accidente Nuclear de Palomares - Consecuencias (1966 - 2016)* (Mojácar 2016)

Higgins, Henry and Jim Myers, *To Be A Matador* (London 1972)

Hoskins, W G, *English Landscapes* (London 1973)

Iglesias, Javier Adolfo, *Juan & John* (Almería 2013)

Jackson, David, *Turre, A History* (Turre 2015)

Jacobs, Michael, *Andalucía* (London 1998)

Jacobs, Michael, *In The Glow Of The Phantom Palace* (London 2000)

Lodé, Joël and Andrés Soler Navarro, *Guía de Fauna y Flora: Desert Springs Resort & Golf Course* (Almería 2013)

Lopez, Barry and Debra Gwartney *Home Ground: Language for an American Landscape* (San Antonio 2006)

López de Haro, Paco, Antonio Martínez Cano and Paqui Tomás Ruiz, *El Levante Almeriense 20 excursiones a pie y en bicicleta* (Murcia 2002)

López Galán, Juan Salvador and Juan Antonio Muñoz Muñoz, *Guías de Almería, Territorio, Cultura y Arte: Arquitectura Tradicional* (El Ejido 2008)

MacCaig, Norman, *The Poems of Norman MacCaig* (Edinburgh 2005)

Mackie, Jim, *Boogieman and his Cat in Andalucía* (Milton Keynes 2015)

Maconie, Stuart, *Adventures On The High Teas: In Search Of Middle England* (London 2009)

Maillard, Phil, *English Writers on Andalucía* (essay in manuscript 2010)

Map, Triangle Postals, *Almería*, 1:235,000 (Almería 2013)

Marin, José Manuel F and Macarena Molina Hernández, Cabo de Gata-Níjar: Guia Oficial del Parque Natural (Andalucía 2009)

Marsden, Philip, *Rising Ground: A Search for the Spirit of Place*, (London 2014)

Mather, A.E., J.M. Martin, A.M. Harvey and J.C. Braga, *A Field Guide to the Neogene Sedimentary Basins of the Almería Province*, South-East Spain (Oxford 2001)

Measures, John, Wild*life Travelling Companion Spain* (Marlborough 1992)

Moldenhauer Carrillo, Federico, *El Tren minero Bédar-Los Gallardos-Garrucha dio su primer viaje a finales del XIX*, La Cimbra Nº 10 (Los Gallardos 2001)

Moreno Izquierdo, Rafael, *La historia secreta de las bombas de Palomares* (Spain 2016)

Mullarney, Killian, Lars Svensson, Dan Zetterström and Peter J Grant, *Collins Bird Guide* (London 1999)

Newspapers and journals: Actualidad Almanzora, Axarquia, Costa Almería News, El Afa, El Pais in English, Ideal, Ideal Levante, La

Cimbra, Levante Información, La Voz de Almería, The Advertiser (various dates)

(No named author): *65 aniversario de la instalación del Cristo (1)*, Ideal Levante (Sept/Oct 2014)

Ortiz, Domingo, *La Vera Vieja vista por el viajero Münzer*, Ideal Levante (Sept/Oct 2013)

Papadimitriou, Nick, *Scarp* (London 2012)

Pérez Pérez, Andrés, *Infraestructuras y Proceso Alfarero*, El Afa N° 10 (Sorbas 2004)

Piqueras Valls, Rosa María, *La Casa del Duque de Alba*, El Afa N° 22 (Sorbas 2010)

Pritchard, Matthew, *Scarecrow* (2013)

Pritchard, Matthew, *Broken Arrow* (2015)

Rihuete Herrada, Cristina, *El Argar and the Beginning of Class Society in the western Mediterranean*, Archäologie in Eurasien N° 24 (online, 2011)

Robertson, Struan and Anne Harling, *Murder Under The Sun* (2015)

Robertson, Struan and Anne Harling, *Deadly Duplicity* (2015)

Rodriguez Agüero, Ana María, *La Matanza del Cerdo: Una Costumbre y Un Oficio Casi Desaparecidos*, El Afa N° 19 (Sorbas 2009)

Rodriguez Agüero, Ana María, *Milagro de la Virgen de Fátima en Sorbas*, El Afa N° 25 (Sorbas 2012)

Ruiz García, Alfonso (Coordinador), *Guías de Almería, Territorio, Cultura y Arte: Arquitectura Tradicional* (Almería 2008)

Ruiz García, Alfonso (Coordinador), *Guías de Almería, Territorio, Cultura y Arte: Cine* (Roquetas de Mar 2011)

Ruiz García, Alfonso (Coordinador), *Guías de Almería, Territorio, Cultura y Arte: El Litoral Mediterráneo* (2a edición, El Ejido 2006)

Ruiz García, Alfonso (Coordinador), *Guías de Almería, Territorio, Cultura y Arte: Naturaleza Almeriense, Espacios del Interior* (El Ejido 2011)

Simpson, Alan, *Naked In The Snow* (Mojácar 2004)

Sterry, Paul, *Complete Mediterranean Wildlife* (London 2000)

Stewart, Chris, *Driving Over Lemons* (London 1999)

Stewart, Chris, *A Parrot in the Pepper Tree* (London 2002)

Stewart, Chris, *The Almond Blossom Appreciation Society* (London 2006)

Stewart, Chris, *Last Days Of The Bus Club* (London 2014)

Suiter, Bud, *A Year in Andalucía: An American's Point of View*(2015)

Tremlett, Giles, *Ghosts of Spain: Travels Through a Country's Hidden Past* (London 2006)

Union of Democratic Control, *How The German Fleet Shelled Almería* (London 1937)

Villalobos Megía, Miguel, *Geology of the Arid Zone of Almería* (Andalucía 2003)

Webster, Jason, *Andalus* (London 2004)

Wickman, Roy, *Spanish Insight: Spain's unprotected protected parks* (in *Costa Almería News* June 2014)

Wilkinson, Steve, *Flamingo Summer* (2014)

Woolsey, Gamel, *Death's Other Kingdom* (London, originally 1939, new edition 2004)

Zoido Salazar, Said and Iván Zoido Salazar, *Almería in Film: Movie Walks And Routes* (Andalucía 2015)

Websites

This is by no means an exhaustive list but these websites may be helpful to anyone looking for more information about some of the topics and places mentioned in this book:

www.almerianature.guide Wildlife and nature guide and photographer Jesus Contreras, offering tours with a very knowledgeable local expert.

www.almeriawesternfilmfestival.es Details of the film festival held in the Tabernas area each October.

www.amigosdesorbas.com/revistaelafa The website of the 'Friends of Sorbas' particularly useful for digital editions of past issues of the journal El Afa.

http://www.azimuthspain.com/en/calar-alto/ Visits to the observatory at Calar Alto in the Sierra de las Filabres.

www.cabodegata.net The website (in Spanish) of the Asociación Amigos del Parque Natural Cabo de Gata-Níjar, very active supporters and conservationists of the Natural Park.

http://www.campinglasmenasdeseron.com The campsite at Las Menas and some details of the mining history there.

www.costaalmeriatours.com A local family-run company offering bespoke tours and trips, mainly in Almeria, and promising to show you 'Secret Spain'.

www.cuevasdesorbas.com The Sorbas Caves, offering underground visits in the Gypsum Karst area. The website offers an English language option.

www.dgseturismoactivo.com Javi Rodriguez's sustainable tourism and development company, offering mountain biking, kayaking and guided walks (Spanish speaking).

www.farodebedar.com A useful source of historical information (in Spanish) about Bédar and surrounding area.

www.faydon.com Don Gaunt's site, very good on Almería's old railways and industrial archaeology

www.finncampbellnotman.com/birds/ Finn Campbell-Notman's Almerían bird paintings

www.geogata.com David Monge's 'responsible tourism' company, offering 4WD tours to show you wildlife, geology and astronomy.

www.ign.es The website of the Instituto Geográfico Nacional (in Spanish). You can buy maps through the online shop on this site.

www.pitaescuela.org The website of Europe's only Agave School, offering courses and workshops in how to use agave wood. Run by Timbe Bernhardt in Los Molinos.

www.pulpituristico.es/index.php/es/llegar-a-pulpi/item/180-visita-virtual-a-la-geoda Details of virtual visits to the Pulpí Geode.
www.sunseed.org.uk Sunseed Sustainable Technology offers courses and retreats, providing practical education in sustainable, off-grid living. They also accept volunteers and interns. Based in Los Molinos. Website in English and Spanish.
www.youtube.com/watch?v=5NlxVC89mN8A short video showing film sets near Pechina.

Index to selected people, places and subjects

Italians (supporting Franco) 128, 132
IUCN Red List (of threatened species) 276

Jackson, David 42, 155-156
Jacobs, Michael 41, 117, 121, 252, 281-282, 389
janissaries (Turkish infantry) 79
jarapas (rag rugs) 230
Jardines de Agua, Los 290
Jews 33, 280
Jiménez Barrios, Manuel 270
José and Aurora 237-238
Juan & John 392
Juan of Austria, Don 337
Juana La Loca 249
juniper 383-384, 386

Kafka, Franz 298-299
Kampschulte, Anne 234
Karst en Yesos de Sorbas 55, 161-162, 210, 217-219, 235
Kerouac, Jack 281
Kerry, John 70
kilns 101, 240, 243-244
Kindler, Arthur 66, 74
Kingdom of Granada 79, 232, 248, 337
kingfisher 55, 64, 136

La Piza forest cafe 389
La Voz de Almería 50, 168, 179, 221, 367
ladder snake 376-377

Langle, Guillermo 130
Lark, Sarah 160
Las Amoladeras Visitor Centre 169
lavadero (public washing place) 192, 205-206, 208, 308, 359-360
Law of the Coasts (see Ley de Costas)
Lawrence of Arabia (film) 148-150, 270, 397
Lawrence of Arabia (person) 125, 150
lead mine 53
Lean, David 148-149, 397
Lennon, John 125-126, 151, 392-393, 398
Leone, Sergio 38, 392, 400
Lester, Mark 38
Lester, Richard 151
Levante (east wind) 187
Levante Almeriense (environmental group) 271
Levante Información 221
Levy, Deborah 159
Ley de Costas 22, 88, 96, 270
Libro Guinness de los Records, El 366
lichen 161
Lijar 310-311
Limonium 22
Lindholm, Tobias 398
Little Venice 56
lizard 256-257
Llamas Yeste, Miguel 386
Llano de la Alfahuara 388-389

Lightning Source UK Ltd.
Milton Keynes UK
UKOW04f2313251117
313353UK00003B/21/P

9 781788 760409